Britain and the International Committee
of the Red Cross, 1939–1945

Britain and the International Committee of the Red Cross, 1939–1945

James Crossland
Lecturer in History, Murdoch University, Australia

First published 2014 by
PALGRAVE MACMILLAN

Palgrave Macmillan in the UK is an imprint of Macmillan Publishers Limited, registered in England, company number 785998, of Houndmills, Basingstoke, Hampshire RG21 6XS.

Palgrave Macmillan in the US is a division of St Martin's Press LLC, 175 Fifth Avenue, New York, NY 10010.

Palgrave Macmillan is the global academic imprint of the above companies and has companies and representatives throughout the world.

Palgrave® and Macmillan® are registered trademarks in the United States, the United Kingdom, Europe and other countries.

ISBN 978–1–137–39955–7

This book is printed on paper suitable for recycling and made from fully managed and sustained forest sources. Logging, pulping and manufacturing processes are expected to conform to the environmental regulations of the country of origin.

A catalogue record for this book is available from the British Library.

A catalog record for this book is available from the Library of Congress.

Typeset by MPS Limited, Chennai, India.

Transferred to Digital Printing in 2014

*To my parents, in gratitude for all
they have done*

Contents

Plates

Acknowledgements

I would like first and foremost to acknowledge the support I have received over the years from my friend and mentor Michael Durey who, despite this, probably still owes me a coffee. I should also like to thank Neville Wylie for the invaluable advice he gave me during my research, and my PhD examiner, Joseph Maiolo, for first suggesting that this book could and should be written. Reinhard Kühnel was of great help over the course of this project, both as a research assistant and constant source of encouragement. The author gratefully acknowledges the permissions given to reproduce material by: The Archives of the International Committee of the Red Cross, Geneva; The Archives of the International Federation of the Red Cross and Red Crescent Societies, Geneva; The British Red Cross Museum and Archives, London; The Churchill Archives, Cambridge; The Hampshire Records Office, Winchester; The Longmore Family; and The National Archives of the United Kingdom, London. I should also like to acknowledge the assistance given to me by Fabrizio Bensi at the ICRC and Grant Mitchell at the IFRC in Geneva, so too Isabel Trueb and Lorenz Heiligensetzer at the University of Basle archives. Emily Oldfield and Sarah Cox were also very accommodating of me during my visits to the British Red Cross archives. My thanks to both Melanie Oppenheimer, for allowing me to bend her ear on all things Red Cross, and Rebecca Gill, who so kindly gave me an advanced copy of her book on British humanitarian war relief. James Boyd was also good enough to read through draft sections of my book and offer useful feedback. My colleagues at Murdoch: Michael Sturma, Andrew Webster, James Trotter and Alex Jensen have all offered me various forms of wisdom and guidance over the course of the last five years and for that I thank them. To my editors at Palgrave Macmillan, Clare Mence and Emily Russell, my sincerest thanks for ushering me through the final stages of this project and helping to bring it to fruition. I have been fortunate throughout my life to have a wonderful, supportive family. It is to them that I owe everything, including my eternal gratitude. Finally, I should like to acknowledge the love and support of my wife, Sarah, who I thank for her willingness to look after a husband who so often forgets to look after himself.

Abbreviations

ACICR	Archives of the International Committee of the Red Cross, Geneva
AFHQ	Allied Force Headquarters
Agency	Central Agency for Prisoners of War
ARC	American Red Cross
AWA	Allgemeines Wehrmachtsamt
BEW	Board of Economic Warfare
BRC	British Red Cross
CCPS	Concentration Camps Parcel Scheme
CHURCH	Churchill Archives
DPW	Directorate of Prisoners of War
FO	Foreign Office
HRO	Hampshire Records Office
IACPR	Inter-Allied Committee on Post War Requirements
ICRC	International Committee of the Red Cross
ICRC Report	*Report of the International Committee of the Red Cross and Its Activities during the Second World War*, 3 vols (Geneva: ICRC, 1948)
IFRC	International Federation of the Red Cross and Red Crescent Societies, Geneva
IHL	International Humanitarian Law
IPOWC	Imperial Prisoners of War Committee
IRC	International Red Cross
IRO	International Refugee Organisation
IWM	International War Museum
JRC	Joint Relief Commission
JRC Report	*Final Report of the Joint Relief Commission of the International Red Cross: 1941–46* (Geneva: ICRC, 1948)

LRCS	League of Red Cross Societies
MEW	Ministry of Economic Warfare
MOC	Man of Confidence
NKVD	People's Commissariat for Internal Affairs
NSV	Nationalsozialistische Volkswohlfahrt
OFRRA	Office of Foreign Relief and Rehabilitation
OKH	Oberkommando des Heeres
OKW	Oberkommando der Wehrmacht
OSS	Office of Strategic Services
'POWs in WWII'	Harry J. Phillimore, 'History of the Second World War: Prisoners of War 1939–1945' (unpublished, 1949)
PP	Protecting Power
PWD	Prisoner of War Department
PWE	Political Warfare Executive
PWIB	Prisoner of War Information Bureau
SAARF	Special Allied Airborne Reconnaissance Force
SEP	Surrendered Enemy Personnel
SHAEF	Supreme Headquarters of the Allied Expeditionary Force
SS	Schutzstaffel
TNA	National Archives of the United Kingdom
UNRRA	United Nations Relief and Rehabilitation Association
VAD	Voluntary Aid Detachment
UB	Universität Bibliothek
WL:RAM	Wellcome Library, *Papers of Sir Thomas Longmore*
WO	War Office
YMCA	Young Men's Christian Association

Introduction

In 1946 Winston Churchill was preparing to journey to Switzerland for one of his many post-war speaking tours. Included in the events on his itinerary was a visit to Geneva, where he was to be the guest of honour at a luncheon hosted by Max Huber, the international lawyer, academic and occasional advisor to the Swiss Federal Council, who had been the president of the International Committee of the Red Cross (ICRC) during the Second World War. Although the ICRC's members had carried no arms and its main base of operations on the tranquil banks of Lake Geneva, the Villa Moynier, had suffered no air raids, many carried scars from the conflict not unlike those of the man whose decisive contributions they were honouring. The 179 delegates recruited by the ICRC during the war – Swiss volunteers whose only protection from harm in the field was a white armband emblazoned with a Red Cross and the willingness of belligerents to adhere to International Humanitarian Law (IHL) – exerted themselves tremendously on behalf of Allied and Axis soldiers, and the many civilians caught between their clash of arms. The delegates' status as neutral, impartial humanitarian actors having been codified in the 1929 Geneva Convention, the men and women of the ICRC traversed the globe throughout the conflict and its aftermath, delivering food and medical relief to Prisoners of War (POWs) and civilian internees, inspecting the camps in which they were detained and reporting on the status of their health and well-being to belligerent governments. In all, between 1939 and 1945, the ICRC collected the details of 30 million civilians and POWs, made 11,000 visits to places of internment and delivered 445,702 tonnes of food and medicine to victims of war, many of whom – had they not received such succour – would undoubtedly have perished.[1]

1

One of the main beneficiaries of this relief, from the opening of hostilities in Europe to the repatriation of prisoners in the Far East, were citizens of the British Empire. Approximately 365,000 British and Commonwealth soldiers and civilians were lost to captivity during the Second World War, many to the perilous abyss of the Japanese camp system, where their captors in the main ignored both the Geneva and POW Conventions and the humanitarian sentiments that underpinned their articles.[2] Other prisoners suffered the comparably less inhumane, though certainly arduous and dangerous, experience of captivity in the Third Reich and Italy; fed into the Axis's colossal POW camp system from battlefields in Europe, North Africa and the Balkans; the seas of the Mediterranean and the Atlantic; or from the skies above. All those detained by the Axis relied, some to the utmost extent, upon the delegates of the ICRC, whose delivery of food and inspections of the camps made them, as one inmate of the infamous Oflag IV C (Coldtiz) recalled, nothing short of 'angels'.[3]

The POW who made this assessment was Giles Romilly, nephew of Winston Churchill. It was with Romilly, and the hundreds of thousands of other British prisoners who felt similarly in mind, that in August 1945 the War Office suggested that 'it would be appropriate to express the gratitude of His Majesty's Government' to both Huber and the delegates of his Committee 'for their unremitting zeal in assisting British prisoners of war at every stage and in every aspect of their captivity'. Reflecting on his wartime work in 1950, Harold Satow, the head of the Foreign Office's Prisoner of War Department (PWD), also expressed gratitude for the 'inestimable services to Commonwealth prisoners of war' given by the ICRC and National Red Cross societies.[4] Beneath these plaudits, however, lay a more complex attitude towards the ICRC. Within pages of his words of praise for the Committee's relief work, Satow remarked that the delegates' reporting on conditions in the camps was not always up to standard, and throughout the war 'care had to be taken' by the PWD and others in Whitehall 'to ensure that, in their zeal, the International Red Cross Committee did not exceed the role allotted to them by the Convention'.[5] Reflecting in December 1945 on the character of the ICRC, David Roseway of the War Office declared that:

This Committee, which is responsible to nobody but itself and which in its most exalted moments tends to claim an authority independent of all other authority in the world might, if it ever ceased to be controlled and inspired by men and women actuated by the high principles and the neutral spirit have so far guided the Committee, become a dangerous body.[6]

Although Roseway's sentiments lay at the extremity of negative views in Whitehall, British officials of the Second World War – despite their appreciation for its work – tended to regard the ICRC with a mixture of apathy, confusion, indifference and, at times, barely concealed hostility.[7] In any manifestation, the result was disenchantment and disagreement between one of the key belligerents and the primary provider of humanitarian relief during the Second World War.

The sentiment existed at the very top of the British leadership. As he prepared for his luncheon with Max Huber, Romilly's uncle, the former Prime Minister, requested of the Foreign Office a 'brief history of the International Red Cross and also a few notes about the chief personnel of the Red Cross'.[8] It was as if the ICRC – the protector of British war victims and indeed of his own kin – had slipped the mind of Britain's wartime leader. This was particularly odd, not only because of Churchill's well-documented 'Napoleonic memory',[9] but also because he had much experience of the ICRC and was very aware of the global Red Cross movement to which it was central. His wife Clementine had organized Red Cross relief to Russia during the Civil War, and was a long-time supporter of the National British Red Cross Society (BRC), with whom she returned to Russia in 1945 on similar humanitarian business.[10] Moreover, Churchill himself had been engaged at a diplomatic level with the ICRC's leadership throughout the war, most prominently in the Katyn Affair of 1943, when the Committee was requested by Berlin to confirm that Britain's ally, Joseph Stalin, had ordered the massacre of 15,000 Polish POWs. The reciprocal shackling of British, Canadian and German POWs in 1942 – the last on Churchill's orders – also led to intense diplomatic engagement between the British Government and the ICRC's Vice President, Carl J. Burckhardt, who exerted himself in an effort to mediate an end to the shackling crisis. These specific incidents, as well as the manifold occasions in which the ICRC petitioned the British to slacken their blockade of occupied Europe – a cherished wartime strategy of the Prime Minister's – meant that Churchill was not ignorant of the ICRC or, indeed, of its wartime work. He was, however, indifferent and aloof towards the Committee and in this he was representative not only of many within Whitehall but also of those who would come after him in governments the world over.

Whether it be representatives from the ICRC, National Red Cross Societies, Médécins sans Frontières or the United Nations, even today humanitarians in war are often viewed with, at best, ambivalence by military forces and their governments. At worst, their neutrality and apparent desire to do no harm in violent contexts engenders suspicion of their motives, perhaps even a fear from one belligerent that these seemingly impartial humanitarian actors are being used – either willingly or unknowingly – by their foe as a source of food, medicine, intelligence or as a shield from attack.[11] Although these assessments of the ICRC's relationship with belligerent states apply to our own times, the same has been true, in varying forms, since the middle of the nineteenth century. The French had spoken of Red Cross volunteers as saboteurs at the First Geneva Conference in 1864 and hidden their forces behind the supposedly sacrosanct Red Cross flag in their war with Prussia in 1870–1. The Bolsheviks, though outwardly welcoming of the ICRC's work during the Russian Civil War, had little time for the Red Cross ethos of 'humanity for all' and made it clear that they would only support the ICRC if it approved of the creation of a new Soviet Red Cross Society and turned its attentions to the sufferings of 'Red' rather than 'White' war victims first and foremost.[12] The British had also been reluctant to embrace ICRC intervention during the Boer War and, despite the countless diplomatic interactions between the British Government and the Committee, and despite all the latter did on behalf of British citizens in both the First and Second World Wars, as late as 1949 'Whitehall nevertheless found great difficulty in knowing exactly how to regard and to deal with the ICRC.'[13] The questions of why this was the case and how the British attitude shaped the ICRC's approach to its activities during the Second World War lie at the heart of this book.

* * *

The ICRC was, and still is, unique. It began informally in 1863, as a five-man committee of concerned Swiss citizens engaged in debate over how best to protect wounded soldiers from unnecessary death on the battlefield. From these meetings a Europe-wide humanitarian movement was established, at the centre of which lay a small Geneva-based organization that, in 1876, was officially named the International Committee of the Red Cross. Today, the ICRC is the most widely recognized humanitarian organization on earth. It has a staff of 12,000 based in over eighty countries, many of which are plagued by endemic political instability and violence. The field humanitarians – known as 'delegates' in Red Cross parlance – who work in these war-torn environments handle one of the two main streams of the ICRC's operations: active humanitarianism. This includes the supplying of food and medicine to war victims, monitoring the conditions of POWs and civilian detainees and attempting, through myriad other techniques, to infuse humanitarian practice into the conduct of war and bring succour to those affected by it. The Committee's legal experts and leadership pursue the second stream of its activities: the development and promotion of International Humanitarian Law (IHL) as a means of regulating the conduct of belligerents in future and ongoing conflicts.[14] In both endeavours the ICRC – a neutral, impartial, nongovernmental organization – has to abide by the will of states, while simultaneously striving to pursue its own humanitarian agenda, often in the face of the contradictory force of military necessity.[15] In this respect, the ICRC has long been the arch-agitator for moderation in war, a thorn in the side of those who would wish to conduct 'total war' bereft of restraint. It is an unenviable and seemingly disempowered role to assume; historically, however, the ICRC's efforts have by no means been futile. This is because, beneath the lofty ideals of humanity preached by the Red Cross movement, its representatives have always possessed, to highly variable degrees, both political awareness and a willingness to adapt to difficult situations. As one historian has remarked, 'the ICRC can undertake its unique responsibilities only if it acts with great tact and discretion' in its dealings with belligerents in times of war, or state parties to IHL in times of peace.[16] The humanitarian impetus of the Red Cross, in short, has always and still is tempered by the realities of war, either as policy or in practice. Although much has been written on the post-1945 problems of the ICRC striking this balance in civil conflicts, the Committee has, since its very inception, walked this tightrope.[17]

During the Schleswig-Holstein War of 1864, Prussian forces refused the Committee's first ever delegate, Louis Appia, access to their front lines despite the Red Cross armband he proudly wore. Prussia had signed the First Geneva Convention in August 1864 and, in theory, had agreed to respect the neutrality of those wearing the Red Cross armband. In practice, however, there was little to be gained by allowing an unwanted, unarmed civilian into a war zone. It was only once Appia could offer something of tangible benefit to his hosts, namely, his skills as a surgeon, that he was permitted entry into the Prussian camp. Having gained this modicum of trust, he assumed the role of Red Cross missionary, spending his evenings with the soldiers, talking of Red Cross ideals and humanitarianism, promoting the 'Geneva project'.[18] In this Appia established a practice that is still expected of ICRC delegates to this day: always to push just that little bit more to achieve a humanitarian end, while remaining mindful that to push too far would be to lose the compliance of belligerents and thus the mandate to carry out humanitarian action.

This need to push ahead while being sensitive to states' interests has a long history in the ICRC's practice, not only in the field but also in its role as 'the main driving force behind the development of international humanitarian law'.[19] Having presided over the presentation and signing of the First Geneva Convention, the Committee's leadership began almost immediately to consider revisions and improvements to the document. Implicit in this process was the cajoling of states, which were frequently urged by the ICRC throughout the late nineteenth century to come to Geneva to discuss new IHL proposals. When this process came to fruition at the Geneva Conference of 1906 the ICRC, having performed so much preparatory work, was required – grudgingly – to stand back and stay silent. The ideas having been suggested by the worthies of the Committee, it was left to the will of the states' representatives to shape the new IHL to meet, as much as possible, their own military concerns.[20]

It is one of the contentions of this book that the role played by Britain, as the enforcer of pragmatic restraint upon the ICRC's humanitarian ambition, was decisive in shaping the latter's practices during the Second World War. This dynamic was not a phenomenon of that specific conflict. Long before 1939 Britain had been playing a key role in the development of the Red Cross movement. Florence Nightingale, the champion of British wartime humanitarianism, both influenced the thinking of the ICRC's founder, Henry Dunant, and, when displeased at the sum of the latter's thoughts, opposed his vision for the Red Cross on the grounds that neutral humanitarian volunteers – irrespective of their noble motives – had no place on the battlefield.[21] This contrary influence of Nightingale on the Red Cross movement was also manifest in both the development of the BRC and Whitehall's attitude to IHL. The BRC, founded in 1870, became a powerful player in the global Red Cross movement, yet often worked hard to keep itself divorced from Geneva. Like Nightingale, the BRC's founders had little time for the well-meaning Swiss and their lofty, universal ideals of humanity. Instead, like many National Societies of the nineteenth century, they took hold of the Red Cross ethos and shaped it to best serve the interests of their nation, in part by developing close relations with the British military.[22]

There was a similar impetus at work in the British Government and military's engagement with the ICRC over IHL prior to the Second World War. Though reluctant from its first encounter with the Committee in 1864 to embrace the Geneva Convention wholeheartedly – the British representative Sir Thomas Longmore described his participation in the Geneva Conference as 'troublesome' – the British Government nevertheless engaged intensely in the process of new IHL codification that emerged in the decades that followed, an age when 'state practice exhibited increasingly robust-norm-enunciation and procedural institution-building'.[23] Although other states were similarly involved in the process, the fingerprints of the British are clearer than any other on both the 1906 Convention and on its 1929 revision and accompanying POW Convention. This trend continued in 1949 at the conference to revise the Geneva Convention for a fourth time, during which British attempts to monopolize proceedings 'made the UK delegation the most unpopular one there'.[24]

The reader may ask at this point why, given the historical breadth of this dynamic in British-ICRC relations, does this book focus on those relations in the Second World War?

Much of the literature on the ICRC's history during the conflict has focused on its dealings with those belligerents who were vehemently opposed to its mission – those who openly violated IHL and, indeed, the basic principles of humanity and engaged in the very barbarism which is anathema to the Red Cross mission. The ICRC's struggle to carry out humanitarian relief in Japan's 'Greater East Asia Co-Prosperity Sphere', for example, and on the Eastern Front – where neither Moscow nor Berlin permitted the ICRC to operate – have figured prominently in assessments of the Committee's wartime record.[25] A similar degree of attention has been paid to the ICRC's failure to respond effectively to the Holocaust, the most notorious example of which came in October 1942, when the Committee's leadership elected not to speak out publicly about what it knew. The ICRC's fear was that by publicly condemning the Nazi's policies it would both stray from its principle of neutrality and impartiality towards belligerents, and displease the Swiss Federal Council, which at the time was endeavouring to maintain amicable relations with Berlin.[26] More so than its dealings with Tokyo or Moscow, this controversial episode has dominated recent histories of the ICRC, which in turn has led to much criticism of the Committee's overall record during the Second World War.[27] As the historian of the ICRC and the Holocaust, Jean-Claude Favez, has noted, since the opening of the Committee's archives to the general public in 1996 – primarily as a means of addressing public condemnation over its lack of action in the Holocaust – the former 'angels' of humanitarianism have joined the Swiss Government, Swiss banks and Swiss big business in being scrutinized for their complicity in the crimes of Hitler's regime.[28]

This narrative has been important, both to the wider scholarship of the Holocaust and as a counter to the often self-righteous official

8 *Britain and the ICRC*

histories provided by the ICRC and its delegates since 1945.[29] However, it by no means provides the full picture of the ICRC's wartime mission which, rather than being a crusade against barbarism in all its forms, was mostly dominated by the 'day-to-day' duties of its delegates: providing as best they could food and medical relief for POWs, civilian internees and, as the conflict escalated, non-interned civilians living under the yoke of the Axis. A broad, global overview of these less scandalous, though no less important, aspects of its wartime campaign has been provided not only in the ICRC's three-volume *Report of the International Committee of the Red Cross and Its Activities during the Second World War*, published in 1948, but by historians with connections to the ICRC – André Durand, François Bugnion among others – who have used the official report extensively as a basis for their works.[30] The independent researcher, Caroline Moorehead, also offered a sweeping overview of the ICRC's wartime work in her 1998 book, *Dunant's Dream: War, Switzerland and the History of the Red Cross*, which condensed the global history of the ICRC and the Red Cross movement since 1864 into a single volume. The intention of this book is to take a contrary, more constrained approach. By focusing on a key belligerent whose relations with Geneva, though touched on in the aforementioned works, have never been fully explored, this book provides nuance to extant historical narratives of the ICRC's wartime work and provides a greater understanding of how the Committee was able to bring a modicum of humanity to the twentieth century's greatest conflict.

The choice of Britain as the belligerent in focus is not an arbitrary one. Throughout the war the ICRC had to work very closely with Whitehall who, as masters of the blockade – the campaign to restrict the flow of food and medical relief into territories occupied by the Axis – wielded the power to deny relief to POWs, civilian internees and other objects of the Red Cross's concern. In order to understand how the ICRC, despite these restraints, was able to establish its relief campaigns and to construct a POW relief system that sustained both British and non-British prisoners over the war's duration, its relations with Whitehall must be examined. The second reason for a focus on British–ICRC relations is to contribute to the emerging discourse on Whitehall's wartime humanitarian policy – if indeed, such a term is appropriate. As Meredith Hindsley has concluded, Whitehall's thoughts on humanitarianism were scattered at best, and 'at no time during the war did the Allies consciously formulate a specific policy covering humanitarian activities'. This may have been true in the wider regard to British blockade policy which, in the main, was built upon Churchill's declaration of

20 August 1940 that no relief would be permitted into Europe until Hitler was defeated.[31] The fact, however, that there were exceptions to this rule – Greece and Vichy France – indicates that British humanitarian policy was not as unbending as it first appeared. The same is true of British humanitarian thinking in regard to POWs. As Neville Wylie's work on the 'POW regime' in Anglo-German wartime relations has shown, Whitehall's POW policy – though ostensibly as straightforward as its policy for civilian war victims – was in practice, complex, multifaceted and, as it evolved, impossible to divorce from the wider context of the war.[32] This was particularly true of British POW policy in the Far East where, owing to the collapse of the norms of the POW relief system, a certain degree of unusual flexibility permeated Whitehall's thinking.

In both these broad areas of humanitarian policy – for civilians or POWs – the British necessarily had to engage with the ICRC which, by treaty and custom, was recognized by most belligerents as a key mitigator of human suffering in war, in particular the suffering of POWs.[33] The Committee's right to carry out humanitarian action on behalf of civilians was, however, less recognized and its struggle with the British blockade authorities for such recognition was a central aspect of the ICRC's wartime campaign. As will be argued, the ICRC's continuous – at times volatile – disputes with the British over this issue were a significant factor in its wartime growth from small philanthropic agency to global humanitarian institution. This expansion of the ICRC raised the spectre of long-held concerns in Britain over the Committee's freedom of action, prompting a concentrated campaign by Whitehall to curtail the ICRC's ambitions to extend its scope for humanitarian action. In this endeavour, however, the British also had to be mindful that the ICRC provided a lifeline to its citizens in captivity. In this respect, the British had to perform a balancing act: keeping the Committee active in working for British interests, while restraining the attempts by its leadership, in particular its maverick Vice-President Carl J. Burckhardt, both to raise the Committee's international profile and to extend its operational purview into new areas that were not prescribed to its delegates in extant IHL. The exploration of this dynamic of dependence and divergence in British–ICRC relations will form the backbone of much of the discussion in this book.

The pre-Second World War relationship between the ICRC and Britain forms the first part of this book and the necessary background to British–ICRC wartime relations. In Chapter 1, the origins of the Red

Cross movement and its development during the late nineteenth century are explored in conjunction with the evolving attitudes of British Governments and their militaries towards the ICRC and, in particular, the latter's campaign to develop new IHL. Included within this examination is a consideration of the origins and development of the BRC which, though far from completely embraced by the British Government, was nevertheless regarded as a more useful and less troublesome manifestation of the Red Cross movement than its 'parent' organization in Geneva.

Chapter 2 provides an assessment of the ICRC and the British Government's preparedness for the humanitarian challenges of the Second World War. Particular attention is paid to the approach both parties took to POW welfare, upon which foundation British–ICRC wartime relations were built. The corpus of existing literature on British attitudes to POW policy – which in the main have offered a damning assessment of Whitehall's 'blind bureaucracy' – is contrasted with the ICRC's own responses to the outbreak of war and the need to establish a workable system of relief, inspection and monitoring for POWs.[34] The ICRC's response to these challenges was more proactive than that of the British departments concerned with POW welfare and, although relations between Whitehall and Geneva were stable and healthy during the Phoney War, malaise and a lack of forward planning were endemic in Whitehall's handling of POW matters and proved destabilizing to British–ICRC relations.

Chapter 3 explores the breakdown of British–ICRC relations and the POW relief system in Europe in the wake of the capture of over 40,000 British soldiers in the summer of 1940. The plight of these prisoners – whose captures were not reported to the ICRC by the Germans in a timely manner and whose access to POW parcels was very limited during the first six months of their internment – engendered a public backlash against the British Government and the BRC, which had been given the task by the War Office in 1939 of organizing relief for British POWs. The means by which Whitehall, the BRC and the ICRC recovered from the POW crisis and, in so doing, constructed a stable and resilient POW relief system that would maintain the health and well-being of many POWs in Europe until the collapse of the Third Reich is explored, with particular emphasis on the importance of the maturation of British POW policy and the increasing professionalism of the ICRC's operations during 1941. In Chapter 4, the outcome of these 'evolutions' in Whitehall and Geneva's POW policies – the sum of which was the creation of a dynamic of British dependence on the

ICRC, while still holding divergent views towards the latter's war aims –
is examined against the backdrop of the Committee's work in the Far
East and the attempts by the ICRC to expand its operations into new,
non-traditional fields.

The extent to which Whitehall was willing to back the ICRC in its
campaign in the Far East, and in so doing increase its dependence upon
Geneva, is contrasted in Chapter 5 with the stark divergence of each
parties' conception of the blockade of Europe. This examination charts
the evolution of Geneva's anti-blockade policy – from clumsy, utopian
acts of defiance against British wishes in 1940 to the more thoughtful
and professional scheme to construct its own 'White Ships' relief fleet in
1942. The wider ramifications of this engagement with Britain are discussed, in particular the extent to which the ICRC's agitation on behalf
of civilians solidified British views that the Committee, by expanding
its operations into new areas, was becoming 'too big for its boots' and,
possibly, compromising British wartime strategy.

This new, more agitated phase of British–ICRC relations is covered
in Chapter 6, via an analysis of the spread of the ICRC's operations
across the world and the resulting suspicions over ICRC neutrality that
emerged, not only in British minds but also increasingly in the minds
of the United States military and intelligence services. The efforts of
Carl J. Burckhardt to address the Allies' concerns over the credibility
and trustworthiness of himself and his Committee – by attempting to
make himself indispensible to the British during the Shackling Crisis of
1942–3 and by steering the Committee away from the politically volatile Katyn Affair – are also discussed. Through this a wider assessment
of the ICRC as practitioners of humanitarian diplomacy is made. It is
concluded that by 1943 the ICRC, having laboured since the start of the
war under the label of 'amateurs', was now set on a campaign to become
a more professional and pragmatic humanitarian agency. The extent to
which the ICRC achieved this is assessed in Chapter 7, by examining
the Committee's response both to the disruptions caused to its operations by the Allied invasion of Europe and to the breakdown of supply
lines and forced evacuations of hundreds of thousands of Allied POWs
over the winter of 1944–5. The often maverick nature of the ICRC's
work in the final months of the war, and the responses of the British
and United States governments as well as the Supreme Headquarters
of the Allied Expeditionary Force (SHAEF) to such an approach, is also
discussed. Finally, in Chapter 8, it is argued that, despite its manifold wartime achievements and operational expansion, the ICRC was
marginalized in the post-war relief effort by the Allies, who favoured

their own humanitarian organization – the United Nations Relief and Rehabilitation Administration (UNRRA). The extent to which this decision was coloured both by Allied experience of the ICRC during the war and early Cold War politics is also assessed.

This book concludes that, despite the apparent negative influence of its often disparaging views of ICRC personnel and its unwillingness to co-operate with certain Committee initiatives, the British Government also made a positive contribution to the ICRC's wartime record and, through engagement with the Committee, was forced to consider aspects of humanitarian policy that Churchill's 'victory before relief' stance belied. To explain how this complex interaction between Britain and the ICRC developed, it is important first to establish how the foundations upon which British–ICRC relations in the Second World War were built and the extent to which – despite their apparent robustness – these foundations were, from the outset, riddled with cracks.

Part I

1
Britain and the Red Cross, 1864–1929

A conference in the city of Calvin

The 8 August 1864 was an ostensibly momentous day for those gathered at the Hôtel de Ville, in the heart of Geneva's old town. It was the final day of an international conference, attended by twenty-four beribboned representatives of sixteen European states, at which the First Geneva Convention for the Amelioration of the Condition of the Wounded Armies in the Field would be signed. The occasion was presided over by the conference's proud instigators, the fledgling International Committee for Relief to the Wounded, the first incarnation of the organization that, in 1876, would be renamed the International Committee of the Red Cross (ICRC). For the founders of this Committee – five Swiss private citizens – the signing of the First Geneva Convention marked the end of an eighteen-month-long road of negotiations, the aim of which was to call together the heads of the most powerful states in Europe to sign a document that would outline regulations on how to care for wounded soldiers and protect those who tended them on the battlefield. Although the ICRC's founders could lay claim to having these practices codified in such grandeur, the idea of establishing such a set of rules for states to abide by in times of conflict was not a radical one. Informal codes that regulated the practice of war had developed over the course of the preceeding centuries and, in the immediate decades prior to the signing of the First Geneva Convention, several quasi-formal codes were put into practice on American and European battlefields. Far from being a pioneer, the Committee's attempts to regulate the practice of war dovetailed completely with the sentiments of an era that marked the 'high tide' of legal positivism.[1] The conference was, all the same, somewhat unique, if only for the fact that the man who gave birth to the idea of

15

the summit was no political figure of authority or international standing but a struggling Swiss businessman and philanthropist by the name of Henry Dunant.

Raised in a conservative Genevan household, Dunant was, from the youngest age, a Samaritan. By his early 20s he was already highly active in the city's many humanitarian circles and, prior to entering the agriculture business in the 1850s, he spent much of his time volunteering for the Young Men's Christian Association (YMCA), sacrificing his weekends to read to illiterate prisoners in Geneva's jails. It was on a business trip across Lombardy, however, that Dunant experienced the true turning point of his career as a humanitarian. On 24 June 1859, he was startled to witness the Franco-Sardinian army clash with Austrian forces near the town of Solferino, a battle which he watched from atop a nearby hill. Reflecting on this experience in 1862, Dunant wrote not only of the 'hand-to-hand struggle in all its horror and frightfulness' of the Battle of Solferino proper but also of the disturbing aftermath of the Franco-Sardinian victory, which left a glut of wounded and dying. 'Some, who had gaping wounds already beginning to show infection, were almost crazed with suffering. They begged to be put out of their misery, and writhed with faces distorted in the grip of the death-struggle.'[2] It was this wastage of life and indifference to the suffering of those who could have been saved in Solferino's wake that moved Dunant to write *A Memory of Solferino*, a provocative account of the battle and its horrors in which he outlined his vision of how similar human catastrophes could be averted in future. This vision – which called for the establishment of neutral, voluntary societies to provide medical assistance to wounded on the battlefield – in turn inspired another Genevan: a high-minded, if at times cantankerous, lawyer named Gustav Moynier. A less emotional and more cynical character than Dunant, Moynier nevertheless saw the harmony between the former's ideas for humanitarianism in war and his own civic-minded utilitarian views of philanthropy as the basis upon which to encourage moral progress in society. For if humanity could somehow be infused into the conduct of war then surely it could find its place in the gutters, backstreets and factories of European cities, areas of concern that Moynier had been working on for years via the Geneva Society for Public Welfare.[3] Using Moynier's contacts in that organization and the wider world of Swiss philanthropy, he and Dunant built up support for their cause, and before long they were joined by three others who had read *Solferino* with interest and were determined to act upon it. These were the French-born Swiss doctor Louis Appia, his colleague Théodore Maunoir and a retired General of the

Swiss Army, Guillaume-Henri Dufor who, together with Dunant and Moynier, formed the International Committee for Relief to the Wounded in February 1863. With this 'Committee of Five' in place and in agreement, Dunant took to the road in order to urge Europe's heads of state to gather in Geneva for a conference, at which the Committee's vision would be presented with the aim of securing an international agreement to bring succour to the war wounded.[4]

His proposal was, in the main, well received, particularly by the German states and Emperor Napoleon III of France, who became one of Dunant's most important early supporters. This response was not surprising. Since the sixteenth century the notion of applying chivalric values, hitherto reserved for nobles, to the treatment of common soldiers had gradually become adopted by most modern professional armies. In the years immediately prior to the founding of the 'Committee of Five', this concept of humane treatment for soldiers had become manifest in the work of Florence Nightingale in the Crimea and, as Dunant traversed Europe in 1863, in the United States, where President Lincoln applied the recommendations of lawyer Francis Lieber on the treatment of prisoners of war to the conduct of soldiers in the Union Army.[5] Dunant's initiative therefore, was very well timed to meet a favourable response.

In addition to the fifteen other states moved – or at least made curious – by Dunant's request, Britain sent delegates to both the initial Geneva conference of October 1863 and the concluding conference of August 1864 at which the Geneva Convention was signed. Despite this, however, the British Government was among the most reluctant of participants in Dunant and Moynier's enterprise. The delegate sent by Whitehall to the 1863 conference – Dr William Rutherford, Deputy Inspector of Hospitals attached to the War Office – was chosen at the last minute, spoke little French and was briefed that he was attending a sanitary conference, not, as he soon found out, a meeting of 'a kind of international amateur society to assist the sick and wounded'. He was also given instructions to abstain from participation in the discussions, take notes on the views of others and report back. Nothing more, nothing less.[6] This order to remain detached from proceedings turned out to be well advised. The other British attendee, Dr Twining, was present not on behalf of the Government but of the London Social Sciences Association, an extra-parliamentary think-thank that 'melded the political, administrative and intellectual elites of mid-Victorian Britain and believed itself to be uniquely representative of the social concerns of the period'.[7] Despite this liberal pedigree, Twining sparked one of the more controversial moments of the discussions by opining that the best way to address the problem of treating the wounded on the battlefield was with a mercy shooting that would avoid them dying 'with a fevered brain and blasphemy on their lips'. Although there was laughter from some of those present, it remains unclear how serious this suggestion was.[8] Whether joke or not, it was an inauspicious start for British relations with the Red Cross.

For the concluding conference of 1864 at least, Whitehall had prepared. At the request of Lord De Grey, the Secretary of War, both Rutherford and Sir Thomas Longmore, the Surgeon General, were given a brief by Britain's doyen of battlefield succour, Florence Nightingale. Unfortunately for Dunant and Moynier, Nightingale was no fan of the 'Geneva project', which she regarded as noble in intent but 'absurd' in practice, emanating as it did from 'a little state like Geneva, which never can see war'. Britain, by contrast, had already successfully blended the spirit of volunteerism into the practice of war and as a consequence boasted one of the most well-established military medical units in Europe – the Medical Staff Corps – which had been developed during the Crimean War before becoming a permanent service in 1856. With such a resource already at its disposal, the idea of non-British civilian volunteers running across battlefields to tend to wounded was viewed by Nightingale, Rutherford and Longmore as being an unnecessary complication to the practice of conducting modern, professional war which, to the parties concerned, had already been mastered by the forces of Queen Victoria. Longmore and Rutherford were not shy in putting forward this view. Upon their arrival at the Hôtel de Ville in August 1864, they presented Moynier with a copy of the *Queen's Regulations for the Management of British Army Hospitals*, so as to educate their host in alternative forms of battlefield succour to those being proposed. The British position going into the conference was clear: in regards to medical assistance for soldiers 'the whole procedure is military and under the direction of the general commanding the forces'.[9] Britain's armies had nothing to gain from neutral, voluntary humanitarianism.

It seems odd, given this clear position of opposition to Dunant and Moynier's vision, that Longmore and Rutherford agreed in principle to the main points laid down in the Geneva Convention. These were that all ambulances, medical personnel and civilian volunteers who wore the emblem of a Red Cross on a white background would be granted neutrality on the battlefield; that through this neutrality the emblem would be recognized by belligerents as being sacrosanct; and that wounded and sick soldiers should be recovered, cared for and then repatriated as quickly as possible. The British delegates' willingness to agree was no doubt encouraged by the fact that, like the representatives of several other states, neither Longmore nor Rutherford had been given authorization by their government to actually sign the Geneva Convention. As was the case with the initial talks the year before, the British wished to tread carefully. Their representatives were to take notes on who signed and what was agreed to, before reporting back. Therefore, when prompted to sign by Moynier, Longmore claimed he could do no such thing without a royal seal. This hesitancy was countered by General Dufour, who produced his penknife, cut a button from Longmore's tunic and declared 'there, your Excellency, you have the arms of Her Majesty'. Longmore, no doubt concealing the affront he would have felt at the dissection of his garment, played along with the stamping of the document, safe in the knowledge that without an official signature and ratification by his government the gesture was near meaningless.[10] It was with a degree of caution and a sprinkling of farce, therefore, that Britain commenced its relations with Dunant and Moynier's 'international amateur society'.

Humanity begins at home: the development of the British Red Cross

The British Government ratified the Geneva Convention on 18 February 1865, five months after France and a little over a month after Prussia had done likewise.[11] Of the great powers present at the signing ceremony, Britain had waited the longest to ratify the Convention. Nevertheless it had done so despite the logical, if somewhat self-serving, objections that its representatives had raised at Geneva. These objections amounted to two simple questions that would hang over the Committee's relations with Britain into the twentieth century and particularly at times when the latter went to war: what did the Government have to gain by entering into a principled agreement with the Committee? Why should an empire at the apex of its power, with a military well equipped to address concerns for its soldiers' welfare, involve itself in a Swiss humanitarian exercise? One of the clearest reasons was that the British generally viewed the 'Geneva project' as both noble and, importantly, harmless. Writing to Longmore upon his return from Geneva, even Nightingale remarked that, despite her personal reservations over its substance, the Convention amounted 'to nothing more than a declaration of humanity' and so was worth ratifying as a gesture of British moral worth.[12] For their part, the Committee's founders also recognized the appeal that their project's blend of Christian morality and Enlightenment values would hold for most European states. Agreement to the Geneva Convention was presented as a solemn duty which, as General Dufour declared at the signing of the document, was 'demanded by the present circumstances of civilisation and real Christian charity'.[13]

Arguably more important than this impulse to appear civilized and moral was the states' practical sense of the cost and benefit of infusing humanity into the practice of war. Longmore, for one, was very mindful that, as a consequence of the communications revolution and the narrowing gap between the battlefield and the home front in modern warfare, information on the welfare of soldiers was now more freely available to their families than at any other time in history.[14] In such changing circumstances, so Longmore believed, not only did medical responses to battlefield carnage have to improve but also state indifference to soldiers' welfare could also no longer be tolerated. Open and codified cooperation with an international organization like the Committee, however amateur they viewed it, would give the British Government a means of showing the average Briton that it was acting in the best interests of those who fought and died on the nation's behalf. This reason alone, in Longmore's mind, justified the Government's participation in the 'Geneva project'.[15]

Beyond the signing and the ratification, the question of how this participation would change anything in Britain itself in regards to humanitarianism remained open. As Longmore was well aware, Dunant was passionate about a proposal he first raised in 1863 – that states party to the Convention 'shall have a committee whose duty it shall be, in time of war and if need arise, to assist Army Medical Services by every means necessary in its power'. In other words, a National Red Cross Society. Fearful that such a demand would sour the opinions of conference attendees, Moynier had the matter removed from the agenda of the 1864 conference. The idea nonetheless continued to be promoted by Dunant in the years that followed.[16] Despite the official British view of National Societies as superfluous to the work of the Medical Staff Corps, outside Whitehall this aspect of the 'Geneva project' had fertile ground in which to grow. In the decades prior to the signing of the Convention, many Britons, from the landed and middle classes in particular, had endeavoured to construct a national culture of humanitarianism and volunteerism. The London Social Sciences Association was the primary body within this movement, the grass-roots momentum of which had pushed the development of other volunteer societies devoted to, among other things, the abolition of slavery, women's rights, the protection of children, and the maintenance of the 'concert of Europe' for the purposes of preserving peace, order and civilization. In the wake of the Crimean War – from the battlefield hospitals of which came lurid reports of the wounded and dying – this enthusiasm for humanitarianism and volunteerism permeated more than ever into concerns for the victims of war.[17]

When hostilities broke out between France and Prussia in July 1870, this desire to do good for soldiers became manifest in Britain through the creation of the British National Society for Aid to the Sick and Wounded in War, the precursor to what would later become the British Red Cross Society (BRC). The British Society's specific origins can be traced to a series of appeals to the British public in *The Times* during the summer of 1870. The most emphatic of these appeals came from a Crimean War veteran, Colonel Robert Llyod-Lindsay, who had been recruited to act as a British mouthpiece for Dunant's vision by both Longmore and Sir John Furley, a man so inspired by the Red Cross ideal that he had translated into English Moynier and Appia's *La Guerre et la Charité* in an effort to rouse support in Britain for a National Society. The sentiments of this work were channelled into Llyod-Lindsay's appeal, which was also thick with allusions to the moral duty of British citizens. Speaking as both a military man and a humanitarian, he reminded readers of Britain's ratification of the Geneva Convention, its tradition of 'contributing aid and succour' in prior conflicts and the unacceptable fact that, despite this rich and noble tradition, it had been left to many of the other nations of Europe to form National Red Cross Societies in the years since 1864.[18] Writing in support of Lloyd-Lindsay on 11 August, the Earl of Shaftsbury turned the former's sentiments into a humanitarian call to arms by declaring that:

> secure as we are in this, by God's mercy, inaccessible island, and enjoying in abundance so much wealth and so much comfort, we ought to do something to show our humanity and a great deal more to show our Christianity, in the midst of such mental and bodily tribulation as now afflicts so large a portion of the Continent of Europe.[19]

The public responded well to this appeal and by the middle of August the British Society had received the official endorsement of Queen Victoria. Within a matter of weeks several buildings in London had been requisitioned as storehouses for food and medicine donations and by the end of September sixty-two surgeons had been recruited to serve as Red Cross volunteers in France. By the time the Franco-Prussian war concluded in May 1871, the British Society had collected a total of £300,000 in donations from the public and had taken receipt of twelve ambulances from the War Office. The fact that these ambulances were sold to the British Society rather than donated was not without significance. For all the apparent embrace of the Red Cross ideal by humanitarian-minded Britons outside Whitehall, the War Office continued to hold the view, first espoused by Nightingale, that Dunant's vision was both 'utopian and impractical' and that the British Society volunteers were an unnecessary appendage to the Medical Staff Corps.[20]

This negative view of the British Society lingered into the dawn of the twentieth century. Attempts in the 1870s and 1880s to integrate its volunteers into military operations better – cautiously at first as providers of transport between field and base hospitals – had done little to alter the view that such volunteers were, ultimately, unneeded. As Surgeon-Major W. G. MacPherson reported to Whitehall in 1896, the British Society was both poorly provisioned and amateur compared with the more elaborately structured and efficient National Societies established on the Continent, and was in no position to offer a practical contribution to the endeavours of the British military.[21] The appeals made by both the British Society's leadership and the War Office during the Boer War for adventurous volunteers to stay at home and show their support by sending money to pay for relief supplies fell on deaf ears.[22] Instead, MacPherson's assessment of the British Society was confirmed as waves of well-meaning though unprepared and undisciplined humanitarians flooded into South Africa, many of whom were devoid of even the most basic medical training. More worryingly, some volunteers used the neutrality of the Red Cross emblem as a cover for distinctly non-humanitarian activities. A male British volunteer was accused of sexual assault while wearing the Red Cross armband and at least one group of over fifty volunteers from the American Red Cross, upon reaching South Africa, tore off their emblems and took up arms alongside the Boers. This incident merely added to concerns already prevalent in Whitehall that the Boers had adopted a policy of using the Red Cross emblem as cover to move arms and soldiers.[23] In Whitehall's eyes, therefore, not only its own National Society but also the Red Cross movement writ large came out of the Boer War looking enthusiastic but amateur, its volunteers unfit for the tasks they had set themselves and, most dangerously, susceptible to abuse by the enemy on the battlefield. An official report compiled in 1900 by the Foreign Office concluded that 'irresponsible civil aid societies' could never be seen 'on the same footing as the regular military medical service, with its responsibility to authority and its long and honourable record'.[24]

In the wake of the Boer War, an effort was made by the British Society to address its image problem, improve relations with the military, and, in the spirit of international competition, to 'obtain greater respect and support' and 'a position more in harmony' with the status enjoyed by National Societies on the Continent, which had been more successful in wedding themselves to their nations' militaries.[25] To this end, in 1905 the various volunteer and nursing organizations in Britain were reorganized into the British Red Cross Society (BRC), with Queen Alexandra as its president and King Edward as its patron. This reorganization, royal endorsement and subsequent push for greater integration between the BRC and the military greatly improved the former's status by finding – or rediscovering – a common ground on which to build relations between itself and the British Government; namely, concern for the welfare of British soldiers and the need to serve British interests.[26]

It was on this basis that the BRC carried out its work in the First World War with the endorsement of Lord Kitchener himself, who recognized the role that could be filled by BRC volunteers as stretcher bearers and nurses. These duties were extended once it became clear that the war would not end quickly. By the end of September 1914, the BRC had four hospitals established in Paris, staffed by 150 nurses who had been given training under the Voluntary Aid Detachment (VAD) scheme, a programme that had been introduced in 1909 by the General Director of the Army Medical Department in order to better integrate the BRC's work into the military's operations. By 1916, VAD detachments were present on almost every front in which British soldiers were engaged, performing tasks as varied as changing soldiers' bandages, transporting X-ray equipment, handing out cricket sets and making lemonade. With the authorization of the War Office, the BRC also established a tracing agency for missing prisoners and was accredited as the packer and provider of Red Cross food parcels for prisoners of war (POWs). Both of these tasks acutely married its activities to British military concerns.[27] Although there were protests from certain quarters of the War Office throughout the war over the permeation of the BRC into military affairs, in general the latter came out of the conflict with an enhanced reputation. This confirmed the degree to which, since the blunders in South Africa at the turn of the century, the national Red Cross movement in Britain had been rejuvenated and, in Whitehall's eyes, rehabilitated as an effective component of Britain's military.[28]

The question that had first been asked by Longmore and Nightingale over how Dunant's call for neutrals on the battlefield could be reconciled with British military humanitarianism was thus answered by the start of the First World War. That the process of finding a common ground between the BRC and the military had involved the former all but surrendering its neutrality – the very font of its volunteers' right to carry out their tasks – was not without significance. By subordinating the BRC in this fashion the British confirmed the basic assumption that had underpinned their dealings with the Red Cross since 1864: that neutral humanitarianism was not compatible with practical relief for victims of war. Humanitarianism in the national interest, however, was achievable, indeed, necessary. The BRC had, arguably, been a willing participant in the 'militarisation of humanity', a process which, notably, was not at all unique to the British Government and its National Society.[29] For its part, the ICRC kept itself distant from these developments. Moynier, in particular, had chosen to take a very hands-off approach to the growth of the National Societies and had been little troubled by the increasing trend of their aligning, to the detriment of Red Cross neutrality, with their nation's militaries. The full consequences of this aloof attitude to its 'children' would come back to haunt the ICRC after the First World War. The consequences in the late nineteenth century, however, were similarly important for the Committee.

Unlike the various National Societies, the ICRC was neither an agent for wartime relief nor an entity that could be corralled into serving the national interest of a belligerent state. The Committee's Louis Appia and a retired Dutch officer named Van de Velde had tried their hands at ICRC 'field work' in the Schleswig-Holstein War of 1864, during which they proudly wore the first ever Red Cross armbands. Both men were viewed suspiciously by the belligerents and, although they travelled widely through the front lines and rear areas as observers, the practical achievements of their mission were not clearly evident. In the decades that followed only a handful of Committee delegates carried out practical relief and it was not until the outbreak of the First World War that the notion of the widespread deployment of ICRC delegates in belligerent territories as relief agents became normalized. In its formative decades, therefore, the Committee did not view itself as a practical humanitarian actor. That role – viewed in Britain as much as in any other European state as the only real service offered by the Red Cross – was to be assumed by BRC volunteers.[30] Consequently, although the benefits of this Red Cross activity were slowly becoming apparent to the British by the end of the nineteenth century, the role played by the ICRC itself, and the value to Britain of its work, remained unclear.

Britain and International Humanitarian Law

As the Committee saw it, its primary task after 1864 was to build upon the success of the first Geneva Conference and in so doing refine and expand the corpus of International Humanitarian Law (IHL), a role that is central to the ICRC's existence to this day.[31] The ink had barely dried on the First Geneva Convention when Moynier began to lay claim to this role. In October 1868 representatives from twenty countries, including Britain, returned to Geneva to discuss, among other things, the extension of Red Cross emblem protection to relief and hospital ships; mandatory identity tags for soldiers and restrictions on the looting of bodies. The discussions were taken seriously by the attendees and by the British in particular, who examined the proposals relating to maritime warfare very closely.[32] The willingness of Britain and others to resume the 'Geneva project' so soon after 1864 was the result of context as much as it was an acknowledgement of the ICRC as the driving force and 'guardian' of IHL.[33] In the late nineteenth century, previously held conceptions of war and peace were changing and sharper distinctions between the two states of existence were being made. The idea that two separate legal regimes existed – one for times of peace and one for times of war – and that there needed to be clear distinctions between combatants and non-combatants and neutrals and belligerents were becoming the norm. The support of international jurists engaged in this thinking, combined with acknowledgement by states themselves of the significance of the Geneva Convention as the first definite step towards 'civilising' war were part of a process that was soon to grow bigger than the ICRC.[34]

Even in his capacity as a private citizen, Dunant did his bit to contribute to this process. The glories of 1864 long past him, at the turn of the decade Dunant was in a bad way. His involvement in the collapse of the Crédit Genévois bank in 1867 had left him both destitute and estranged from Moynier, who, already frustrated by the utopianism of the Red Cross founder, gladly accepted Dunant's resignation from the Committee in the wake of the scandal. Despite his parlous state and divorce from Geneva, Dunant, having heard of the manifold violations of his treasured convention during the Franco-Prussian War, went on a one-man humanitarian crusade in the early 1870s. In this he endeavoured both to strengthen the existing articles pertaining to the protection offered by the Red Cross emblem and to develop new articles to cover a glaring omission from 1864: protection for POWs.[35] There had been a notably practical effort by the Committee to address this issue during the Franco-Prussian War via the creation of the Basle Agency, a centralized office at which information on captured soldiers was compiled, food and medical supplies stored and letters from loved ones received and distributed.[36] Dunant's goal was to ensure that this expedient measure would be codified as standard practice for future conflicts. So determined was he to make these changes that in 1874, despite still being penniless and suffering from poor health, he travelled to Britain to drum up support for this initiative. His proposal to extend the Convention into the realms of POW protection was accepted in principle by Longmore, the Social Sciences Association and the Peace Society of London, albeit with the acknowledgement from all that the idea might be too radical for Britain's military leaders. By now indisputably recognized as the elder statesman of the Red Cross movement despite his personal calamities, Dunant was gratified at the special treatment he received as an honoured guest of his British supporters. Beyond the praise, however, it was clear to the old philanthropist that the groups that welcomed him, ten years after the triumph in Geneva, had lost much of their fire, direction and influence in government circles – casualties of the emerging crisis of liberalism within Britain in the final decades of the nineteenth century. His request that the British Government call for an international conference, as the Swiss Federal Council had in 1864, was rejected.[37] The increasing powerlessness of his supporters was, however, only part of the reason why Dunant's mission failed. The real problem lay in the fact that, for those in Britain enthused by the idea of new IHL, there were new avenues available besides Dunant or his erstwhile friends in Geneva to make the practice of war more civilized.

During the 'golden age' of codification in the late nineteenth century, the main challenge to the ICRC's role as guardian and chief architect of IHL came from St Petersburg where, in 1868, the very year Moynier tried to get the Geneva Convention revised, Tsar Alexander II called for his own international conference. On the agenda would be new regulations for the use of exploding (dumdum) bullets, the conduct of maritime warfare, and the protection of partisans and POWs. The source of these humanitarian proposals – a nation that, unlike Switzerland, was much involved in the power politics of Europe and, indeed, was pursuing a policy of expansion to the detriment of British interests in eastern Europe and Central Asia at this time – led to a cool response not only in Britain but also throughout the Continent. Nevertheless, pulled by the same forces that had taken them to Geneva, delegates from across Europe gathered in Brussels between July–August 1874 to attend the

Tsar's humanitarian soirée. Although the Brussels Conference was a far grander affair than the concurrent speeches being made by Dunant in Britain, Alexander's efforts were generally interpreted by his guests as amounting to little more than a 'code of conquest' that served only to legitimize Russian expansionism. That impression, combined with the disorganized nature of proceedings, and the mass of new regulations put forward, ultimately led the fifteen attendees to come away from Brussels with no binding agreements.[38] For Dunant and Moynier, both of whom felt that their reputations were being damaged and their efforts sabotaged by Russian meddling, there were greater threats to come.[39]

Undeterred by his predecessor's lack of success, Tsar Nicholas II called in 1898 for a new conference to discuss regulations for the conduct of war and arms reduction. Once again, suspicion of Russian motives swept through European corridors of power. Yet the excitement engendered by Nicholas's initiative, the outcome of which optimists believed might amount to nothing less than a new golden age of peace, all but ensured that the conference would be well attended. In Whitehall, the themes in pre-conference discussions were similar to those that had preceded the 1864 Geneva Conference – focused less on the humanitarian imperative behind the occasion and more on the question of how best to appear civilized, while making sure not to give up any military advantage to rival powers. It was primarily this motivation, in addition to growing unease over the developing arms race in Europe, that prompted the British to send a delegation to what became the Hague Conference of 1899. Although the proceedings confirmed the agreements made over POWs in Brussels in 1874, the loftier ambitions of the occasion were not met and, in a sign of the changing political context and wearied expectation of war, the focus was shifted from discussions of peace and IHL onto the need to strengthen the principle of military necessity – the point at which humanitarian concerns have to give way to the efficient and expeditious conduct of war.[40] This cycle of IHL proposals, clarification and conference continued into the new century and, in the wake of the First Hague Conference, discussions soon began over the need for both a second Hague Conference and a new Geneva Conference, which were held in 1907 and 1906 respectively.

What role did Britain play in this complex era of intense IHL codification, carried out against the backdrop of a world that seemed to yearn for peace while preparing for war?[41] Moreover, what effect did British involvement in the development of IHL have on its views of the ICRC and the 'Geneva project' writ large? A cursory glance suggests a certain degree of British aloofness towards IHL, tinged ever so slightly with annoyance, at both the development of 'Geneva Law' (the laws governing the treatment of war victims) and the emerging corpus of 'Hague Law' (the laws governing the means of waging war). In addition to the persistence of Longmore and Rutherford's basic argument – that humanitarianism in war was the responsibility of the military, not of civilian volunteers – at the 1899 Hague Conference the British delegation brought an attitude that was as wary as it was unremarkable in the minds of the representatives of other states. This was that IHL had already gone too far and that agitators for further regulation were no more than pacifists bent on interfering in crucial military affairs at a time of increasing rivalry between states. Consequently, much British focus at The Hague was on the need to preserve the Royal Navy's pre-eminent position on the high seas, a task which fell to Admiral John 'Jackie' Fisher. Throughout proceedings Fisher worked to ensure that no agreement would be reached that would affect the Royal Navy's ability to develop long-range guns for heavy battleships. Similarly, the British representative of the Army, Sir John Charles Ardagh, argued for the necessity of using dumdum bullets as a means of disabling enemy soldiers and thereby making them *hors de combat* – a characteristic of the ordnance which, he unconvincingly proposed, made dumdums humane rather than unnecessarily cruel.[42]

Although the British fully understood that Hague Law was a separate stream of IHL to Geneva Law, the stances taken to both were premised on the same notion.[43] Whitehall was willing to consider the gradual adoption of new regulations on the assumption that such codifications both embodied civilized principles and offered the Government some tangible benefit. There was, however, a limit to how much the British would embrace new IHL and that limit lay at the point of convergence between a principled acceptance of the humanitarian ideal and the perceived political and military needs of the nation. This principle – which only hardened as the development of IHL became more normalized, the need to appear more civilized than other nations less important and fears of war more grave – meant that Britain became more concerned in the process of IHL development as the new century dawned. As the ICRC had weathered the storms of the Russian challenge, both by continually pushing for the codification of new articles of Geneva Law and defeating a motion raised at The Hague that the Geneva Convention should be folded into the corpus of Hague Law, the Committee was still recognized by Britain as an important player in IHL.[44] This meant that, if the British wanted to become more active in IHL development, they would have to engage with the ICRC more closely than ever before.

This latter obligation was not generally welcome, particularly by Charles Ardagh and Sir W. G. MacPherson, Whitehall's two primary interlocutors with Geneva at the turn of the century. Although Ardagh acknowledged that the Red Cross movement had 'risen into such an important position' that the activities of its volunteers and the articles by which they carried out their work had to be respected, he also believed that 'the material and personnel' of the Red Cross could only operate 'so far as military exigencies permit'.[45] The BRC, long seen as the manifestation of this very problem, was being co-opted into the British military thus solving the problem of how the 'Geneva project' could be practically applied to a wartime context. However, the tricker problem of reconciling the other main area of the project – the ICRC's pursuit of IHL – with British interests remained. To MacPherson's mind, the Committee performed no real function beyond holding conferences and maintaining the 'high ideal' of the Red Cross movement. Moreover, although MacPherson acknowledged the ICRC's centrality to the process of IHL codification, he still felt that its leadership had no 'special qualifications' to engage in 'international questions of the laws and customs of war'. The slapdash fashion in which the ICRC had ensured Boer ratification of the Geneva Convention – without notifying Whitehall or following the established procedure for new adherents – was but one example of the worryingly undisciplined attitude the Committee could take when it came to pursuing such aims. In an age in which war seemed imminent, the ICRC was viewed by the British – and other nations party to the 'Geneva Project' – as simply too 'irresponsible' to be trusted with spearheading the practice of regulating conflict.[46]

Although the British had always been thoughtful in their consideration of new IHL, dating back to the discussions between the Admiralty and the Foreign Office over the 1868 amendments, it was the processes at The Hague, the calls for a new Geneva Convention and the sense of distrust of the ICRC to handle the latter that sparked not only a greater level of engagement and consideration but also a firmer sense that Britain could and should 'own' the process of IHL development. There is strong evidence of this in British attitudes towards the 1929 Geneva Convention and its accompanying POW Convention.[47] The sinews of this policy of dominating the 'Geneva Project', however, can be traced back to the drafting process of the preceding Geneva Convention of 1906. In a report on the Conference compiled by MacPherson, who was one of a five-man delegation sent by Britain, he rather snootily noted that certain other attendees at the conference had not even studied the Convention, preferring instead to waltz into the Hôtel de Ville with 'larger humanitarian ideas which are not always possible of realisation in war'. One nation's representative, unnamed, had also 'naively admitted in private, that his only instructions were to vote with the majority'. The British delegation, in contrast, had been preparing draft articles of its own since Moynier had called for a new conference three years before and had a very clear idea of what they wanted to achieve even before arriving in Geneva. One of the key aims of the delegation was to introduce practical amendments to the Convention rather than push for a full revision based on lofty ideals. In this exercise the British and the Japanese – who, fresh from the Manchurian War, offered support for the pragmatic aims of the British – were opposed at the conference by what MacPherson dubbed the 'Red Cross party'. Blaming both these more idealistic state representatives and the Russian representative, who insisted on adding references to Hague Law to the revised document, MacPherson conceded that, although the new Convention's articles cleared up some of the deficiencies of 1864, confirmed the alignment of National Societies with their nation's militaries and 'in the main agreed with those contained in the British project', it was still 'hastily drafted' and as such had many new contradictions and imprecise moments.[48]

It was with this limited piece of IHL and its Hague counterpart in hand that many nations party to these agreements set to war in 1914. The results were predictable. With civilians practically unmentioned in extant IHL, POW regulations loose and barbarism an incremental norm of the conflict, adherence to IHL during the First World War was patchy at best. Moreover, although the focus in 1906 on defining the purposes and scope of action for Red Cross volunteers had led to some clarification on the status of the National Societies in wartime, the ICRC's prescribed role in conflict was still limited and the legal foundations upon which it could operate 'very thin'.[49]

To the British, the Committee's value in the conflict lay broadly in two main areas. First, in its work as a collector of POW capture information and forwarding agent for food and comfort parcels, which the War Office arranged to be packed by the BRC for despatch to Geneva, whence the supplies would be delivered into the camps by ICRC delegates.[50] The second valuable offering from Geneva did not manifest until 1915 when the British agreed to the suggestion made by the new ICRC president, Gustav Ador, that, in addition to delivering supplies to the camps, ICRC delegates should be permitted to report on conditions therein, including any breaches of the Convention. As with so much of its wartime work, the ICRC had little legal basis upon which to carry out this duty, which, by the custom of established norms, lay within the purview of the Protecting Power. This was the neutral state which, at the outbreak of war, would be assigned the task of looking after the interests of belligerents' citizens in enemy territory. This included POWs, whose camps were to be inspected by staff from neutral embassies acting as representatives of the Protecting Power.[51] As this was an accepted norm, when Ador offered the British the services of his delegates as camp inspectors the Foreign Office initially resisted. However, the timing of Ador's appeal – the moment when concerns in Whitehall were heightening over the variable standards of treatment applied to British prisoners in Turkey and Germany – led the British not only to set up a committee to investigate instances of British prisoner maltreatment but also to agree to reciprocal inspections of POW camps by ICRC delegates. This agreement was made all the easier by the fact that the British regarded the Committee's inspector of camps in Britain, Edouard Naville, as pro ally.[52] As a consequence, by war's end the ICRC's delegates had made 524 visits to POW camps and in so doing had expanded the Committee's scope of action well beyond that prescribed in the Convention as an information collection agency and delivery agent for relief.[53]

The acceptance of the ICRC as a complement to the Protecting Power marked the limit, however, of British willingness to allow the Committee to step outside its Convention-prescribed role. Attempts throughout the war by Ador and his delegates to engineer an exchange of fit prisoners between Germany and Britain were rebuffed and, when the ICRC called in April 1918 for a conference of the various National Red Cross Societies, Whitehall forbade the BRC to attend on the grounds that it was not only a pointless exercise but also possibly dangerous, as representatives of the German Red Cross would be in attendance and might seek to open peace negotiations.[54] Ador's attempts in February 1918 to prohibit the use of gas by the belligerent states was also unwelcome. Poisonous gas was a form of ordnance that was forbidden by the articles of the Hague Convention, to which both Germany and Britain were signatories.[55] Ador's appeal put before the British a stark decision: to abide by IHL or to defer to military necessity. Although there was some sense that British officials were torn between the desire to agree to the ICRC's request to cease using gas in order to uphold a standard of morality, the problem was tackled principally from a military rather than humanitarian perspective. Consequently, the prospect that Germany had either overtly pressured or subtly manipulated the ICRC into launching the appeal with the aim to disarm the Allies of chemical weapons was a factor in their considerations.[56] In the end it was decided that a united response from the Entente would be sent to Geneva, within which the Allies' belief in the ICRC's principles would be reaffirmed, the fact that the Germans had used gas first pointed out and the onus shifted onto Berlin to make the next move. The Allies, in short, would only cease to use gas once the ICRC convinced the Germans to do likewise. The opening of this door to a prohibition on the use of gas was slammed shut, however, by the fact that the Germans waited until September 1918 to send their response, which similarly reaffirmed their commitment to the 'spirit of humanity', blamed their enemies for forcing them to use gas and declared that the Entente would have to abandon chemical warfare before Germany did likewise. The resulting stalemate meant that over the course of the war's final year 61,000 tonnes of gas was used, double the amount unleashed in 1917.[57] As a consequence it was not until 1925, after years of labour on the issue by the ICRC and the League of Nations, that a substantive international agreement prohibiting the use of chemical weapons was signed by thirty-seven states, including Germany and Britain, who ratified the Gas Protocol in 1929 and 1930 respectively.[58]

The ICRC's campaign to prohibit the use of gas during the war was a failure, one that clearly displayed the extent to which its role in wartime was a limited one that would be defined, more than anything else, by the acquiescence of the belligerents to its proposals. The permission given by the belligerents did not, however, guarantee that the ICRC's prestige would rise or its scope of action would grow. Within the War Office there was a sense that, for all the help the Committee's delegates gave Britain via their POW camp inspections, the existence of the Protecting Power made Geneva's exertions mostly 'redundant'. As the British Prisoner of War Information Bureau's (PWIB) post-war report concluded, it was only in the interests of encouraging the Committee's relief work on behalf of British POWs that the War Office tolerated the duplication of tasks by the Protecting Power and Geneva, which the report's author colourfully described as 'an old man of the sea'.[59] This marginalization of the ICRC emerged in tandem with a greater assertion during the war by the belligerents themselves in humanitarian matters. It was a series of direct negotiations between the British and the Germans that led to POW exchanges and mitigation, to varying degrees, of prisoner privations. This belligerent-to-belligerent form of humanitarian diplomacy cut the ICRC out of an equation that its leadership felt lay within its purview. Was not the ICRC the 'initiator of humanitarian law and the guardian of Red Cross principles?'[60] The fact that neither role guaranteed the ICRC a place of prominence in the humanitarian diplomacy of the First World War was symptomatic of the trend towards marginalization of the Committee that had been in play, arguably, since the signing of the First Geneva Convention. The end of the war brought little respite for the ICRC in this respect.

It was acknowledged by the British themselves that their handling of POW matters during the war had been inconsistent at best; at worst, inept.[61] Administrative strife and interdepartmental quarrels had frustrated the Government's attempts to construct a clear POW policy; maltreatment of British servicemen had gone unpunished and there was much criticism of the Government from the relatives of the prisoners. As soon as the guns had fallen silent, reassessments began in Britain on a wave of renewed interest in the idea of redrafting and expanding pre-existing codes on POW treatment.[62] The outcome of this consideration led to Britain playing a decisive role in shaping both the revised Geneva Convention and its accompanying POW Convention, both of which were presented in draft form, debated and signed at an international conference in Geneva in 1929. In Britain, both the IHL-minded think-tank, the Grotius Society, and the man in charge of investigating the maltreatment of British POWs during the war, Lord Justice Robert Younger, had begun their preparations for this conference even before the war had ended. The sum of this was that by 1921 the International Law Association – comprising lawyers from across Britain, Europe and the United States and headed by Younger himself – had drafted a comprehensive code for POW treatment in future conflicts. In recognition that the 'Red Cross code will probably be the one on which the delegates work', it was decided as early as 1926 that Younger's code would have to 'follow the arrangement of the Red Cross code' in order to smooth the way for British suggestions to be put forward.[63] More so even than in 1906, therefore, the British were determined to take the leading role in shaping post-war IHL.

The ICRC had, likewise, taken much care in preparing for the Conference. It's legal expert, Paul Des Gouttes, worked closely with Max Huber, a new ICRC member and former judge at the League of Nation's Permanent Court of International Justice, in drafting new codes throughout the 1920s.[64] Although ostensibly this thought and preparation by both parties boded well for British–ICRC co-operation, there were some clear points of divergence between the ICRC and the representatives of Britain and the United States at the Geneva Conference. Informed by the ILA's report, Sir Horace Rumbold, the head of the British delegation – who was a last-minute replacement for Lord Cecil and was irritated at being given the assignment – held to the prevailing view in Whitehall and, indeed across Europe, that reprisals against POWs should be permitted, something that Des Gouttes was adamant should be prohibited in any future code.[65] Although the ICRC was able to obtain a remarkable concession on this point, namely, in Article 2 of the POW Convention which banned reprisals, the overall outcome of the 1929 Conference engendered defeat for the ICRC's broader aspirations, which were aimed in the main at achieving exactly what the British had sought to curtail during the war: the expansion of the Committee's wartime duties.[66] Such hopes were all but buried under the weight of objections from Rumbold – the same man who believed that the Germans had manipulated the ICRC into launching the gas appeal – and his American counterpart, Hugh Wilson. Both men dismissed out of hand the proposal for the ICRC to be the primary mediator in disputes between belligerents over POW maltreatment; to investigate violations of the Convention; and, if need be, have such matters forwarded to the League of Nations Court of International Justice. Rumbold's partner in the British delegation, Sir George Warner, also opposed, unsuccessfully, the codification of the requirement that the ICRC act as the central hub for collecting and storing POW capture information and mail, on the grounds that the Committee's exertions in this area during the war were 'not very satisfactory'. Warner also bristled at Des Gouttes, who 'went out of his way to make every possible difficulty' by attacking the process of belligerent-to-belligerent that was, for the British, a far preferable procedure for conducting humanitarian diplomacy than deferring to neutral mediation.[67] The British intention was clear and more overt than it had ever been in relations with the ICRC: the Committee's role was to be reduced, not expanded, in future conflicts.

Des Gouttes's other objective, to 'tighten up' IHL pertinent to POWs through more precise wording and articles of minutiae, was also out of step with the Anglo-American position, which favoured a more concise guideline on how to treat prisoners. The purpose of this idea was to provide belligerents with the flexibility to respond to the changing conditions of future wars, that more detailed articles would lack. The freedom for belligerents to balance humanitarian codes with military necessity, in other words, would have to be maintained. Although the final product – signed by forty-seven states, including Britain and the United States, on 27 July 1929 – was more detailed than the Americans in particular had intended, the basic principles outlined in both the POW Convention and the revised Geneva Convention were generally in keeping with those espoused by Rumbold and Wilson.[68] One of the main reasons why the Anglo-Americans were able to eclipse so many of Huber and Des Gouttes's ambitions was that the initiative had been taken from the ICRC long before the delegates took their seats at the Palais du Conseil Général's conference table. The proactivity of Younger's ILA had allowed the British to set the framework for the discussions in 1929 and, in so doing, influence the views of many participants in the Geneva Conference.[69] Against such a strategy the Committee was, inevitably, placed right in the position where the British wanted it – on the periphery.

Although the degree of British preparation for the Conference was to an extent the product of decades of British wariness at the dangers of letting the Red Cross – be it in the form of National Societies or conference callers in Geneva – run amok, the containment of the ICRC's ambitions reflected a wider post-war trend in the relationship between states and humanitarians. The need for humanitarianism in war and codification of norms of conduct was widely recognized, but so too was the need for boundaries to be set. The 'golden age' of IHL codification was at an end and, in the face of the burgeoning peace movement of the interwar years, there were few statesmen who wished to get into the business of codifying war. Even when humanitarian action was accepted by states as a crucial component of the post-war order, practical support was thin on the ground.[70] Though over fifty years old by the end of the First World War and recognized by most as the largest humanitarian organization in the world, the ICRC was to be treated no differently. Recognition of its importance as the key humanitarian actor in war was struck from the League of Nations charter and, despite the combined efforts of Des Gouttes and Huber, the only new IHL produced in the interwar years was the 1925 Gas Protocol and the 1929 Conventions. By any measure it was a poor response by the architects of IHL to the barbarism of the First World War.

In terms of its relations with the British, there was also little for the ICRC to be happy with. The BRC, long maligned both in Geneva and in its own country as the ill-equipped black sheep of the international Red Cross family, ended the First World War with a rejuvenated reputation and a place of great prestige within the global Red Cross movement. British humanitarians were proud of this achievement, in comparison with which the work of the ICRC seemed 'a near irrelevance'.[71] A similar view of the ICRC was also present in Whitehall. Though of great value as a monitor of POW welfare, the ICRC had proved meddlesome, at best, in its attempts at mediation and forays into humanitarian diplomacy. It was, in part, on account of this, that the British continued during the post-war period to actively 'manage' the ICRC's campaign to broaden IHL and, in so doing, its scope of action. Through careful planning and consideration of how humanitarian principles could be applied to broader military and strategic concerns, the British had done much to eclipse the utopianism that had underpinned much of the ICRC's work – utopianism that would only further fade as Europe inched towards a second, more barbarous, war.

2
Grandeur, Tribulation, Apocalypse, 1919–40

Geneva challenged: the road to 1939

In the years after the First World War, the ICRC was beset by a number of challenges, both internal and external, that greatly shaped the character and composition of the organization that would attempt to bring humanity to the twentieth century's bloodiest conflict. The first such challenge came in 1919 from within the Red Cross family itself, when a rival body – the League of Red Cross Societies – emerged to claim leadership of the movement and in doing so question the past record and future effectiveness of the ICRC. The seeds of this split had been sown decades earlier by the Committee's founders. Although Dunant's talk in the 1860s of the need for 'societies in each country'[1] had been fulfilled in the years after the signing of the First Geneva Convention, the process by which these National Red Cross Societies were created and their relationship to the ICRC were never clearly defined. It was not until 1876 that the notion of the ICRC having to officially recognize and endorse new National Societies became systematic. By that time, however, the independent character of and distance between the first National Societies and the ICRC had become deeply entrenched and the former was bound to the latter by little more than a 'community of principles' well into the first decades of the twentieth century.[2] In some cases this estrangement grew to open schism. The British National Society's founder, Robert Loyd-Lindsay, was so unwilling to take direction from Geneva that he refused to attend the Moynier-chaired International Red Cross Conferences of the 1860s and 70s. As far as he was concerned, the Society's genesis may have lain in the 'Geneva project' and it may have been a branch of the Red Cross family tree, but in practice it was a British organization that embraced British humanitarian values and was in no way beholden to distant Geneva.[3] This attitude, combined with the growing closeness between the National Societies and their governments, was re-enforced by the experience of the First World War, during which the ICRC delegates' battlefield usefulness was brought into question by the work done by National Society volunteers.[4]

Considering this history, it is unsurprising that during the post-mortem of the Red Cross's wartime effort – which concluded that more needed to be done in order to meet the humanitarian challenges of modernity – the National Societies were seldom troubled by the idea of a full divorce from the ICRC as a way of revitalizing the Red Cross movement and making it more professional. This notion was raised as early as February 1919 by the head of the American Red Cross (ARC), Henry Davison, who called for the establishment of an international League of Red Cross Societies to supplement – or, possibly, supplant – the activities of the parent organization in Geneva. Davison was a man of great ambition and aptitude, a wealthy banker who had used his skills in finance to help raise over three-hundred million dollars for the ARC during the First World War. He had every reason therefore, to approach the question of reorganizing the Red Cross movement with both self-confidence and vision of purpose. What he wanted was 'a truly international' Red Cross movement that could respond not only to the plight of war victims but also to peacetime natural disasters, child health and poverty. This idea was unsettling for Geneva. Davison's vision would raise the status of the National Societies within the Red Cross movement and strengthen the already firm ties that existed between them and their nation's military leaders. These outcomes, combined with the suggestion from the BRC's Sir Arthur Lawley that the five National Societies representing the victorious Allied powers form their own committee to achieve these ends – excluding both the ICRC and the National Societies of the defeated Central Powers – gave the proposal a flavour that was anathema to the internationalism that the Committee espoused. The proposal to have this new Red Cross movement led by someone from outside Switzerland was also perceived by the ICRC as a threat to its long-held principle that, for all its differences with its international brethren, the Committee in Geneva was the shining star around which the National Societies should revolve. This notion had deep roots in the ICRC's history. Attempts by the French Red Cross in 1868, for example, to have the Committee's headquarters transferred to Paris were rejected out of hand by Moynier on the not unreasonable grounds that a significant aspect of the ICRC's right to action was derived from its location within Europe's premier neutral state. His successor, Ador, took a similar line with Davison, whose visit to Geneva in February 1919 was used by the former as an opportunity to educate the ambitious American in the rich history and traditions of the Committee whose authority his proposal challenged.[5]

Reliance on precedent and history, however, was no longer enough to sustain the ICRC's position. Keen to link his organization with the newly founded League of Nations, Davison not only gained the approval of President Woodrow Wilson for his proposal but also made a Dunant-like flying tour across Europe at the end of the First World War in order to drum up support from within the National Societies. Having all but circumvented the ICRC and brushed aside its protests, on 5 May 1919 Davison's League of Red Cross Societies (LRCS) was officially established in Geneva with a retired British commander of the Royal Air Force, Lieutenant-General David Henderson, appointed as its director.[6] The desired official recognition from outside the Red Cross movement was also forthcoming in the form of the Covenant of the League of Nations, which impressed upon its member states the need to:

> encourage and promote the establishment and cooperation of duly authorised voluntary national Red Cross organisations having as purposes the improvement of health, the prevention of disease and the mitigation of suffering throughout the world.[7]

Although it enjoyed a good working relationship with the League of Nations, the ICRC was not granted any such official endorsement. Moreover, by 1939 the founding societies of the LRCS – those of the United States, Britain, France, Italy and Japan – had welcomed a further 54 National Societies from across the world into their movement. Today, its successor, the International Federation of Red Cross and Red Crescent Societies, comprises 186 National Societies and has offices in almost every country on earth. The ICRC's claim in 1919 that the new organization was merely a 'transitory organism' has thus proved to be as much self-delusion as fallacy.

Only 154 days separated Davison's initial meeting with President Wilson from the day of the LRCS's birth in Geneva.[8] If the idea of a new international Red Cross organization was not challenge enough, then the rapid speed of its creation highlighted the extent to which the ICRC seemed to be being left behind by its more forward-thinking, youthful, internationally minded sons and daughters. A glance at the Committee in the post-war years is illustrative of this. At the time the LRCS was formed the ICRC was led by the 74-year-old Gustav Ador, a

40-year veteran of the Committee and nephew of its co-founder, Gustav Moynier, who had only vacated the presidency when he passed away in 1910, nine weeks before Dunant. The death of the ICRC's founders and the coming of Davison's League did engender some changes in the Committee's leadership, albeit tempered by familiarity. Although the lawyer and historian Renée-Marguerite Cramer, the first woman to be part of the ICRC's leadership, was appointed in 1918, she was, in character, background and place of birth little different from any man who had sat on the Committee since 1863. Born and raised in Geneva, Cramer came from an upper-middle-class Protestant family; her political persuasion was conservative; she had close familial bonds with her colleagues (she became Frick-Cramer after marrying fellow delegate Edouard Frick); and her approach to her work at the ICRC was legalistic and cautious. Arguably more radical than Frick's appointment was the appearance of the first non-Genevans on the Committee in 1923. Among them, in yet another break from tradition, was a Catholic, Giuseppe Motta, from the Italian-speaking canton of Ticino in southern Switzerland. German-speaking Swiss were also appointed in the form of a lawyer and legal theorist from Zurich, Max Huber, and the Basle-born historian, Carl J. Burckhardt. Within the closeted world of the ICRC, the inclusion of non-Protestants and non-Genevans was something of a breakthrough. Indeed, these changes represented the first significant alteration to the composition of the ICRC's leadership since 1863. More than anything, the changes signalled an acknowledgement by Geneva that the organization had grown stale and had been, to an extent, left behind by developments within its own movement and across the wider world. The time had come to reinvent the ICRC as not just the world's premier humanitarian organization but also as the moral conscience of the post-war humanitarian movement.[9]

Max Huber both presided over this period of transition and would go on to lead the ICRC during the Second World War. A lawyer by trade, Huber had represented Switzerland at the Second Hague Conference in 1907, helped the Swiss Federal Council to untie the Gordian Knot of reconciling Swiss neutrality with that nation's entry to the League of Nations and sat for seven years as a judge at the Permanent Court of International Justice before becoming its president in 1925. His legal background and devotion to humanitarianism, framed as they were within a truly internationalist perspective, drew him almost inevitably into the world of the Red Cross. During his tenure at The Hague, he became close to both Gustav Ador and Paul Des Gouttes, with whom he worked on preparing for the revision of the Geneva Convention. With

Ador's sponsorship, Huber officially joined the ICRC in July 1923 and, when the former died in 1928, there was no question that his protégé would become the organization's next president.[10]

With regards to tackling the ICRC's post-war crises of purpose and status, Huber proved more than capable of filling his predecessor's well-worn shoes. Building on the earlier work of Ador and Davison to find rapprochement – more often couched in niceties and pledges of solidarity rather than genuine reconciliation – one of Huber's first acts as president was to broker a truce with the new LRCS president, Colonel Paul Draudt.[11] This came on 26 October 1928 in the form of the proc- lamation of an International Red Cross comprised of the LRCS and the ICRC, and agreement between the two leaders on a list of commonly held statutes. In addition to laying down the uniform principles of both organizations, specified lines of demarcation were agreed which, broadly speaking, placed war relief within the purview of the ICRC and peacetime relief in the hands of the LRCS.[12] Although it by no means knocked the bad taste out of the ICRC's mouth, the rapprochement was an important step in the Committee's post-war rebuilding, in as much as the agreement acknowledged that the LRCS was now a reality of the Red Cross world.

Huber's efforts to narrow the divide between the two organizations were spurred in no small part by the need to address concerns that, in the global sense, were of greater importance for the ICRC's future. Mindful that the 'Red Cross path' was currently 'filled with grandeur and tribulation' in an age that was 'apocalyptic', Huber came to reject much of the international post-war sentiment on the maintenance of peace to the detriment of preparing for war. Instead, as the 1920s unfolded, he increasingly held to the view that 'as long as states have not laid down their arms, the Geneva Convention is not without purpose'.[13] In terms of its role as IHL's architect therefore, the ICRC had much work to do to ensure that the next war – when it inevitably happened – would be fought within the codified constraints of humanitarian principles. This interpretation of the post-war world – imbued in equal measure with dark pessimism, grim determination and an unshakable faith in the Red Cross mission – would characterize Huber's reign at the ICRC. Such sen- timent underpinned his efforts both to revise the Geneva Convention and to draft further regulations prohibiting the use of poisonous gas throughout the 1920s, campaigns which, by and large, were successful. The ICRC's other main interwar IHL initiative – to extend the articles of the Geneva Convention to protect civilians – proved, however, to be a dismal failure.

Though concern for the plight of civilians in modern war had first been officially raised in 1921 at the Tenth International Red Cross conference, it was not until 1934 that the Committee was able to prepare a draft of new civilian-protecting IHL for consideration. Presented at the Fifteenth International Conference of the Red Cross in Tokyo, the draft resolution, penned primarily by Des Gouttes, recommended that civilians be treated in accordance with the Geneva and POW Conventions and be permitted to receive food and medical relief from ICRC delegates. The setting for the presentation of the Tokyo Draft – only the second International Conference of the Red Cross to be held outside Europe – was attended by 252 delegates from 57 National Red Cross Societies and looked to be a grand and significant occasion, one that would herald a new epoch in the Red Cross's global work on behalf of civilians. In practice, however, the Tokyo Conference exemplified the extent to which the ICRC's campaign for new IHL was increasingly out of step with the political will of the world's great powers. The conference's host nation had still not ratified the POW Convention and, as the ICRC well knew, Japanese troops in Manchuria were at the time conducting themselves in a manner far removed from the sentiments contained in the draft under consideration. The document was nevertheless accepted in principle by the Red Cross delegates and discussions began in earnest for a new Geneva Conference at which the proposals could be signed and ratified by state representatives. However, the 'firm and definite refusal' from the French and the general dissatisfaction expressed by most other governments, including Britain's, with the wording of the document meant that the intended conference remained uncalled and articles for civilian protection unratified when war broke out in 1939.[14] Aside from the challenge the draft's articles posed to the conduct of states – particularly those which embraced aerial bombing as a linchpin of war strategy – the document was also condemned by bad timing. Although its content was noble and support for the draft from the recently reconciled LRCS forthcoming, its presentation to a world in which the authority of the League of Nations was crumbling, totalitarian dictatorships were in the ascendency, and instances of barbarism in war increasing made the whole enterprise seem disconnected from the drift to war. Thus when Huber requested the Swiss Federal Council to call a new Geneva Conference in 1937, it refused on the grounds that the gesture was pointless.[15] For all Huber's efforts, there was to be no new, civilian-encompassing epoch for IHL.

Attempts by the ICRC to demand adherence to pre-existing IHL – or, at least, to the basic tenets of humanity – were also increasingly

unsuccessful as the 1930s wore on. Both Italy and Germany had ratified the 1929 Geneva Convention and the POW Convention. The very
nature of Fascist ideology and Hitler and Mussolini's deliberate spurn-
ing of the norms of international conduct, however, inevitably led to a
clash between the dictators and the ICRC – a clash that the latter came
away from bruised and callow. The most notorious example of this
came in the Italo-Ethiopian war of 1935–6, during which Italian pilots
ignored the sanctity of the Red Cross emblem by deliberately attacking
Red Cross installations. Testament to how callously years of hard work
in IHL development could be compromised by the whim of a belligerent, the Italians also violated the 1925 Gas Protocol by dropping mus-
tard gas on Ethiopian soldiers and civilians. This action was not born
out of military necessity. Rather, the notion of using gas in Ethiopia was
unflinchingly embraced by Mussolini and his generals during the initial
planning stages of the invasion with no regard to the existing prohibitions on the deployment of chemical weapons. It was an expression of
Fascist militarism in the purest sense.[16]

Despite its concern over these flagrant breaches of IHL, the ICRC's
response was both timid and indicative of a prevailing belief in Geneva
that, contrary to the mounting evidence of the 1930s, no civilized
European state could so wilfully engage in such barbarism.[17] When
an effort was made by the ICRC to address these breaches of IHL, in
the form of a meeting between the Committee's senior figures and
Mussolini in Rome on 20 March 1936, the issue of gas was not raised for
fear of upsetting il Duce and overshadowing the delegation's attempts
to address the attacks on Red Cross personnel and installations. This
tactic led to no tangible outcome. At the end of the meeting, which
lasted little more than ten minutes, Mussolini assured the delegates that
Italy respected the sanctity of the Red Cross emblem and the principles
and values it represented. The degree to which the delegates accepted
this lie at face value is debatable. What can be concluded, however, is
that in the face of a totalitarian regime the ICRC was shown to be both
politically impotent and bereft of the moral platform on which it had
previously entreated other nations to adhere to IHL. Mussolini had no
reservations, moral or legal, over trampling on the laws of war, nor
did he feel the need to display his nations' liberal qualities or moral
authority to the rest of Europe. On the contrary, such principles were
anathema to a man who, like Hitler, sought to intensify, rather than to
mitigate, the barbarism of the First World War.[18]

This ideological gap between Geneva and Rome was also present
in the ICRC's concurrent dealings with Berlin. After nearly a year of

negotiations with the German Red Cross – which had become incorpo-
rated into the Nazi regime and by May 1936 was under the leadership of
Reichsarzt SS Ernst Grawitz[19] – the ICRC was permitted to visit the 'special punishment camp' at Esterwegen, the first of three planned visits by
the ICRC to Hitler's burgeoning concentration camp system. Upon his
arrival at the camp the Committee's inspector, Carl J. Burckhardt, found
that many detainees were off limits to him, despite his prior insistence
that he be given free rein. Furthermore, those inmates he was permitted to see showed signs of intimidation and abuse. Burckhardt's view
that Esterwegen was 'brutal, militarist' and run in a 'pointlessly harsh'
fashion resulted in little material change to the camp. Moreover, his recommendation that its commandant, Hans Loritz, be removed was interpreted in a perverse manner by Burckhardt's host, SS-Gruppenführer
Reinhard Heydrich, who responded by re-assigning Loritz to Dachau
which, under his supervision, became the model concentration camp
of the Third Reich. When Burckhardt visited Berlin a year later he
concluded that conditions in the camps had improved, a perception
facilitated by the front put on as part of the regime's efforts to present a
glowing image of the Third Reich in the lead-up to the Olympic Games.
The subsequent inspection of Dachau by the ICRC's Guillame Favre in
1938 produced similarly fabricated results.[20] The sum of these inspections was a dubious endorsement by the Committee of the conditions
in the camps, made at the expense of addressing the fact that concentration camps as a concept were an affront to the very principles of the
Red Cross movement. As Jean Claude Favez has argued, this divergence
between Geneva's principles and the principles that governed the conduct of totalitarian regimes led to the Committee's leadership favouring broad public statements over practical action when addressing the
barbarism unleashed by the dictators – a dangerous precedent for the
later impotence the ICRC would display when faced with, among other
things, the Holocaust.[21]

In addition to its treasured Conventions coming under fire, the ICRC
was also in a 'precarious' financial position by the late 1930s. Donations
from its traditional sources outside the Swiss Federal Council – namely,
foreign governments and their National Societies – dropped significantly during the interwar years and by 1939 the ICRC had a provisional
budget of SFR24,000 per annum, supplemented by capital accrued from
the First World War, to pay for its SFR130,000 per year peacetime operating costs.[22] This weakening of its financial position reflected a similar
decrease in the ICRC's other form of capital – its moral authority. In
addition to its failed dealings with Berlin and Rome, the ICRC's strict

policy of impartial, apolitical conduct pushed it further to the fringes of humanitarian discourse as the storm clouds of war gathered. Huber, despite his pacifist tendencies, was silent on the issue of the seemingly inevitable path to a new Europe-wide conflict, in response to which he could only advise the Committee to prepare and watch as the brief lacuna of interwar humanitarianism was 'warehoused'.[23] The 1930s, therefore, was a decade in which the ICRC – the mitigator of war's excesses – ostensibly belonged and yet, owing to its increasingly futile appeals to basic humanity and its inability to meet the challenges posed by ideological conflict, seemed completely out of place. Such was the Committee's status when the Second World War began.

Forgotten lessons and phoney war

Max Huber had twenty-three Committee members and three part-time administrative staff at his disposal on the morning of 1 September 1939. Taken together with trusted volunteers from Geneva who, during the interwar conflicts, had contributed part-time to the operation of relief centres and manned the desks of various administrative departments, the Committee in total had no more than fifty people ready to work as the first Polish prisoners were taken into captivity. In terms of the Committee's preparedness for the conflict, a full year before the invasion of Poland the Villa Moynier, the organization's picturesque headquarters on the banks of Lake Geneva, had been put on a war footing – of a sort. Mindful of the drift to war, in 1938 the ICRC had established the Commission for Work in Wartime, a loose-knit body that met every month to discuss how best to prepare for the conflict ahead. One of the Commission's first duties was to recall the Red Cross faithful, and, before long, those already in Geneva coordinating the ICRC's relief operations in Spain were reinforced by the arrival of Committee veterans from past conflicts. Requests were also put out for new volunteers and Huber, determined to lead by example, donated his entire salary to the ICRC and moved permanently from his home in Zurich to be closer to the centre of operations at the Villa Moynier.[24]

The months of preparation and gathering of new and old blood in Geneva could not, however, mask the sense of anxiety and foreboding that pervaded the minds of many ICRC members. One delegate who was particularly concerned by both the gaps in existing IHL and the barbarity of modern war was Marcel Junod, a surgeon from Neuchâtel who had joined the ICRC during the Italo-Ethiopian War and, in his years of ICRC service to come, would earn a reputation as 'an example to emulate in training new delegates'.[25] From the chaos of Addis Abbaba's fall in 1936, Junod was to spend the better part of the next decade travelling across war-torn Spain and the Third Reich, inspecting POW and civilian internment camps, delivering relief supplies and witnessing atrocities first hand, before arriving in the ruins of Tokyo in August 1945, where he took up the unenviable position of chief ICRC delegate to Japan within days of the destruction of Hiroshima and Nagasaki. With the gift of hindsight furnished by this incredible journey through the twentieth century's nadir, Junod reflected in his post-war memoirs on the sense in September 1939 of 'tragic hiatus between our weak powers and the magnitude of the drama unleashed all around us'.[26] Yet, inspired in no small part by Huber, who refused to 'let a word of pessimism pass his lips', Junod set off to Warsaw in the first days of the war, a determined man. His re-activation was followed by that of other interwar conflict alumni. Roland Marti, who had earned a reputation for being able to deal with ruthless military commanders, had the unenviable, if well-appointed task of establishing the ICRC's delegation in Berlin. Lucie Odier, the head of the ICRC's Relief Division in Spain and, notably, only the second female member appointed to the Committee, also set about expanding her operations to coordinate the distribution of food and medicine for war victims across any territory into which war spread. The mobilization of these experienced delegates, combined with Huber's leadership in Geneva and the arrival of a small army of volunteer Swiss from the surrounding Cantons, underpinned the sense of pluck and determination that characterized the Committee's response to the outbreak of war. Come what may, the ICRC, ennobled by its principles and ideals and backed by the Swiss people, was determined to weather the storm.[27]

In keeping with this attitude, the ICRC's national desks sprang to life within the first week of hostilities, opening diplomatic channels to Berlin, Paris, Warsaw and London. The ICRC's wartime work on behalf of the last began officially on 14 September 1939, with the establishment of the British Section, a department tasked with handling all cases of internment involving subjects of the British Empire. Like all national desks, the British Section fell under the auspices of the ICRC's Central Prisoner of War Agency (the Agency), the internal body that had been established during the First World War to collect information on POWs and whose duties, including the maintenance of relations with the POW bureaux of belligerent nations, had been codified in the POW Convention. When the Agency was revived, therefore, on 3 September 1939, in the offices of the Palais du Conseil Général, its staff inherited not only the burden of keeping records of those captured and monitoring their well-being but also the significant task of acting as the ICRC's first point of contact with the nations now at war. The man appointed to head the Agency was Jacques Chenevière, a brooding poet who had volunteered as a camp inspector during the First World War, at the conclusion of which he officially joined the Committee as a full-time member.[28] It was he, along with Max Huber, who opened relations with the British Government shortly after Chamberlain's declaration of war by way of a letter-writing campaign, which requested of Whitehall information on German civilian internees, as well as presenting details of how the Agency intended to forward similar information regarding Britons being held in Germany.[29]

Historians have been critical of the lack of British preparedness for the housing, feeding and overall treatment of POWs and civilian internees – the very objects of concern that were central to British–ICRC relations during the Second World War.[30] This malaise seems peculiar if one considers both Whitehall's increasing engagement in IHL codification in the decades prior to the conflict and the fact that, seemingly, the mistakes made by the British in POW matters during the First World War had been addressed. In 1920, Major-General Sir Herbert Belfield, head of the War Office's Prisoner of War Directorate, compiled a report which, acknowledging the swiftness of the descent to war in 1914 and the resulting unpreparedness in his department, outlined comprehensively how Whitehall could prepare a POW administration for future conflicts. In addition to containing recommendations for bureaucratic organization, the Belfield Report also outlined how to set up camps and relief systems, how to manage any public outcry at POW maltreatment and, notably, reinforced the need to 'keep strict control of the many philanthropic organizations that spring up on the outbreak of war'. The Army Council noted that the report was 'a valuable departmental record and contains valuable suggestions for future guidance'.[31] This acknowledgement did not, however, prevent the report from being left to gather dust in the 1930s, to the extent that, by 1939, few within the War Office even knew of its existence. Far from having its recommendations implemented upon the outbreak of war, the report was not even circulated. Consequently, British POW policy in 1939 was a sketchy affair at best, determined in the main by the individual concerns of the various departments. Neither the Air Ministry nor the Admiralty took steps to organize an administration to handle POW matters, preferring instead to liaise with the War Office and MI5 on their pre-eminent concern: establishing procedures for the transit, processing and, most importantly, interrogation of enemy prisoners. At the urging of the Ministry of Agriculture and Fisheries and the Ministry of Supply, the idea of POWs being used for labour was also raised during the first months of the conflict.[32] This marked the extent of British consideration for enemy POWs.

Beyond the assumption that the POW Convention would be adhered to by Germany on the basis of reciprocal adherence, the subject of British and Colonial prisoners attracted even less consideration in Whitehall. The POW Convention specified that 'at the commencement of hostilities, each of the belligerent Powers and the neutral Powers who have belligerents in their care, shall institute an official bureau to give information about the prisoners of war in their territory', a Prisoner of War Information Bureau (PWIB).[33] Despite the Convention's allusion to immediacy, and Huber's repeated requests that they abide by it, the British only set up this most basic agency of POW administration on 9 October 1939, later than both the Germans and the ICRC.[34] The PWIB was to be the focal point for handling POW matters in Whitehall, yet, owing to the small number of British prisoners taken and enemy prisoners captured during the so-called Phoney War, it remained understaffed well into 1940. As the War Office's Colonel Harry Phillimore candidly admitted in his post-war account of Whitehall's POW departments, the small workload engendered by the lack of active fighting fronts – as late as March 1940 the British held only a few hundred German POWs and civilian internees in conditions that, though spartan, were generally satisfactory[35] – was no excuse for such a lack of development in Britain's POW administration. Reflecting on the war's early years, albeit with the gift of hindsight, Phillimore regretted the fact that, rather than using the lull of the war's first winter to reform and refine the POW administration and to adopt the pre-war recommendations of the Belfield Report in an incremental and ordered manner, Whitehall instead grew complacent thus laying the foundation for future failings.[36] A component of this complacency was the passing of POW matters to agencies outside Whitehall proper, specifically to the BRC. At a meeting on 31 October it was agreed that the BRC would handle the lion's share of POW-related duties, including the packing of relief parcels for British POWs and the receipt of prisoner capture information and reports on the missing and wounded. For its part Whitehall would send representatives to any future meetings of a like character, provide funding for the BRC and keep the PWIB running as an agency that would forward POW information to the appropriate government departments. There was little or no discussion of the setting up of a more comprehensive POW administration and no mention of the ICRC outside its usefulness as a source for collecting POW capture information. The entire programme, as was admitted at the meeting, was little more than a reactivation of the same arrangements that had existed during the First World War.[37]

As POW welfare had been established during the First World War and its aftermath as the common ground upon which British–ICRC relations were built, the handing over of POW matters to the BRC did little to make Whitehall alive to the Committee's early wartime work. This explains not only why there was a sense of confusion over why the likes of Huber and Chenevière were bombarding Whitehall with missives but also why, when in September the ICRC sent a report on the numbers of civilian internees held in Germany and the conditions of their captivity, the Foreign Office Consular Department – unsure of the Committee's right even to compile such reports – opted to send no reply to Geneva. Moreover, when the ICRC sent a German translation of the POW Convention to be put up in camps in Britain, the War Office decided the best place for the document was 'in the library' for future reference. As the ICRC's delegate in London observed during his first weeks on the job, there was also a sense that the PWIB was not much bothered with the ICRC and that, if possible, it hoped to avoid having to use the latter's good offices where possible.[38]

In terms of building some form of relationship therefore, it was left to the ICRC to take the initiative. In this endeavour actions spoke louder than words to Whitehall. Having been informed by Huber of Marcel Junod's inspection of Oflag XA (Itzehoe) on 23 September, the British were quick to accept the ICRC's request that its delegate be allowed to carry out a reciprocal inspection of British camps holding German internees, the first of which was to take place on 6 November.[39] This success in negotiating reciprocal camp inspections was rightly viewed by the Committee as a significant moment in its wartime relations with both London and Berlin. After accepting the ICRC's offer to inspect places of internment – a duty that, by the terms of the POW Convention, required the consent of the belligerents – both governments set a precedent which in theory guaranteed that 'the freedom of action of the delegates was not in question'.[40] The basis of reciprocity established, the onus was now on the ICRC to normalize the practice of camp inspections and ensure that the belligerents would accept the notion of the Committee's delegates regularly inspecting camps for the duration of the war. The best way to do this was to make sure that the inspections went as smoothly as possible.

The man charged with carrying out this crucial task in Britain was Rudolphe Haccius, an experienced ICRC delegate who had performed outstanding work on behalf of political prisoners detained in Hungary after the First World War. His successful negotiation for the release of those detained in Bela Kun's camps, as well as his shrewd handling of Republican and Irish Free State officials during his visit to detention centres in Dublin in 1923 proved Haccius's credentials as both a man with a keen eye for prisoner maltreatment and a capable and resolute negotiator.[41] These skills had been recognized by the ICRC leadership as early as July 1939 when a decision was made that, should war break out, Haccius – who lived in West London and spoke good English – would be Geneva's man in Britain.[42] By September therefore, Haccius was prepared to take on his assignment, which began by his setting up offices at St James's Palace, the headquarters of the BRC. His orders from Geneva were forthcoming. In addition to being instructed to follow up Huber and Chenevière's queries with Whitehall over its POW administration, he was told to form a link both between the BRC and Geneva and between the latter and Whitehall so as to coordinate the tripartite effort on behalf of British POWs and, if need be, other victims of war. The primary means by which these links were to be forged was by negotiating with Whitehall officials for the right to inspect camps and to help organize the despatch of relief parcels for British prisoners in coordination with the BRC. Beyond these basic directives, however, Haccius's mission – like that of all ICRC delegates since Louis Appia was first despatched to the Prussian lines in 1864 – was, by design, a fluid one. His other duties, loosely defined, included gathering information on POWs and civilian detainees held in Britain; exploring possibilities for new relief initiatives; conveying messages from the ICRC leadership to the Foreign Office; and, in general, keeping his eyes and ears open to any points of intersection between war and humanitarianism that might be raised in Whitehall. This gave Haccius, and all other ICRC delegates of the Second World War, the quality of an envoy, devoid of official diplomatic status and yet tasked with engaging with government officials on a quasi-diplomatic level and gathering what amounted to 'humanitarian intelligence' on prisoner and camp conditions, for transmission back to the Committee.[43]

From the point of view of the ICRC, this fluidity in the delegates' mission was a necessary component of any Red Cross work beyond the ordered and stable world of Geneva. In the field – be it in the form of diplomatic or military engagement – the Red Cross delegate had always to respond to changes in circumstances, to seek out new means of carrying out humanitarian action and, above all else, to adapt. As the celebrated delegate Sidney Brown told Junod when both men set out for Ethiopia in 1935, the best and only guide the ICRC delegates had to their duties was a sense of the 'spirit of the thing' that they were doing.[44] The ICRC's purposely ill-defined conception of a delegate's duties meant that, although Haccius's primary activity in Britain – the inspection of camps – was made known to Whitehall as early as September 1939, the further purposes of his mission were not fully explained to his hosts. This neglect on the part of Geneva, combined with the slow start of Whitehall's POW administration and its already distant attitude towards the ICRC, led to some understandable confusion over the questions of who this man was and what exactly he was doing setting up a Red Cross office in London. Owing to the location of his office at St James's Palace, the Foreign Office originally believed that Haccius's role was only to act as liaison between the ICRC and the BRC which, some British officials initially believed, was simply a regional branch of the Geneva organization rather than an independent National Red Cross Society. The BRC quickly – and, one suspects, with great irritation – corrected this misapprehension. Confusion about his standing still reigned for some weeks after Haccius's arrival, however, and it was not until February 1940 that the Foreign Office officially approved him as the primary conduit for communications between itself and the ICRC.[45] In the interim Haccius set to his task diligently, visiting German detainees and captured airmen over the winter of 1939–40 as Junod did likewise in Germany. Haccius's eye for detail as an inspector shone through in his reports. Complaints of poorly applied paint being used in lieu of blackout boards at the internment camp in York, or of the large numbers of under-18- and over-60-year-olds at Lingfield were raised, so too an observation that German officers had yet to receive the pay to which they were entitled by the terms of the POW Convention. Despite these crisp observations, Haccius found that the British camps, though rustic and ad hoc in their composition, were for the most part acceptable and that, despite a prevailing 'lack of interest' on the part of the British in applying the Tokyo Draft, the '1929 Convention is almost entirely applied by the English' to civilian internees.[46]

Haccius's reports seem to have lifted some of the fog from Whitehall's thinking on POWs. The recently retired former Minister in Berne – and British representative at the 1929 Geneva Conference – Sir George Warner – remarked that, as Junod's reports had indicated the standard of camps in Germany were higher than in Britain, the War Office had to lift its game lest the Germans decide to drop their standards as a means of reprisal.[47] Haccius's efforts also drew the attention of a 60-year-old First World War veteran named Major-General Sir Alan Hunter who, as head of the PWIB, assumed the informal role of government liaison with the ICRC over the winter of 1939–40. The two men immediately struck up a good relationship. As Hunter wrote in late November 1939 to Marcel Junod, his dealings 'with Monsieur Haccius are of the pleasantest' and, when Junod had the chance, he too should visit Britain so that relations between the War Office and the ICRC might be further strengthened. Hunter also expressed his 'great satisfaction' at the rate at which the Agency sent information on captured airmen to Whitehall and, when this service was disrupted by problems with the postal system in early January, he assured the ICRC that he understood that the French Postal Service, rather than Geneva, was to blame. This comprehension of such basic, yet crucial aspects of the ICRC's operation, combined with the geniality of his dealings with Haccius, made Hunter a significant source of stability in the embryonic British–ICRC relations of the Phoney War.[48]

Facilitating this amiable state of affairs was the fact that, in the months prior to the German invasion of Western Europe, both Haccius and Hunter had little to do beyond monitoring the welfare of a few hundred, mostly well-treated, prisoners and keeping themselves appraised of the BRC's parcel packing operations. On this issue the War Office's only intervention was to advise against the BRC expanding its operations to Hove, where it intended to set up a second parcel distribution centre in April 1940.[49] The recommendation was in line with the trend set from the war's outset in Whitehall of forsaking forward planning in POW matters, on the understanding that adherence to the POW Convention and expectation of conditions similar to those of the First World War would be satisfactory. Bereft of hindsight, this notion had some merit. Few in Whitehall could have predicted the collapse of France in 1940 and the resulting changes in both the strategic dynamic of the war and the situation for British POWs. One of the few who did urge caution was Hunter, who in December 1939 lamented the fact that 'it seems as if the War Office had only visualized prisoners of war materialising in France, when (*sic*) we hope everything will go like clockwork'. George Warner also voiced concerns in March 1940 of the 'impossible' conditions in which officials would be forced to operate 'should large numbers of prisoners be taken'.[50] Such prophecies had little place in Whitehall. Prisoner numbers were low, the PWIB's relations with both the ICRC and the BRC were healthy and uncomplicated and there was no apparent need to alter the status quo or prepare for any future developments. Haccius – having overcome his first battles to get both recognition and a functioning phone line from Whitehall – also had a calm time of things. Most of his work over the winter months was focused on organizing food parcels for Polish POWs and civilian internees, and ingratiating himself with his hosts from Whitehall and the BRC.[51]

The leisurely pace of wartime events and the cordiality of British–ICRC relations contributed to a similarly contented view of the situation from the Villa Moynier. In January, Huber wrote to the British Foreign Secretary Lord Halifax, expressing an optimistic forecast for future British–ICRC relations and the workload of the Committee on behalf of Britain. So assured was he of this latter issue that Huber declared he was:

> now under the impression that a number of important points have been settled owing to the collaboration of our Delegate [Haccius] with the various Government Departments concerned as well as with the War Organisation of the British Red Cross Society and Order of St John of Jerusalem. It would appear to us that in so far as has been possible in the period of his stay in England, the objects of his mission have been accomplished or are well on the way to accomplishment.[52]

Such optimism was grievously misplaced. On 10 May 1940 the Wehrmacht pushed into Western Europe, an offensive that resulted in the cornering of the British Expeditionary Force around Dunkirk later that month. Although over 300,000 soldiers were evacuated from Dunkirk's beaches, during the subsequent weeks of France's capitulation close to 40,000 British POWs were marched into German captivity. The Germans' preparations for such an avalanche of prisoners were wholly inadequate and the attitude taken towards their charges reflected both the brutality of Hitler's regime and the dominance of his armies. This turning point in the wider history of the war was also a key moment in the history of the Red Cross movement's role in the conflict. The sudden emergence of so vast a workload not only opened a difficult chapter in the BRC's wartime history but it also blew apart any considerations Huber may have had that the ICRC's mission in Britain had ended or needed scaling back. On the contrary, the events of the summer of 1940, and the humanitarian crisis they engendered, brought forth the first significant test of British–ICRC wartime relations.

Plate 1 'ICRC Vice-President, Carl J. Burckhardt, President Max Huber and the head of the Central Agency for Prisoners of War, Jacques Chenevière, Geneva 1939' © Photothèque CICR (DR).

Plate 2 'Rudolph Haccius visits German officer prisoners of war at the No. 1 POW Camp (Derbyshire), October 1940' © CICR.

Plate 3 'British POWs in Libya, 1941' © CICR.

Plate 4 'Preparing for the worst: a parcel-packed ICRC warehouse in Geneva, 1944' © Photothèque CICR (DR).

Plate 5   'A small, Red Cross-marked white ship leaves Lorient, 1945' © Photothèque
CICR (DR).

Plate 6 'The first White Ship meets its end – the SS *Kurtulus* run aground in the Sea of Marmara, February 1942' © Photothèque CICR (DR).

Plate 7 'The "White Angel" trucks arrive in Moosburg, 1945' © CICR.

Plate 8   '"White Angel" trucks assist in the repatriation of French POWs – a task for which the trucks were not originally intended, April 1945' © CICR.

Part II

3
Prisoners and Parcels, 1940–1

Relations transformed: the prisoner of war crisis of 1940

The author of the ICRC's official history took an unusually blunt tone when he conceded that, for all its preparations and good intentions, the sudden difficulty in obtaining information on the tens of thousands of Allied prisoners captured during the fall of France and the pressing need to organize relief on a massive scale left the Committee thoroughly 'over-whelmed'.[1] This was despite the fact that, amidst the tumult of June 1940, Jacques Chenevière emerged as one of the first, in either Geneva or Whitehall, to grasp fully the scale of the humanitarian disaster engendered by the German conquest of Western Europe. Although Chenevière's dour nature probably had him prepared for the worst, it is clear that he had also learnt much from his experience of the war's first weeks when, following the influx of Polish POWs into Germany, the Agency's system of reporting captures was beset by the same disruptions to transport and communications as would occur in the summer of 1940. In the case of Poland, the destruction wrought to postal systems and the ill-preparedness and unwillingness of the Germans to report POW captures efficiently, if at all, rendered obsolete the Agency's preferred method of using the information given them by the detaining power to compile long lists of prisoner details for periodical forwarding to the detainees' government.[2]

Chenevière was under no illusion that the war's base standard for human catastrophe and material destruction had been set in the fall of Poland, and that the ICRC would have either to adapt to this harsh reality or run the risk of lagging behind in response. During the Phoney War, therefore, he reintroduced an innovation that the Agency had first experimented with during the First World War: the POW capture card.

This was a postcard-sized document which was filled in with the capture details of each individual POW and forwarded immediately to the Agency, thus cutting out the time-consuming list method of reporting. The first of the near 13,000,000 of such cards to be received by the ICRC during the war arrived in Geneva – from a captured British airman – on 26 March 1940. The practice of using the POW capture card had thus already been adopted as the preferred method of POW information gathering before the panzers rolled west and, by the time the French surrender was signed, the Palais du Conseil Général's storerooms were packed with boxes of blank capture cards in anticipation of the worst occurring. Provision had also been made for the distribution and filing of these cards. In the first weeks of May, Chenevière increased the number of volunteers at the Agency to the extent that, by the end of June, he had close to one thousand workers at his disposal. Most of these Swiss had volunteered on a casual basis, taking a few hours each week out of their private lives to embrace the Red Cross spirit. Although this enthusiasm was laudable and, indeed, necessary for the Agency to function, Chenevière realized that further assistance would be needed to turn this body of volunteers into an efficient workforce. This assistance came in the form of the Hollerith Machine, a card-punching tabulator developed by the New York-based International Business Machines (IBM). Ironically, at the same time that Chenevière took delivery of six of these machines as a gift from IBM, German concentration camp administrators were using their own Holleriths as a means of recording information on their prisoners. In Geneva, the Holleriths were used for the more savoury purpose of cataloguing and sorting the POW capture cards in a mechanized and more efficient manner and before long they became indispensable tools at the Palais du Conseil Général.[3]

For all these preparations, the success of Chenevière's Agency was, ultimately, dependent on the willingness of the Germans to uphold their commitment to IHL both in spirit and in practice. Ostensibly, there was cause to believe that such adherence would be forthcoming. In addition to the fact that, from a racial point of view, Western Allied soldiers held a privileged position in National Socialist eyes, the 1929 Geneva and POW Conventions had been signed and ratified by Hitler's regime in 1934, and their basic tenets were understood by the staff of both the German War Office, the Allgemeines Wehrmachtsamt (AWA) and the Oberkommando der Wehrmacht (OKW). Within the latter there was also an Inspekteur für das Kriegsgefangenenwesen im OKW (camp standards inspector) whose job was to make sure that camp commandants were aware of their obligations under IHL. There were, however, two main problems which complicated German attitudes to the POW Convention. The first was that, though both the principles of the Convention and the importance of reciprocity were understood, the humanitarian sentiment that underpinned the regulations was in general lacking. This was both owing to National Socialism's championing of violence and rejection of human rights – a problem in many of the younger soldiers who had come of age in Hitlerite Germany – and, more so in the officer corps, to the adherence to articles of the Convention that were most in harmony with traditional, Prussian codes of military conduct. Practical standards of treatment, and the notion of maintaining a 'correct' attitude to prisoners in order to preserve the honour of the German soldier were therefore more keenly embraced than the more intangible Red Cross spirit. There was little room for viewing the prisoners as victims of war in ways that the POW Convention implied. Indeed, throughout Germany's POW administration there was a prevailing mindset, left over from the First World War, of the prisoners as enemies of the Reich, rather than as strictly being *hors de combat*, even when disarmed and in captivity. The second complicating factor in German attitudes was Hitler, whose omniscience applied as much to the fate of the POWs as it did to any other denizen of the Third Reich. Though, much like his officers, Hitler was aware of the POW Convention and its principles, he was prone, for reasons of ideology or personal whim, either to adhere to it inconsistently or, in the case of the Eastern Front, ignore it altogether.[4]

Although Soviet POWs suffered most glaringly, Western Allied POWs were also not immune from the vagaries of internment in the Third Reich.[5] Hitler's personal interventions in particular were fateful for many an Allied prisoner. These occurred mostly in the war's later years, primarily via his issuing of the infamous 'Commando Order', involvement in the shackling of British and Canadian POWs in 1942, and his handing over of POW affairs to the Schutzstaffel (SS) in the autumn of 1944. However, the brutal and lawless nature of the regime he had constructed and the influence of its ideology had an immediate impact on the prisoners taken in the summer of 1940. The lack of humanity in applying the POW Convention and the intoxication of victory over those who had shamed Germany at the end of the First World War were apparent as the Wehrmacht marched the prisoners into the Reich, committing a host of crimes against their charges as they went. In addition to unprovoked beatings, circuitous routes designed to sap the prisoners' morale and strength, and arbitrary shootings of stragglers, increasingly meagre rations were a constant feature of the POW capture experience of 1940. Some prisoner columns marched for over a week on little more than boiled soup-bones and black bread. On one occasion, when a Red Cross delegate attempted to hand out food parcels to the prisoners, the Germans insisted that this could only be carried out if they too received parcels.[6] At best this was a perverse interpretation of Article 11 of the POW Convention, which decreed that prisoners should be allocated the same rations as their guards.[7] More likely such obstruction was one of many examples of the victors revelling in their domination of the vanquished, whose maltreatment extended beyond the privations of the march itself to the nature of their processing and accommodation.

Following a headcount after capture, the prisoners were marched to the nearest Frontstalag, which was often little more than a barbed-wire ringed field, where a report on the number of prisoners was compiled. From there the prisoners would again be marched to a mass transit camp, or Dulag, for interrogation, medical examinations and a final sorting according to their rank and health before at last being transferred, usually by poorly ventilated rail cars, to their permanent place of internment. This journey to either a Stalag (for non-commissioned officers and enlisted men) or Oflag (for officers) in Germany and Poland, was pock-marked by a system of hastily built transit camps housed within the shells of old barracks, sports grounds or schools, at which accommodation generally ranged from huts and tents to open-air sleeping. Food at these stops was also in short supply and of poor quality. In some cases one loaf of mould-ridden bread was shared between thirty men and both medical care – often needed for those who had been existing on such fare for days – and running water were rarely available.[8]

Beneath the privations of the march into captivity, there lay the labyrinthine bureaucracy of Germany's POW administration, the dysfunction of which – combined with the German suspension of the postal system over much of June and July – made the prospect of information on the prisoners getting to the ICRC in a timely fashion very slim. At the Dulags, the Oberkommando des Heeres (OKH) officially handed the prisoners over to OKW and, within that office, the AWA who, in turn, having processed the POW information passed it onto the Auswärtiges Amt (German Foreign Office). It was this last body which usually transmitted POW capture information to the Protecting Power and/or the ICRC. The sum of this set-up was that, in contrast to the under-staffed and ad hoc British POW administration, the Germans had by mid-1940, constructed a bureaucratic quagmire that only became more muddied as the war progressed.[9]

An inefficient administration was not the only thing Britain and Germany shared when it came to POW matters. Both parties tended to view the capture, processing and transit aspect of the POW experience as a means of intelligence acquisition first and humanitarian administration second. With British attentions focused on establishing interrogation 'cages' for enemy POWs and addressing the parlous state of interrogation training in the army, the notion of constructing a more comprehensive POW administration – one that would make humanitarian provision for the long-term housing of prisoners after interrogation – was seldom considered. Arguably, this lack of planning and centralization in Britain's fledgling POW administration contributed to the development in 1940 of a culture of secrecy and abuse within certain British 'cages' which, bereft of oversight from the ICRC – which was not made aware of the facilities' existence until after the war – operated outside the boundaries of IHL.[10]

In Germany, the establishment of the Dulags as centres of interrogation had also been conceived before the war began and, by the time of France's fall, Dulag Luft (Oberusel) had a special interrogation facility attached to it, through which passed close to 25,000 Allied airmen over the course of the conflict.[11] It is little surprise that, owing to the preeminent concern to interrogate prisoners and the clutter of the German POW administration, article 8 of the POW Convention – which decreed that the detaining power was to supply the Agency with information on the captured prisoners *as soon as possible* – was seldom adhered to in the summer of 1940.[12] Although the number of prisoners taken over the summer and the number of deaths that occurred on the marches was reported to the Wehrmachtsauskunftsstelle (Armed Forces Information Office), this information was primarily kept for German records and broadcast over the radio for propaganda purposes. Despite this evident capacity for such reporting, this crucial information was often not forwarded to the Agency for transmission until the prisoners arrived at their permanent camps. That was only in certain cases. For some prisoners, the period between their capture and the transmission of their details to Geneva was as long as six months. Moreover, during this time those prisoners deemed of value, such as officers and pilots, were often kept for interrogation in solitary confinement within the Dulags and denied access to Red Cross inspectors or parcels.[13]

This denial of humanitarian assistance in the Dulags served a more calculated purpose than simply making life more miserable for the prisoners. In place of the genuine article, officers from the Gestapo sometimes took to impersonating ICRC inspectors and issuing bogus Red

Cross information forms. This clumsy ruse, Pilot Officer Idrwerth Patrick Bentley Denton recalled, involved a sit-down interview, the offering of imitation British cigarettes and constant references to Denton as 'old chap' in an effort to befriend him and gain information about the type of plane he flew and his mission. Denton, and many others, were not fooled. The practice, however, continued in certain Dulags until early 1944, even after the ICRC had lodged a formal complaint with Berlin.[14]

Faced with the loss of 40,000 men to the morass of the German POW system, the question of what could be done for the prisoners weighed heavy on the minds of many in Geneva and – not before time – Whitehall. The two men who were placed at the forefront of the British Government's response to the POW crisis were Alan Hunter and Sir George Warner. As mentioned, the former had acted as the British liaison with Haccius during the Phoney War, and was a logical choice to become head of the War Office's Directorate of Prisoners of War (DPW), which was created on 25 May 1940 in response to the emerging crisis. Warner was also well chosen, at least in terms of his credentials. In addition to his wealth of experience in crafting IHL, he had been British Minister in Berne in the late 1930s, in which capacity he had come to know the future ICRC vice-president, Carl J. Burckhardt.[15] Despite retiring from his position in Berne shortly after the war broke out, Warner nevertheless acted as a Foreign Office consultant on POW and ICRC matters and believed deeply in the importance of a robust POW administration. As much can be gauged from the fact that, in addition to coming out of retirement in mid-1940 to head the newly formed Prisoner of War Department (PWD) at the Foreign Office, he also agreed to forfeit his pay for taking on the burden. Duty to British prisoners was Warner's paramount concern.[16]

The two-pronged POW administration was an admirable attempt by Whitehall to get its house in order, the more so because the new regime was established in the midst of the trauma of France's collapse and the resulting threat of German invasion of the home islands. Typical of bureaucratic expedients in a time of crisis, however, both the PWD and the DPW were beset by teething problems. In Lucie Odier's opinion, the fledgling DPW was a poorly run and understaffed department whose officials were too overcome with tackling the administrative side of POW policy to have a genuine sense of humanity about what they were doing.[17] Though Odier's expectations may have been too high in terms of expecting humanitarian sentiment on a par with the ICRC, she was at least correct about the department's dysfunctionality. The DPW remained officially leaderless until the middle of June, when Hunter was finally appointed its director. His presence, however, did little to solve the organizational problems. Despite being tasked with holding POW information that had been transmitted via the Central Agency, the DPW initially possessed no-one on its staff who could speak either French or German – the preferred languages of the ICRC. This resulted in the information having to be sent back to the PWD for translation, all of which added further delays to the process of transmitting what little POW information there was to worried relatives. Both the DPW and the PWD were also encumbered by the constant input of numerous other Whitehall departments, the effect of which was to strangle any notion of bureaucratic efficiency at precisely the time when such efficiency was needed.[18]

In the haste of Whitehall's reorganization, British–ICRC relations took a battering. The breakdown centred in no small part on relations between Haccius and Warner, who brought to the PWD long-standing reservations over the usefulness of the ICRC. Warner's jaded view of Geneva had been shaped by his dealings with Huber and Des Gouttes during the 1929 Conference. The agitation of De Gouttes for a greater acknowledgement of the ICRC in the Convention had led Warner to conclude that the Committee, despite its pretensions to the contrary, was very much the 'fifth wheel' of an already complicated POW relief system.[19] Of the humanitarian players in this system during the Second World War – the ICRC, the National Red Cross Societies, the Young Men's Christian Association (YMCA) and the Vatican among others – Warner placed his faith in the Protecting Power for British interests, a role that until December 1941 was assumed by officials from the United States Embassy in Berlin. Warner's reasons for preferring to deal with the Protecting Power on POW issues were understandable. As a key participant in the 1929 Geneva Conference, Warner was well aware of and in full agreement with the Convention's emphasis on the Protecting Power being the primary inspector of POW camps, collector of POW information and reporter of violations of IHL. The ICRC by contrast, though mentioned in the Convention, was clearly positioned as the junior partner in the system for maintaining POW welfare. Its duty was to forward Red Cross parcels to the camps and receive and transmit information via the Central Agency.[20] That and nothing more was what Warner expected of the ICRC in 1940.

This perception was soon tested. Though he 'took it for granted that as the P/W population increased they [the Protecting Power] would visit the new camps',[21] shortly after the onset of the POW crisis United States officials informed the British that they both lacked the manpower to fulfil this task and were being hindered by German restrictions on visiting the Dulags. They therefore suggested to Warner that the ICRC be asked to assist by sending its own inspectors. Warner agreed, albeit grudgingly, making sure to note to his colleagues that he preferred the more 'independent position' of the United States officials to that of the 'body of Swiss', whose work was 'supplementary to the work carried on by the United States' diplomatic missions' and 'not of great importance for His Majesty's Government'.[22] This interpretation was valid in the context of the pre-summer period, when POW numbers were small and channels of information transfer functional. By June, however, reliance on the Protecting Power alone was too limited a response to the POW crisis. An allowance for such flexibility had, ironically, been the main thrust of the Anglo-American argument at the 1929 Geneva Conference. Yet, despite his presence at that conference, Warner's view of the POW Convention was rigid, and his perception of the ICRC as a commodity of limited value remained entrenched, even as Marcel Junod and Roland Marti began their visits to the camps and Odier set off to front-line hospitals containing those POWs too wounded to be marched from France. A month later the reports came in. Junod and Marti, having visited all camps to which they could gain access in Germany and France, concluded that despite the lack of adequate food, mail and parcels and some instances of thievery by guards, actual conditions in the Stalags and Oflags were on the whole 'generally satisfactory'. The situation in the Dulags, however, was still precarious. The fact that Marti and his partner from the Berlin delegation, Pierre Descourdes, were even able to gain access to the Dulags was itself a small victory, given that the existence of the camps was often kept from the delegates and extensive negotiations with camp commandants required before entry could be assured.[23] Following such negotiations, Marti and Descourdes visited Dulag VID and Dulag Luft (Oberusel) in late August. At both Dulags the picture painted by the inspectors' reports was one of inadequate food, poor accommodation and near-constant interrogation. This impression of a spartan and at times cruel camp system that lacked all but the most basic necessities was confirmed by other reports received in the months that followed from the Protecting Power and the YMCA, which also lent its assistance in an effort to expedite the camp inspection crisis.[24]

Although they helped to paint a clearer picture of the situation in the camps, the inspections did little to improve the Committee's standing with Warner, whose continued preference for the Protecting Power rubbed the usually convivial Haccius up the wrong way. Prompted in June by Chenevière to provide a report on his relations with Whitehall's POW administration, Haccius spoke of Warner as the bane of British–ICRC relations. A man who was 'naturally inclined towards the PP [Protecting Power]' and so disposed to resist new ideas that Haccius found himself having to work around, rather than with him, in order to achieve anything. The delicacy of Haccius's position – a pseudo-diplomat tasked with maintaining cooperation between a private humanitarian organization and a government facing the greatest threat to its national security in centuries – in part explains his frustrations. His response was to strive to keep British–ICRC relations stable, to which end he endeavoured to position the ICRC as the most credible and active respondent to the POW crisis. For example, in the wake of Whitehall's receipt of the first batch of camp reports from the Protecting Power, the ICRC and the YMCA, he passed on information to Geneva – told to him in confidence by Hunter – on which camps the United States inspectors had been unable to gain entry, presumably so that the ICRC could step into the breech. He also implored Geneva to speed up its transmission of POW information to Hunter, for fear that delay might adversely affect the latter's view of the Committee's competence.[25] This campaign, though in practice aimed at achieving an effective humanitarian response, was also driven by Haccius's own fear that, under the weight of Warner's indifference to the ICRC and the burden of an increased workload, his hosts might soon view him as unsuitable for his task and send him packing. He expressed as much to Odier when, in the midst of a growing public backlash in Britain in December 1940 over the lack of parcels reaching POWs, he angrily complained that the Agency's inability to provide him with information on parcel delivery had 'placed my position in peril'. So on edge was Haccius over the issue of Geneva providing him information that he felt the need to send the Committee a terse complaint about inconsistency in telegram numbering.[26]

What Haccius failed to realize was that no degree of bureaucratic efficiency or humanitarian zeal was going to change Warner's mind about the ICRC. This was because, although the camp visits were conducted relatively efficiently, other responses from Geneva to the crisis seemed to confirm Warner's opinion of the ICRC as out-of-their-depth amateurs. Faced with the breakdown of the postal system over the summer, Haccius petitioned Warner to allow Red Cross planes and ferries to operate between Britain and France for the purposes of carrying parcels, mail and facilitating POW exchanges. The proposal was rejected on the not unreasonable grounds that the Channel was now the frontline of the war and the British had received reports of the Luftwaffe using its own

Red Cross-marked planes over English skies for surveillance purposes. The fantastic nature of the idea, given the reality of the military situation, did very little for Haccius's standing with both Warner and Hunter who, despite his early enthusiasm, had increasingly come to regard the Red Cross delegate as being 'not a very live wire'.[27]

The second proposal from the ICRC to remedy the breakdown of the postal system was to improve telegraphic communications between Geneva and London. Although more practical than the planes and ferries proposal, the request brought to the surface additional concerns held by Warner about both the focus of the ICRC's mission and the organization's future as the war spread across Europe. Prior to the invasion of France, the transmission of POW information by the Agency to the PWIB was conducted free of charge via the Swiss and French postal services, an agreement that had been included in the terms of the 1935 Cairo Postal Convention. This system in general ran smoothly until the postal system broke down in May, from which time the Agency began, gradually, to abandon its reliance on the post in favour of sending what little POW information it received via telegraph. As more information was gathered, this method of communication placed an extra financial burden on the ICRC to such an extent that Haccius was soon paying for return communications to Geneva out of his own pocket. Having been informed of this, the BRC asked Warner to speak to the Treasury about funding for the ICRC, which until then had received only minimal financial contributions from the British Government and the BRC, compared with donations from other belligerents.[28]

For Warner the issue was more about purpose than money. Specifically, he was concerned that British funds might be spent on non-British interests. Informed by a report from Chenevière in April, which indicated that the lion's share of the Committee's funding was being spent on Polish POWs, Warner minuted to his colleagues that 'the essential expenditure of the IRCC on objects in which we have a real interest cannot be considerable. We are really being asked to contribute to the maintenance of *Allied P/W* to a great extent.' He further called Geneva's pleas into question by opining to C. G. L. Syers at the Treasury that the ICRC's 'claims to services rendered are very exaggerated'.[29] The fact that the number of Allied POWs held by the Germans had swelled to over two million by the summer of 1940, and the further fact that 40,000 of that total were British did little to move Warner or Syers, who agreed with the former that the Committee was making a mountain out of a molehill and was capable of absorbing the extra expense for the telegrams itself. Although ostensibly petty, there was some reason for this reluctance to contribute to the ICRC's expenses: the fear that the Committee might not exist by year's end. Syers for one viewed Switzerland in mid-1940 as an imperilled 'neutral island surrounded by enemy seas', an impression that was heightened by intelligence reports from Zurich, which indicated that German divisions were massing on the border with the aim of invading Switzerland on 16 May. So great was the fear that the British Minister in Berne, David Kelly, burned his papers and temporarily evacuated his family to the supposed safety of France along with other British officials from Zurich and Basle.[30] Warner, for his part, had given some prior thought to the prospect of a German invasion of Switzerland. When asked to prepare a brief on this scenario in early 1940, he informed colleagues that the brave Swiss would put up resistance. A repulse could only be successful, however, 'pending the arrival of the strong support which they can expect from the other side of the Jura'.[31] With the capitulation of France in late June this scenario became untenable and the notion of Switzerland falling into the Nazi abyss a distinct possibility. It is testament to rising British concern over POWs that, despite prior indifference to the Committee, the issue of how the fall of Switzerland would affect the ICRC's capabilities was considered in Whitehall. At the height of the invasion scare, David Kelly was instructed to take the matter of invasion up with Chenevière who, in a misguided attempt to assure the British of the ICRC's resolve, made clear that in the event of Switzerland's neutrality being compromised it would neither evacuate nor allow German occupation to impede its mission. This point was clarified by Carl J. Burckhardt as Geneva's official policy on the day before France's capitulation.[32] The ICRC's senior figures were therefore in agreement that, even with Switzerland under Nazi occupation, the Committee would go on.

Much like the planes and ferries scheme, the ICRC's intention to continue its operations – with its neutrality supposedly intact – within Hitler's empire was not viewed by Whitehall as evidence of the Committee's intractable determination, but as an example of the misunderstanding it had of both its own limitations and the realities of the war. There was little to be gained therefore by increasing financial support to such an apparently doomed organization and it was only with reservation over the ICRC's 'precarious' financial position that Warner and Syers agreed to donate £4,000 (SFR70,000), on the condition that the Germans made a reciprocal donation.[33] It was left to an embarrassed David Kelly to point out to the Foreign Office that this total donation barely made a ripple in the Committee's £200,000 monthly administration costs, much of which was being covered by the Germans and the

French. Nevertheless, it was not until April 1941 that the ICRC received another donation, for the same amount, from the British Government. This was despite the latter's acknowledgement that the amount proffered left little spare for the Committee to spend on miscellaneous British POW matters once the costs of the telegrams to Whitehall had been paid.[34]

Although it was far from adequate, the tentative financial investment in the ICRC reflected a wider trend in British attitudes in the aftermath of the summer of 1940. The Committee had begun the war viewed by Whitehall as a useful, though limited, humanitarian commodity that, in conjunction with the Protecting Power, could be left alone to handle the small problem of maintaining POW welfare. The events of the summer changed this paradigm of relations significantly and presented new challenges for both the ICRC and the British – challenges that neither party was adequately equipped to deal with. Although Haccius laboured under the notion that energy and ideas would overcome operational constraints, the Committee lacked the necessary funds, personnel and compliance from the Germans to respond effectively to the POW crisis. The ICRC's main achievement in 1940 – instituting the practice of regular inspections of POW camps – was made possible by the agreement of the belligerents out of necessity. Although this practice helped to ensure that the prisoners were not completely cut off in their first, shambolic months of captivity, it was by no means as comprehensive a response to the POW crisis as the Committee believed it was capable of making.[35] The ICRC's need for more delegates and more funding was matched by Whitehall's need to revise its First World War-era conceptions of POW policy. For this the established practices for monitoring POW welfare and ensuring that prisoners received food parcels had to be modified. As it was the most important humanitarian agent behind the Protecting Power, the ICRC also had to become more central to the thinking of the PWD and the DPW. The problem was that such adjustments to mind-set had to be made in circumstances of extreme pressure, when the very relief system upon which the prisoners relied for humanitarian assistance began to collapse and public furore in Britain began to rage.

'One parcel, per man, per week'

Pilot Officer Maurice Butt, a prisoner at Stalag XXA (Thorn), spoke for the vast majority of POWs when he stated that during the long years of captivity 'the food situation was a dominant thought in most minds'. Although the basic rations issued to Western Allied POWs – thin cabbage and potato-based soups, ersatz coffee and black bread being staples – prevented starvation, the calorie and vitamin intake of such fare was insufficient to maintain good health over a long period of captivity. This deficiency, lack of variety and meagre portions meant that even in the better-supplied Oflags 'nothing could rival food as a subject for talk'. It is therefore unsurprising that the role of the ICRC – the primary external provider of food and medical relief for the prisoners – has figured prominently and fondly in the post-war recollections of POWs. Armed with parcels supplied by prisoners' relatives and national Red Cross societies, ICRC delegates assumed, in the minds of many prisoners, the role of 'angels', whose arrival heralded not only a much needed supplementing of rations but also an equally necessary boost to morale.[36]

The ICRC's mandate to act as supplier of parcels was codified in the POW Convention, and the right of its delegates to enter the camps in order to deliver the parcels was further bolstered by the establishment of regular ICRC inspections to POW camps in 1940. As we shall see, the Committee often tried to broaden its range of services beyond inspecting camps, collecting information and delivering parcels. It was in these three fields of work, however, that Geneva was primarily engaged on behalf of POWs. Though other POW issues may have eluded Whitehall in the war's early months, the importance of the Committee's parcel delivery work was well understood by British officials and provision had been made from the outset of hostilities to keep the ICRC's 'angels' supplied. As had been the case in the First World War, the BRC, with partial funding from Whitehall, had its position confirmed by the War Office as 'the accredited authority for packing and despatching parcels to British prisoners of war' in September 1939. In adherence to this duty, the BRC helped to pay for, pack and despatch parcels, via the General Post Office, across the Channel, through France and to Geneva, where they were stored in the ICRC's warehouses until information on the numbers and names of prisoners at specific camps was received by the Central Agency. It was only once this information was processed that the ICRC's delegates set off to the camps with trucks of parcels and the names of those for whom they were intended in hand. Until the fall of France, this POW relief system ran well and was a cause of little concern to the War Office, which trusted that the BRC would maintain the flow of parcels to Geneva and that the ICRC would be able to distribute the parcels to the camps, irrespective of what twists and turns the war might take. When France fell, however, the entire POW relief system had to change abruptly and the original cross-Channel shipping route was diverted south to neutral Lisbon for onward carriage through Spain, Vichy France and, ultimately, to Switzerland.[37]

The new route's functionality was hindered by a host of problems, the first of which was the suspension of all mail traffic in France on the orders of the Germans on 15 June. Not only did this inhibit the transmission of POW capture information but also cut off the BRC's parcel warehouses from the ICRC's depots in Geneva, leaving a significant gap in the flow of parcels to the Continent. Even when the mail routes were reactivated in the middle of July, the parcels' seaborne journey from Britain was disrupted by the intensifying military situation in the skies over the Home Counties and in the Channel, beneath the waves of which the Red Cross lost 16,296 parcels by the end of 1940. The fate of the parcels that made it to Lisbon was no less precarious than the journey of the ships that ferried them there. The key neutral European port during the war, Lisbon was as much a busy hub for refugees, ships and spies as it was 'decaying, shabby and in desperate need of reinvention'.[38] The docks themselves were chaotic and overburdened by the amount of shipping that had to be accommodated, and the capabilities of the ICRC's man on the quayside, Colonel Frédéric Iselin, were also questionable. Overwhelmed by his duties, Iselin's updates to the BRC warehouses in London on the status of the shipments were sporadic and, under his watch over the course of 1940 thousands of BRC parcels went missing from Lisbon's docks. Parcels also disappeared during the overland journey to France which, owing to the lack of rolling stock and the parlous state of a Spanish transport system that was still recovering from civil war, was deemed both unreliable and unsatisfactory by the ICRC.[39]

Compounding matters was the fact that, in June 1940, Geneva had only a small stockpile of parcels from which not only to supply the influx of new Allied POWs but also to maintain the flow of parcel to the hundreds of thousands of other prisoners captured since 1939. These parcel stocks, distributed by delegates visiting the camps only after negotiations with the Germans, soon ran dry and by the end of July the prisoners in Stalag XX (Thorn) were having to ration their Red Cross supplies to one parcel for every group of twenty-five men until the next, small, delivery arrived in mid-September. At Stalag Luft IV (Gross Tychow) the prisoners had only two parcels each over the course of the same period and at Stalag XXI-D (Posen) no parcels were received until late September and even then only at a rate of one for every two prisoners. The ICRC lacked both the stockpile required and the transport infrastructure to keep its supply lines stable and respond effectively to the crisis. Having received reports on this situation and the sporadic deliveries to the camps, the PWD grimly concluded that 'no parcels could have reached the prisoners between the middle of June and the middle of September'.[40] This was an exaggeration, though not by much. Fuelled by the helplessness of the situation and encumbered by the lack of clear information on the plight of the POWs, however, exaggeration and confusion took hold in both the British Government and the British public's understanding of the POW crisis.

The British public's main source of information on the unfolding drama were the POWs themselves, whose letters to loved ones began arriving in the wake of the resumption of mail services in late summer. Tales of parcel deprivation, cruel guards and overcrowded camps led outraged relatives to demand answers of both the government and the BRC. One of the more vocal critics was Winifred Coombe-Tennant, the mother of a captain in the Welsh Guards being held at the dilapidated Oflag VIB (Warburg) who, despondent at the plight of her son and his comrades, wrote personally to Clementine Churchill on the matter and so peppered Whitehall with her demands for answers that she earned a reputation as a semi-deranged troublemaker. The problem for the Government was that Coombe-Tennant could not be ignored – in fact she was only the most vocal of many.[41] As winter descended, the public pressure grew such that the question of why the task of keeping the prisoners supplied had been left to an independent, voluntary organization like the BRC was raised in Parliament. The outcome of the ensuing debates was a reassurance on 26 November from Anthony Eden that a 'one parcel, per man, per week' rate of delivery was about to begin. Although clearly aimed at diffusing public tension, Eden had some cause to believe that this pledge might soon be fulfilled. The backlog of POW capture information had been clearing in the weeks prior to his announcement and there were also tentative signs that the parcel delivery routes were starting to recover. The most encouraging development in this regard was the devising of a plan to speed up the delivery of parcels once received in Lisbon. The agreement reached between the ICRC, the BRC and Whitehall was to begin a feeder service by ship from Lisbon to Marseilles, where the Committee would establish a parcel warehouse and supervise the shorter rail journey north to Geneva. With Churchill's endorsement, the Ministry of Transport agreed to pay three-quarters of the cost of the seven feeder ships, the first of which, the *Juleta*, sailed from Lisbon on 22 December.[42]

The probability of success for the new Lisbon–Marseilles route – one of the few clear examples during the POW crisis of tripartite

cooperation – was increased as a result of other initiatives that ema-
nated from Geneva and St James's Palace once the shock of the summer
subsided. Prior to the fall of France, the individual Red Cross parcel – a
5 kg package of food or clothing that was usually packed by a prisoner's
relatives or National Red Cross Societies for despatch to specifically
named prisoners – had been the primary form of parcel received by
POWs. The exceptions to this norm were Polish prisoners who, owing
to the destruction of their country, had few relatives or relief agencies
left to pack such parcels. The ICRC's response to this problem was to
switch the primary form of relief for Polish POWs from individual to
collective parcels. These were bulk consignments of unmarked packages
that were sent to the camps for distribution by the prisoner's primary
representative, the Man of Confidence (MOC).[43] In response to the
similarly chaotic conditions in the summer of 1940, the Committee
phased out the individual parcel in favour of collective shipments,
negotiations for the despatch of which Haccius began as early as July
with the British authorities. Roland Marti was also busy in Berlin trying
to keep channels of information from the camps to the outside world
open. In December he helped to bring some measure of consistency to
POW mail by obtaining agreement from the Germans for a minimum
of two letters and four postcards a month for each prisoner. He was also
given support from Geneva in the form of a permanent four-member
strong delegation, which allowed for further consistency in the gathering of information on new prisoners, transfers and the production of
reports on camp conditions. The means by which this information was
analysed was also reviewed, leading the ICRC to set up a liaison staff in
order to better disseminate the information to the Committee's relief
and missing inquiries departments.[44]

For its part, the BRC tried to improve its capability to produce the
number of parcels required by the POWs. To this end, eight new parcel
packing centres were established in Britain over the latter half of 1940
and, when the output from these centres was still deemed unsatisfactory, the Canadian Red Cross was approached to supply enough parcels
to make up the shortfall while the BRC's new facilities completed their
'running in' period. The BRC also took steps to make sure that parcels
would no longer disappear into a black hole once they arrived on the
Continent. On 23 November it sent one of its representatives, Judith
Jackson, to Lisbon to meet Iselin and get to the bottom of the manifold
problems there. She swiftly concluded both that the parcel transport
system was cluttered with individual parcels, rather than bulk shipments, and that the overland route via Spain was no longer tenable as a

means of getting the parcels to Geneva. In addition to Jackson's report contributing to the establishment of the Lisbon–Marseilles route, she also ensured, by procuring extra warehouse space at the port, that the BRC would have a permanent presence in Lisbon and a parcel stockpile ready for use once the new shipping arrangements were in place.[45] Based on these developments the BRC assured Whitehall that as winter descended the worst of the parcel crisis was near to being over and that Eden's 'one parcel, per man, per week' pledge would probably be fulfilled.

Although Eden responded by projecting confidence in his performance to the House, others in Whitehall, quite rightly, held a more sceptical opinion of the BRC's assurances. Alan Hunter in particular expressed exasperation at the BRC's repeated claims to have the parcel situation under control despite the fact that the new warehouses and the Lisbon–Marseilles route were not yet fully operational. This led him to suggest that the War Office should assume the task of packing next-of-kin parcels – personal parcels that could contain food, clothing and mementos from home – thus freeing up the BRC to focus on making sure food-only parcels were produced. When public criticism of the Government and the BRC's handling of the parcel crisis reached its height at the end of 1940, Hunter also tried, unsuccessfully, to have any BRC statement intended for public consumption vetted by the War Office's censors. This suggestion served only to unnerve the BRC further, which grew concerned that the Government was attempting to compromise its autonomy and take over its operations.[46] These fears became manifest when, in January 1941, the War Office forced the BRC to take on a new director of POW affairs, both as a means of assuaging public fury and guaranteeing that the BRC's promise of a revitalized parcel system would not be empty.

The man appointed for the task, Stanley Adams, was the Chairman of Thomas Cook travel agents and, purportedly, an expert on all continental transportation matters. Ever sensitive to Whitehall's attempts to control it, the BRC received Adams frostily and, following a year of frustration and concern over 'his authority being whittled down', he resigned in January 1942. Although he was criticized by some of his colleagues at the time, it is difficult to argue that Adams's appointment was not of benefit both to the BRC and the burgeoning POW relief system. With regards to addressing public criticism, one of Adams's first priorities was to meet Coombe-Tennant and her supporters and assure them that all would now be well. It was timely in this respect that his appointment coincided with the receipt in Geneva of a bulk delivery of 20,000 parcels, products of a Lisbon–Marseilles route that was stuttering into life. Though this made it seem that Whitehall's appointment had been decisive, the happy event of the parcel delivery in January 1941 was the product of the expectations of November 1940 at last coming to fruition, rather than any effort on the part of Adams personally. His primary contribution to improving parcel delivery was, nonetheless, significant. Fearing the emergence of another parcel crisis in future, Adams insisted that the BRC's stockpile – which by May 1941 numbered close to 1 million parcels in Britain and Lisbon – be continually maintained. Bruised by the events of 1940, the ICRC also developed a similar, preventative policy, and by mid-1941 had amassed a stockpile of 300,000 parcels in Geneva.[47] With shipping along the Lisbon–Marseilles route also stabilized, following a bottleneck of congestion in the spring, by the end of 1941 nearly 3 million parcels had been despatched to mainland Europe – 1.5 million more than in 1940. It had taken over a year but by the middle of 1941 the foundations of a stable POW relief system had been laid. In the years that followed, British prisoners in Europe received parcels, in the main, at the promised rate of 'one parcel, per man, per week' or, sometimes, even higher.[48]

This stable means of parcel delivery was only one facet of the POW relief system that sustained many POWs and civilian internees – British and otherwise – over the duration of the war. The system's other aspects were the receipt and processing of POW capture information by the Agency – crucial for the BRC in determining how many parcels needed to be packed – and the practice of ICRC delegates visiting the camps both to deliver parcels and ensure that they were reaching their intended recipients. The role played by the ICRC in this POW relief system was far larger than anything that had been anticipated by Whitehall in 1939. Although the collection of POW information and the inspections of camps were expected, the notion of the Committee acting as the coordinator of the Lisbon–Marseilles route was an unforeseen development, which led to it becoming involved in matters of shipping, warehousing and general logistics on a near-continental scale. The agreement made by Whitehall in late 1940 to allow the ICRC to assume these burdens was highly significant. Not only did the adopting of the Lisbon–Marseilles route mark an important move away from the 'unimaginative'[49] approach to POW matters hitherto practised by Whitehall, but, in acknowledging the increasingly vital role played by the Committee, the door was opened to a new phase in British–ICRC relations.

Whitehall becomes 'POW minded'

The year 1941 was pivotal not only for British–ICRC relations but also for the growing British POW population. By the end of that year the POW relief system in Europe had been stabilized; conditions in the camps had begun to improve; parcels and letters from home were being received more regularly; and the prisoners themselves had begun to settle into a dull, yet relatively safe, life of captivity that for most would last until 1945.[50] Outside the Reich, however, new POW problems emerged, first in Greece and North Africa and then, more desperately, in the Far East, where 130,000 prisoners were taken following the dramatic collapse of British forces in Hong Kong, Malaya and Singapore. Against the backdrop of these crises, many changes came both to Whitehall's POW departments and to the philosophy that had hitherto guided their conduct.

In April 1941, George Warner – exhausted and embittered over the lack of staff in his department and the increased workload over the winter – was politely moved on from his position as head of the PWD, a development he seemed to welcome with relief.[51] His replacement, Sir Harold Satow, was a man far better suited to the task of his office, possessed of greater energy than his predecessor and an aptitude for bureaucracy that enabled him to untangle some of the confusing threads that had developed in British–ICRC–BRC relations since 1939.[52] Change also came in 1941 to the DPW, albeit in more dramatic circumstances. Shortly after Warner's retirement, an internal investigation began into allegations that Alan Hunter and his deputy, Colonel Nick Coates, were involved in a scam to seize money and jewellery that had been sent to German POWs. Owing to the fact that some of the money stolen had come via the ICRC, its London Delegation was in danger of having its integrity and neutrality questioned should news of the scandal reach Berlin. Mindful also that the news might lead to reprisals against British POWs, Haccius was taken into British confidence and asked to keep the matter quiet, which he agreed to do, even after Hunter was stood down and replaced by Major-General Cyril Gepp as head of the DPW. Haccius was undoubtedly acting first and foremost in the interests of maintaining his and his organization's reputation for neutrality and discretion. The notion of ICRC neutrality being preserved was, however, difficult to reconcile with Haccius's actions in favour of British interests. The fact that he was trusted with this delicate matter indicates that Hunter's claim that Haccius was 'an International Delegate, accredited to FO (and to DPW) for a particular purpose' was no empty proclamation. In fact, by the time the scandal around him broke Hunter had come to view Haccius as nothing less than a member of Whitehall's POW administration.[53] Although he possessed a more tempered opinion of the delegate than his predecessor, Satow was nonetheless highly aware of Haccius's growing importance and the need to keep British–ICRC relations healthy. With the support of Anthony Eden Satow expedited arrangements for the enlargement of the Committee's London Delegation over the summer of 1941 – including a personal secretary for Haccius – on the grounds that such a development could only help British interests.[54]

Cooperation of this nature reflected a wider trend that developed in British–ICRC relations in the wake of the POW crisis and the reorganization of the DPW and PWD. Though at first damaging, the travails of 1940 led ultimately to a better understanding between Haccius and his Whitehall associates. In public, the Government certainly projected confidence in the ICRC's abilities, primarily in order to assuage criticism of the POW relief system on the home front and maintain the prestige of the Committee as an important humanitarian actor.[55] Although in the initial stages of the POW crisis this sentiment masked a more critical view of the Committee, by early 1941 there had been a genuine improvement in British–ICRC relations, albeit one that stemmed from a negative factor: a shared sense of weariness towards the BRC. The latter had enjoyed good relations with Whitehall for many years and clearly had the trust of Government in 1939 when it was appointed chief agent for the maintenance of British POW welfare. The problem was that the POW crisis had exposed certain frailties within the BRC, not the least of which was a form of institutional insecurity over its independence and centrality to POW affairs. Throughout 1940 the BRC constantly harangued Geneva and Whitehall over such matters as whether its staff had the right, as Haccius had, to use the Swiss diplomatic bag, as well as making frequent demands to receive duplicate POW capture information from the Agency. This engendered a shared sense of frustration within the ICRC and Whitehall. So exasperated was the Committee that the usually convivial Max Huber wrote a scathing missive to Stanley Adams, in which he argued that the ICRC had better things to spend its precious financial resources on than facsimiles of POW information for the benefit of the staff at St James's Palace.[56]

For its part, Whitehall – irritated by the BRC's apparent inability to get its parcel packing operations in order – endeavoured over the winter of 1940–1 to deflect blame for the collapse of the POW relief system onto the BRC in order to protect itself from public criticism.[57] The ICRC, too, played this blame game and in so doing all but 'sided' with the British Government against the BRC. In the autumn of 1940, neither Haccius nor Hunter corrected the false impression, conveyed by an inmate of Oflag VIIC (Laufen) in a letter home, that, as the prisoners were receiving parcels marked 'ICRC' rather than BRC, the latter must have been dragging its feet.[58] The Government and the ICRC also continued to exclude the BRC from its discussions, even on matters of parcel despatch information, much to the latter's chagrin. The extent to which this became a sore point in ICRC–BRC relations is evident in the Committee's official post-war report which, though a dry read for the most part, noted that 'some of the National Societies were disturbed to find that, side by side with their contacts with the Committee, the ICRC was in direct and regular touch with the Government of their own countries on questions of importance'. Though unnamed, this is clearly a reference to the BRC, whose own confidential – and more candid – history records the irritation felt by its leadership at being cut out of British–ICRC discussions.[59]

In one respect the BRC had every right to carry a chip on its shoulder over this exclusion. Leaving aside the damage such practice did to any notion of a coordinated tripartite response to the POW crisis, the accepted protocol during the Phoney War had been for the BRC to act as a conduit between Whitehall and the ICRC, so as to protect the image of the Committee as being apolitical and 'above' liaison with governments. In the scramble to get hold of any information on the prisoners in 1940 this rule was abandoned and most of what information there was passed between Haccius, Hunter and Warner without consultation with the BRC. This practice soon became normalized. Indeed, as late as May 1941 Haccius received explicit instructions from Geneva to continue working to this effect.[60] So normal had exclusion of the BRC become that, when Geneva announced its intention to send Junod and Odier to Britain in April 1941, the BRC, though eventually included in talks between the Government and the ICRC delegates, only received word of the visit 'casually from one of our government departments'. Subsequent efforts by the BRC to involve itself in preparations for the visit, by warning the ICRC of the extent to which public opinion in Britain was sour towards the Red Cross and by preparing parliamentary questions on the ICRC for the War Office, served only to annoy the latter parties further and to re-enforce the divide between Whitehall and the Committee, on the one side, and the BRC, on the other.[61]

As the seemingly less troublesome member of the Red Cross family, both the ICRC's stock and that of its delegate rose in Whitehall as a consequence. When Geneva proposed in late 1940 that Haccius be recalled and that Junod travel to Britain both to inspect POW camps and to help smooth over the cracks in relations with the BRC, Hunter reacted defensively. Rather than view the idea for what it was – an attempt to repair the damage by sending a more senior delegate – he instead suspected a BRC-inspired plot to replace Haccius with someone who would be more critical of the Government. This scenario was viewed by Hunter as a 'tragedy', both because it would lead to Haccius becoming a 'cat's-paw' in the BRC's contretemps with Whitehall and also because by this time he had grown to trust Haccius and, as the latter proudly reported to Geneva, had 'necessary confidence' in his standing.[62] The PWD's Walter Roberts also criticized the BRC – 'a pale shadow of its more brilliant rival, the ICRC' – for its suggestion that it send a liaison to Geneva better to open the lines of communication, citing the view that the BRC had no one on its staff capable of assuming such a role. David Kelly also opined, more diplomatically, that the workload in Geneva was too small for the BRC to appoint a delegate and that, owing to their good relations with the ICRC, the British embassy staff could handle the task of liaison themselves.[63]

This negativity towards the BRC, born in no small part of the POW crisis, could not last forever. As more soldiers were marched into captivity from battlefields in North Africa and the Far East, both the demand for parcels and the need for tripartite cooperation increased. By March 1942 the Government was looking to the BRC to produce 90,000 parcels per month.[64] It was no coincidence that, as the number of British servicemen in captivity grew, Whitehall, through a combination of increased funding, greater involvement in BRC policy and the use of the latter's publication, *The Prisoner of War*, as a propaganda tool to quell public concerns, became closer to the BRC than it had ever been. This led to an improvement in relations upon common grounds of interest. When, for example, following Stanley Adams's resignation public criticism of Whitehall and the BRC intensified, both parties worked together to keep an inquiry into Adams's tenure from being discussed in Parliament.[65] The practical intervention of Whitehall in BRC matters also rose greatly in the war's middle years. When parcel production rates dipped in February 1942, the War Office began a 'steadily increasing watch and control over the actual work of the Society' which, probably, contributed to the fact that by year's end the BRC reached the height of its wartime production – 5,552,151 parcels packed and despatched.[66] Though the marriage between Whitehall and the BRC was never truly a happy one, with over 200,000 British soldiers and civilians in captivity by the end of 1942 neither side could realistically avoid increasing their level of cooperation with the other.

The same need to reconcile with the BRC was pressing for Geneva, whose capacity to deliver parcels was reliant on the POW relief system being fed from the BRC's warehouses. Consequently, though questions over who should receive what information and talk to which Whitehall official continued to hum in the background of ICRC–BRC interactions, in December 1941 the BRC's Sir John Kennedy and Carl J. Burckhardt, in a frank acknowledgement of the parlous state of their organizations' relations, came to an agreement that 'mutual confidence between the International Red Cross Committee and the British Red Cross' had to be restored. This was followed by Haccius finally agreeing, at the request of Harold Satow, to forward all camp inspection reports received from Geneva directly to the BRC.[67]

Satow's intervention in this matter was not arbitrary. Indeed, his many attempts to clarify tripartite relations – a campaign he fought throughout 1941 – was part of a wider effort on the part of Whitehall's POW administration both to coordinate itself with the Red Cross more effectively and refine its POW policy in response to the spread of the war, the new waves of prisoner captures and the threat of yet more public scrutiny lest the prisoners should not receive a regular supply of parcels. Under the weight of these challenges Whitehall could no longer afford to treat POW welfare as a peripheral concern, to be dealt with in a reactive manner.[68] The time had come for Whitehall to become more pervasively 'POW minded'.

The clarification of relations with the Red Cross was only one of the steps taken in this process. At the same time Satow was tackling the problems in tripartite relations, in April 1941 moves were also being made to centralize the bureaucratic side of British POW affairs by forming an Imperial Prisoners of War Committee (IPOWC). The purpose of this was both to respond to public criticism by putting forward a more organized front and to acknowledge the growing involvement of Dominion troops – those of Australia, New Zealand, Canada and South Africa – in the conflict. Though it seemed like a medium through which to coordinate POW policy across the Empire, in practice the IPOWC was something of a flop. It met only three times during the war and in practice the handling of POW affairs remained firmly in the grasp of the PWD and DPW. The very fact, however, that the IPOWC had been created was indicative of an acknowledgement by Whitehall that the expansion of the war into new theatres and the increase in captures that came with these developments required a response.[69] A more tangible example of this came with regards to British policy towards Axis POWs. Between autumn of 1940 and the spring of 1941 British forces in North and East Africa captured close to 300,000 Italian troops. Like the Germans a year before, the British were completely unprepared for this prisoner influx.[70] There were only two POW transit camps in North Africa, and in East Africa food was scarce, to the extent that the prisoners had to be fed on their own captured rations. The decision was thus made to transport the POWs out of Africa for use as labourers in Britain and throughout the Empire. This plan marked a significant turning point in Britain's policy towards enemy prisoners, who hitherto had been considered as security risks first and potential 'assets' to the British war effort second.[71]

In addition to shipping Italian prisoners across the Empire, Whitehall was also keen to see its own men on ships bound for Britain. The question of POW repatriation, pertinent since the start of the war, was raised to new heights of consideration in 1941. The discussions between Berlin and London over the exchange of sick and wounded POWs – a practice carried out during the First World War and codified in the 1929 Conventions – culminated in a frustrating eleventh-hour cancelation of a planned exchange, on Hitler's orders, on 6 October 1941. Nevertheless, over the course of these negotiations POW matters had been raised to the highest levels of discussion in Whitehall. Moreover, such considerations stayed there. In early 1942, new policies on censorship in the negotiations with Berlin were adopted and two interdepartmental committees were formed in Whitehall – one concerned with repatriation policy, the other with administration – in order to push the repatriation question forward. The result was a protracted series of negotiations over POW exchanges that continued until the end of the war.[72]

What, in British eyes, was the ICRC's role in this new, more engaged, phase of POW thinking? In one respect, little had changed in the British view since 1939. The PWD and DPW still approached POW problems within the framework of a strict adherence to the Convention, lest a disregard of this norm open the way for retaliatory measures by Berlin against British prisoners.[73] What this adherence meant in terms of British–ICRC relations was that the latter's role, as laid down in the Convention, was the one preferred by the British – a supply agent for POW relief and assistant, at most, to the Protecting Power. As Satow himself put it, although the ICRC became increasingly important to the maintenance of British POW welfare in the war's middle years, 'care had to be taken to ensure that, in their zeal, the International Red Cross Committee did not exceed the role allotted to them by the Convention'.[74] When this role was expanded beyond the Conventions' articles – to camp inspections and more hands-on logistical work in the organization of the POW relief system – acquiescence from Whitehall was furnished, more than anything else, out of desperation for a remedy to the POW crisis. What would prove decisive in British–ICRC relations and what mattered to Whitehall increasingly as new battlefronts opened was the ICRC's ability to repay the trust placed in it during the crises and to match its own expectations as a humanitarian agent par excellence. In the wake of a succession of British military setbacks during 1941–2 – in North Africa, Greece and the Far East – Geneva was proffered the opportunity to make good on this promise.

4
Dependence and Divergence, 1941–2

The system tested: the ICRC in the Mediterranean and the Far East

On 20 April 1941, Greece – having resisted the invasion launched by the Italians in October 1940 and the arrival of the Germans in the spring of the following year – finally capitulated to the Axis. In the days that followed, the Wehrmacht rounded up the remaining British and Colonial soldiers that had been sent to Greece's defence, taking, by the time of the fall of Kalamata on 29 April, a grand total of 11,000 British POWs. A little over a month later, these were joined by an additional 12,000 of their comrades who, following evacuation from the mainland, had fought on in the subsequent battle for Crete, only to surrender on 1 June. Though the total number of POWs taken in the Greek campaign was less than the intake in Western Europe in 1940, the same problems of transportation, housing and food soon emerged. The two main transit camps in the region – Dulag 183 (Salonika) and the 'Corinth Cage' Frontstalag – were ramshackle facilities in which prisoners were beset by dysentery and untreated infections and, in some cases, shot by overzealous guards for such trivialities as attempting to use the open-ditch latrines at night. The experience of capture for Allied prisoners taken in North Africa during the same period was little better. The main transit camp at Benghazi – 'The Palms' – was little more than a dust-choked, barbed-wire-ringed enclosure, in which the sanitation was non-existent and the rations consisted of watery macaroni and hard tack biscuits, supplied in measly quantities. Transit camps in Italy were comparably bad. The camp at Capua, bereft of adequate water supplies and functional latrines, was notorious as a breeding ground for malaria and beri beri.[1]

Administration of camps in the Mediterranean also left a lot to be desired. Viewed as good for little more than guard duty, the Italians were charged by their senior German partners with the task of running the transit camps in North Africa and Greece and handling the processing of the POWs through to their places of permanent internment, usually within northern Italy or the Reich itself. In this the Italians soon earned a reputation for cockiness, cruelty and incompetence. Reporting to Geneva from the transit camps happened rarely, if ever, despite the fact that the Italian Red Cross – in theory close to ICRC – was given this duty by Rome. As late as November 1941 the Agency was still waiting on capture cards for prisoners taken in April who, by year's end, had been transferred from North Africa to permanent camps in Europe.[2] In terms of privation therefore, the capture and transit experience for British prisoners of the Italians in 1941 was eerily reminiscent – and, for the most part, worse – than that experienced by their comrades the year before.

Aspects of the POW experience in Greece that did differ from that of France were the more coordinated and expedient response of the ICRC and the understanding and support proffered by Whitehall to its enterprise. The PWD was informed by Haccius in the first week of May 1941 of the number of prisoners captured in Greece and the rate at which they were expected to be transferred to permanent camps in Germany. The BRC acted on this information by releasing funds to the ICRC for purchases of food and clothing in Turkey and sent a representative, Edward Hogg, to Ankara in order to coordinate relief efforts with Marcel Junod.[3] Standing at the centre of this response from the Red Cross was the ICRC delegate Robert Brunel, a man widely regarded as one of the Committee's finest servants during the war.[4] Brunel had first been despatched to Athens at the outset of Mussolini's failed Balkan adventure in the autumn of 1940 and so was well established in the capital in the spring of 1941 when the Germans finished what the Italians started. Following the cessation of hostilities, Brunel – adopting the spirit of Junod and Marti's visits to the camps in France the year before – opted to gather information on the newly captured POWs in person rather than wait for the compliance of the Axis authorities, whose competence to handle POW affairs he already doubted.[5] This direct approach led to more expedient and detailed reporting of capture information. His initial report, which was received by Haccius on 13 June, presented gram-by-gram information on the quantity and type of food available as well as details of the numbers of those affected by dysentery and diarrhoea following its consumption. This depressing picture was enhanced by further reports of the number of wounded in various Greek hospitals, their condition and the time expected for the prisoners to be transferred to permanent camps in Germany.[6]

As the prisoners awaited their transit, the parcels began to arrive. Fearful of a second POW crisis, Brunel's delegates took no chances in resupplying the camps as often as possible and, in the case of one delegate, André Lambert, risked physical confrontation with camp guards in order to get the parcels through to the prisoners.[7] So thorough was the distribution of parcels that by January 1942 the handful of prisoners remaining in Crete told ICRC inspectors that they were content with their provisions and did not want to be transported to Germany, lest they have to share their bounty with a larger prisoner population. Still, caution reigned, the parcels kept coming and it was not until the summer of 1942 that Whitehall, the ICRC and the BRC all agreed that the parcel situation was satisfactory in Greece and Crete and that no further bulk consignments, except for those that could be stockpiled for future POW captures in North Africa, should be sent.[8]

The ICRC's results in Italy were not as impressive, though this was not for want of trying. Poor hygiene in the permanent camps, lack of water and inadequate food were compounded by irregularities in the supply of Red Cross parcels, which were either pilfered by the guards or simply lost in the shambles of the Italian transport system. Although certain commandants and guards undoubtedly acted against their charges with overt malice, to the mind of one ICRC inspector, Colonel De Watteville, it was the Italians' laissez-faire attitude and complete negligence in planning for POW housing and provision that underpinned the problems in Italy. Still, the ICRC persevered. The head of the ICRC's Rome Delegation, Hans Wolfe De Sallis, visited the camps regularly and was 'considered to be very good' at his job by the prisoners, who – existing on a diet of poor quality bread and tiny morsels of cheese – came to depend on personally delivered Red Cross parcels for their daily survival.[9]

British enthusiasm for the ICRC's work in the Mediterranean was far more forthcoming than it had been in 1940. The British Ambassador in Ankara, Sir Hughe Knatchbull-Hugessen, was quick to respond to Brunel's reports and did his best to facilitate the ICRC's mission. When, for example, he received from Geneva an unusual request from the Athens delegation to use caiques in order to reach coastal islands where POWs were held, Knatchbull-Hugessen advised the Foreign Office to back the initiative. This was despite the fact that others – particularly in the Ministry of Economic Warfare (MEW) – viewed it as another typically outlandish ICRC idea that, technically, violated the British effort to blockade Axis-occupied territory. The Foreign Office, fearing a renewal of public backlash, however, agreed to the ICRC's proposal.[10] The work done by the ICRC in Italy was also greatly appreciated. Whitehall officials laid the blame for the poor conditions endured by the prisoners on the Italians rather than on a lack of effort from the Committee's delegates. Accounts from British prisoners which 'emphatically' endorsed the ICRC's efforts and noted the importance of parcels in averting starvation and malnutrition also greatly influenced British views of the ICRC's performance. The reward for Geneva was more than validation of its ambitions. The hitherto unsatisfactory level of British funding for the ICRC was increased in September 1941 to £30,000 per month and, in August 1942, Haccius, in addition to enjoying 'the very greatest courtesy' from his hosts, also began to receive a monthly donation of £1,725 for the upkeep of his delegation. As Satow wrote after the war, such gestures needed to be made in order to avert 'the risk of curtailment of Committee's valuable work' on behalf of British interests.[11] Whitehall, in short, understood that as long as new waves of British soldiers were sent into captivity, its dependence on the ICRC would only grow and with it the need both to support and to invest in the POW relief system. This support, combined with the ICRC's increasing ability to run its humanitarian enterprise efficiently, provided a stable foundation for a new, more positive epoch in British–ICRC relations in the war's middle years.

The effectiveness of the POW relief system was still, however, highly dependent on external factors – not the least of which was the agreement of the Axis to allow the system to function. Although ICRC delegates may have had difficulties getting into certain camps in the Mediterranean and, in the case of those in Italy, keeping them well supplied, the notion that the delegates had the right to carry out such duties or agitate for better conditions was never flatly rejected by the Italians, despite their ambivalence to the ICRC's work. Negotiations were completed between Rome, Geneva and London for the shipping of relief parcels across the oceans and complaints of prisoner maltreatment were reported to the Protecting Power and the ICRC, whose inspectors were permitted to interview prisoners during visits without fear of Italian commandants looking over their shoulders.[12] Moreover, the prisoners, once established in their permanent camps, could expect a way of life and standard of treatment that broadly fitted within the framework prescribed by the POW Convention. The waves of new prisoners taken in the Mediterranean were, therefore, absorbed into the

POW relief system that had been constructed over the course of 1940–1 without compromising accepted norms or complicating British–ICRC relations.

In the Far East, in contrast, no such normalcy or stability existed. The ICRC's work was constantly impeded by the Japanese authorities and, as it conceded after the war, 'up to August 1945, the ICRC had to make very strenuous efforts, even to secure results which were in no way proportionate to these exertions'.[13] This humanitarian crisis – arguably the greatest challenge faced by the ICRC during the war – was engendered by the swift collapse of Allied forces in Hong Kong, Indo-China, the Malay Peninsula and, finally, in Singapore itself in February 1942, which led to the march of 132,000 British and Colonial soldiers and 130,000 Allied civilians into Japanese captivity. The Committee's subsequent struggle to provide succour to these war victims has been well documented; so too the extent to which, in addition to rejecting the authority of the ICRC, the Japanese view of POWs – as objects of derision rather than of humanitarian concern – lay at the heart of Geneva's difficulties.[14] Though a signatory to both the 1929 Convention and the POW Convention, only the former had been ratified by Japan at the time of its entry into the war on 7 December 1941. Moreover, the Japanese Red Cross, which had been among the most active of National Societies in the interwar years, was all but silent in the weeks following the attack on Pearl Harbor, confirming the trend of subordination to the Japanese military which had first been observed by ICRC delegates during Japan's invasion of Manchuria in 1931.[15]

Despite these worrying signs, as Japanese forces carved their way southwards towards Singapore in early 1942, the Committee found cause for hope that the humanitarian norms that had been broadly applied in Europe would find traction in the Far East. The day after Pearl Harbor, Huber wrote to Tokyo, Washington and London, calling on all three belligerents to agree to exchange details on civilian internees and POWs, and to expedite the repatriation of diplomats, to which the Allies quickly agreed. Although it came a little later, Tokyo's response, that it had set up the Huryojohokyoku (POW Information Bureau) in accordance with the POW Convention and had agreed in principle to the appointment of an ICRC delegate in Japan, Dr Fritz Paravicini, ostensibly boded well. So too did the fact that, as in Greece a year earlier, the ICRC already had a foothold in the Far East when the new front opened. During the Sino-Japanese War of the late 1930s, the Committee and the American Red Cross (ARC) set up a relief base for Chinese civilians in Shanghai, under the leadership of a former League of Nations official and ICRC delegate, Colonel Charles de Watteville, and the Swiss doctor, Louis Calame. When the base was abandoned by the ARC in the aftermath of Pearl Harbor, the stockpiles of food and medicine were quickly purchased by the ICRC delegates and, bereft of supplies from outside the region, the food and clothing became crucial to the subsequent Red Cross relief effort in 1942. At the time of the Japanese drive south, ICRC delegations also existed across South East Asia, where the Committee had been carrying out relief work on behalf of civilian internees of Axis countries since 1939.[16] The foundations for building a new POW relief system in the Far East were, therefore, quite well established.

Promising as it seemed, signs that such a foothold would count for little in practice were ominous. Huber, having requested for a second time that the Japanese confirm their adherence to the POW Convention, at least in principle, received the following response from the Japanese Legation in Berne on 5 February 1942:

> Since the Japanese Government has not ratified the Convention relative to the treatment of prisoners of war, signed at Geneva on 27 July 1929, it is therefore not bound by said Convention. Nevertheless, in so far as possible it intends to apply this Convention *mutatis mutandis*, to all prisoners of war that may fall into its hands, at the same time taking into consideration the customs of each nation and each race in respect of feeding and clothing of prisoners.[17]

The true meaning of this statement was soon confirmed when reports were received from those who escaped the fall of Singapore, of atrocities being committed against surrendered soldiers, nurses and civilians. Similarly sourced reports of dysentery outbreaks, violent requisitions of food and arbitrary shootings of soldiers and civilians in Hong Kong were also received by Whitehall, in response to which the Foreign Office demanded that an ICRC delegate be despatched immediately to 'exercise restraining influence' on the occupation authorities, gather information on the captured, wounded and killed, and organize for the distribution of relief supplies. Importantly, the British also requested that the ICRC inform Tokyo that reciprocity would be guaranteed to Japanese prisoners and internees and that Whitehall was prepared to organize a Red Cross ship to immediately set sail from Sydney to Hong Kong in order to facilitate a relief operation.[18]

This prompt response was indicative of the extent to which Whitehall's capacity for 'POW mindedness' had grown since the last major crisis in 1940. Having agreed to the exchange of diplomats and reciprocal treatment for Japanese prisoners, as early as 16 December 1941, relief schemes for the Far East were being discussed by DPW, PWD, BRC and ICRC representatives. By late January 1942 a concrete plan had been formed for a coordinated relief operation to be carried out under the auspices of the ICRC and the Protecting Power, with the assistance of the Australian, American and Canadian Red Cross societies.[19] The Allied governments, their National Societies and the ICRC were, therefore, more swiftly mobilized and better prepared in the Far East than they had been either in Western Europe, Africa or the Mediterranean, for the challenge of responding to the unfolding humanitarian crisis. Such preparation, however, could not overcome the fact that every facet of the European-style POW relief system – be it administration, purchasing and shipment of relief supplies, camp inspections or the forwarding of POW information – was, on account of the very different context of the Far East, highly problematic to implement. With Japan now master of the region, entire new rules of humanitarian practice would need to be written.

The cracks in the system began at the most basic level of liaison between the ICRC and Tokyo. Throughout the war the Japanese Gaimusho (Foreign Office) either ignored or waited several months to acknowledge requests of a humanitarian nature. Moreover, unlike the similarly tardy Italians (who, despite delays in communications, usually let the ICRC carry out their duties), more often than not the reply from Tokyo would be framed around the principle that, as Japan had not ratified the POW Convention, it was unreasonable for the ICRC to expect cooperation. Consequently, in the first six months of 1942, Paravicini received a total of only four short, negative replies to his seventeen inquiries, and staff from the Huryojohokyoku – in theory the primary liaison office with the ICRC – refused even to meet him in person.[20] This trend emerged acutely in the wake of the Allied–Red Cross proposal for relief. Although sent to Tokyo in January, it was not until the summer of 1942 that the reply – a flat refusal – was received. The sum of Japan's argument was that relief ships could not be permitted to operate in waters that they regarded as 'active military zones' for fear of enemy agents using such vessels for infiltration. Despite this setback the ICRC responded, notably by attuning its efforts to the clearly altered context of the Far East.

During talks with the BRC in April 1942, Haccius raised a suggestion made by Paravicini that, should the Japanese refuse to establish a dedicated shipping route for relief, it might be worth proposing that the ships being used for exchanges of civilians also be used to transfer parcels for Japanese and Allied prisoners. The PWD and DPW rejected the idea. They believed that not only would the scheme take too long to organize but also, by agreeing to a plan that would openly contravene the regulations for the use of ships as laid down in the Hague Convention, the British would be validating Japan's dismissive attitude to IHL. Testament to the gravity of the situation, however, the ICRC was actually somewhat willing to embrace a scheme that ran counter to IHL, and in so doing to acknowledge that new norms of humanitarian practice would be needed in the Far East. So too was Tokyo, which agreed to Paravicini's suggestion that the exchange ships could be used to transport food and medical supplies.[21]

If the use of these ships in this way was not out of the ordinary enough, the conditions imposed by Tokyo stretched the accepted practice of the POW relief system to the limit. The Japanese demanded that ships coming from Allied ports would have to tranship their cargo at a neutral location – Portuguese Macao or Lourenço Marquez being the main suggestions – onto a Japanese ship for on-carriage to a Japanese-held port. Understandably, the Allied governments held deep concerns over this scheme. In addition to compromising IHL norms, it would require the handing over of tens of thousands of dollars' worth of relief supplies to an enemy who, by this point, was more distrusted than the Germans. It was a suggestion that was anathema to the British and yet, bereft of an alternative that fitted within accepted practice, they agreed to the plan, provided that a dual Protecting Power/ICRC delegate be on board to supervise the first leg of the journey and the exchange of the goods into Japanese hands. What was built out of this peculiar agreement was a less stable, though no less important, Far Eastern equivalent of the Lisbon–Marseilles route, the first two ships to service which – the *Asama Maru* and the *Gripsolm* – completed an exchange of 22,160 food parcels for Allied internees at Lourenço Marquez in July 1942.[22] For this exchange and the three more that occurred between early 1943 and Japan's surrender in September 1945, the ICRC had great difficulty in ascertaining how many parcels actually got through. This was because the Japanese refused to adhere to yet another norm of the POW relief system – the signing of receipts for individual parcels. Consequently, although the ICRC could confirm the delivery of some parcels to the camps, its delegates had no idea of knowing whether the prisoners ever received them or whether, as happened in several camps, the parcels were simply stockpiled by the Japanese for their own purposes.[23]

What made the supervision aspect of this already unsatisfactory relief system even harder was the fact that the ICRC delegates were usually peripheral to proceedings. In keeping with the principle that no humanitarian action could be carried out in 'active military zones', Japan refused to acknowledge the right of the delegates, some of whom had been on the ground since 1939, to carry out their work. Indeed, Tokyo approved of only three ICRC delegates during the war, all of whom were located in the north of its burgeoning empire in either China or Japan. Following Paravicini's official recognition in February 1942, a businessman named Edouard Egle was given permission to set up a delegation in Shanghai and take control of the ARC supply base there. This was followed, in June 1942, by the approval of Rudolf Zindel, a twenty-year resident of Hong Kong, as the official ICRC representative in that city. A fourth delegate, Werner Salzman, was approved in Bangkok by the local authorities. His accreditation, however, was overruled by Tokyo. The remaining delegates, scattered across South East Asia, were left in the unenviable position of being appointed by Geneva but unrecognized by Tokyo. Even the Japanese Red Cross, when requested by the ICRC to safeguard its people in South East Asia, replied frostily that, as far as Japan was concerned, the only delegates in the region were the three men approved in the north. Not that such recognition counted for anything comparable to the status enjoyed by the likes of Haccius, Junod or Roland Marti. In addition to day-to-day obstructions and being subject to near-constant observation from the Kempeitai (Japanese Secret Police), the accredited delegates had to fight hard for permission to carry out the other key facet of the POW relief system: routine inspections of camps.

Of the 102 known POW camps in the Far East, the ICRC was only able to visit forty-two over the course of the war and, even then, only after lengthy negotiations with the camp authorities. The form of the visits also bore little resemblance to those conducted in Europe. The delegates were only permitted a maximum of two hours to visit the camp and were always accompanied by a Japanese officer, even when interviewing the MOC. Talk of the Geneva and POW Conventions or any protests at the treatment of prisoners were rarely made, as the delegates learned early that the mere mention of such things annoyed most Japanese commandants and could result in the inspection being abruptly ended. Visits to civilian internment camps were, generally, easier to organize, and conditions within the camps themselves were not usually as horrendous as places of POW internment. This was primarily because civilians were not regarded with the same disdain by the Japanese as captured soldiers and, more than likely, because the Japanese feared reprisals against their own nationals interned in the United States.[24]

This comparatively mild stance towards civilian internees did not, however, negate the fact that the basic principles of humanity were so lacking in Japanese internment policy that the ICRC was rendered powerless in a way that was comparable only to its failed campaign to bring succour to war victims on the Eastern Front.[25] As was the case in the latter theatre, the basic problem was that the military authorities rejected not only IHL and its associated norms of conduct but also the very principle of the ICRC's much cherished right to initiative – the medium through which the likes of Junod, Marti and Brunel had negotiated their way into otherwise off-limits Dulags in Europe. By mid-1942 therefore, it was clear that the three crucial aspects of the POW relief system – stable supply lines, delegates on the ground and recognition of their right to act on behalf of the prisoners – would be lacking in the Far East. This meant that, unlike in Europe, where the Committee's objectives had been to stabilize the POW relief system and gain wider recognition from the belligerents by working within the framework of the Convention, Paravicini and his companions were forced to adopt controversial measures – often in direct violation of Japanese wishes – in order to achieve even the most basic humanitarian goals.[26]

The ICRC's representative in Singapore, Hans Schweizer, epitomized this unorthodox approach. A Germano-Swiss businessman with no pre-war career in philanthropy to speak of, Schweizer had been managing director of Diethlem & Co., an import/export company based in the port city at the time of the Japanese arrival in Malaya. Like the other delegates in South East Asia, Schweizer was never officially recognized by Tokyo. Not that this gave him much pause for thought. No sooner had the Japanese occupation of the newly proclaimed Syonan (formerly Singapore) begun than Schweizer set forth towards Changi Barracks, with little more than a cavalier attitude and a copy of the Convention. Having presented himself to the commandant, Schweizer demanded of the guards the names of every internee and the right to distribute food parcels to them. Undeterred by the blunt Japanese refusal, he wrote a personal letter to the conqueror and military governor of the island, General Yamashita, to request an audience. Two days later the Kempeitai arrested and interrogated Schweizer in their Singapore headquarters which, ironically, was the old YMCA building. A similar sequence of events was repeated over the next three years, during which Schweizer was routinely kicked out of camps, had his activities suppressed and was detained by the Kempeitai on suspicion of being, among other things, a British spy. Yet he persevered. When news of Japan's lack of response to the Allied–ICRC relief scheme came through to him – itself a small miracle considering the difficulty he had in getting the Japanese to allow him correspondence with Geneva[27] – Schweizer resorted to working as what could best be described as a 'humanitarian private contractor'. To this end, he used funds from his own company and donations from neutrals in the region to import foodstuffs from India and purchase a truck to deliver supplies across the island personally. He also managed to set up a clandestine network of helpers to facilitate delivery to the camps, more often than not via bribery and smuggling. Included in this network was one Sergeant-Major Fujibayashi of the Kempeitai who, though apparently assigned to monitor Schweizer, ended up helping him as an interpreter and, undoubtedly, shielding him from more severe repercussions for his actions.[28] Although it was far from stable, Schweizer did manage, through a blend of ingenuity, courage and sheer luck, to construct some form of relief system for civilian internees and POWs in Singapore, despite having no right in the eyes of the Japanese to do so.

The basic characteristics of Schweizer's humanitarian campaign – adaptability, guile, unorthodoxy – were adopted elsewhere across South East Asia, where the variable conditions in certain regions and camps required the delegates to 'tailor make' their work. Werner Salzman, another employee of Diethlem & Co. turned ICRC delegate, was based in Bangkok and, like Schweizer, never received official recognition from the Japanese and, sometimes for months on end, was cut off from communication with the Committee. Although, like Schweizer, Salzman had to rely on local networks and donations from neutrals to purchase goods on the black market, he also had certain advantages denied to his Singapore counterpart. These included the assistance of a Protecting Power representative and the Thai Red Cross, which had managed to keep itself relatively free of interference from the Japanese authorities by agreeing to restrict its work to helping civilian internees. Salzman also achieved more than Schweizer in regards to POWs, for whom he was able to organize the despatch of more than 11,000 food parcels and 400 cases of medicines during the war. In addition to this, Salzman's greatest achievement – other than not being arrested – was successfully to send a report to Geneva in 1943 on the appalling state of the prisoners being forced to construct the Burma Railway, an act that, had he been caught, would surely have led to any further activities on his part being swiftly curtailed. Of the unrecognized delegates, Salzman and Schweizer were the luckiest and most successful. Joseph Bessmer, the delegate in Manilla, was never able to visit the camps either as an inspector or deliverer of supplies. Moreover, what little he could achieve – the sending of money to prisoners and lending assistance to YMCA relief agents who had better luck distributing parcels – was brought to an end in October 1944 under threat of arrest. Bessmer, at least, survived such a threat. Not only were Matthaeus and Betty Vischer, the unrecognized husband-and-wife delegation in Borneo, unsuccessful in their efforts to set up a relief system in their region, but in December 1943 they were detained by the Japanese on suspicion of espionage and summarily beheaded.[29]

It is interesting to note that, for all the talk of adherence to principles, certain ICRC delegates appear to have opted for a form of retaliation against Japanese practices. At Bikaneer camp in India, for example, Japanese POWs were given smaller rations than the Italians interned there and, according to the prisoners themselves, were treated coldly by British doctors. To these complaints the ICRC generally turned a blind eye, initially claiming that Japanese prisoners did not need as many calories as Europeans and that any 'brusque' attitude on the part of the British doctors was on account of their sizeable workload and was, therefore, understandable.[30] Such incidents were the exception rather than the rule, which continued to be that the ICRC had to bow to the wishes of the Far East's conquerors. Even the recognized delegates, Edouard Egle and Rudolf Zindel, had to tread cautiously around Japanese sensitivities, and a common feature of both men's work was their carefully worded POW camp reports. These were sent back to Whitehall, via Geneva, and, as the delegates well knew, were subject to intense scrutiny by the Japanese censors. For this reason, criticisms of Stanley Civilian Detainment Camp in Hong Kong, for example, were deeply buried under niceties and wordplay. References to the 'summer camp' quality of the facility and the encouragement of 'physical exercise' by the guards were used to explain the fact 'that the majority of internees had probably lost weight'. Those internees who 'grumbled' about conditions were portrayed as simply being unused to life without champagne, batmen and beefsteaks, and the fact that 'some people may feel a little crowded with six people in one room' was 'not such a great inconvenience' because, it being Hong Kong in the summer, the windows and doors would be open anyway in order to let a breeze through. Similar wordplay was employed when trying to explain to Geneva the overtly glowing descriptions of life under Japanese detainment. Having admitted that some in Britain might 'contest the veracity of my reports', Egle made clear that he could not speak for what conditions were like prior to his visits and could only report what he saw with his own eyes. The inference – that much of what was presented to the inspectors was a front by the Japanese – was confirmed by Zindel after the war when, unfettered by Tokyo, he confirmed that his and Egle's reports 'had to leave unsaid many matters of considerable interest if the reports concerned wished to have a chance to pass the Japanese censorship and reach Geneva'. For his part, Schweizer, fearing 'the risk to life and limb that any factual report in my possession' would pose, was similarly restrained in his communiqués.[31]

Egle's concern that his reports might be either misconstrued or dismissed out of hand was justified. The Canadian Government was certain that the reports 'were too good to be true' and that the Japanese must have tampered with them before they were sent to Geneva, while Whitehall and the BRC both concurred that Egle's reports had to be taken with 'pounds of salt' and Zindel's were 'too optimistic' to be taken seriously.[32] This scepticism was understandable in context. For a POW administration already floundering for an effective response to Tokyo's policies, these peculiar reports of British subjects enjoying holidays behind barbed wire under the benevolent gaze of an enemy known for its contempt of the Conventions probably only added to the otherworldliness of the situation. What is interesting, however, is that throughout the Committee's campaign in the Far East, the British were seldom prone to the type of criticism that had been previously directed at Geneva for its naivety or shortcomings. Although the word 'unreliable' was often used to describe Zindel and Egle's reports, there was no implication that the delegates themselves were to blame. In the main, British officials understood the delicacy of their position. A report to the Foreign Office, compiled by a repatriated civilian nurse in August 1942, summed the situation up bluntly: 'Zindel not liked by the Japs and Egle under constant surveillance.'[33] Remarking in 1943 on the 'unsatisfactory' outcomes in the ICRC's work on behalf of British and American POWs in the Far East, the British Ambassador in Switzerland, Clifford Norton, was nevertheless at pains to stress to his colleagues that such failures were 'due not to inefficiency or remissness on their part, but in the main to Japanese character and attitude towards Convention and prisoners of war questions generally'. In some cases the ICRC's record was even defended by the British, who found greater fault in the Canadian Government for constantly 'throwing stones' at the Committee over its manifold setbacks.[34]

The BRC also defended Geneva in the first half of 1942, when Whitehall came the nearest it ever did to slighting the ICRC's efforts in the Far East. Despondent at the lack of response from Tokyo to the Allied–Red Cross relief proposal, the British approached the Vatican – without telling the ICRC – with the suggestion that its representatives in the Far East take over the position of coordinator for relief. Although the suggestion of engaging the Vatican was floated into 1943, the initial idea to approach the Holy See without consulting Geneva was condemned by the BRC, which pointed out that the Committee was the only credible channel for sending POW relief and, as such, could not be undermined. Having recognized the need to preserve what little credibility the ICRC had in the Far East, Whitehall eventually dropped the Vatican proposal.[35] Underpinning the decision, and the support for Geneva that came with it, was a clear appreciation in Whitehall's POW administration of the challenges that the delegates were facing. Satow, in particular, was aware from a very early point in the ICRC's Far East campaign that the delegates' work would be not only difficult but fundamentally different from that carried out elsewhere. Although he believed that the 'strengthening of the Committee's representation in the Far East is obviously a matter of urgency', he also acknowledged that, unlike in Europe and North Africa, the appointment of new delegates would not simply be a matter of obtaining agreement from the belligerents but, rather, would take time, effort and money.[36] To this end, in mid-August 1942 the British Government agreed to a monthly donation of £10,000 – increased to £15,000 in January 1944 – to be paid to Zindel, so that he could purchase whatever supplies he could acquire in Hong Kong. When moves were made to try to expand his administrative staff in 1943, the British also agreed to pay the full wages of the new staff rather than 'haggle' over percentages of donations with the Americans, whose detainee population in Hong Kong was much smaller.[37] Such gestures usually came with few stipulations. When, for example, the Indian Government suggested that it would donate to the ICRC on the condition that it provide details of what its delegates were actually doing, Satow not only rejected the demand by pointing out that the nature of the ICRC's work in the Far East was 'impossible' to catalogue but also argued that 'after a slow start, for which they are not to blame, the International Red Cross organisation is doing very good work in the Far East' and that its delegates 'deserve every assistance'. The message was clear: despite the fact that the 'no one can estimate the return' such donations would bring, the funds nevertheless had to be provided, faith had to placed in the ICRC, and the best had to be hoped for.[38]

To what extent was this faith repaid? Judged by the standards of its efforts in Europe, the ICRC failed in the Far East. The limited exchange/parcel ship route was never stable enough to maintain a consistent line of supply to the camps and the variable conditions on the ground, combined with inflated prices in Hong Kong and Shanghai in particular, made local procurement similarly irregular. Even taking into consideration the temporary bolstering of the parcel delivery service – by Japanese agreement in 1944 for a dedicated relief vessel, the *Hakusan Maru*, to ship supplies from Vladivostok to Osaka – the ICRC, at most, was only able to deliver 225,000 parcels over the course of the entire war to over 300,000 POWs and civilian internees in the Far East.[39] Moreover, owing to the absence of parcel receipt reporting, it is still unclear just how many of these parcels got through to the prisoners. Unsurprisingly, POWs in locations where the ICRC delegation was recognized had a better chance of actually receiving the relief they needed. On average, prisoners in Hong Kong, Shanghai and Japan received four or five parcels over the entire period of their detainment; that is to say, four or five parcels over the course of nearly four brutal years behind Japanese barbed wire. In Singapore and Bangkok, by contrast, prisoners could expect only one-sixteenth of a parcel over the duration of their internment.[40] Such figures highlight the importance of the ICRC delegates' efforts to acquire goods locally – by any means at their disposal, including the black market – in order to supplement both the prisoners' pitiful rations and the sporadic parcel deliveries from abroad. British financial assistance and the unusually flexible attitude proffered in this respect were very important. Whitehall approved, without conditions, of the ICRC's proposal to use funds from the same pool for civilian internees and POWs at the discretion of its delegates on the ground.[41] The BRC also agreed to transfer both £10,000 a month to Schweizer, despite the fact he was not an officially recognized delegate, and £23,000 to the Vatican, for further distribution to ICRC and YMCA workers across the region. This cavalier funding was implicit in Whitehall's policy for relief in the Far East, which was set out in March 1944 as follows:

> It is a fixed commonwealth policy to continue supplying relief for British prisoners of war and civilian internees in the Far East so long as there is the least possibility that all or some of the relief will reach those for whom it is destined. This of course, does not mean that all possible measures must not continue to be taken to ensure that it does reach them.[42]

This unconditional support for the ICRC's work, combined with the understanding given to Egle and Zindel in regards to their otherwise spurious reports, indicates that the British Government both recognized the extent to which it was dependent on the ICRC in the Far East and appreciated the need for its delegates to work beyond the boundaries laid down in the Conventions.[43] It is testament to how far up the POW learning curve the British had progressed since 1939 that this dynamic in British–ICRC relations in regards to the Far East emerged so quickly and with so few complications.

Important as it was in engendering the handful of humanitarian successes the ICRC could claim in the Far East, this more cooperative and flexible attitude from Whitehall by no means marked a watershed in British–ICRC relations. It was the unique circumstances in the theatre that forced the British into a state of relatively unqualified dependence on the ICRC, whose delegates reciprocated by going above and beyond the limits of norms of their duties. In Europe and North Africa, by contrast, British concerns over the need of the Committee to work within the boundaries of both the Conventions and the POW relief system were still paramount. In this respect, the Far East was a humanitarian lacuna in British–ICRC relations. In the wider scope of the war's middle years Britain's relationship with the ICRC was characterized not by unfettered cooperation but by the dynamic of dependence on Geneva's good offices for providing succour to captured British soldiers and divergence of opinion over the Committee's wider wartime ambitions – ambitions which only grew as the humanitarian crises of the Second World War escalated.

The limits of humanity

The ICRC's impetus to provide, in as impartial a fashion as possible, assistance to *all* victims of war had always been at the heart of its working ethos. As one of the more romantic accounts of the ICRC's wartime effort argues, for the delegates the view of war victims was simple: 'I am blind to the uniform you wear, and see only your wound, that I may tend it. I am deaf to the language you speak, and hear only your cry, that I may bring you comfort. I know not who you are; I only know your distress.'[44] The humanity of Geneva, therefore, was supposed to be without limits. No belligerent state – let alone Britain – had ever fully accepted this utopian concept of the ICRC's work. This applied as much to the British campaign to restrict the ICRC in regards to IHL codification in times of peace as to the practices of its delegates in the field in times of war. In the case of the latter, the decades-old view that neutral humanitarians had no place on the battlefield was edged during the Second World War by concerns that unrestrained universal humanity might imperil British interests, specifically the welfare of British POWs.

This attitude came to the fore in 1940 when George Warner had voiced his reservations over donating British money for the benefit of Polish and French prisoners at a time when British POWs were also *in extremis*. For other officials in Whitehall, the need to curtail the ICRC's 'relief for all' ethos was not simply in the interests of preserving the welfare of British prisoners. Officials from the MEW, tasked with cutting off Hitler's Europe from food and medicine imports, regarded the idea of allowing the ICRC to deliver bulk deliveries of parcels into the occupied territories as nothing less than a threat to the British blockade strategy. This was particularly true in cases where the locations of the camps to which the parcels were destined were unknown and the actual status of the prisoners themselves was in doubt. For these reasons, in the midst of the POW crisis of 1940, efforts were made by MEW to curtail shipments of parcels intended for French POWs. This action was tempered, however, by the Ministry's deference to British prisoners, who were duly granted the right to receive parcels in quantities denied their French allies.[45]

The ICRC, for its part, was appalled by what it viewed as a double standard. The French captured at Dunkirk had after all suffered the same privations as their British allies: forced marches, poor rations, humiliation, interrogation and the cutting of their lines of communication and access to Red Cross parcels. To the minds of Geneva, this suffering was all that mattered. The fact that in the autumn of 1940 the Germans were in the midst of brokering agreements with the Vichy authorities to release hundreds of thousands of French POWs for use at labour camps within the Reich was immaterial to the ICRC, so too the fact that many of the Polish POWs taken the year before were already being used in such a capacity.[46] In defiance of British concerns that the sending of relief to these prisoners would be tantamount to feeding Hitler's labour force, Lucie Odier complained bluntly to Whitehall that it was favouring the welfare of its own POWs over those of its fallen Allies. This was followed by a more subtle approach, taken by Carl J. Burckhardt, who leaked to David Kelly information that French dockworkers at Marseilles, having been made aware that their labours were going towards the provisioning of British POWs rather than their countrymen, would soon refuse to unload parcels. This argument was bolstered by the ICRC pointing out that British and American POWs were also being used as labourers within the Reich and that to deny other Allied prisoners bulk parcels on this principle was only to push the double standard further.[47] In the end, extrinsic factors in the war forced Britain's hand. In November 1942 German forces occupied Vichy and in so doing removed any considerations of keeping Marshal Philippe Pétain's government neutral. In the wake of this development, and following a slight disruption to the Lisbon–Marseilles route on account of the German occupation, French POWs were at last granted a similar relief service to that enjoyed by the British. This was a significant breakthrough for the French prisoners, whose parcels – the calories within which were lower than those of British prisoners – had been arriving at a rate that had been sporadic at best since October 1940.[48]

Throughout its negotiations with Britain over relief for Vichy the ICRC found an ally in the United States. Even before the attack on Pearl Harbor and, despite his sympathy and support for Britain, President Roosevelt and many in his administration held a dim view of Churchill's blockade strategy. This was on account of not only the misery it inflicted on the civilian population of Europe but also the capacity it had to foment negative public opinion in the United States and, by depriving certain nationalities of prisoners of parcels, to damage Allied unity. It was Washington's voicing of this displeasure and bewilderment over British policy on relief for French POWs that ultimately added the weight necessary for the Committee's arguments to be listened to.[49] As we shall see, this was the only time that the United States' displeasure towards British humanitarian policy dovetailed with the ICRC's 'relief for all' ethos and helped the latter to break down some of the barriers to humanitarian assistance thrown up by Whitehall. Nor was POW relief policy the only area in which United States' involvement in the war affected the ICRC's work.

When the United States entered the war in December 1941 it lost both its neutrality and its role as Protecting Power for British interests, which it had held since September 1939. The Swiss Federal Council – representative of the longest-standing permanent neutral state in Europe – was a logical and favoured choice of Whitehall to assume the role previously held by the Americans. This was not only on account of its history and the highly regarded work it had performed as Protecting Power for German interests since 1939 but also because, as the British well knew, the Swiss Federal Council had close ties to the ICRC. Not only did the former provide nearly half of the Committee's funding but the two parties, at various times during the war, also shared everything from members, to premises, to official letterhead. This closeness was owing to both the long history of relations between the ICRC and the Swiss Government, which dated back to 1864, and the fact that Marcel-Pilet Golaz, the Swiss Foreign Minister, had embraced the idea of linking Geneva and Berne on the common ground of humanitarianism in order to enhance the value of Switzerland to the belligerents. To this end in January 1942 he appointed the ICRC member, Edouard de Haller, to the newly created post of Federal Delegate for Humanitarian Affairs. In an unconvincing attempt to preserve the notion of ICRC independence and neutrality, de Haller resigned from Geneva and was given the position of 'honorary delegate of the ICRC' by Max Huber. In truth, de Haller became little more than the Swiss Federal Council's agent within the ICRC and was instrumental in guiding the Committee's decision-making in areas where its humanitarian mission intersected with Swiss foreign policy, a facet of a relationship that was defined as much by cooperation as conflict, depending on the issues at hand.[50]

The view from Whitehall of Berne and Geneva's closeness was initially positive. Not long after the announcement of de Haller's new role and the appointment of the Swiss as Protecting Power for British interests, Cyril Gepp from the DPW wrote to Huber expressing the view that Berne and Geneva's convergence of responsibility for British POWs and civilian internees could only be good for Britain. He thus urged Huber to 'secure closer collaboration between the Protecting Power and your Committee'. The British hope was that, with both parties coordinating their inspections of POW camps, a more consistent and fuller picture of British POW life behind the wire would emerge.[51] It was also hoped that closer liaison between Geneva and Berne might overcome a trend that had first emerged during the POW crisis, whereby the ICRC's inspectors would both turn up at the camps within a matter of a days of US officials and send reports that, by the time of their receipt in Whitehall, were sometimes considered to be 'valueless' compared with those compiled by the Protecting Power.[52]

Any hope that the ICRC had of correcting this flaw in its work and, in so doing, chipping away at the entrenched British perception of its delegates as the well-meaning junior partners of the Protecting Power's inspectors was, however, soon dashed. Although some of the problems in overlap inspections were remedied, incidents of ICRC inspectors carrying out their tasks in apparent ignorance of Swiss inspectors persisted and the British still continued to hold the Protecting Power in higher regard than the ICRC.[53] The success of the Swiss inspectors in gaining entry to camps that had been closed by the Germans to both Geneva's delegates and US officials, as well as the contributions made by the Swiss to the negotiations with Berlin over POW repatriations, played a part in this glowing recognition.[54] So too, however, did the ICRC's response to its new arrangement with Berne.

Rather than establish a distribution of workload with the Swiss along lines prescribed in the IHL, the ICRC instead continued to step beyond the bounds of what the British thought was acceptable. The ICRC's persistent belief that it, rather than the Protecting Power, could forward complaints over breaches of the Convention directly to Berlin was criticized by the British as yet another example of Geneva's meddling. This criticism was not born simply out of a lack of enthusiasm for the ICRC straying beyond its customary duties. Whitehall had been mindful since 1941 that the more protests and threats levelled at Berlin over POW treatment the less force such sentiments would carry. On this basis, British policy was to use only the Protecting Power to launch protests with the Germans in certain, necessary cases.[55] The ICRC's efforts to the contrary – like its agitation for more relief for non-British prisoners – were viewed as not just an attempt to 'usurp functions which under other articles of the Convention are specifically confided to the Protecting Power', but as something that could imperil British interests.[56]

The same was true of ICRC interference in the negotiations over POW repatriation. These negotiations had begun in the war's first months under American auspices, only to collapse following Hitler's intervention in October 1941. In 1942 these negotiations were revived with the inclusion of the Swiss Federal Council's Marcel Pilet-Golaz, who jumped at the opportunity to enhance his government's reputation in the eyes of the belligerents. Following the process laid down in the Convention, the Protecting Power had the authority, if recognized by the belligerents, to act as the mediator in these discussions between Berlin and London. The ICRC, though confined to the marginal role of proffering assistance where needed – supervision of the exchange, and acting as courier agent on the ships – nevertheless tried to introduce itself into the repatriation talks as a mediator.[57] To this the DPW argued that the ICRC, far from being authorized as a negotiator, should not even be told of where, when and by what means the exchanges were taking place. At most it was agreed that the ICRC could help to set up the Mixed Medical Commission – the body that inspected the prisoners in order to determine their eligibility for repatriation – and provide delegates to supervise the exchanges. Although these expectations on the part of the British were made clear to the Committee and the view that its delegates held 'no diplomatic status' remained unchanged in Whitehall's considerations, over the course of the negotiations 'both the Vatican and the International Red Cross Committee had at times to be restrained from meddling in affairs with which the Swiss government were dealing'.[58]

Unsurprisingly given this attitude, when Max Huber offered in August 1943 to negotiate an Anglo-German exchange of POWs who had been held since 1940, his proposal went nowhere. Though received 'sympathetically' by some Whitehall officials, the idea was flatly rejected by the Admiralty, who were reluctant to return potential U-boat crews to Germany. For their part, the Foreign Office saw problems in allowing the ICRC a foot in the repatriation negotiation door, specifically because it might disrupt Pilet-Golaz's efforts to effect the exchange of wounded and sick prisoners.[59] Similar attempts by Burckhardt to intrude upon the mediation work of the Protecting Power over the shackling of POWs by the Germans and the British in 1942–3 – which will be discussed in depth below – were also rebuffed by the British Minister in Berne, Sir Clifford Norton, on the grounds that the Protecting Power was the only credible medium through which to engage with Berlin on such a delicate issue. In response to Burckhardt's attempts to prove otherwise, an exasperated Norton wrote to his colleagues in Whitehall that 'I cannot too strongly emphasize that only reports of protecting power can be regarded as really authoritative.'[60]

These objections to ICRC intervention in Protecting Power matters marked the extent to which Whitehall, for all its appreciation of the Committee's work on behalf of POWs, was reluctant to countenance it stepping beyond the role of provider of relief and reporter – not mediator – of POW treatment. There was much to justify Whitehall's policy, at least, in Europe. Although possessed of a glut of Italian POWs, Britain still possessed only a third of the total number of British and colonial POWs held by the Germans. Until equalization began as a result of the Allied invasion of Europe in 1944, this disparity in numbers weakened Britain's position with Berlin with regards to reciprocity.[61] In such circumstances the maintenance of a strict reading of the Convention and, consequently, the campaign to restrain ICRC attempts to bend or go beyond its articles by carving out new roles for its delegates was understandable. The problem with this limited conception of the ICRC's role was that it ignored the extent to which, no less than Whitehall, the Committee also had to adjust to the expansion and escalation of the war and, together with the Protecting Power, develop a new, more comprehensive programme for humanitarian action from 1942 onwards.[62] In tackling this burden the ICRC may have erred in its forays into humanitarian diplomacy. Its pursuit, however, of greater flexibility from the blockade authorities to import relief into Europe for POWs was justified. Although some in Whitehall may have doubted that the Committee's policy of 'relief for all' could be reconciled with a

'British POWs first' mentality, the fact is that, though subject to many privations while in captivity, no British POW in Europe was ever put in danger of starving on account of the ICRC's pursuit of equivalent relief for non-British POWs and civilian internees. Indeed, once the POW relief system stabilized, British POWs and civilian internees received as much as thirty kilos of food per month from the ICRC – nearly three times the amount received by French prisoners.[63] Despite their ostensible divergence of priorities, therefore, both Whitehall and Geneva were in practice united by a shared common goal: to ensure that British POW welfare was maintained for the duration of the war. The ICRC's work on this issue – be it in Europe, North Africa or the Far East – ensured that, for all the divergence that existed in British–ICRC relations, some level of support would be forthcoming from the increasingly dependent British. Unfortunately for the ICRC, this harmony of interest was absent in its dealings with Whitehall on another humanitarian issue that became as weighty as the war dragged on as any concerns over POWs: how to provide relief for non-interned *civilian* victims of war.

5
Civilians and Ships, 1940–3

'Victory before relief'

Having resolved upon a policy of 'no surrender' in the months after the fall of France, the British Government was faced with the problem of how to continue the fight against Germany until, as the architect of the 'no surrender' policy intoned, 'the New World, with all its power and might, steps forth to the rescue and the liberation of the Old'.[1] The loss of the British Expeditionary Force removed the capacity for terrestrial military engagement in Europe, and the North African theatre, though strategically important, was at the time viewed as too peripheral to carry the full weight of Churchill's favoured policy of striking at the heart of the enemy. Though embraced by some in Whitehall as a war-winning strategy, aerial bombing on a scale required to deliver the fabled 'knock-out blow' to Germany was a relatively untested means of engagement and it did not take long for the Royal Air Force's limitations to become apparent. Another means of continuing the fight was to harness one of Britain's clear strengths in 1940 – the Royal Navy – to tighten the blockade that had first been imposed on Germany in September 1939 further. Unlike bombing, there was precedent enough for a blockade to be implemented at the outset of the conflict with a clear conscience and an expectation, albeit slender, of success.[2]

The practice of restricting the importation of food, medicine and war material into Germany had been implemented by the British during the First World War and, in the minds of some officials, it had played a crucial role in ensuring victory.[3] Owing to this pedigree, within days of the invasion of Poland the British began negotiations with continental neutral governments with an aim to restrict their importation of conditional contraband (food and other supplies that could be used for non-military purposes) and absolute contraband (materials intended specifically for military use) that was destined for Germany. The means used by Whitehall to regulate the import of these materials was by issuing navicerts, documents which granted permission for merchant vessels to ship goods into European ports only once their cargoes had been assessed and deemed acceptable for importation. The task of enforcing these measures fell to the Ministry of Economic Warfare (MEW), described by one early employee as a 'bewildering organisation' of 'many deluded optimists' which, owing to a combination of inter-departmental disagreements, lack of available intelligence on German food and resource stocks and the difficulties of ensuring cooperation from neutral governments, achieved mixed results in its blockade during the Phoney War.[4]

Underwhelming as its efforts were regarded in Whitehall, MEW was thrust by the events of the summer of 1940 into a key position in Britain's strategy. The Ministry's hardline chief, Hugh Dalton, was bellicose in his embrace of the challenge to break the Third Reich's war economy and resolved, in the face of the blockade's apparent ineffectiveness and mounting public criticism in both Britain and the United States over the moral aspect of depriving civilians of food, to make the MEW 'much more combative, more true to its name'. This involved making the issuing of navicerts compulsory at points of departure for all ships heading to European ports, seizing contraband at the source, restricting the amount of goods that could be imported into neutral nations and extending the blockade to cover territories under German occupation.[5] Dalton's measures were enthusiastically supported by Churchill, who outlined this new, more robust, blockade policy on 20 August 1940 by declaring that, as occupiers, it was the Germans who had the responsibility to feed the civilians of the territories they had conquered. The British, therefore, would refuse all attempts to send relief supplies into either occupied or Axis-affiliated territories and would countenance only the stockpiling of food and medicine in expectation of military victory. The sum of this was a relief policy that called, not for sustained humanitarian action on behalf of Germany's victims, but for the preparation of relief operations that would be carried out in the wake of Europe's liberation. The task of organizing this post-war relief was duly bestowed upon the newly created Inter-Allied Committee on Post War Requirements (IACPR), headed by one of the more moderate members of MEW, Sir Frederick Leith-Ross.[6] There, it was hoped, the question of Allied commitment to humanitarian action would lie until the defeat of Germany.

Responses in Geneva to Churchill's 'victory before relief' policy ranged from bitter consternation to vocal moral outrage. This was despite the fact that, in terms of IHL, the Prime Minister was justified in his stance. The Hague Convention specified that it was the duty of the occupying power to maintain the well-being of the population under its control. Thus the burden of feeding the conquered was, as Churchill claimed, Hitler's alone until the cessation of hostilities. The tactic of blockading those territories until such time as relief could be freely distributed was also a well-established means of making war. The practice of blockade, first used in 1584 by the Dutch against Spanish ships operating out of Flemish ports, had been employed by belligerents increasingly as the age of sea power unfolded until it was accepted into the customary laws of war via the Declaration of Paris in 1856 and, subsequently, codified in the Declaration of London in 1909.[7] Owing both to this IHL and the precedent set by its use in past wars, blockade was something that the ICRC entered the Second World War in full anticipation of it being utilized. This did not mean, however, that the Committee considered the practice to be in any way morally legitimate and it was on this point that the ICRC and MEW differed most starkly.

This disagreement was of a very different type from that which emerged between Whitehall's POW administration and the ICRC, where poor relations and a lack of cooperation were shaped by personalities, external pressures and differing approaches to the shared goal of preserving the health and well-being of British POWs. In the case of civilian relief, this latter thread of harmony in particular was lacking. Instead, the same principle of divergence that existed in British–ICRC relations over non-British POWs was pervasive. MEW's mission was to restrict the importation of food, materials and medicine into Europe in order to place extra burdens on the Third Reich and hasten its defeat, irrespective of the humanitarian costs to those civilians under the German yoke. This was a strategic goal that would never converge with the humanitarian mission of the ICRC, which viewed the very principle of deliberately restricting the importation of supplies that could benefit civilians as abhorrent and inhumane. This affront to humanitarian considerations was all the more acutely felt by the ICRC because of the failure of the Tokyo discussions in 1934, the outcome of which had left the Committee with only the principled approval of governments party to the talks, which included Britain and Germany, as a basis upon which to request, at the outbreak of the war, that the draft's recommendations on civilian protection be adhered to. The response to this request was very different to that conveyed in peacetime: not one of the belligerents agreed to abide by the draft articles in their entirety. The only point on which both the Germans and the British agreed was that the Red Cross would have the right to organize relief for civilian internees – foreign nationals detained in enemy territories at the outbreak of the war. This decision was an uncomplicated one for Whitehall to make, not only because it benefited British civilians in enemy territory but also because it did not threaten the integrity of the blockade. Like POWs, the civilian internee population in Germany was both kept in secure camps and too small in size for any relief sent to it to imperil British strategic objectives. Moreover, the camps that held the internees could be visited regularly by ICRC and Protecting Power inspectors, who could monitor the distribution of supplies therein and ensure that pilfering by the Germans – an issue of great concern to MEW officials – was kept to a minimum.[8] The ICRC was thus given permission in late 1939 by both London and Berlin for reciprocal deliveries of relief in the form of food parcels to civilian internees. Agreement was also made that goods imported for POWs and civilian internees be exempt from the quota of imports assigned by MEW to Switzerland. Once these provisions had been agreed, most civilian internees were catered for by the ICRC in a similar way to that for POWs for the duration of the war.[9]

The notion of shipping relief through the blockade for the other, larger category of civilians in Europe – those living outside the camps in the occupied territories – presented greater problems for Geneva. In addition to The Hague regulations and precedent, MEW was able to argue that, unlike in the camps where relief distribution could be monitored, no guarantees could be made that supplies sent to the occupied territories would not simply be requisitioned by the Wehrmacht, which had been issued with orders to live off the land so as to avoid straining Germany's food supply.[10] Any relief sent for the benefit of non-interned civilians, therefore, was deemed to be a threat to the success of the blockade – a tactic that fell within the much defended realm of military necessity in British IHL considerations. On this point of military necessity, the British resisted efforts made throughout the war by the ICRC, a number of National Red Cross societies, Quakers and a variety of other humanitarian organizations to obtain concessions for relief. There were only three exceptions made to this stance. The first was on behalf of Vichy France, which received two shipments of milk and four of wheat over the winter of 1940–1. The second concession was made to Greece in late 1941, from which point a systematic relief effort was put in place for the duration of the war in an effort to mitigate the effects of a famine that killed as many as 450,000 Greek civilians between 1941 and 1944.

The third concession came very late, in early 1945, when a handful of relief ships and a series of food drops were used in the Netherlands in an effort to mitigate the effects of the *Hongerwinter*. Although in the case of Greece in particular, the plight of those affected by lack of food was considered with sympathy in Whitehall, all three decisions to compromise the blockade were made principally on strategic and political, rather than humanitarian, grounds.

With regards to the Netherlands, the decision was made with one eye on imminent victory and the other on a starving populace that the Allied liberators would soon have to feed. The decision to begin what was, in many respects, simply the opening phase of 'victory before relief' for the Netherlands was thus a straightforward one to make in the winter of 1944–5.[11] Earlier in the war, the impetus to allow a limited number of ships to unload cargo for civilians in Vichy France lay in the British wish both to gain the favour of the neutral Vichy Government and honour the wishes of President Roosevelt, who was a supporter of the idea of a relief scheme for civilian children in occupied and unoccupied France. In the case of Greece, concessions were granted primarily as a means of highlighting the Germans' ruthless requisition practices and strengthening Britain's reputation in a region that was considered a sphere of influence. The predominance of these political and strategic considerations in the thinking of blockade officials meant that humanitarian agitators for relief were, ultimately, ineffective in altering blockade policy over the course of the war. This outcome was not, however, for want of trying. The former United States President, Herbert Hoover, was the most high profile of the relief agitators and, having engineered a mass relief programme for Belgium during the first war, had a pedigree to back up his demands for similar concessions throughout the second war. His efforts, however, mostly earned him either the condescension of those who viewed him as a man trying to relive past glories or the suspicion of some, Dalton in particular, who saw him as a rabble-rouser for the pacifist, isolationist cause in the United States.[12] For its part, the ICRC struggled similarly to Hoover to introduce relief measures into a strategic paradigm in which blockade was viewed by the British as a military necessity, and thus subordinate to humanitarian concerns. Aside from the concessions given to civilian internees, the ICRC's wartime successes in the area of blockade reform were negligible. The path it took in engaging with Whitehall on this issue was of great significance, however, for the wartime development of the Committee. Indeed, the ICRC was able to use the on-going problem of providing relief to non-interned civilians to expand its role beyond being a relief agent for POWs: to assume, in other words, the exact opposite role to that which the British wished it to play. The first phase of the ICRC's relations with MEW was, like those with the War and Foreign Offices, generally devoid of disruption and conflict. The primary issue of concern for both parties in the war's first months was the Committee's proposal to introduce collective rather than individual parcels for Polish POWs and civilian internees, a change in relief policy that was authorized by MEW on 14 February 1940. Swift approval was also given by MEW for a similar policy for the benefit of British POWs after Dunkirk. As was the case with relief for civilian detainees, the guarantee of supervision for collective parcel distribution in the POW camps, the comparatively small amount of food being sent into Europe via the scheme and the benefit it brought to British detainees meant that the ICRC's requests did not much trouble MEW. It was only on the issue of providing relief equal to that enjoyed by British POWs for other non-British war victims, discussed in the previous chapter, that the first true divergence of perspective between MEW and the ICRC emerged.

Specifically, it was Lucie Odier who took MEW to task on the issue of relief for non-British POWs and civilians. This began with actions, rather than words when, in June 1940, she authorized the despatch of more than one thousand tons of food and medical supplies for French civilian refugees and POWs. Most of these goods were donated by the American Red Cross (ARC) which, notably, had spent the lion's share of its funds prior to this on relief for British civilians.[13] The parcels were distributed by the French Red Cross in occupied France, at the same time that MEW was grappling with the problem of the 'Marseilles Leak', an embarrassing hole in the Royal Navy's Mediterranean blockade which, by year's end, had let 80,146 tonnes of foodstuffs into the unoccupied territories from French African colonies. The Ministry's attempts to seal this leak and implement tighter blockade regulations on Vichy were also being challenged at this time both by Washington and certain officials in Whitehall, who argued for a relaxation of the blockade in order to strengthen relations with Marshal Philippe Pétain's still, technically, neutral regime.[14] With these difficulties on his mind, Dalton was as incensed by Odier's actions as he was unimpressed with her justifications. These Odier described emotively in a letter to MEW, which detailed the plight of starving French civilians, erstwhile allies of the British forced to give up their food to ruthless German requisition parties. She also outlined the various donations made by National Red Cross Societies to remedy the situation. Conspicuous by its absence in her otherwise passionate humanitarian plea was any concrete plan for how the ICRC could guarantee that supplies shipped through the blockade would not fall into the hands of the very same rapacious occupation forces of which Odier complained. Considering that requisitioning was the primary concern of MEW, this was a significant omission. Bereft of an ICRC contingency plan and informed by a report it had received confirming the policy of requisitioning by the Germans, MEW came to the conclusion that no safeguards for distribution could be devised.[15]

There was also concern from some MEW officials that Odier was either deliberately overstating the drama of the situation or ignorant of the fact that, in theory, France was self-sustainable in terms of its food production with the harvest yet to be drawn.[16] This, ultimately, led to the rejection of Odier's appeals for continued shipments of relief to occupied France, albeit with the concession that shipments of medical supplies for those who had been identified by ICRC inspectors as sick or wounded would be permitted on a case-by-case basis.[17] This concession – which ostensibly was at odds with Dalton's efforts to strengthen the blockade – was in part a product of the latter's attempts to distract relief advocates from major anti-blockade campaigns by granting minor concessions.[18] It was also, notably, the product of a recognition by some in MEW of the increasingly important role being played by the Committee in maintenance of British POW welfare. In contrast to Dalton, some MEW officials even suggested that, on account of the need to keep the ICRC 'onside', Odier's ill-conceived shipment to France should not be met with a protest and that any communication with Geneva should make clear that 'there has been no hostile comment on the action of the International Red Cross Committee'. There was also an acknowledgement of the fact that talks were underway at the time for the ARC to deliver two shipments through the blockade to Marseilles as part of Roosevelt and Churchill's campaign to strengthen relations with Pétain. In order to avoid appearing hypocritical or overly favourable to the ARC, it was suggested that 'if one shipment from America was allowed, I think it would be necessary to square the International Organisation first'.[19] Odier's indiscretion, therefore, was permitted to pass with little comment.

This response reflected the extent to which MEW, despite its dismissive attitude to ICRC relief plans, was as aware as any Whitehall department of the impetus to strike a balance between placation of the Committee and restraint of its agitation for wider relief efforts, the objective being simultaneously to support the ICRC's work on behalf of British POWs while maintaining the integrity of the blockade.[20]

The ICRC's policy, by contrast, was to provide relief to all by any means necessary which, after August 1940, meant challenging the blockade the British were determined to enforce. MEW's difficulty in squaring this circle was exacerbated by the fact that Odier continually refused to appreciate the British point of view. As one Whitehall official noted during her and Junod's visit to London in April 1941, the nature of the plans she presented was 'rather confused' by her tendency to view civilians and POWs of whatever nationality as one and the same – victims of war first and foremost. This observation confirmed the fears voiced by Haccius, when he received news of her impending arrival, that her emotional, 'haggling' style of humanitarian diplomacy would do more harm than good to British–ICRC relations. Junod was even more damning in his appraisal, recalling that despite his admiration for her passion, 'her appearance and her voice lent something truly pathetic to all she did'.[21] Junod was overstating the matter. For all her apparent fragility, Odier was as much a passionate believer in the ICRC's mission as she was a seasoned veteran of the practicalities and problems of humanitarianism, having worked for the Committee's civilian relief division in both Ethiopia and Spain. Ostensibly, she had the background to fulfil the role as the ICRC's chief agitator for civilian relief. The problem, however, was that she let her emotions overcome her better judgement and approached this most delicate area of British–ICRC relations with a lack of tact and, in general, a disregard for the policies and processes established by Whitehall.

For example, Odier appears to have taken the fact that she was 'let off' by MEW for her indiscretions over France as carte blanche to push her relief campaign further, launching a fresh appeal in late 1940 for supplies to be sourced from within the blockaded territories for the purposes of a more sustained relief programme. By this time, however, the ICRC's Vice-President Carl J. Burckhardt – who had always taken a dim view of Odier's lack of political acumen – had grown tired of the latter's tactics in dealing with MEW. Accordingly, Burckhardt added a covering letter to Odier's appeal wherein he attempted to show that the ICRC was not so dogmatic in its humanitarianism and in fact understood British strategic concerns and blockade regulations. He demonstrated this by arguing that, by obtaining supplies for the benefit of French civilians from within Europe the ICRC was not only acting in accordance with MEW regulations but also, in effect, denying the Germans the supplies. This – the first step taken by Burckhardt to seize the onus from Odier and attempt to bring a more pragmatic edge to ICRC relief policy – was followed by a letter to Dalton in which Burckhardt stated that he had obtained German assurances that goods shipped through the blockade would not be requisitioned and that the ICRC would have a delegate present at all times during their transit and distribution. Unfortunately for the ICRC, this swift attuning to the concerns of MEW came at the same time that Dalton became aware that 800,000 tonnes of wheat had been sent from Vichy to Germany, thus confirming both his cynicism over the ICRC's assertion that France required urgent relief and his view that any relief shipped through the blockade would, ultimately, end up in Hitler's hands.[22] This proof of the worthlessness of German assurances set in place a dogged stance of refusal from MEW towards ICRC calls for relief at the most inopportune moment: when the civilians of Greece were beginning to starve.

Greece and the White Ships

The onset of famine in Greece in mid-1941 tested the dynamic of proposal/refusal that had come to characterize the ICRC's relations with MEW over the course of 1940. The famine emerged quite suddenly in the wake of the Axis victory, its origins lying in part in the economy of Greece itself, which depended on imports to supply 20 per cent of its overall grain supplies in 1939. These imports from Allied countries and from Germany – one of Greece's key trading partners – ceased on 6 April 1941 when the Wehrmacht invaded the country. It was shortly after the Axis asserted control of Greece and its produce in the spring that the first problems in food supply emerged. Bulgaria, which had joined the Axis in February 1941, was handed the wheat-rich regions of Thrace for plunder, and requisitions of both staple foods and luxury cash crops such as olive oil, tobacco and fruit took place to varying degrees across the remaining German- and Italian-occupied regions in the centre and south of the country. The movement of supplies through these different zones of occupation was also heavily restricted, and trucks, bicycles and railcars were requisitioned, thus hampering efforts to distribute the harvest from the countryside to the cities. When, following the introduction of the 'occupation mark', Axis soldiers were able to purchase food and goods at artificially devalued prices, a black market quickly emerged. Though some cereals were produced in sufficient quantities in certain regions, the dislocation of the transport system and the collapse of the pre-war market led to the onset of starvation within months of the occupation's commencement. Athens itself was immediately affected and in mid-May the German authorities advised Berlin that food needed to be shipped to the capital in order to avert catastrophe. The response to these warnings was a small token shipment of grain from the German food store, followed by a decree that responsibility for the occupation of Greece would now be handed over to the Italians. Though ostensibly more open to the idea of shipping food to Greece than the Germans, Rome had neither the grain stores required for such an enterprise nor the capacity to cease the culture of 'infighting of Byzantine complexity' between its generals, German diplomats and Greek puppet administrators, which threatened any efforts to establish a coordinated response to the unfolding crisis.[23]

Having witnessed firsthand the emergence of the humanitarian disaster during the first days of the occupation, the ICRC's representative in Athens, Robert Brunel, sent a plea to Geneva on 30 May for urgent relief for the capital. As with its response to Brunel's information on the Salonika and Corinth camps, Geneva moved as quickly as possible to organize a relief scheme and, having procured one hundred tonnes of milk from ARC warehouses in Egypt, cabled MEW on 19 June, requesting permission to despatch the goods immediately. Fearing civil disturbance in Greece, Mussolini also agreed to supply 7,500 tonnes of grain and a guarantee to the ICRC that the shipment would be distributed without interference from the occupation forces.[24] MEW's not unreasonable response was initially to reject the idea of such an Axis-dependent operation on the grounds that it had already been burned by Vichy in similar circumstances. Owing to the greater depth of the crisis in Greece and the application of pressure by the Greek Ambassador in London, however, Dalton begrudgingly agreed to the relief plan.[25]

The operation was a disaster. Of the one hundred tonnes of milk despatched only sixty-three tonnes was received by the intended recipients. This, so a report from British sources in Rome believed, was owing to the fact that both the milk and a large quantity of canned meat sent by private donors was pilfered by the occupation forces, possibly with the connivance of the Italian Red Cross. This served to confirm a report received by the Foreign Office in early May that the stories of starvation on the streets of Athens were 'German inspired' as a means of conning the humanitarians into sending supplies for the benefit of the Axis.[26] What is astonishing about this situation is the extent to which the ICRC dug a deeper hole for itself by insisting to the British that the operation had gone smoothly. Having further interjected himself into relief matters at the expense of Odier, Burckhardt requested from MEW that, following the 'success' of the milk shipment, a larger relief effort for

Greece should now be approved. This request he edged with the veiled threat that agreement would:

> counteract a certain resentment which I feel duty bound to mention, is beginning to be noticeable in many countries on the Continent at the sight of so much suffering amongst the innocent especially in countries whose behaviour, as in the case of Greece and Belgium, had been so gallant.

This rather wordy push by Burckhardt to play political commentator and diplomat was written off by MEW as an 'entirely unreal and futile suggestion' from a 'very obnoxious' man who was derided for the fact that, as he was 'penning his second paragraph, the Germans were stealing condensed milk sent to the children of Greece'.[27] As had become typical of the ICRC in its handling of delicate negotiations, enthusiasm trumped common sense. Even Burckhardt, arguably one of the more politically minded Committee members, had difficulty appreciating the fact that the Axis could not be trusted to supervise the distribution of supplies and that this fact would always provide a rock upon which the ICRC's efforts to obtain blockade concessions from the British would founder.

For its part, MEW also possessed a certain tunnel vision in its adherence to the principles of blockade in the face of the escalating crisis in Greece, and the growing evidence that, problematic though a sustained relief mission would be, something would have to be done sooner rather than later. Moreover, this argument for a relaxation of the blockade was increasingly coming from within Whitehall itself, specifically the Foreign Office. The Minister in Cairo, Oliver Lyttelton, was one of the more outspoken critics of the blockade of Greece, warning his colleagues that 'history will, I believe, pronounce a stern judgement on our policy'.[28] His sentiments were matched by those of the Foreign Secretary, Anthony Eden, who sought shades of grey in blockade policy, if only to temper the growing discontent of the heads of the various governments-in-exile in London, to whom he was constantly forced to defend British measures that deprived their citizens of relief. He both openly supported the ICRC's milk-for-Greece scheme and, when it failed, received a blast in Parliament for his troubles from a crowing Hugh Dalton, who dubbed the Foreign Secretary a 'light weight' for daring to weigh in on blockade matters.[29] Dalton's apparent victory over Eden was, however, short lived. In March 1942, he was replaced as head of MEW by the Earl of Selborne, a man who was less belligerent than his predecessor in regards to the blockade and more mindful of the political consequences that Britain might face if it continued to ignore the plight of its erstwhile Greek allies.[30]

Selborne's appointment came at a time, moreover, when attitudes in MEW as a whole towards the blockade of Greece were changing. This was reflected in the MEW-approved despatch to Piraeus in October 1941 of a Turkish freighter, the *Kurtulus*, laden with 5,000 tonnes of wheat and flying under the banner of the Turkish National Red Crescent Society. Although this voyage, and the five that followed until the *Kurtulus* ran aground and sank in February 1942, was vital for the starving Greeks, this one ship was never intended by the British to become the harbinger of a wider, more sustained relief effort. Permission to sail was given by MEW on the grounds that the wheat had come from within Turkey itself and thus was not a breach of the blockade and, with Marcel Junod on-board and present during the principal distribution of the food in Athens, there was at least a modicum of supervision involved.[31] The *Kurtulus* did not, therefore, mark the turning over of a new leaf in Whitehall's humanitarian policy. The despatch of the wheat was viewed by the British as a stop-gap measure and nothing more.

For pro-relief advocates such as the Famine Relief Committee (later Oxfam) in Britain and the American-based Greek War Relief Association, however, the *Kurtulus* mission was viewed as only the beginning. The fact that the famine had not abated and that winter had begun to descend on Greece gave weight to this view and, by the spring of 1942, MEW was beginning to take significant steps to alter its policy on Greek relief, with an aim to construct a more permanent system of delivery. The caveat to this change in policy was that measures had to be taken to ensure that any concession to Greece could not be interpreted by the Germans as a sign of British weakness.[32] The challenge was thus set for MEW: to devise a relief scheme that could be carried out within the blockaded territories, thereby ensuring that no additional foodstuffs would be shipped into Europe; and that would give the impression to the Germans that the scheme was not emanating from Whitehall, but from a third, preferably neutral, party, thus preserving the image of a hard-line blockade policy.

The ICRC certainly thought itself well positioned to play the role of neutral coordinator for this relief programme.[33] In addition to Brunel having been on the ground in Athens from the start of the famine and Junod's recent involvement with the *Kurtulus* mission, since the summer of 1941 Burckhardt had been working on a means of better organizing the Red Cross relief effort on behalf of civilians. This led to the creation on 23 July 1941 of the Joint Relief Commission (JRC), a body that would coordinate the relief efforts of the ICRC with those of

23 July 1941

the League of Red Cross Societies (LRCS). Burckhardt's plan was bold in as much as it required the ICRC to address the long simmering grievances that had existed between itself and the League since the 1920s. The agreement made between Max Huber and Colonel Draudt in 1928 on the formation of the International Red Cross helped in this regard. In particular the acknowledgement made by both leaders that, as the pre-eminent members of the global Red Cross movement, it was incumbent upon the ICRC and the LRCS to coordinate their humanitarian efforts.[34] Despite this decade-old declaration of harmony, Burckhardt still faced strong opposition to the JRC scheme from within the ranks of the ICRC leadership itself. Jacques Chenevière, for example (assuming the role of a Red Cross Cato), took to exclaiming 'la league a tort' at many a meeting on the subject of the JRC. For his part, Burckhardt was determined to press on without the cooperation of Chenevière or Odier. Indeed, in regards to the latter he worked deliberately to undermine her position as the ICRC's head administrator for civilian relief. In his negotiations with the British over the acquizition of ships for the JRC, Burckhardt insisted that the matter should be 'dealt with by me and not by Mademoiselle Odier. I should very much appreciate it if this could be made clear, as I do not want Mlle Odier to have all the onus.' Although this reflected Burckhardt's own personal ambitions – he insisted that he be made the JRC's president – it is likely that he was also mindful both of British displeasure with Odier and the wider concern that, if the ICRC's ability to respond to the escalation of the war in 1941 remained limited, so too would its scope and influence.[35] In pursuing the JRC, therefore, Burckhardt was not simply glory hunting, but also seeking to pick up where Huber and Draudt had left off by using the combined forces of the ICRC and the LRCS to expand the scope and capabilities of the Red Cross movement writ large. The problem of Greece thus presented an excellent opportunity for Burckhardt to demonstrate both the effectiveness of the JRC and engage in what might be termed 'humanitarian empire building'. In order to see his vision implemented, however, Burckhardt had to address two problems: the restrictions imposed by the blockade authorities; and the lack of sea-borne transport possessed by the ICRC to ship the vast quantity of goods required.

It was primarily with these concerns in mind that Burckhardt, with Odier in tow, travelled to London in December 1941 to meet British officials. With the outcome of the *Kurtulus* mission still unclear and MEW in the process of transitioning from the era of Dalton to that of Selborne, the ICRC delegates were, from the outset, viewed by many in Whitehall as unwanted guests. Indeed, even before Burckhardt and

Odier arrived it was decided by MEW to avoid any significant blockade discussions with them, given that the Ministry's 'attitude was necessarily a negative one'.[36] There was, however, something different about this particular visit from Geneva that, in practice, ensured that the delegates would be received well and their voices heard.

The Minister in Berne, David Kelly, was the first to point out the significance of Burckhardt – the former League of Nations High Commissioner and Vice-President of the ICRC – paying a visit to British shores. He urged his colleagues in Whitehall to play into Burckhardt's wish to be viewed as 'an international figure, rather than the philosopher and historian he truly is'. To this end, both Kelly and the BRC put forward suggestions of French-speaking guides for Burckhardt, whose English was poor, and the organizing of hunting trips in Scotland, special treatment that was not extended to any other ICRC visitors to Britain. Though these and other suggestions for rolling out the red carpet generally failed to materialize – on account of time constraints more than anything else – the Foreign Office still concluded that it would be 'impolitic' for Burckhardt to be given the 'cold shoulder'.[37] This obliging sentiment is particularly noteworthy if one considers that, in addition to being the bearer of unwanted Red Cross schemes, Burckhardt was also suspected by some in the Foreign Office of using the journey to London as a means to convey peace feelers on behalf of the Swiss Foreign Minister, Marcel Pilet-Golaz.[38] Despite these concerns – which proved to be unfounded – the fact that the ICRC was represented on this occasion by a former diplomat, combined with the growing acknowledgement in Whitehall that the question of civilian relief needed to be addressed, helped to ensure that Burckhardt's proposals would at the very least be treated more seriously than those put forward hitherto by Odier alone.

It helped that there was broad agreement by all parties that a new, better coordinated relief effort was required. The problem from MEW's perspective was that the ICRC had failed in Lisbon, Vichy and in Athens itself to allay concerns over pilfering. Moreover, Brunel's administrative body in Greece, the Comité de Haute Direction, composed of representatives of the Greek, Italian and German Red Cross societies, was simply not trusted by the Ministry, which feared that, if a more extensive relief scheme were left in the ICRC's hands, it would continue to take the Germans at their word whilst 'contenting themselves with the staff of a man and a boy'. The solution proposed by the British was that the relief effort should be undertaken not by the ICRC alone but by a 'truly' neutral body comprised, in the main, of representatives of the Swedish

Government and the Swedish Red Cross. As the driving force behind
this proposal, MEW argued that although the:

> International Red Cross have done some excellent work, we doubt
> if that body itself is competent to handle a job of this size. It is also
> inconvenient to deal with it, because it has no government behind
> it and no facilities for rapid and secret communication. Moreover,
> it is naturally inclined to pursue its own policy, and also to engage
> in negotiations with Allied governments, whereas we desire to keep
> the strings of any permitted relief action firmly in our own hands.[39]

It is clear from this assessment that for all the Committee had achieved
in POW welfare and for all Burckhardt's attempts to present a more
professional and politically reliable organization to the British,
concerns over both the ICRC's capabilities and its push for greater
autonomy remained. The Committee had simply done too much
damage to its reputation in matters of civilian relief for Whitehall to
entrust it with so delicate a task as organizing relief within the blockade. The Swedes, by contrast, were a seemingly untainted commodity.
The Swedish Red Cross had the necessary humanitarian credentials
in the form of the several limited relief schemes it had running at the
time in Scandinavia and, most importantly, Stockholm possessed a
merchant fleet that had lain near-dormant since the establishment of
the blockade. The fact that the Swedes, despite their neutrality, were
not as beholden to the same tenets of impartiality as the ICRC was also
appealing to the British. Whereas the Committee would have to treat
with both the Wilhelmstrasse and Whitehall as an unbiased humanitarian actor, the Swedish Government, it was hoped, would give the
British 'all the information we need about what goes on'. The Swedes
could also be trusted to propose the scheme to Berlin as if it were their
own, thus protecting the British from any impression that they had
softened their stance on blockade.[40]

   For these reasons, when the relief scheme for Greece was finally
launched in March 1942 the role played by the ICRC was not one of
leader but of 'team player'. The food and medicine was mostly procured
from North America and paid for by the Greek War Relief Association
and the Canadian Greek War Relief Fund. Most of the ships sailed under
the auspices of the Swedish Red Cross and the task of notifying London
of the ship's cargo and Berlin of their movements through U-boat-
infested waters was left in the hands of the Swedish Ministry of Foreign
Affairs. Finally, the food itself was distributed, not solely by Brunel or

Junod, but by a mixture of Swedish, Greek and ICRC delegates operating under the direction of the Commission de Gestion de la Délégation du Comité International de la Croix-Rouge en Grèce, an ostensibly ICRC-run, though in practice a Swedish-controlled coalition body that the British had insisted be formed to replace Brunel's Comité de Haute Direction.[41]

In humanitarian terms, the formation of this new relief system was invaluable to Greece, which received over 600,000 tonnes of food via the Commission de Gestion between September 1942 and May 1945. For the ICRC, however, the passing over of its ambitions in Greece to the Swedes became a sore point in its relations with Whitehall. Brunel, in particular, was aggrieved at what he perceived as British meddling in 'his' relief system, while the Committee's leadership protested by using the flimsy argument that the involvement of the Swedish Government would compromise the neutrality of the ICRC's operation – a claim that both overlooked the presence of Swiss Federal Council members in the ICRC and, by inference, called into question the neutrality of Sweden itself.[42] What was missing from the ICRC's analysis of the situation was a true appreciation of the extent to which its own adherence to impartiality – and with it a willingness to take the Germans at their word – had damaged its credibility in the eyes of the British. The importance of this damage cannot be overstated. The ICRC's right to act was utterly dependent on the willingness of the belligerents to trust that its activities would not impinge upon the military necessity of either side's strategy. In British eyes this right to act had been invalidated by the mounting evidence that, when the ICRC placed its trust in the Axis in matters of relief, breaches of the blockade occurred. This lack of trust, combined with Whitehall's view of the Greek situation as a political, rather than a strictly humanitarian problem, led to the ICRC being marginalized in a relief operation in which it expected to play a central role.[43] As much as this exclusion was a blow to the prestige of both the ICRC and Burckhardt, the negotiations over how to maintain the relief operation did pave the way for the fulfilment of at least one of the latter's ambitions: the creation of a Red Cross fleet.

The idea of an independent Red Cross fleet capable of transporting relief in wartime had been raised at both the Fourteenth International Red Cross Conference in 1930 and with the Commission of Naval Experts in Geneva in 1937. Although there was great support for this from within the Red Cross movement, on both occasions the idea was abandoned owing to 'legal, practical and financial obstacles'.[44] When he set out for London in December 1941 Burckhardt made sure he had a plan for how to overcome these obstacles. Although the need to supply Greece was the reason proffered by Burckhardt for raising the question of a Red Cross fleet to the British, it is clear that for months prior to visiting London both he and Junod had conceived of the fleet as a vital component of the ICRC's overall wartime relief strategy, rather than an expedient measure needed solely for the relief of starving Greeks.[45]

In order to fulfil these grander ambitions, Burckhardt made sure to satisfy British concerns over the neutrality of the fleet, the protection of the vessels and the costs involved, while highlighting to Whitehall the benefits that it would bring to its primary object of humanitarian concern: British POWs. To these ends, Burckhardt suggested that the Belgian freighter *Frédéric*, which had lain dormant at Casablanca since the summer of 1940, be utilised on account of the fact that its crew – comprised mostly of Portuguese – were neutrals. He also agreed both to handle personally the negotiations with the Belgian and Portuguese governments and to provide a clear plan for how the *Frédéric* and other vessels would be marked with Red Cross insignia and signage so as to protect them from attack. In an effort to show restraint for his grander ambitions and play to British self-interest he also emphasized, first and foremost, that the extra tonnage provided by the fleet would strengthen the Red Cross's ability to supply POWs – civilians would come later. Finally, he suggested that, should the British and the Americans agree to release captured French merchant ships to the ICRC, he would also seek to obtain a reciprocal donation of captured Danish ships from Berlin.[46]

Burckhardt's recognition of Whitehall's pre-eminent concern for British interests and the need for reciprocity from the Germans was matched by an equally adroit appreciation of the financial aspect of his enterprise, specifically, the need to ensure that ICRC funds donated to Geneva for the purchase of relief supplies would not be spent on ships. The means of assuring that this would not happen was the formation, on 14 April 1942, of the Basle Foundation for the Organisation of Red Cross Transport. Although the Foundation both had the ICRC delegate Paul Logoz on its board of directors and had been conceived by Burckhardt, Huber and the joint ICRC/Swiss Federal Council member, Edouard de Haller, the organization was legally registered as being an autonomous entity, unattached to the ICRC. This meant that any money spent by the Foundation – much of which was supplied by the Swiss bankers on its board – would not technically be Red Cross money. Through this scheme the ICRC acquired the American freighters *Spokane* and *Oriente*, which, along with the *Frédéric*, were renamed *Caritas I*, *Caritas II* and the *Henry Dunant*, respectively. These, together with the thirteen Swedish vessels chartered to supply Greece, formed the nucleus of what became the Red Cross fleet, dubbed by Junod as the White Ships. Impressed by the proposals and assured of the usefulness of the fleet, the British gave the vessels permission to sail in July 1942. In the years that followed, the White Ships fleet continued to grow. By war's end the 34 ships of the fleet, sourced from four neutral countries, had made 321 voyages and delivered 428,106 tonnes of relief supplies.[47]

Broken visions

The formation of the White Ships, the JRC, the establishment of a permanent relief mission in Greece and the struggles to construct a workable POW relief system in the Far East, all occurred within the space of a year between the summers of 1941 and 1942. In all these pursuits the Committee's approach was characterized by a greater degree of pragmatism, nuance and strategic vision than had hitherto been present in its work, and the focus for its delegates on the ground was increasingly on 'practical and local activities'.[48] Far removed from Huber's small gathering of philanthropists at the Villa Moynier the ICRC was, by the war's middle years, a multi-faceted, global humanitarian juggernaut. The British response to this change was mixed. Although the emergence of a seemingly more professional Committee was welcomed by those in the POW departments who had long doubted the ICRC's capabilities, officials from MEW were concerned over the scope of the ICRC's ambitions which, despite appearing more attuned to the realities of the war, were nonetheless still dictated by the concept of universal humanitarian relief. This was evident in the typically utopian wish of the Committee that the White Ships be used not only for relief supplies for all victims of war – civilians, internees, POWs of any nationality – but also for the delivery of mail and the exchange of prisoners. The British response was also typical, with permission given to transport supplies to Greek civilians, Allied POWs and specific civilian internees in Europe on the proviso that each shipment possessed an accompanying navicert and that the shipping route be communicated to the Admiralty at least six days in advance. The idea of passengers was completely out of the question for security reasons, so too the proposal that mail be transported beyond the reach of the censor – a refusal the British insisted be put in writing before allowing the White Ships to sail.[49]

The fear that the JRC and the White Ships would encourage agitation for larger relief programmes for non-British victims of war was also prevalent. Even before the first ship sailed, W. A. Camps at MEW opined that 'the chief preoccupation of the International Committee is to get space for transport of goods for non-British prisoners' and, as a result, the whole enterprise would bring little benefit to British POWs and stir up the pro-relief advocates. The Admiralty and the Ministry of Transport also expressed fears that the ICRC was manoeuvring to absorb the BRC's own modest fleet of merchant vessels for its grander humanitarian relief schemes. One Whitehall official went so far as to claim that a campaign to discredit the BRC's vessels on the grounds that they had insufficient marking and lighting had been invented by Geneva to further its aims.[50] There were, therefore, at least a few in Whitehall who refused to be taken in by Burckhardt's appeal to British self-interest and who remained beholden to the idea that Geneva's priorities had to remain narrowed to providing succour for British POWs first and foremost. Any schemes that might go beyond that remit had to be discouraged. What is surprising in this respect is that, despite this prevailing divergence of opinion, the Committee was still able to construct a massive system of relief over the course of 1942 and 1943 with the blessing, albeit grudging, of the British Government. Why did Whitehall, for all its reservations, allow the ICRC to expand its operational purview in this manner?

A clear reason was the increasingly present dynamic of dependence and divergence in British–ICRC relations. As the War Office's W. H. Gardner admitted to his colleagues in mid-1942:

> the servicing of British prisoners in Europe and to an even greater extent the servicing of Imperial prisoners in the Far East, would depend increasingly on the goodwill of the IRC [International Red Cross] and the War Office was therefore, greatly concerned that no action should be taken to prejudice their goodwill.[51]

Another reason was that during the war's middle years Whitehall were having to consider the opinions of other, increasingly more senior, voices within the Allied camp. The United States had joined Britain in its blockade of the Third Reich in December 1941 via the creation, under the leadership of Vice-President Henry Wallace, of the Board of Economic Warfare (BEW). The BEW was generally inclined to let the British run the blockade as they always had, while it concerned itself with other facets of economic warfare, such as denying Germany crucial war material by making purchases in South America and blacklisting companies with links to the German manufacturing sector. Relations between MEW and BEW were generally very good and members of the latter sat on a combined Blockade Committee in London, at which

Allied economic warfare policy – usually based on British thinking – was agreed upon. Beneath this otherwise healthy working relationship, however, there were points of divergence in Anglo-American thinking over the blockade. More so in the United States than in Britain, public agitation for food and medicine concessions to Europe influenced thinking within the highest levels of the government.[52] Roosevelt himself was inclined to show sympathy for the plight of civilians in occupied Europe and voiced dissatisfaction with existing relief initiatives. Although this often manifested in him raising with Churchill the suggestion that the blockade be loosened in Belgium and France, the persuasive refusals of the latter, combined with the demonstrative problems of existing relief programmes, meant that in general Roosevelt supported 'victory before relief'. He was, however, determined, to make sure that if this policy had to be followed, it would need planning and forethought to be successful once the fighting was over. To this end, in July 1942 Roosevelt created the War Relief Control Board in order to coordinate the efforts of all American relief societies.[53] He went a step further in early 1943 by creating the Office of Foreign Relief and Rehabilitation (OFRRA), an organization which – despite its initial mandate to prepare for *post-war* relief – called for the immediate distribution of vitamins to Belgian children. The immediate contretemps between OFRRA and MEW only subsided once Roosevelt reaffirmed in May 1943 his commitment to Churchill's view of the importance of the blockade in Allied strategy. By that time, however, the relief genie was out of the bottle and on 9 November Roosevelt, with British agreement, signed into the creation of the United Nations Relief and Rehabilitation Administration (UNRRA), a body tasked with coordinating the post-war relief effort for the benefit of 'nationals of the United Nations, stateless persons, and Italian nationals'. Although its purpose was to prepare for the post-war relief of Europe, the creation of UNRRA reflected a growing sentiment in Washington that Allied humanitarian policy was defective and that a new, better organized approach had to be taken.[54]

Whitehall could not help but be influenced by these moves from across the Atlantic. Despite MEW's predictions, the blockade had not collapsed under the weight of the Greek relief effort and, as news of Roosevelt's flurry of relief planning became known, the manifold charitable relief agencies in Britain and the United States were inspired to agitate in 1943 with a renewed vigour. Although the practical influence of these organizations on British decision-making was minimal, the pressure, particularly from the United States, led some officials within MEW to begin to view the blockade as a 'growing embarrassment'.

The combination of these external and internal pressures led to an acknowledgement by Whitehall that its humanitarian policy – which was supposed to have begun and ended with 'victory before relief' – now needed to be considered in a more open and thoughtful manner, which it was, albeit tentatively, via the first official public debate on the issue in the House of Commons on 8 July 1943.[55]

It is difficult to gauge to what extent this changing context for relief planning influenced British attitudes to the ICRC's concurrent expansion of its relief work. It is hard to dismiss the coincidence of the White Ships proposals – arguably the ICRC's most ambitious relief scheme of the war – being given a more fair and measured hearing by a hitherto unreceptive MEW at the same time that American pro-relief pressure was growing. The Greek famine was also important in awaking British minds to new relief proposals. On both a political and humanitarian level the situation in Greece could not be ignored by Whitehall over the long-term. The need to act on this situation presented Burckhardt with an opportunity, in spite of Whitehall's preference for Swedish control, to outline a broader relief plan (based on the use of the White Ships) that would extend beyond Greece to the rest of occupied Europe. This grander ambition would probably have foundered completely if not for the pressing need to do something about Greece. In this respect, the fact that Burckhardt – though generally distrusted and disliked by the British – had made sure that the White Ships scheme was well thought out and addressed British concerns over relief – was also significant in encouraging a more favourable view from Whitehall.

This receptiveness, however, came with caveats. MEW insisted that it would only countenance the White Ships if their usage was strictly regulated. In the process of developing the fleet, ICRC would also need to ensure:

1. That financial benefit to the enemy shall not result from these transactions.
2. That shipping is not acquired by the Red Cross company which might be or become of service to the United Nations in other ways.
3. That shipping controlled by the IRC do not (*sic*) become a factor in promoting demands for relief shipments which would be of a kind unwelcome to the blockade authorities.[56]

The fact that the third condition was broken by the rise in agitation by the likes of Herbert Hoover and Oxfam was a development the ICRC could not hope to control. What it could control, however, was the extent to which it would adhere to Directives 1 and 2, and in so doing acknowledge Whitehall's reservations and tailor its relief operations accordingly. This need to work within British parameters was, however, cast aside and instead the Committee pushed the boundaries of the agreements too far for British tastes. The result was a swift renewal in Whitehall of the old fears of ICRC amateurism, political unreliability and unfettered ambition.

When, for example, the ICRC attempted to charter a ship from the ARC in September 1943, a scathing missive was sent to the latter from DPW in which Geneva was accused of seeking to procure cargo space for whatever purposes its delegates deemed important – to engage, in other words, in the kind of unregulated humanitarian action that the British had long fought to contain. This raised the ire of those in Whitehall who, from the time of the White Ships' conception, had been 'anxious to guide the initiative of the International Red Cross into convenient channels'.[57] These 'convenient channels' remained, predominantly those which concerned the welfare of British POWs and civilian internees.

The extent to which this concern still governed British attitudes to the ICRC's mid-war expansion can be seen in the decision by the Ministry of Transport to grant the ICRC a ship for its fleet, the *Nancy*, in late 1942. Although the ship was to be presented to the ICRC as part of Geneva's wider relief effort, the terms of its despatch as prescribed by Whitehall were that it operate solely on the Lisbon–Marseilles route under the auspices of the BRC. This would ensure that the 'ship would be used principally in the first place to reduce the accumulation of supplies already around Lisbon for Imperial Prisoners of War'. All other Allied prisoners, however, would have to wait until 'some future date' before being granted the same service by the *Nancy*. Following the inevitable protest from Geneva over these terms, the scheme was cancelled – officially because the upkeep for the ship was viewed as being 'unduly onerous' for the BRC. Although these pragmatic considerations would have played a part in the decision to suspend the *Nancy* scheme, it is likely no coincidence that, following this incident, MEW greatly hardened its stance on the ICRC's relief initiatives. Over the course of the autumn of 1943 new relief schemes from Geneva received increasingly blunt replies from MEW on the grounds that the suggestions were 'a departure from the general blockade principles'. This campaign of refusal reached its crescendo in November 1943 when, in response to agitation from the ICRC's delegate in

Washington, Alfred Zollinger, MEW declared that it would no longer countenance 'entering into any detailed argument' with the ICRC on the matter of relief schemes.[58]

This rhetoric was demonstrative of the fact that, despite engaging in discussions over humanitarian policy during 1942–3, the fundamentals of the British attitude to civilian relief were not altered. As callous as it appeared to the ICRC, Whitehall's emphasis on protecting British POWs first and foremost in 1942–3 was understandable. Although the POW relief system was more stabilized than it had been in 1940, from 1942 onwards material conditions within German POW camps began to decline, and in the spring of that year the Germans cut POW rations, forcing the prisoners to depend on Red Cross parcels alone for 60 per cent of their necessary daily calorie intake.[59] This was followed by the bottlenecking of parcels through Lisbon in June at the same time that 33,000 British and Colonial soldiers surrendered the long-besieged town of Tobruk to the Afrika Korps – a disaster that once again made the British public alive to the Government's apparent failure to care for British prisoners.[60] The summer of 1942, therefore, was a low ebb for the British in regards to POWs and for these reasons the need to channel ICRC attentions away from civilian relief efforts towards the interests of British prisoners was understandable. The idea, however, that the 'the whole programme for servicing British prisoners might seriously be harmed' by the ICRC's effort to construct a more expansive relief operation for civilians was misguided.[61]

For all Whitehall's concerns over the ICRC diverting its attention away from British POWs, the number of parcels received and despatched from Switzerland reached its wartime height of 14,690,625 in 1943, thus more than fulfilling for many prisoners Eden's pledge to deliver 'one parcel, per week, per man'. Moreover, despite this outlay, in mid-1943 the BRC's warehouses still contained a surplus of 200,000 parcels which, combined with the establishment of the White Ships, meant that the ICRC had the means to keep its own massive array of warehouses full in anticipation of any future POW crisis.[62] British fears that the Committee's rolling stock would not be sufficient to handle the extra burden of supplies from the White Ships were also wide of the mark.[63] The amount of rolling stock available to the Committee actually increased over the war's middle years. An extra sixteen trains were acquired in late 1942 and over the winter as many as 1,200 wagons of parcels per month were being sent from Switzerland into Germany. None of these improvements to the ICRC's relief systems were undertaken for the sole benefit of British POWs and yet they benefited immeasurably.[64]

One area of the ICRC's relief plans that did not benefit British POWs was the Concentration Camps Parcel Scheme (CCPS). Concentration camp prisoners – unlike civilian internees – had been viewed by Berlin since the 1930s as objects of domestic concern, beyond the purview of the ICRC. On the handful of occasions prior to the war when the ICRC was allowed to visit concentration camps, the inspectors were shown only what the Germans wanted them to see. The subsequent attempts made by Roland Marti in particular to gain entry to the camps during the war were – with only a few exceptions – unsuccessful, foundering on the same claim from the Germans that the internees were criminals and their detainment a domestic and legal matter, rather than an international, humanitarian concern. This principle was reinforced on 7 December 1941 in the form of Hitler's *Nacht und Nebel* decree, which declared that no information on the fate or location of civilian detainees was to be given to the outside world.[65] The ICRC's initial responses to this problem came primarily in the form of private negotiations with Berlin, the outcomes of which bore little fruit. It was not until the middle of 1943 that an ICRC volunteer named Jean de Schwarzenberg, driven by the aim of providing tangible relief rather than continuing to try in vain to gain permission for inspections, conceived of a means of sending parcels, albeit in small quantities, into the concentration camps. The method he developed utilized the agreement made between the belligerents in 1939 for the ICRC to provide relief to civilian internees. This agreement required that the names of the parcel's recipient and the location of the camps where they were detained had to be known before relief could be sent. Because of the *Nacht und Nebel* decree this necessary information was difficult to come by. Mindful that the names of some foreign nationals detained in concentration camps were recorded at the Central Agency, however, Schwarzenberg, with the assistance of the well-connected Marti, pioneered a system whereby each parcel in a delivery run had an attached receipt on which additional prisoners' names and addresses could be written before being sent back to Geneva for onward transmission. Against all expectation, over the course of 1943 this method began to pay off and by the war's end the ICRC had delivered 1,112,000 parcels to certain concentration camps.[66]

Although initially the Committee was able to procure foodstuffs from Eastern European countries within the blockade, the need for greater quantities of food increased as the CCPS broadened. In August 1943 Zollinger sent a plea to MEW for concessions. As the CCPS offered no demonstrable benefit for British POWs and had all the qualities of a typically outlandish ICRC scheme, the reply from the MEW was unsurprising: to express sympathy for the scheme but a 'particularly painful' refusal to the ICRC's request.[67] Zollinger – a delegate cut from the same purist humanitarian cloth as Odier – was unrelenting in his subsequent campaign, over the course of which he did everything from accuse the British of favouring their POWs over concentration camp internees to informing the World Jewish Congress that he would make public his less than fruitful discussions with Washington and Whitehall on the lack of relief for Jews in Hungary.[68] The advocacy of Zollinger and the development of the CCPS were symptomatic of a wider problem for the British: that not only was the ICRC moving beyond its mandate as laid down in the Convention but also it was becoming more meddlesome and ambitious as a consequence. In this sense, Zollinger's campaign was not helped by the fact that at the same time he was demanding support for the CCPS, the ICRC was pushing – once again – to have the blockade around Belgium lifted in order to send milk and medical supplies to children. These campaigns by Geneva served only to confirm the sentiments expressed by MEW at the time of the White Ships negotiations. That the construction of a broader system of humanitarian relief as envisioned by the ICRC would only give 'rise to demands for relief action to which we cannot consent', the outcome of which could only lead to trouble for the British, both in terms of publicity and blockade integrity. In response to this MEW not only declared its aforementioned blanket refusal to talk to the ICRC about new relief schemes, but it also brokered a new trade deal with the Swiss Government, which included a clause stating that the Swiss were not to approve any more exports on behalf of the ICRC without the prior agreement of the Lisbon-based Mixed Commission, a body of British, American and Portuguese which administered Allied war trade agreements.[69]

If one looks at the Committee's CCPS proposals with this background in mind, it becomes clear that the British attitude was not born simply of callousness. Whitehall had long viewed the plight of the Jews as part of the wider problem of civilian suffering in the Third Reich. Consequently, British policy towards the Jews was little different from policy for other classes of non-British war victims – national and strategic interests were paramount, the need for an immediate humanitarian response was not.[70] With regards to the CCPS, this perception was negatively reinforced by the fact that the ICRC, having already gained permission to establish the White Ships, appeared to be both defying British wishes and, with typical naivety, biting off more than it could chew. Although the overall success of the White Ships in humanitarian terms offers a counter to this view, MEW did have some justifiable grounds for feeling that the Committee's appetite for expansion was growing – problematically – with the eating.

The lack of concern for security arrangements, for example, came to the fore when Geneva proposed that ships plying the Lisbon–Marseilles route be permitted to stop at smaller – less regulated – ports in order to load additional supplies. There was also the case of the ICRC ordering one ship, the *Lobito*, to leave Lisbon without a safe conduct. Both this incident and the notion of greater autonomy for the White Ships that underpinned it were rightly viewed by Whitehall as evidence of the Committee overstretching itself and in the process discarding the security concerns that had been so pre-eminent in the White Ships negotiations.[71] These indiscretions, combined with Zollinger's relentless and often excitable agitation for the ICRC to be allowed to open up another humanitarian front in the problematic area of the concentration camps, galvanized Whitehall into taking the view that the ICRC was 'definitely attempting to obtain an operative control over matters which are entirely outside the supervisory functions of the Committee'.[72] As this both breached the agreement with Geneva over the White Ships and, seemingly, threatened British interests, the reaction from Whitehall to restrict the ICRC's expansion was understandable.

In the end, this hunger for expansion, combined with the fact that 'the Committee refused to take these restrictions (imposed by the blockade authorities) as final' meant that relations between MEW and the ICRC remained tense for the duration of the war.[73]

This necessarily had an impact on the ICRC's plans to expand its role and gain greater recognition as a professional, capable humanitarian actor. Hopes for ICRC delegates on-board parcel-laden White Ships to 'move about freely on the battlefield at agreed times', dispensing relief at will were not forthcoming and the Committee remained devoid of the sort of autonomy that it clearly craved.[74] Despite Zollinger's advocacy, agreement was not reached by the Allies for a plan to send relief to the concentration camps until June 1944, and this was primarily on account of the activism of the American War Refugee Board and public pressure in the United States. The ICRC's contribution, as had been the case in the White Ships proposals, was to provide a system of delivery for relief in the form of the CCPS. The actual ability to activate that system, however, was dependent on the pressure of broader public sentiment and the actions of other, more politically empowered, humanitarian actors such as the ARC.[75] The fact that the White Ships and the concurrent developments in humanitarian planning in the war's middle years did not completely break down the principle of 'victory before relief' or empower the ICRC to the extent that it wished did not alter the fact that, from 1942 onwards, the Committee's scope of action and ambitions grew exponentially. This general expansion of the ICRC not only reignited long-held concerns in Whitehall over the Committee's capabilities but also raised the question of how its delegates – spread out across the world and often acting independently of significant oversight or scrutiny – could maintain their neutrality and impartiality.

6
Prestige and Credibility, 1942–3

Neutrality questioned

Since its inception, the ICRC's prestige and credibility have been decisive in its ability to present itself to belligerents as an impartial and neutral humanitarian actor.[1] As Max Huber himself opined in 1936, the ICRC 'must always afford all parties the guarantee of as unbiased a judgement as possible' and 'avoid every suspicion of partiality, political or other'.[2] Neutrality, as understood and practised by Huber, was a means of detaching the ICRC from the political and strategic concerns of states, for whose soldiers and citizens it sought to provide succour. Through this approach the ICRC could present itself to belligerents as a reliable service agency – one that would abstain from recourse to partisan attitudes; maintain discretion; and carry out its humanitarian duties without interfering in the conduct of military matters. Neutrality in this sense, manifested as a form of operational restriction, confined the ICRC to the role of independent agent for relief work. It did not, as has been argued elsewhere, provide the medium through which the Committee could become an anti-war agitator or promoter of pacifism.[3]

Impartiality implied a contrary value to neutrality, namely, that of expansion. This was because of the ICRC's dedication to provide impartial relief to *all* victims of war, irrespective of their ethnicity, class, age, religion, gender or state allegiance. This policy of 'relief for all' was viewed by Geneva as compatible with its neutrality. By focusing its efforts on the suffering of all victims of war – not as citizens of states but as human beings first and foremost – the ICRC could place itself above the interests of belligerents and instead focus its efforts on the 'higher principle' of humanity, thus remaining neutral while providing impartial relief. The emergence of these two principles as cornerstones of the ICRC's operations in the years leading up to the Second World War was very much a product of the organization's history. In terms of political geography the place of the ICRC's birth, Switzerland – acknowledged as a permanent neutral state at the 1815 Congress of Vienna – was a nation whose very identity was bound to its neutrality. It was an identity, moreover, that the Committee's founders viewed as crucial for giving their organization its credibility and unique status as *the* neutral humanitarian organization in Europe. This sanctity of neutrality became official in 1930 when, under Huber's guidance, the ICRC officially recognized the term 'neutral' as a necessary component of its character and the practices of its delegates.[4]

With the exception of Japan and the Soviet Union, the belligerents of the Second World War in the main recognized the neutrality of the ICRC.[5] Beneath this acceptance of the ICRC as an institution, however, certain belligerents suspected that the individual delegate in the field could not always be trusted. More often than not these suspicions arose from misunderstandings over what the ICRC's neutrality meant in practice and how that neutrality was reconciled by Geneva with its commitment to impartially. The shipping of relief supplies into France by the ICRC and the ARC in 1940 was one of the first instances in which this lack of understanding influenced British perceptions of Red Cross humanitarian operations. In addition to reservations over the supplies being sent into the Reich to feed POW labourers, the British were also uneasy when rumours emerged that the distribution was being handled by the Nationalsozialistische Volkswohlfahrt (NSV), a Nazi 'humanitarian' organization that Hitler had ordered into France in early June in order to promote collaboration by winning the hearts and minds of displaced French. Whitehall's fear was that, owing to the NSV's involvement, any humanitarian goodwill that Britain might have earned by allowing the distribution of food by the ICRC would be snatched from them by the Germans. At the very least, the involvement of a Nazi organization in an ICRC relief operation suggested that the latter could not be trusted to carry out relief work in a truly neutral manner in territories either governed by or under the influence of the enemy.[6]

The reasons for this impression were varied. For some British officials it was formed from the simple fact that the Committee's delegates were unarmed, civilian representatives of a non-belligerent private organization, and as such could only do so much to prevent the pilfering of Red Cross supplies by armed soldiers. Evidence of this problem was manifold. The turning over of Red Cross supplies intended for civilians by the French to the Germans, the endemic practice of the requisitioning of Red Cross supplies by Axis forces in Greece and the Far East, and the inability of the ICRC to get supplies with regularity past the guards in certain camps gave weight to the argument that, when faced with the task of performing humanitarian deeds in areas under enemy occupation, the notion that the ICRC could distribute relief independent of Axis interference was a dubious one. Most British officials saw this as an unfortunate but necessary condition of the ICRC's work, rather than a cause for genuine suspicion of the Committee's motives. Few doubted, for example, that the work done in Greece by Robert Brunel was both admirable and in keeping with the spirit of the Red Cross's mission. What was questioned was the extent to which Brunel's faith in the Comité de Haute Direction – comprised in part of Italians, Germans and Axis-friendly Greeks – compromised the impartiality of his work. Had requisitions not taken place, the noted capability of Brunel's delegates to maintain 'excellent collaboration with the Axis authorities' might have been recognized by Whitehall as an indicator of the ICRC's capability to maintain the principles of its work under the eyes of the enemy. Instead, the willingness of the Committee to engage with Axis authorities on the premise of good faith alone – and in return have their supplies requisitioned – created the impression that the naive humanitarians were letting themselves be exploited.[7]

The MEW was the Whitehall department most concerned with the ICRC's relationship with the occupation forces. Moreover, the Ministry was not beyond acting on its suspicions. In the midst of the discussions over the ICRC's relief plans for Greece, a request was made by MEW for an investigation into 'Red Cross correspondence which throws any light on the International Red Cross being used by the enemy for exploitation of neutrals as intermediaries for the passing of information, particularly in connection with shipping intelligence'.[8] In addition to concerns over the passing of intelligence, there was also suspicion of a scam being run in Greece by members of Brunel's delegation, whereby funds would be requested from private organizations in the United States in order to purchase food supplies, which would then be sold off for a profit on the Greek black market. At the very least there was concern that some ICRC delegates were making 'private arrangements' for the shipment of foodstuffs in the occupied territories and thus breaching the blockade authorities' condition that they be informed how much food was being moved within the blockade and for where and whom it was destined.[9]

The British were not unique among the belligerents in suspecting ICRC delegates of abusing the freedom of movement granted by their neutrality to act with partiality. Marcel Junod was detained by the Gestapo in 1940 after he had discussions with interned French officers. Although this was a requirement of his duties as a camp inspector, the Germans believed he might have been passing intelligence on behalf of the Deuxième Bureau. Japanese suspicions of ICRC volunteers in the Far East were even more serious and had greater consequences. Hans Schweizer was detained by the Kempeitai in the wake of the blowing up of Japanese ships in Singapore harbour in 1943 by agents from the Special Operations Executive, on the suspicion that he had assisted in the sabotage. The murders of Matthaeus and Betsy Vischer, along with twenty-four other civilians, were prompted by the belief that they were plotting a POW-led coup against the Japanese occupation forces in Borneo.[10]

Although no ICRC delegates were subjected by the British or Americans to anything comparable to the aforementioned, the same basic concern over how these humanitarians could be trusted to remain neutral in the occupied territories, and the extent to which the organization's neutrality would provide an opening for enemy agent infiltration, led to similar suspicions of ICRC involvement in espionage. This was particularly the case in 1942, when the Committee opened a number of new delegations in Africa and the Far East. In response to this expansion of the ICRC's presence across the globe, the British not only instituted tougher censorship of the Committee's mail but also laid down a requirement that all new delegates had to be screened by British intelligence more thoroughly than had hitherto been the case, before taking up their overseas postings.[11] Although in one respect such oversight could be seen as a British encroachment on ICRC business, in practice Geneva understood both the reliance it had on belligerent agreement to expand its work and the need to ensure that delegates met the standards of impartiality and neutrality Huber demanded. As a result, the ICRC proved very cooperative with the British on the issue of suspicious and/or troublesome delegates.

Georges Vaucher, the ICRC's man in Cairo, was one such troublemaker. A constant critic of the British administration in Egypt, Vaucher's volatile personality – unique among the generally amiable, upright Swiss who worked for the ICRC – came fully to the surface when a delegate named Phillip Junod was sent to help him manage the increased workload in North Africa in the spring of 1941. Within weeks the two men were squabbling to such an extent that the British – believing that the tumult was affecting the relief effort for POWs – requested that Geneva have Vaucher removed. Somewhat embarrassed at the situation, the ICRC agreed to the British request in the hopes of salvaging its delegation's reputation in Cairo.[12] Haccius offered similar cooperation when the DPW announced new screening measures, and over the course of 1942 he sent a number of requests to the British for new delegations in Cairo, Colombo, Port Au Prince and Hong Kong, among other places. For the most part, these applications for new delegations were approved without difficulty. In some cases, however, the ICRC's choices were questionable.[13] The proposed delegate in Macao, for example, was rejected by the War Office on the grounds that he had known affiliations with the Japanese and was on a British 'suspect list' of politically unreliable figures in the Far East. Similar suspicions were raised over Paul Giroud, the delegate appointed to Diego Suarez in 1942, who was permitted by the British to take up his post, albeit with the requirement that he be put under surveillance until it could be determined that the 'pro-Axis sympathies' he was known to espouse in 1940 had faded. Nothing came of this monitoring of Giroud. In the case of a hotelier-turned humanitarian at ICRC Cairo named Hans Bon, however, deeper cracks appeared in both the ICRC's recruitment policies and British screening measures. Bon was initially approved by DPW on 18 April 1942. Following a further investigation over the course of the next eighteen months, however, MI5 concluded that Bon was the most pro-Nazi in a family that had both a history of allegiance to National Socialism and business ties to several companies that, on account of their connections to the German military, were on the blockade authorities' blacklist. As had been the case with Vaucher, Whitehall and Geneva were in agreement that a mistake had been made and Bon was removed from his post in December 1943, after which new, even stricter measures of screening were introduced.[14]

The Bon affair touched a sensitive nerve not only for the British but also for the Americans, whose strategic focus on North Africa, first as a target for invasion in 1942 and, in 1943, as a base from which to attack Italy, considerably raised suspicions in the Allied camp of spies in the region.[15] In addition to the introduction by British intelligence of new screening procedures for ICRC delegates over the summer of 1943–4, Allied Force Headquarters (AFHQ) advised commanders in North Africa that the ICRC should be 'treated with considerable circumspection' as they were not considered to be 'reliable' from an Allied point of view. Red Cross correspondence sent from Cairo and Algiers to Geneva was also made subject to increased censorship and instructions were issued to American soldiers to confine any conversation with ICRC delegates to Red Cross matters only.[16]

This suspicion that the ICRC could be used as a cover for espionage was not without some foundation. During the 1920s, British intelligence had uncovered a small spy ring in Switzerland whose leader, Dr Serge Batosky, was revealed to be a 'notorious Bolshevik conspirator with Red Cross cover'. Specifically, Batosky was operating a branch of the Soviet Red Cross while simultaneously working for the cause of the Comintern.[17] The Americans also had some experience of humanitarians as spies. In the aftermath of the First World War, Herbert Hoover's relief programme had been used as a cover by the fledgling American intelligence community to monitor the political situation in Central Europe. Moreover, David Bruce, who in 1941 became a key member of the American Office of Strategic Services (OSS), had begun the war as the chief delegate of the ARC in Britain. The idea that the Red Cross could be involved in espionage was, therefore, far from extraordinary to the minds of the OSS, who duly launched an investigation in 1942 into possible links between Berlin and certain ICRC delegates in the Mediterranean.[18]

The report that was eventually compiled by OSS in February 1944 named forty-nine ICRC workers suspected of such links, of whom twenty-one were identified as being not simply volunteers but official delegates from Geneva. In addition to accusations of passing intelligence on Allied troops movements and transporting German spies into North Africa on-board White Ships leaving Spain, one delegate based in Turkey, Giuseppe Beretta, was found to have received gold stolen from Hungarian Jews. Beretta's treasure was discovered by the ICRC and his dismissal from the Committee ordered in February 1945. Though highly inappropriate, Beretta's crime appears to have been one of self-interest pursued under the cover of Red Cross neutrality and was by no means a sign of general corruption within the ICRC. Jean Pagan, a delegate in Algeria, who was arrested in October 1943 by the French military and found guilty of running a spy ring, was a more serious case. Before his eventual execution by firing squad in December 1944 Pagan claimed to have recruited another ICRC delegate, George Graz, and passed information to contacts within the German Embassy in Berne. Graz was himself detained for questioning soon after Pagan's denouncement. He was, however, released with no charge by the French on 18 October.[19]

The 1996 report compiled by the ICRC as a response to the declassification of the OSS files found little basis for the accusations of espionage levelled by Pagan at others, most of whom – contrary to OSS's claims – were volunteers rather than fully fledged members of the ICRC. Indeed, Pagan had left the ICRC in 1942, a full year before he was arrested for passing information to the Germans. Based on the decision by the French to release him after interrogation in October

1943, the Committee also concluded that George Graz was not an asset of German intelligence and was instead simply 'imprudent' in his handling of sensitive information. The other man implicated in Pagan's supposed spy ring, an ICRC volunteer named Jean Sublet, was found guilty only of having been less than impartial in his efforts to help a French collaborator working for the Germans to avoid execution in Morocco. When this story was uncovered by the ICRC in November 1944, Sublet was dismissed. All in all, the ICRC's findings concluded that, with the exception of Pagan and Beretta, the indiscretions of the accused ICRC workers were either minor or non-existent and many of the accusations were based on no more than the OSS's 'total ignorance of the organization's role and work'.[20]

If one considers the number of basic mistakes made in the OSS reports, there is little reason to doubt the Committee's conclusion that ignorance was a key factor in shaping American suspicions. This ignorance appears to have in part developed from the fact that North Africa was the first theatre of the Second World War in which American soldiers experienced the peculiarity of Swiss in neat suits with Red Cross armbands asking – as if possessed of some inviolable right – to see and speak with Axis prisoners. As had been the case in 1940 with the British, this first exposure to the ICRC's way of doing things led to confusion and misunderstanding. The very fact that ICRC delegates had contact with German consular officials, for example, perplexed some of those attached to the investigation, as they worked from the erroneous premise that 'the Germans gain little from the humanitarian side of IRC activities. The Germans must be getting some compensatory advantages.'[21] For this reason, routine discussions between crew on-board White Ships docked at Lisbon and the ICRC delegate François Ehrenhold were interpreted by the OSS as an exchange of shipping intelligence between Red Cross workers and pro-Nazi Portuguese. The deployment of Jean Duchosal to Cairo in mid-1942 for the purposes of pleading the case to visiting Soviet officials for the establishment of a Moscow delegation was viewed as a possible attempt by the Committee to snoop on the Cairo Conference. Finally, Paul Burckhard – a junior ICRC volunteer in Naples suspected of passing information to the Germans – was confused by the OSS with Carl J. Burckhardt, on which basis the Americans concluded that the ICRC had been infiltrated by the enemy at the highest level of its leadership![22]

These more outlandish accusations had little basis in reality. The very fact that this investigation was launched, however, indicates that for the Americans the ICRC delegate was regarded not only as a possible pawn of the Axis but also as one who would be willing to work to the detriment of Allied interests. In this respect the Americans were not alone in their suspicions. George Warner – whose pre-war experiences in Berne and at the Geneva Conference of 1929 made him one of the better informed British officials on the ICRC – held to the belief that the Committee was not only susceptible to manipulation but was possibly inclined to favour non-British, specifically German, interests deliberately.[23] Although this was informed in part by his opinion of the ICRC as a naive and amateur organization, his knowledge of Burckhardt was also probably of significance. Warner was aware that Burckhardt shared a long-standing friendship with Joachim Ribbentrop's deputy, Baron Ernst von Weizsäcker, and the German Consul in Geneva, Wolfgang Krauel. These connections, combined with the sympathy Burckhardt showed for the German's arguments over Danzig in the late 1930s led Warner to caution his former colleagues in Whitehall in 1944, that the ICRC Vice-President was 'possibly pro-Fascist' and on this basis rejected the suggestion that Burckhardt become the new Swiss Minister in London. Warner's opinions, outlandish though they seemed, were an understandable construct of his pre-war experience of Burckhardt. The latter's closeness to top German officials while High Commissioner in Danzig was widely known in the Foreign Office. So too were Burckhardt's efforts, in the final years of peace, to broker some form of agreement between the British and Hitler – whom he met personally at the Berghof in 1939. Because of this, Warner and certain mandarins such as William Strang and even Anthony Eden found it difficult to reconcile their pre-war conception of Burckhardt – the non-English speaking, Nazi-meeting, peace deal seeking, highly political man of affairs – with his wartime incarnation as vice-president of a humanitarian organization that abided by a strict code of neutral impartiality.[24]

For his part, Burckhardt also thought very little of the British. As an ardent anti-Communist and peace seeker, he viewed the alliance between Churchill and Stalin as an unnatural partnership which might possibly lead to a post-war Europe turned over to Communism. On a personal level, Burckhardt – who was a friend and supporter of the former Foreign Secretary, Lord Halifax – also disliked and distrusted his successor, Anthony Eden. This was not only because Burckhardt regarded him as 'an advocate of a decidedly pro-Soviet orientation' in British foreign policy but also because of his memory of the 'condescension' Eden had shown towards him during his time as High Commissioner in Danzig.[25] In truth, Eden's view of Burckhardt was more one of circumspection than derision. It was not so much Burckhardt's politics that

seemed to have troubled Eden as his irritating proclivity to play amateur diplomat both in Danzig and particularly during the war, when he
was supposed to be concerning himself only with Red Cross matters.[26]
In this respect, Eden's views were typical of most others in Whitehall:
Burckhardt was no collaborator, but he was a meddler who needed to
be treated with caution.

The extent to which Foreign Office wariness of Burckhardt could
affect British–ICRC relations was evident in the autumn of 1941 when
he and Odier travelled to London for a week of meetings with Whitehall
officials. On the agenda for discussion were the state of British POW
welfare, the ongoing disputes with the BRC over jurisdiction and information sharing and the thorny issue of concessions for the blockade,
particularly as it pertained to Greece. Despite the validity of these matters, one of the first reactions in Whitehall was to regard Burckhardt's
visit as cover for a peace feeler. This impression was not an irrational
one. In early 1939, Burckhardt had conducted a roving peace mission
across Europe on behalf of the then Foreign Secretary Lord Halifax and,
more grievously, in July 1940 – by which time Burckhardt had supposedly become a non-political actor – he had discussions with David
Kelly about the possibility of the British coming to the negotiating
table with Hitler.[27] Based both on the memory of these prior events
and, to a lesser extent, Czech intelligence reports received from Berne
in the weeks before, it was thought that Burckhardt might be carrying
to Britain peace proposals either from Hitler or on behalf of a middle
man, such as the Swiss Federal Council's Marcel Pilet-Golaz. So palpable
was the concern that David Kelly was advised to warn Burckhardt that
permission for the visit would only be granted if the latter agreed to
confine himself to discussion of Red Cross matters alone. In the end, the
meetings did go ahead, albeit in an atmosphere of tension that did little
to better each party's negative view of the other. Burckhardt was more
than aware that he was a *bête noire* in Whitehall and he believed that he
was watched by British intelligence during his journey from Geneva to
London.[28] It is highly likely also that Burckhardt, vain as he was, would
have taken umbrage at the fact that neither Eden nor Churchill was
willing to meet him, and for much of his journey he was chaperoned by
the comparatively lowly Walter Roberts from the PWD. As it turned out,
these supervisory measures were not entirely unwarranted.

Although the British were not made aware of his machinations until
after the war, Burckhardt had been active in peace discussions since
mid-1940 with associates of Herman Goering and members of the
German opposition to Hitler. Discussions with the latter, conducted

principally through the former German diplomat, Ulrich von Hassell, had even drawn Burckhardt into Rudolf Hess's disastrous peace mission to Scotland in May 1941. Moreover, despite the reassurances he gave to Kelly, it appears that Burckhardt did set out to London in late 1941 with the intention to talk something other than Red Cross business. He had told Pilet-Golaz that he only wanted Odier to accompany him in order to maintain the façade to the British that the journey was a strictly ICRC affair. There is also evidence to suggest that while in London he found time to meet with his old associate from the Danzig days, the pre-war appeaser R. A. 'Rab' Butler – by this time a marginalized Minister of Education in Churchill's government – with whom he probably discussed, albeit with futility, the need for a peace deal between Germany and Britain. Despite this meeting, however, there is no evidence that Burckhardt performed any function as a genuine peace emissary during his visit to London in 1941. At best, he was simply entertaining his long-held pretences to be a mediator of belligerents and bringer of peace.[29] The extent to which suspicions lingered over his official business, however, can be gauged by the fact that Walter Roberts was asked to provide a brief report after Burckhardt had returned to Switzerland, the purpose of which was to confirm that the latter had confined himself to Red Cross-related discussions.[30] The fact that Burckhardt did not launch a genuine peace feeler is not surprising. By this stage in the war the chances of Burckhardt, or anyone else for that matter, brokering some form of accord between Britain and Germany had faded. This did not mean, however, that he had forsaken either his desire to play the role of diplomat or his penchant for politics. Indeed, from 1942 onwards Burckhardt appears to have channelled this proclivity more so than ever into his work with the ICRC, endeavouring both to improve his own reputation in Whitehall and inject a new sense of pragmatism into the Committee's work.

Carl J. Burckhardt's 'Realpolitik Humanitarianism'

Regarded by those who worked closest to him as the 'grand politician' of the ICRC, Burckhardt was never satisfied with being a mere humanitarian. For much of his professional life he had yearned to be an international figure of importance and, indeed, in 1940 he came close to turning away from the ICRC in order to pursue a position on the Swiss Federal Council. When this opportunity did not eventuate he returned to the Committee, though his ambitions for a grander role in the drama of the war remained.[31] Bereft of the opportunity to play peacemaker or politician, Burckhardt channelled his energy into the ICRC, muscling Odier out of her role as primary blockade agitator, developing the JRC, founding the White Ships and contributing to the creation of Schwarzenberg's Concentration Camp Parcel Scheme.[32] In this respect, Burckhardt's restlessness and ambition were well matched to the ICRC's imperative to expand its purview in the war's middle years. The problem for Burckhardt was that the ICRC was still a humanitarian organization, mandated to provide succour to victims of war. It was not an arena for high politics. The only avenue open to him in this regard was that of humanitarian diplomacy – the act of negotiating with belligerents with an aim to get them to adhere to IHL and/or principles of humanity – which the ICRC has always, and still does, practice in various forms.[33]

Burckhardt's visit to London to negotiate on blockade matters was a stand-alone venture into humanitarian diplomacy. On a day-to-day basis the ICRC was still subordinate to the Protecting Power, which was prescribed in the Convention to carry out mediation between belligerents if they requested neutral assistance in a dispute. Officially, therefore, the scope for the ICRC delegate to play the role of mediator between belligerents was very narrow. Max Huber's attempts to interject himself into the negotiations between Berlin and London over POW exchanges were mostly unsuccessful and, when exchanges did take place, the ICRC's involvement was usually confined to providing supervision for the transfer operations.[34] The ICRC's advocacy for a greater role – already hampered by Allied preference for the Protecting Power – was further damaged in the eyes of the Allies by the fact that the Germans and the Italians were generally more amenable to Geneva's forays into mediation.[35]

For Burckhardt, the inability of the ICRC to assert itself in this field and the subordination to Berne in matters of humanitarianism had led to an 'irreparable loss of prestige'. This assertion, made by him in December 1942, reflected a wider crisis of functionality, purpose and direction that beset that Committee during that year. The ICRC may have expanded its operations, but there was still an undercurrent of amateurism in its day-to-day activities. The relief departments had poor liaison with the Central Agency, Haccius was 'not as up to date' on POW information as he wanted to be, and the leadership – as was evident in the recruitment of the likes of Pagan and Berretta – no longer possessed the same close, almost familial, oversight it once had over delegates. As Chenevière wrote to Huber in the summer of 1942, there was 'a deplorable lack of liaison, of discipline' throughout the

Committee.[36] As the war spread, the bombing of cities intensified and details of the Holocaust began to emerge, Burckhardt also worried that the ICRC was failing to keep up with the pace of the war, failing to use its resources wisely and that, when the fighting ended, the Committee's use and effectiveness would, as had occurred in 1919, be called into question.[37] In response to these rising apprehensions, a meeting of the ICRC leadership was held in May 1942, at which the sinews of a new, more pragmatic policy of humanitarian action were formed. As with so much change in the ICRC, alterations to its character and practice were gradual. It took most of 1942 in fact for the internal dysfunction of bureaucratic liaison to begin to be addressed and for the idea of dispensing with the utopianism of the war's early years in favour of a focus on achievable goals and 'practical and local activities' to permeate into the Committee's practice.[38] Nonetheless, the conscious effort to address its failings was a big step in the ICRC's wartime evolution.

Burckhardt's role in steering the Committee in this direction was very important. Increasingly beset by poor health – which was probably engendered by the stress of seeing the Red Cross ideal consumed by barbarism – Huber all but handed the day-to-day running of the ICRC over to Burckhardt in the autumn of 1942. This transfer came at one of the most crucial and controversial moments in the ICRC's wartime history. At a meeting at the Hôtel Metropole on 14 October 1942 – unattended by Huber, who was convalescing in Nyon – the ICRC leadership agreed, in defiance of the wishes of some Committee members, that it would not launch a public démarche to Berlin in protest against the atrocities being inflicted upon Jews. The decision to opt for silence was made for two main reasons. The first was to conform to the wishes of the Swiss Federal Council, whose representatives at the meeting, the honourary ICRC delegates Edouard de Haller and Philippe Etter, argued that an appeal of this nature would compromise the ICRC's neutrality and impartiality. Despite his anxieties over the Protecting Power, Burckhardt supported the appointment of de Haller and Etter to the Committee and backed their argument in favour of silence. He reasoned that speaking out over the atrocities would do nothing more than squander the ICRC's prestige and credibility in the eyes of the Germans. Better, Burckhardt believed, to abstain from grand gestures and instead work discreetly on practical measures that could ameliorate the sufferings of Jews and other victims of war. Huber, who was especially concerned about the possibility of the démarche being seen as a breach of the ICRC's apolitical impartiality, also let it be known, from afar, that he supported the motion for silence.[39]

This episode remains the most controversial in the ICRC's history, and has been used as a locus for criticism of the Committee's institutional inflexibility, weakness and/or subservience to the Swiss Federal Council.[40] The intention here is not to repeat these arguments, but to contextualize the 'non-appeal' within the wider crises that beset the ICRC in the war's middle years. Although it smacked of selective humanitarianism, the 'non-appeal' was indicative of the ICRC's wider turn – despite the concerns of some attendees at the meeting over the long-term implications of silence for the ICRC's reputation – away from idealism. This turn was prompted by immediate wartime considerations, held by Burckhardt in particular, which demanded that the right of ICRC delegates to visit POW and civilian internment camps be safeguarded. At the heart of the 'non-appeal' therefore, lay the notion of preserving the ICRC's prestige and credibility and maintaining good relations with Berlin, as a means of ensuring that the Committee's day-to-day work in the many camps of the Reich would not be curtailed by a government incensed by accusations of atrocity. That this impetus dovetailed with the concerns of the Swiss Federal Council to keep the Germans pacified all but guaranteed that the suggestion to speak out about the Holocaust was shelved at the behest of senior ICRC members at the October meeting.[41]

For Burckhardt, this turn to 'realpolitik humanitarianism' served an even wider purpose than the maintenance of good relations with Berlin. At the time of the 'non-appeal', he was endeavouring to address two related problems that had bedevilled both the ICRC and himself for much of the war: the political amateurism of the Committee and his own reputation as a troublemaker in the eyes of the British. Burckhardt's golden opportunity to address these issues began a week prior to the 'non-appeal' via his engagement in the so-called Shackling Crisis. This began on 8 October 1942 when the German Government announced that 1,376 British and Canadian prisoners of war had been shackled and would continue to be so for twelve hours a day for an indefinite period as an act of reprisal against Allied violations of the Convention. The first violation had occurred during an Allied raid on Dieppe on 19 August, in which captured German prisoners were bound and blindfolded. Although the Germans initially accepted the British pledge to launch an inquiry into the matter, a more severe violation of the Convention in the aftermath of a similar raid on the Channel Island of Sark on 4 October prompted Berlin to respond with the shackling order. This, in turn, was met by a reprisal from the British, who on 9 October coerced the Canadian Government into shackling 1,100 German POWs held in

Canada. Driven both by Hitler's desire to use the POWs as bargaining chips for better conditions for German prisoners on the Eastern Front, and by Churchill's need to promulgate the ethos of never backing down, the situation rapidly escalated beyond the scope of the original incidents.[42]

Sensing an opportunity, Burckhardt moved swiftly to involve himself and on 9 October the Foreign Office received a message from Clifford Norton, conveying an offer from the vice-president to mediate in the matter. Less than an hour after hearing from Burckhardt, Norton received a similar offer of mediation from Marcel Pilet-Golaz on behalf of the Swiss Federal Council.[43] In the race to be confirmed as mediator, Pilet-Golaz had a significant head start, not only on account of British preference for the Protecting Power but also because of a change in the British diplomatic corps in Switzerland. David Kelly, the British Minister in Berne, was a friend of Pilet-Golaz: however, he also enjoyed a relationship of 'great cordiality', 'friendship and hospitality' with Burckhardt, to whom, when Kelly was reassigned to Buenos Aires in April 1942, he saw fit to compose a parting letter of personal thanks.[44] No such sentiments were forthcoming from Kelly's replacement, Clifford Norton, who had been the Foreign Office's chargé d'affaires in Poland during Burckhardt's tenure as High Commissioner in Danzig. As an adamant supporter of the Poles it is probable that Norton, like many other British officials, found Burckhardt's seemingly pro-German conduct unsettling, or, at the very least, gained the not unreasonable impression of Burckhardt as a wearisome would-be diplomat.[45] Norton was, however, a fan of Pilet-Golaz and was sympathetic, as many in Whitehall had been since 1940, to Switzerland's geographical plight in the jaws of the Third Reich. This sympathy for the Swiss Federal Council, plus the undoubted successes Berne had in tending to the welfare of British prisoners over the course of 1942, further bolstered the Protecting Power's reputation in Britain.[46]

With regards to the Shackling Crisis, however, neither Berne nor Geneva was embraced by the British. Indeed, both the Swiss Federal Council and the ICRC were thought to have had 'a misconception of the position they held in the matter'. On this basis, both offers of mediation were refused. Churchill took this rejection a step further, by implying that a consideration of either offer was 'only a step to mediate peace', characteristic – so the Permanent Under Secretary at the Foreign Office, Alexander Cadogan, believed – of the Prime Minister's 'silly fighting mood' in discussions on what to do about the shackling.[47] More so than any reservations over Swiss peace making or ICRC amateurism, there was a genuine concern in Whitehall that to seek mediation – and thus show weakness – in the face of Berlin's actions would only exacerbate a worrying trend towards callousness and brutality in the treatment of POWs that had emerged in the previous year. This had begun by Hitler issuing his infamous Commando Order in October 1941, which prescribed execution for soldiers or espionage operatives caught in German territory. This was followed in December by the order to reduce rations for Allied POWs by a third, on the premise that Red Cross parcels would make up the calorie shortfall. Over the course of 1942 in some camps POW mail was also suspended or delayed. The British, for their part, had also contributed their fair share to compromising the norms of treatment for POWs. In March 1942 German officers on-board a transport ship bound for Durban were beaten and denied access to their personal belongings by their captors, and in camps in Palestine German POWs were, on British orders, placed into the hands of Polish guards and habitually maltreated. Owing to this context, the Shackling Crisis – far from being regarded as an anomaly – marked a significant point in the war's escalation, at which the British were determined to draw a line in the sand and seek retaliation, rather than mediation, as a means of ensuring that the Germans backed down.[48]

Burckhardt's intentions were entirely different. First, there was a clear sense of ambition in his actions, to expand upon the 'humanitarian empire building' he had begun with the JRC and the White Ships by pushing the ICRC into the Protecting Power's territory. A second, more justifiable, reason for Burckhardt to get involved was the need to preserve the belligerents' adherence to the Convention, the articles of which had been incrementally violated in the months prior to the shackling order. Burckhardt recognized early that if the practice of reciprocal shackling escalated the sanctity of the Convention might be further jeopardized and with it the ICRC's very authority to act. A picture of the effect such a renunciation would have on the ICRC's operational effectiveness had already been painted in the Far East and on the Eastern Front. As Burckhardt pointed out to the British – in an attempt both to convey his fears and to appeal to British self-interest – the escalation of the shackling 'might seriously jeopardize the entire question of prisoners of war and affect Red Cross work for them'.[49] This argument, however, did little to persuade Whitehall, where the onus remained on first matching the Germans and then beating them at their own game.

Much like the blockade concessions granted the ICRC, it was influence from across the Atlantic, rather than an acknowledgement of Geneva's viewpoint, that eventually altered the British view.

Specifically, agitation from the Canadian Government – whose soldiers were among those captured at Dieppe and who had agreed, with reservations, to shackle German prisoners in Canada – was a key factor in the British agreeing to seek third-party mediation. Unsurprisingly, Pilet-Golaz was the preferred agent for this task. As the British Consul in Geneva, Harry Livingston, made clear to Huber, the British saw the ICRC's duty as being to investigate the extent to which the Convention had been breached and inform the Protecting Power of its conclusions.[50] Actual involvement of the ICRC in negotiations to end the shackling was neither anticipated nor welcomed. Burckhardt remained undeterred, stridently so. On 15 October – the same day Livingston informed Huber that the Protecting Power was the preferred mediator – Burckhardt telephoned de Haller to inform him that he was also active in a mediation capacity. Specifically, Wolfgang Krauel, Burckhardt's old friend and German Consul in Geneva, had begun to contact 'competent military authorities' in Berlin on Burckhardt's behalf as part of what Ernst von Weizsäcker called a campaign of 'guerrilla diplomacy'.[51] So began Burckhardt's thirteen-month-long effort to end the Shackling Crisis, extend the Committee's purview into humanitarian diplomacy and prove his worth as a mediator.

Burckhardt's efforts were far from subtle and more than a little cavalier. Attempts made by Livingston in late October to rein in the would-be diplomat – with a polite reminder that the Protecting Power was Whitehall's chosen mediator – were ignored by Burckhardt, who instead drew on every contact he had in the German administration in an effort to get the ICRC positioned as the key mediator in the Shackling Crisis. To this end, he wrote to the president of the German Red Cross, the ruthless SS Grüppenfuhrer Ernst Grawitz, suggesting that the shackles be removed in an incremental fashion, under ICRC supervision and with no publicity. As Roland Marti reported, this proposal soon reached the ears of no less a figure than Hitler, who, supported by his ever sycophantic Chief of Staff, Field Marshal Wilhelm Keitel, thought Burckhardt's letter was a 'reasonable document'.[52] This clandestine approach to solving the crisis was complemented by the organizing of a more traditional response on the part of the ICRC: inspections of the camps where the shackling was taking place. In November Burckhardt instructed Haccius to visit camps in Britain and, in the interests of reciprocity, inspections were also organized for Marti in Germany and Ernst Maag, the ICRC delegate, in Canada.[53] Although ostensibly these inspections were a case of the ICRC carrying out its traditional duties, for Burckhardt their purpose was to form a basis upon which to suggest to the belligerents that, as the prisoners were not being maltreated, the matter could be resolved quietly by the simultaneous removal of the shackles.[54] By early December these endeavours seemed poised to bear fruit. Not only did word reach Geneva from Odier that officials in Berlin were in favour of Burckhardt's efforts but also Krauel informed Burckhardt that Hitler was willing to consider removing the shackles over Christmas, a development that the no doubt exuberant vice-president quickly passed on to Livingston in order to ensure a reciprocal gesture from the British.[55] At the very moment when he believed he had brought the crisis to an end, however, Burckhardt's efforts were trumped by Pilet-Golaz, who launched his own successful appeal on 8 December for both sides to unshackle their prisoners over Christmas. It turned out to be a small victory. On 26 December the Germans reapplied the shackles to their charges and the cycle of retaliation began anew.[56]

The Pilet-Golaz initiative greatly irritated Burckhardt, prompting his aforementioned lament over the loss of the Committee's prestige to the Protecting Power.[57] The question is, was Burckhardt right to feel that his thunder had been stolen? There was certainly some support for his view from MI6, which in early December compiled an assessment of the most likely avenues in Berlin through which the crisis could be solved. Discounting the influence of the likes of Keitel and Ribbentrop on Hitler's thinking, MI6 instead reported that Grawitz – Burckhardt's primary contact – had the best chance of softening Hitler's stance and getting the shackling to end, an assessment that seemingly confirmed Burckhardt's wisdom in using this channel to the Führer.[58] The fact, however, that MI6's recommendations were ignored until early 1943, when it became clear that the Pilet-Golaz Christmas cessation had not led to a permanent solution, is indicative of the extent to which Burckhardt was not viewed as a viable mediator by the British. This was reaffirmed by Norton in the spring of 1943 when he derided Burckhardt's reliance on Krauel and complained that the former's interjection into Pilet-Gloaz's initiative in December had 'upset the delicate negotiations'.[59] With this negative perception of Burckhardt's efforts in mind, it is difficult to believe that he could have solved the crisis in December 1942. To do so would have required the agreement of not only Berlin but also London, where trust in Burckhardt's judgement – beyond the MI6 report – was hard to find.

For his part, Burckhardt seems to have acknowledged his credibility problem and made sure to coordinate his efforts with those of Pilet-Golaz better.[60] There was much in the inspection reports of the ICRC and the Protecting Power to encourage a new initiative to solve the crisis in 1943. At Oflag VIIB some of the supposedly shackled POWs had taken to 'carrying their manacles and swinging them nonchalantly as their hosts tried to count them'. The opposite, however, was true at Stalag VIIIB, where heavier chains had been applied and forced labour imposed upon one shackled prisoner who had a medical certificate prescribing only light work.[61] The inconsistency of these measures, combined with information from Grawitz on the increasing discontent within the Oberkommando der Wehrmacht and the Auswärtiges Amt over the reprisals, painted a picture of discord in Berlin. In response both Burckhardt and Pilet-Golaz reignited their efforts in early August with the latter informing Norton that both Keitel and Ribbentrop were planning to confront Hitler to suggest ending the reprisals.[62] Owing to Burckhardt's direct line into Berlin and the similarity of this report to that which Krauel provided in 1942, it is more than likely that this information was given to Pilet-Golaz via Burckhardt, yet the latter's name was not mentioned in the telegram. The reason for this becomes apparent when one considers Burckhardt's comments to Livingston in November 1943. The former reported that he had been asked by Grawitz to visit Berlin to meet the German Government, which 'desired to treat through Red Cross channels', a proposed resolution for ending the shackling. Notably, Burckhardt also emphasized to Livingston that while in Berlin he would 'have no contacts or discussions on political matters or any approaches outside [the] scope of Red Cross business'. Clearly Burckhardt realized that his reputation as a peacemaker was a source of British apprehension over his involvement and so, having obtained the initial information of a possible resolution in August, he asked Pilet-Golaz to act as the official negotiator in order to receive British approval. As the German Government's preference was to use the ICRC as the diplomatic channel, however, it was Burckhardt who ultimately had to go to Berlin for the talks, the outcome of which was an agreement that the Germans would remove the shackles and that Marti would visit all camps to confirm that the order had been carried out.[63]

The involvement of Pilet-Golaz in the Shackling Crisis helped to raise the profile of the Swiss Federal Council in the eyes of Whitehall.[64] Given his exertions in a similar vein, the question must be asked, how did Burckhardt's generally unwelcome involvement affect British perceptions both of the ICRC and of its vice-president? As with British rationale for bringing the Swedes into Greece months earlier, Whitehall's reaction to the shackling was to limit the involvement of the ICRC as much as possible in favour of embracing a more credible alternative – in this instance, the Swiss Government. This decision led the British to dismiss Burckhardt's efforts in favour of those of Pilet-Golaz, even after the latter all but admitted in February 1943 that his discussions with the Germans had broken down and his attempts to reach out to Grawitz had failed.[65] At the very least this admission should have prompted the British to consider the alternative; the Foreign Office, however, guided in its judgement by Norton in particular, continued to ignore Burckhardt's machinations.

The British had some good cause to be wary of Burckhardt's intervention. His prior instances of dubious diplomacy threatened the status of the Protecting Power as the credible, Convention-sanctioned conduit through which to conduct humanitarian diplomacy. This should not, however, have precluded making use of Burckhardt in an unofficial capacity, particularly if one considers that by the time the shackles were reapplied in early 1943 it was obvious that the quickest way to resolve the issue was via the kind of closed-door negotiations on which Burckhardt thrived. Burckhardt, moreover, recognized early that for Berlin and London the need to save face had to be the linchpin of any deal. It was this conclusion that dictated his efforts to resolve the issue, ultimately culminating in his meeting with Ribbentrop at which the latter made clear that no public declaration was to accompany the removal of the shackles – a condition to which the British agreed. In the wake of this agreement the British finally recognized Burckhardt's efforts, instructing Norton to pass on their gratitude, notably with the acknowledgement that Burckhardt's German contacts had played a pivotal role.[66]

Oddly, Burckhardt was restrained in taking credit. On 7 December the British indicated their desire to make a statement in Parliament on the end of the shackling to which he grudgingly agreed, but only on the proviso that the British should not express any gratitude towards either himself or the Committee.[67] Burckhardt's request was as clear an example as any of the degree to which he had adapted his political instincts to humanitarianism. His fear was that any trumpeting of each side backing down would both raise again the spectre of non-adherence to the Convention and damage his campaign to establish the ICRC as a credible mediator in POW issues.[68] His promise to Ribbentrop that the back down would not be acknowledged was also no doubt a factor in his wish not to be associated with it, and in so doing maintain good relations with Berlin. This intention to use the situation to strengthen the ICRC's reputation was not, however, exclusively targeted at the Germans. The extent to which Burckhardt exerted himself on behalf of the British during the Shackling Crisis and his agreement, against his better judgement, to the public declaration, indicates that he viewed the episode as a means of building a similar relationship with Whitehall to that which he enjoyed with Berlin. The outcome of this campaign to improve his reputation was, however, mixed. As much as his involvement in solving the Shackling Crisis displayed his worth to the British, it also highlighted the concern still held in Whitehall about not only the man himself but also his policy of steering the ICRC more stridently into the realms of humanitarian diplomacy. With the grim discovery in April 1943 of a mass grave of Polish POWs, Burckhardt was handed a timely opportunity to address these concerns.

On 13 April 1943, Berlin Radio announced that German authorities on the outskirts of Smolensk had discovered a mass grave in the nearby forest of Katyn. The initial inspection of the grave site by the Germans revealed the bodies of 3,000 Polish officers who had been missing since the German-Soviet invasion of Poland in 1939. As the radio broadcast claimed and, as Moscow finally admitted in 1990, the POWs had actually been executed by agents of The People's Commissariat for Internal Affairs (NKVD), on the orders of its chief, Levrenti Beria, during the summer of 1940. When the initial accusation of cold-blooded murder was made by the Germans in April 1943 the Soviets replied via their own propaganda medium, the Sovinformburo, declaring that the Poles had in fact been executed by the 'German-Fascist scoundrels'.[69]

This was not the first time the fate of the POWs had been raised. Moscow's forty-nine-year denial of the truth about Katyn began following the German invasion of the Soviet Union in 1941 and the subsequent resumption of Soviet-Polish relations – now as allies rather than enemies. The first inquiry was made by General Wladyslaw Anders of the Polish Army, who had been released by the Soviets from Lubyanka prison in August 1941. When he realized that many of the men he had served with were not released at the same time, he questioned his new allies as to the whereabouts of the Polish officers who had been held in Soviet POW camps since 1939. The series of denials, evasions and alterations to the lie that the Soviets had simply 'lost track' of the Poles continued until the discovery of the graves in April 1943, by which time the unresolved question of their fate had grown into one of the most significant of many sore points in Soviet-Polish relations.[70] Alive to this schism, the Reich Minister for Propaganda, Josef Goebbels, saw the discovery at Katyn as an opportunity to snap the already strained relations between the Soviets and the Poles. As part of his campaign to conduct 'anti-Bolshevik propaganda in a grand-style', Goebbels ordered both journalists and members of the Polish Red Cross to Katyn to validate Berlin Radio's claims of Soviet barbarism. The chances of this propaganda tactic bringing success were greatly increased on 16 April, when it was announced that the investigators had uncovered another 1,500 bodies.[71]

The day before the announcement on Berlin Radio of this new find the German Red Cross, undoubtedly under orders from Berlin, requested the ICRC to send a representative to join Goebbels's team. The request was a clear attempt by Berlin to legitimize its claims of Soviet barbarism by including an organization that was regarded as being truly neutral by the rest of the world. Ironically, Berlin may also have sought the ICRC's assistance for the opposite reason. From the war's outset Berlin had displayed a preference for intervention by the ICRC on matters pertaining to POW welfare. The support shown by the Germans for Burckhardt's efforts to diffuse the Shackling Crisis in the months prior to the Katyn discovery indicates that this opinion of Geneva as being useful was still prevalent in Berlin in 1943. In seeking to validate their claims of Soviet guilt, therefore, the ICRC was a logical choice of investigator for the Germans to make, the more so once Waclaw Lachert, the Polish Red Cross representative at Katyn, refused to be drawn into what was clearly a propaganda exercise. Despite being informed of the Soviets' guilt by what he saw at Katyn, Lachert evaded Berlin's request by insisting that to issue a definite statement he would need two witnesses to each of the murders. It was only after Lachert's refusal to cooperate with Berlin that the ICRC was contacted. The Committee was also suddenly in demand across the Channel. On 17 April the Polish Government-in-Exile, which had been based in London under the leadership of General Wladyslaw Sikorski since 1939, instructed the Polish Red Cross representative in Geneva to request that the ICRC launch its own independent inquiry into the Katyn affair.[72] Noting that it 'suits us perfectly', Goebbels, with Hitler's blessing, duly sent the ICRC a telegram urging them to cooperate with the Polish request.[73]

The reaction of the British to this development was one of disappointment edged by a small, yet very real, dose of fear. The latter emotion was owing to Britain's alliance with the Soviets who, in the spring of 1943, were in the midst of a massive offensive to capitalize on their recent victory over the Germans at Stalingrad. At such a crucial moment in the European conflict it was perceived as disastrous by the British for the Russians to be accused of mass murder comparable with that committed by their enemies. Accordingly, the response of the Foreign Office when informed of a pending ICRC investigation was to have a sentence placed into the official British statement indicating that the accusations against the Russians could simply be a construct of German propaganda. This was despite the fact that privately many within Whitehall suspected that the Soviets were indeed guilty.[74] Tempering these suspicions, the British decided that the only way to preserve their alliance and overcome Goebbels's plan was cautiously to follow the Soviet line. As part of this display of solidarity with Moscow, Churchill opted to attack the ICRC when he wrote to Stalin on 25 April saying that Whitehall would 'certainly oppose rigorously any "investigation" by the International Committee of the Red Cross *or any other body in any territory under German authority'*.[75] Although he showed little support for Stalin's absurd theory that the Poles, the Germans and the ICRC were using Katyn to construct an anti-Soviet conspiracy, Churchill clearly sought to tap into this paranoia by taking the Soviet line that the ICRC was susceptible to influence from Berlin and so could not be trusted.[76]

One wonders whether Churchill was being sincere in his suggestions of ICRC–German collusion. In addition to this idea having been raised intermittently since the start of the war by Whitehall's POW departments and the MEW, Churchill and the entire Cabinet had more recently shown displeasure at Burckhardt's close dealings with the Nazi leadership. That, coupled with knowledge from those British officials who worked alongside Burckhardt in Danzig of his hatred of Communism and distrust of the Soviets would have made the idea of the ICRC being sympathetic to the German cause one worth considering.[77] That said, there is no evidence that this thought – if indeed it was considered – was ever sincerely committed to paper. What is clear, however, is that there was definite concern in Whitehall that the Committee, already deemed to be, at the very least, susceptible to German influence, would follow its tendency to involve itself in matters beyond its concern by agreeing to Berlin's request.

The degree to which the ICRC was put under a microscope by the British as a response to this situation is evidenced by the production of a special report on the Committee's involvement in the Katyn Affair for the benefit of the Foreign Office on 29 April. This document, compiled by the Political Warfare Executive (PWE), contained a series of intelligence and media reports outlining the progress of the ICRC's deliberations over whether or not to respond to the German and Polish requests, as well as analysis of what the outcome of the ICRC's reply would mean for Polish-Soviet relations.[78] The reason for such scrutiny was that by this stage in the affair the question of ICRC involvement had taken on a new and more potent significance. As a measure of how little Moscow trusted the ICRC and how much it feared what the Committee's investigation might uncover, an enraged Stalin threatened to cut diplomatic ties with the Poles on 24 April unless Sikorski retracted his appeal to Geneva. Sikorski refused, and so ties were officially severed between the two allies on 25 April. As the PWE gathered its intelligence, Anthony Eden began frantic attempts to persuade Sikorski to withdraw the request to the ICRC; a campaign that did not bear fruit until 4 May.[79]

It is apparent from this sequence of events that the ICRC's involvement in the Katyn Affair was a significant factor in Whitehall's handling of the issue. Indeed, it was the opinion of the Foreign Office that the Polish request for ICRC intervention was nothing short of being 'the immediate cause of the crisis'. There was more to Whitehall's concern, however, than simply keeping its Allies at peace. The British quite rightly suspected their Soviet ally of guilt and were themselves aware of their own complicity in covering up the crime by following Stalin's line. As Alexander Cadogan confided to his diary, 'how can *we* discuss with Russians execution of German "war criminals", when we have condoned this?'[80] Apprehension over this delicate situation being made public, plus the lingering suspicions in Whitehall over the Committee's apparent closeness to and, more importantly, capacity to be manipulated by Berlin would only have added to the British sense of anxiety over what the ICRC might uncover. Based on past experiences, the British fear that the ICRC would throw itself with typical enthusiasm into the Katyn issue was understandable. It was fear of the truth – perhaps more so than fear of the Committee being manipulated by Berlin – that served as the catalyst for the PWE's report, which eventually calmed British concerns on 29 April by stating that the ICRC's 'reply is really a negative one'.[81] Until this report was received Whitehall waited anxiously, expecting the meddlesome ICRC to answer positively to the Polish and, possibly, German requests. It is clear from ICRC sources, however, that the British had nothing to fear.

Much like Lachert at the Polish Red Cross, the Committee was mindful from the beginning of the political weight attached to the Katyn Affair. At a time when the ICRC was trying to ingratiate itself with the British, while shifting to a focus on practical activities, this burden was unwanted. Despite Goebbels's expectation that the 'cantonal diplomats' would tow the line, the Committee never had any real intention of getting involved in either German propaganda games or Polish attempts to uncover the truth.[82] In coming to the decision to reject both appeals for an inquiry, the ICRC's reasoning was notably pragmatic, politically minded and self-serving. As early as 19 April the Committee's leadership concluded that any affirmative response to the German request might anger the Soviets. This was of particular concern for Geneva as, since the invasion of the Soviet Union in June 1941, it had been campaigning unsuccessfully for Moscow to allow the ICRC to conduct relief activities on behalf of POWs on the Eastern Front.[83] Kid-glove treatment of the Soviets was, therefore, the order of the day for the Committee. As part of this policy, the ICRC had recourse to Huber's solidly legalistic argument that it was not authorized to conduct a unilateral investigation of this nature without the consent of all belligerents involved.[84] This rationale formed the backbone of Geneva's official reply to both the Poles and the Germans on 23 April, which stated that the Committee was

> willing, in principle, and provided that all parties concerned ask them to do so, to lend their assistance in the appointment of neutral experts, in accordance with the memorandum which the Committee sent on 12 September 1939 to the belligerent states, and by which, immediately upon the outbreak of the war, the Committee established the principles according to which they would be able to take part, if need be, in making investigations.[85]

Put simply, the Committee would only involve itself in the Katyn investigation – and then only with the participation of other neutral bodies – if 'all parties', meaning the Soviets, agreed to its involvement.

For a number of reasons, this was one of the ICRC's most shrewd and calculated diplomatic moves of the Second World War. For one thing it caused Goebbels to put 'the whole matter of the Red Cross on ice' in regards to Katyn, lest German bullying affect the services the ICRC provided to German POWs.[86] The Katyn refusal was also a deft way of handling the Soviets. Huber's demand for Soviet involvement, to which the ICRC knew that Stalin would not agree, was designed to be rejected.[87] As much as the response was intended to preserve what remained of the ICRC's flimsy relations with Moscow, it was also intended, albeit subtly, as a statement of purpose. The clever wording made it clear to any who doubted the ICRC's resolve that it was indeed authorized, capable and willing to investigate Katyn. This not only placed the ICRC above the issue but implied that the fault for a lack of investigation lay, not with the Committee, but with the squabbling governments involved. Mired in Polish-Soviet antagonism and German propaganda, the Katyn Affair was an unwanted diversion for the ICRC at a time when it was tackling the Shackling Crisis and the general rise in POW maltreatment. Mindful of this wider context, the Committee was aware that to respond affirmatively to the Polish and German requests was to pursue an idealistic course that may have proved disastrous to its relations with the British and the Soviets. Much like the 'non-appeal', therefore, Katyn was a complex and difficult issue from which the increasingly pragmatic ICRC chose to walk away, albeit with a more convincing argument for so doing.

There may also have been a realization, in Burckhardt's mind in particular, that in choosing not to participate in the Katyn Affair the ICRC could earn a much needed boost to its credibility in Whitehall. Prior to the 'non-appeal' meeting, Burckhardt had rejected the proposal for a blanket appeal to all belligerents to temper their conduct towards civilians, on the grounds that such a pronouncement would not only annoy Berlin but also, with its tacit reference to aerial bombardment, be received poorly by the British. More overt efforts to improve the ICRC's standing in Whitehall came only a few months prior to the discovery of the graves at Katyn, when the ICRC leadership agreed to enlarge Haccius's delegation.[88] This was followed by Burckhardt throwing himself into the Shackling Crisis, and agreeing to the British wish to make a public statement when that crisis ended. Moreover, when the decision was made not to become involved in the Katyn Affair, Burckhardt chose to notify Moscow via the Foreign Office rather than Geneva's usual line to the Soviets in Ankara, that the Committee had been 'absolutely correct in the matter'.[89] It seems, therefore, that in conjunction with the push to gain greater prestige and credibility, Burckhardt was also actively trimming his and the Committee's sails to Allied winds. He certainly wanted to make sure that both the Russians *and* the British knew that the ICRC was on 'their' side in the Katyn Affair.

It is also probably no coincidence that at this time Burckhardt also began to provide information on conditions within Germany to Allen Dulles, the head of the OSS in Switzerland. Dulles noted that during a recent visit by Burckhardt to Berlin on Red Cross business – presumably his meeting with Ribbentrop over the Shackling Crisis – he had taken soundings about the mood in Germany, the prospect of Hitler being usurped by Himmler and, most importantly, the possibility of the Germans making a secret peace deal with the Soviet Union. Burckhardt further noted, with his usual sense of fatalism, the 'self-delusion' of those in Germany who could not realize that defeat was inevitable.[90] Neither Burckhardt nor the Committee suffered from any such delusion. On 17 December 1943 the ICRC leadership met to discuss the challenges that would await them once Germany and Japan were, inevitably, defeated.

The prevailing sentiment at the meeting was that, although much had been achieved, both the war's end and the coming of peace would provide the ultimate test of the Committee's capabilities. For all his efforts, Burckhart's fear that the test would be failed and that the ICRC would emerge from the conflict cloaked in derision had not been quelled.[91] What was needed was the most unlikely of panaceas – a humanitarian miracle amidst the chaos of the Third Reich's denouement.

7
Humanity and *Götterdämmerung,* 1944–5

Planning for liberation

As the armies of the Western Allies pushed into France, following their successful landing in Normandy in June 1944, thoughts in Whitehall began to turn to the question of how best to safeguard Allied POWs during the forthcoming collapse of the Third Reich. These considerations were not new; in fact they were as old as the plan for D-Day itself. In June 1942 the DPW had first raised the issue by suggesting that, once the invasion was underway, the prisoners should receive arms and food drops in order to 'control chaos' in the liberated territories and defend themselves from German reprisals. Although it was dismissed as ill-advised on the grounds that widespread violence against Allied POWs was 'improbable', by 1944 the idea of reactivating the prisoners as combatants was once again raised by the DPW. The suggestion was born of a heightening concern that, should 'fanatics' within the Nazi regime gain control of the prisoners during Germany's *Götterdämmerung,* arbitrary acts of violence and the movement of POWs to a secret location where they could be used as hostages might be possible outcomes.[1]

The notion that the Germans might discard the Convention was a lingering fear in Allied minds. This fear had been fed by a series of ICRC and Protecting Power reports received from mid-1943 onwards, which suggested a pattern of escalation in incidents of prisoner mal-treatment. In keeping with Josef Goebbels's branding of captured airmen as *Terrorfligers,* camp inspectors reported that certain prisoners at Dulag Luft (Oberursel) were deliberately deprived of Red Cross parcels and were being held for extended periods of solitary confinement inside windowless cells with the radiators turned up high. The inspectors also noted the increasingly jittery and trigger-happy nature of guards at

Stalag Luft III (Sagan) and Stalag VIIIB (Lamsdorf) where, over the course of 1943, there were twenty-eight shootings of would-be escapees, a grim precursor to the execution of fifty Allied POWs in retaliation for the 'Great Escape' from Sagan in March 1944.[2] Less overt, though no less sinister, incidents were also noted in April, when captured airmen were forced to operate anti-aircraft batteries and fire on their own planes as part of the defence of factories in the Rhone Valley. Further instances of POWs being used as a component of the Reich's defence were observed during an ICRC inspection of the newly constructed Dulag Luft at Frankfurt am Main in November 1943. Although the facility was well provisioned, the inspector could not help but conclude that the choice to construct the camp in such close proximity to the city was a deliberate attempt to leave the prisoners 'exposed to aerial attack'. If the idea was to shield the city from bombing then it was a cruel miscalculation. In March 1944 the Dulag was destroyed by Allied bombs, the camp becoming one of thirty estimated by the ICRC after the war to have been attacked from the air. Although only two prisoners died in that particular raid, they were part of the combined death toll of approximately one thousand POWs who were killed by their compatriots in similar circumstances during the war's final year.[3]

The response of the ICRC and the British Government to these reports was indicative of each party's differing conception of how best to maintain POW welfare and keep the POW relief system functioning in the midst of intensifying pre-invasion military activity. The Committee's capacity to respond to the maltreatment, beyond launching protests with Berlin, was very limited and the degree to which it could mollify German intentions was constrained by arguments of military necessity. Berlin's response to protests over the use of POWs as gunners, for example, was to argue that, since ordinary German citizens were now being forced to take up arms, enemy prisoners could no longer expect preferential treatment. In the face of this twisted claim of military necessity the ICRC's push to embrace more pragmatic forms of humanitarianism could only take them so far. Overwhelmed by the intensification of the bombings, Huber reverted to a protection scheme that had first been raised and rejected in 1939 – reciprocal marking of camps and notification by each belligerent of their location. An even older proposal – first espoused by Henry Dunant during the Franco-Prussian War – was for the establishment of immunity zones within the fighting fronts that would not be subject to either aerial or terrestrial attack. The replies from the belligerents indicated that such proposals had no place in the context of the final, bitterly fought months of the war. For the Germans, who were demonstratively willing to place POWs in harm's way in defence of the Reich, there was nothing to be gained by agreeing to the suggestion of marking and protecting camps and thus they rejected Huber's request outright. The Americans, mindful of the impact such restrictive measures would have on the strategic bombing campaign, though inclined to show sympathy to the ICRC's proposals, offered an amicable written refusal. The Soviets and the British neglected to reply at all.[4]

This rejection by the British did not mean, however, that the issue of POW protection had been dropped in Whitehall. It was more that the measures envisioned by the ICRC were judged to be so incompatible with the reality of the military situation that they barely warranted comment. What was needed instead were plans that would neither be disruptive to Allied military operations nor would be so reliant on the assumption that the Germans would maintain a 'correct' adherence to the norms of prisoner treatment. With these problems in mind, three measures were proposed by the Joint Intelligence Committee. These were to issue a warning to the Germans that those who did harm to POWs would be punished after the war; to maintain contact with the camps using radios dropped from the air; and, if necessary, to drop either soldiers near the camps or rations and arms so that the prisoners could defend themselves from their captors.[5] It is notable that the last scheme, despite having first been posited in 1942 during the initial invasion discussions, had been left to linger with little to no tangible development for years and was only seriously resurrected *after* D-Day. Moreover, once the suggestion was raised it became mired in bureaucratic wrangling and redrafting to the extent that it did not come to fruition until March 1945. Even then this was only in the highly bastardized form of the Special Allied Airborne Reconnaissance Force (SAARF), a combined initiative of the British Special Operations Executive and the American Office of Strategic Services whose primary objective was to make sure that Anglo-American prisoners did not fall into the hands of their 'allies' in the Red Army.[6] The SAARF was but one example of the extent to which, for all the concerns over German reprisals and Churchill's claim to Roosevelt in March 1945 that 'we have long foreseen the danger to these prisoners', few in Whitehall seriously considered how much the collapse of the Third Reich would impact on the well-being of their captured soldiers and sought practical and adaptive schemes in response. As such, when this collapse began to accelerate from autumn 1944, any plans for maintaining POW welfare necessarily had to be made haphazardly, as had been the case in the wake of France's fall four years before.[7]

This repetition of recent history was all the more remarkable considering that, only a year earlier in Italy, the consequences of poor POW policy had been manifestly demonstrated. Following the landings in Sicily, the overthrow of Mussolini in July 1943 and the arrival of the Wehrmacht in Italy to stiffen its defence, the Allies were faced with the prospect of 80,000 Allied prisoners being forcibly transferred to Germany or, worse still, made victims of mass reprisals. Owing to a lack of clear policy, conflicting messages were sent to the prisoners, not just from different Whitehall departments but from within MI9 – the department tasked with assisting POWs in escape and evasion. The MI9 section chief in Cairo was adamant that the organization live up to its billing and help the POWs to break out and escape back to Allied lines while Norman Crockett, the chief of MI9, was beholden to General Bernard Montgomery's 'stay put' order, which demanded that the prisoners stay in their camps and await liberation. Adding to this confusion was the request made by Churchill to his new ally, Marshal Pietro Bagdolio, that the POWs be protected from the Germans by Italian troops and, if necessary, shepherded over the border to safety in Switzerland. Bereft of clear orders, many of the prisoners took an ill-executed middle route. Most opted to stay in the camps in anticipation of liberation, only to be transferred to the Reich once the Germans consolidated their occupation of Italy in September 1943. Those who fled the camps fared little better. Few made it to Allied lines or to Switzerland, and most of those who roamed Italy over the winter of 1943–4 were eventually rounded up by the Germans.[8] It was a costly demonstration of how a lack of clarity in POW policy could affect the prisoners at the very moment when their liberation was at hand.

A year after the fiasco in Italy, however, inertia still dominated Allied thinking on the issue of POW protection. This thinking grew murkier following the execution by the Gestapo of fifty POWs following the 'great escape' from Sagan in March 1944. On the one hand, the crime smacked of the long-anticipated shift in German policy, confirmation of the fear that the Convention would be thrown out of the window and the influence of Nazi diehards on the camp system would become decisive in determining the fate of POWs in the war's final year. Conversely, the German justification for the murders – that the prisoners were shot while trying to escape for the purposes of joining resistance movements – led Anthony Eden to re-emphasize to Berlin in an official statement that the Allies had no such policy of 'escape and resist', that those responsible for the killings were war criminals who would be hunted down and that the British would continue to abide by IHL. Whitehall's strategy, therefore, was to emphasize the illegality of the act in order to ensure that the Germans continued to adhere to the Convention. With such a strategy adopted for protecting the prisoners, there was little room for radicalism or the implementation of schemes that might rattle German nerves and give further provocation for violent acts. The arms drop plan, therefore, faded into greater obscurity in the lead up to D-Day and the 'stay put' dictum, despite its manifest imperfections, not the least of which was the difficulty of actually communicating the order to the camps, was left in place for want of anything better as the official Allied policy for POW protection.[9]

On the question of how to maintain the supply lines to the camps, British thinking was similarly conservative. The 'stay put' policy was very much in harmony with 'victory before relief', the sum of which thinking was that the best way to maintain the health and well-being of POWs was for them to stay in their camps, keep their heads down and continue to receive parcels until such time as they were liberated. This policy for POWs would be little different from that prescribed for civilians, be they interned or under occupation. Although care for these war victims would ultimately fall under the auspices of UNRRA once the war was ended, immediate provision for relief in the wake of the invasion was to be provided principally by the ARC, which was authorized in March 1944 by Washington to accompany the Allied armies into Europe to provide relief to the liberated. Whitehall also authorized the despatch of delegates from the BRC and other voluntary aid agencies, such as the Friends Relief Service and the YMCA, into the liberated territories, and as early as January 1943 began training them for the task of deployment to Europe once the invasion had begun.[10] These measures were to be implemented, however, only after D-Day and were premised on the idea that where Allied boots marched humanitarian assistance would follow. Military activities could, therefore, find harmony with humanitarian action should the former precede the latter.

As progressive as this realization was, new plans for how to keep humanitarian channels open *before* the arrival of the Allied forces were seldom factored into the plan. Moreover, when schemes to this effect were posited they invariably foundered on divergences of opinion between Whitehall and Washington, particularly with regards to the role to be played in such initiatives by the ICRC. When, for example, the State Department proposed in May 1944 that the MEW relax its 'unnecessarily stringent' blockade conditions so that White Ships could deliver larger cargoes of medicine and food – to be distributed by the ICRC in the soon-to-be liberated territories – the British replied that, while the proposal 'would appear to dispose from the operational point of view of the difficulties connected with safe conduct and the use of a European port, those involved in internal transport and distribution would remain to be solved'.[11] The British, as always, did not trust the ICRC's capabilities to supervise and distribute the supplies and, having appointed the BRC and the ARC as the liberation's relief agents, felt no need to bring the ICRC into the fold or encourage 'the opening of further channels of importation into Europe at the present moment'. This would, so Churchill opined to Roosevelt, 'be wholly incompatible with the naval and military situation which is developing'.[12] This attitude was both a manifestation of 'victory before relief' and reflective of the fact that Allied humanitarian thinking in 1944 was measured, restrictive and primarily focused on, first, maintaining German adherence to the Convention and, second, coping with humanitarian crises after liberation. The ICRC's policies in contrast were, from 1943 onwards, increasingly reactive, adaptive and, ultimately, quite radical, with an emphasis on the need for greater freedom of action for delegates, more supplies and more transport options. In order to understand why this approach to humanitarian action developed in the Committee's thinking it is necessary to appreciate the extent of the challenges it faced as military action across Europe intensified, its capacity to work within pre-existing norms became more limited and the integrity of the POW relief system began to weaken.

'War exists for the International Committee too'

By 1944 the ICRC's volunteers, be they in mobile hospitals, within the camps or on the decks of the White Ships, had come fully to understand that, irrespective of the apparent protection offered by the Red Cross emblem, 'war exists for the International Committee too'.[13] As early as 1941, the Italian air force – in a return to the practice of attacking Red Cross installations it had followed in Ethiopia in 1935–6 – bombed, more than likely deliberately, Greek Red Cross hospitals and buzzed a number of Red Cross trucks en route to the camp at Salonika. These incidents were followed by an even more overt act in June 1942, when a squadron of Italian dive bombers torpedoed and sank a clearly marked ICRC vessel, the *Stureborg*, which led to the loss of tonnes of relief supplies and the death of all but one of the crew, including the Committee's agent on-board, Richard Heider.[14] As this act both undermined the Convention and disrupted the Greek relief effort, Whitehall was quick to support the ICRC's official protest to Rome. This did not mean, however, that the British were devoid of responsibility for similar attacks. In November 1942, for example, incendiary bombs dropped from a squadron of Royal Air Force planes severely damaged the parcel ship *Padua* while it was at anchor in Genoa. Having been repaired and refloated, it was sunk almost a year later by a submerged mine off Marseilles in the Golfe du Lion, resulting in the loss of six men and all the parcels in her hull.[15]

The attack on the *Padua* was the first major instance in which Allied, rather than Axis, military actions inflicted significant damage on Red Cross shipping. Perhaps owing to the fact that, unlike the Italians in 1941, the Allies were in effect sponsors of the White Ships, the ICRC showed restraint in dealing with this infraction, confining itself merely to notifying the British of what had happened and accepting both the swift apology offered by Whitehall and the proposition from the Admiralty that all relief ships plying the Lisbon–Marseilles route henceforth be degaussed to lessen the chances of their being hit by magnetic mines. That it took over a year of negotiations to decide on where, how and who would pay for the degaussing reflected the fact that, despite the apparent earnestness of its offer, the Admiralty's attitude to attacks on Red Cross vessels was that no guarantees could be given or safeguards devised. The fate of the *Padua* was viewed as the clearest example one could encounter of humanitarianism having to bow to the realities of war.[16] This conclusion, that little could be done to protect Red Cross vessels, was proven over the course of 1944, during which there were numerous attacks by aircraft from both Axis and Allies on clearly marked Red Cross ships and installations in the Netherlands, Albania, Romania and, to a great extent, along the Lisbon–Marseilles route.[17]

The cumulative outcome of these incidents was not apparent until one of the most serious pre-D-Day attacks occurred on 6 April 1944, when the parcel ship *Embla* was bombed by British planes off Port Vendres, resulting in the loss of twenty-five tonnes of goods through fire and water damage. Like the *Padua*, the *Embla* was twice a victim. After being repaired and refloated on 20 April, the ship was attacked once again by British planes, the outcome of which this time was not only her sinking with a full cargo hold but also the death of another ICRC on-board agent, Marcel Reutter. This was followed on 6 May by an attack on another White Ship, the *Christina*, while at anchorage in the port of Sete, not far from where the *Embla* sank. The response from Geneva was swift and highly reactive. Citing the increased threat to its ships and personnel, the ICRC declared on 31 May that shipping along the Lisbon–Marseilles route would be suspended until such time as the safety of Red Cross ships and personnel could be guaranteed. British POWs would, therefore, be cut off and forced to rely on parcel stockpiles in Switzerland. Although this ban on shipping was short-lived – it ended on 2 June – it was the start of a radical trend in the Committee's management of the POW relief system. On 14 June, barely a week after Allied forces had landed in Normandy, the ICRC announced that, owing to a spate of attacks on rail yards in northern Italy, rail services from Marseilles to Geneva would have to be suspended. This was followed on 20 June by a further decree that Marseilles could no longer safely receive Red Cross ships. These two decisions effectively severed the parcel routes from Lisbon to the camps by land and sea, leaving the Committee's storehouses in Marseilles packed full of increasingly valuable parcels which were unable to be transported by either train or ship to a more suitable transhipment location.[18]

These actions on the part of the ICRC marked a clear change in its relief policy. Whereas in the past its efforts had always been overwhelmingly proactive and expansive, focused on acquiring as many ships and trains as possible in order to distribute relief on a mass scale, the Committee chose in June 1944 to contract its operations, and in so doing sought to send a clear message of protest that attacks on its installations, personnel and vehicles could not be tolerated, irrespective of the intensification of military operations. This stance – a far cry from the usual formal written protest favoured by Geneva – caught both Whitehall and the BRC off guard. The fact that, unbeknownst to the Committee, its initial suspension of the shipping routes threatened to cut off the POWs only a matter of days before the Normandy landings, led the Admiralty to conclude that Geneva was being 'reckless' in its regard for British prisoners. The BRC also expressed consternation that the ICRC's 'unhelpful attitude' meant that ships bound for Marseilles would now have to be redirected to Casablanca at great cost in time and money.[19] The ICRC's action was not, however, as callous or as reactive as it appeared. The Committee only suspended shipping on account of the fact that, with a stockpile of up to ten weeks' worth of parcels in Switzerland, it believed it could continue to supply the POW camps, while both demonstrating its displeasure towards the British and, if possible, shocking them into an acceptance that something needed to be done to protect White Ships.[20] In this respect, the Committee's move was a calculated and audacious one. The success of the tactic, however, was negligible. Although attempts were made by the Admiralty to lay the blame on ICRC delegates in Lisbon for lax reporting of the vessels' movements, the Foreign Office was quick to realize that the question of who was to blame was mostly immaterial and that as 'we have more to lose than the Axis by the curtailment of shipping' a swift and sincere apology needed to be sent to Geneva, after which, to the relief of the Foreign Office, the ban was lifted.[21]

Beyond earning some recognition for its difficulties in Whitehall, the shipping ban did very little to alter British views of the ICRC's work during Europe's liberation, which continued to be relatively uninfluenced by the fact that the lines between the Committee's relief efforts and the Allies' military actions were becoming increasingly blurred. Despite the impetus to maintain the norms of the POW relief system, few in Whitehall grasped, until the Committee's suspension of the parcel routes, that each attack on the White Ships not only further eroded the apparent sanctity of the emblem and thus the integrity of the Convention but also, by sending so many parcels to the bottom of the ocean, endangered the supply lines upon which British prisoners relied. Similarly, scant regard was paid to the effect that military operations in southern France – specifically the Operation Dragoon landings of 15 August – would have on the delivery of parcels to British POWs via Marseilles. This owed as much to the prevailing lack of adaptability in Whitehall's humanitarian thinking as it was to the delayed planning of Dragoon, the purposes and execution of which was argued over by the British and the Americans until the final acceptance of the plan in June 1944.[22] Even after the plan's approval, however, and the first attempts by the ICRC to suspend its operations in southern France, the British continued to believe that the Committee's operations in Marseilles would not be gravely imperilled and that, at worst, the disruptions caused would be minor and swiftly overcome. The grimmest scenario envisioned was that the rail service to Geneva would be only 'intermittently open for traffic', in which case existing stockpiles would ensure that the POW relief system did not completely collapse. This optimism was buoyed by the expectation that, in the wake of the Dragoon landings – one of the objectives of which was the capture of the Marseilles docks to service the Allies' supply lines – shipping operations would be quickly restored.[23] Bearing in mind the importance of Marseilles to the welfare of POWs, this was a weighty and reckless assumption to make. It also turned out to be an erroneous one. Although the city was captured, the docks were so badly damaged in the fighting that, when a new route from Lisbon was finally established in September, ships had to be diverted to nearby Toulon. This might have sufficed as an expedient had it not been for the fact that Toulon had little in the way of the warehousing and trans-shipment facilities needed by the ICRC.

The establishment of parcel delivery from this port was, therefore, sluggish at a time when it needed to be anything but.[24]

The British handling of the Marseilles problem is illustrative of the extent to which the pursuit of victory and the need to keep relief efforts as restricted and unobtrusive as possible shaped Whitehall's humanitarian thinking. In this respect, there are echoes in 1944 of the views on relief in 1940–1, when the blockade was first extended, delivery of parcels to British POWs favoured to the detriment of a wider relief programme for Britain's allies, and ICRC initiatives aimed at expanding the scope for relief were routinely shot down. As both 1944 and 1940 were years of intense military action in Western Europe, the need to focus on military rather than humanitarian concerns was understandable. The key difference between the two phases of increased Allied military action on the Continent, however, was that, unlike in 1940, the Allies had time in the lead-up to D-Day to better integrate humanitarian thinking into their military strategy for the benefit of the POWs. It was only once it became clear that the POW relief system would be disrupted during and in the immediate aftermath of D-Day that the ICRC's concerns gained some traction. Even then support was only initially forthcoming from across the Atlantic. Washington and the ARC both backed Geneva's proposal that a new parcel route through the Baltic be organized in order to keep supply lines open should Marseilles be compromised. This idea had first been raised by Burckhardt as early as November 1941 as part of his vision for an expanded ICRC shipping programme. Walter Roberts at the PWD saw the potential. As he predicted, however, the proposal was rejected by both his colleagues and MEW.[25] For the latter the resurrection of the suggestion in 1944 engendered yet another ICRC-inspired headache. Not only did the notion of increased shipping into Swedish waters appear insensitive to Allied attempts to curtail Stockholm's trading relations with the Reich, but a new shipping route would require fresh negotiations over navicerts and safe conducts; the procurement of additional shipping from Sweden; and, as the ICRC unrealistically proposed German-occupied Stettin as a port of destination, a return to British concerns over the Committee's supervisory capabilities, the integrity of which the Americans were more inclined – their reservations over certain ICRC delegates North Africa notwithstanding – to place their faith in.[26]

In addition to the disruptions the scheme presented to the maintenance of the status quo in humanitarian policy, the answer to the prevailing question of what exactly was in it for the British was also far from apparent. Even if the worst did happen after Dragoon, and

Marseilles was put out of commission for some time, Whitehall was satisfied that, owing to the size of the Committee's parcel stockpile in Switzerland, British POWs would 'not be in immediate jeopardy'. For these reasons, the Baltic route – having been proposed at a time when the MEW was already entangled in a frustrating debate with the ICRC over exemptions for civilian parcels from the Swiss national import quota – was destined to fall on unreceptive ears.[27] It was simply too much bother for too little gain, and its implementation was viewed as an unnecessary backup for the ever-reliable Lisbon–Marseilles route. The most the British offered in response was a suggestion that Gothenburg be used as a terminal port for White Ships in the Baltic and that the ICRC charter a small, emblem-marked ferry as a shuttle service from there into German territory.[28] It is probable that the only reason this suggestion was put forward was because of the pressure Washington exerted on Whitehall. As the British Ambassador to the United States, Lord Halifax, reported earlier in the year, opinion on the other side of the Atlantic, be it among the American public or in some quarters of Roosevelt's administration, was generally based on the understanding that restrictions on relief imports into Europe were held in place by an obstinate Britain in the face of 'the better judgement of the United States Government'. This negative view of British relief policy was sharpened by Washington's own concerns for American POWs who, unlike their British allies, had in May 1944 only enough parcels stored in Geneva to keep them supplied until 15 August, and only then if there was not another wave of captures following D-Day.[29] Mindful that this issue had not been factored into Whitehall's considerations over the Baltic route, the State Department opted for the ICRC's often-used tactic of appealing to British self-interest. The Foreign Office was reminded that a quarter of the parcels on-board the two vessels the Committee wanted to send to Gothenburg – the *Mangalore* and the *Travancore* – were intended for British POWs. In the end it was this pressure from Washington and the fear of 'very high level political repercussions' should the ICRC's proposal be refused outright that led to the agreement of 5 August that the two ships originally scheduled to dock at Marseilles would now sail to Gothenburg for on-carriage to their final port of destination, Lübeck.[30]

Although the ICRC could count it as a success, the establishment of the Baltic route was a hollow victory. The crucial support of Washington, far from representing a fundamental change in Allied perceptions of humanitarian policy, turned out to be an aberration, almost certainly prompted by short-term concern for American POWs rather than a wider appreciation of the Committee's increasing demands for more parcel routes and a more fluid humanitarian policy. Such changes were demanded in particular by Alfred Zollinger, who tried frantically from 1943 onwards to prepare the ICRC for Europe's liberation. In the wake of the losses to rolling stock made available to the Committee in that year on account of German requisitions and air raids, Zollinger, warning of dire consequences for parcel-starved POWs and civilian internees, requested from the Americans that 600 rail cars be immediately shipped to Lisbon for use in southern France. When that hopeful appeal failed Zollinger next insisted, in the wake of D-Day, that trucks, fuel and spare parts be donated to the ICRC in order to keep supply lines to the camps operational in instances where rail lines were cut. Zollinger also joined Burckhardt in calling for the establishment of large parcel-supply depots within key camps across the Reich and requested of MEW that Red Cross parcels henceforth be distributed to whomsoever the ICRC's delegates encountered who needed them – be they POWs, civilians, British subjects or otherwise. The sum of these suggestions was a vision of the ICRC's 1944 activities that blended the fluidity and adaptation of its work in the Far East with the lofty hopes that had been vested in the White Ships in 1942, a vision in which the ICRC's delegates would operate with something close to autonomy, traversing the roads of the crumbling Reich in a fleet of Red Cross-emblazoned, Allied-donated trucks, dispensing parcels at will to any and all victims of war they encountered.

Far from impressing the Allies as a display of foresight and ingenuity, this vision of fluidity was seen by Washington and Whitehall as the latest and most comprehensive example of ICRC utopianism. The Allies rejected as untenable both the supply depot idea and the requests for rolling stock. They shared concerns that the ICRC's stores of parcels would simply be seized by the retreating Wehrmacht. The request for trucks did evoke some thoughtful discussion, albeit tempered not only by further concerns over German requisitioning but also by the problem of how to reconcile the arrival of American trucks on European soil for neutral ICRC use with existing blockade provisions. In the light of these reservations – which were seldom addressed by Zollinger with little more than impassioned insistence – the Red Cross trucks scheme left the British put out by the 'many administrative difficulties' it raised. The Americans for their part, having secured a new means of keeping supply lines open for their POWs, were also more sluggish in their advocacy of the ICRC's plans than they had been for the Baltic route. It was not until 20 September 1944, therefore, that fifty American trucks finally arrived in Barcelona on-board the *Caritas I*. These, however, were only shipped on the proviso that they would be stored there until MEW approved their despatch to Switzerland. It took an additional three months after that approval was given for the vehicles to reach the Spanish border, during which time a second consignment of twenty-three trucks arrived at Marseilles to form a shuttle service between there and Toulon where another fifty trucks, donated by the Canadian Red Cross, arrived soon after. The sporadic arrival of these vehicles, and the restrictions placed on their movement once unloaded, meant that it was not until early 1945 that the ICRC received something close to the number of trucks requested by Zollinger almost a year before – by which time the rail service between Marseilles and Switzerland had been stabilized.[31]

It seems clear from the outcomes of Zollinger's proposals that the ICRC, despite its best efforts to equip itself to respond to the ebb and flow of events, was forced by the Allies to work instead within the confines of a more conservative humanitarian policy, in which it was required to continue its operations in the manner it had since 1940. This expectation of the Committee's role encouraged resistance towards the ICRC's more imaginative proposals and contributed to the Allies' distant view of the problems 1944 would bring to POWs. One outcome of this was that it was not until the eve of D-Day that the Allies even questioned whether the ICRC had enough delegates in Berlin to cope with any influx of prisoners. The response to this request – that the Berlin delegation was well equipped with cars and petrol, and was in the process of enlarging its delegation to twelve full-time members – was indicative of the extent to which the Committee, despite the Allies' views, had no intention of taking a business-as-usual approach to its operations during the year of invasion.[32] In addition to enlarging the Berlin delegation, across Switzerland the ICRC had assembled a staff of over three thousand volunteers, five hundred of whom were attached to the JRC and stationed at various facilities across the country, one of which, the Palais des Expositions, sat astride the supply line from Marseilles to Berlin, 'piled high with pyramids of cases of parcels'. The gradual creation over the course of 1943 of a separate stockpile of medical parcels in Geneva and stockpiles of food parcels at Sagan and at two of the Frontstalags in France provided further indications that the Committee had learnt from the parcel crisis of 1940 and was determined not to see a repeat. In consideration of Haccius's difficulties during the aforementioned crisis, Nicholas Burckhardt (cousin of Carl) was also redeployed to London in March 1944, ensuring that the delegation at St James's Palace would have a full complement of staff.[33] What these preparations indicate is that, having accepted that it would be limited in its ability to curtail acts of violence against war victims or protect them from attack, the Committee chose to stick to what it did best – the provisioning of relief – albeit within a framework that was designed to give it as many options as possible to respond to changes in the military situation. That the ICRC's preparedness was justified and its conception of a fluid humanitarian policy more appropriate to *Götterdämmerung* than the more conservative attitude taken by the Allies would soon be made apparent.

Finest hour? The ICRC and the collapse of the Third Reich

On 25 September 1944 Hitler, incensed at the recent Warsaw Uprising and fearful of the threat of similar acts of armed insurrection being taken by escaping POWs, ordered that the administration of all POW camps be handed over to the Reichsführer SS Heinrich Himmler, who in turn passed the role of arbiter of POW affairs in Germany into the hands of SS Obergruppenführer Gottlob Berger. Though Berger would ultimately carry out this task with less brutality than was feared, at the time of his appointment the Allies were convinced that this development would herald the nightmare scenario of mass reprisals and hostage taking that had been predicted months earlier. This new threat to POW safety coincided with the issuing of another worrisome Führer decree that camp commandants puncture tins of food in their stockpiles, so as to deny partisans and escaped POWs the temptation to raid the camps for sustenance.[34] Taken in consideration with the breakdowns to the Lisbon–Marseilles route, it was clear by the autumn of 1944 that the norms of the POW relief system in Europe were starting to crumble.

The ICRC was mindful that a great test of its capabilities, one possibly comparable to that faced in the Far East, was in the offing. As the Berlin delegation reported in October, the question of whether the norms of POW treatment adhered to by the Germans could be maintained as conditions on the ground deteriorated was now of the utmost importance.[35] This disconcerting turn of events in Berlin's POW policy coincided with the onset of two additional crises that would influence the nature of the ICRC's work during the war's final months. The first and most pressing concern was the temporary breakdown of the parcel delivery system, engendered by the Dragoon landings, the lack of trains and trucks and the increased bombing of transport infrastructure in southern France. The sum of these disruptions was that, by the time that Hitler ordered camp stockpiles to be spoiled, British POWs had been placed on half-rations on the recommendation of the BRC, and thoughts of food deliveries via air-drop were being discussed in Washington and Whitehall, albeit on the proviso that this could only occur after liberation.[36] The second problem that arose at this time was the emergence of a trend of evacuation of POW and concentration camps in the eastern territories of the Third Reich. The Protecting Power had given a hint of what was to come as early as February 1944, when it reported that 1,500 prisoners had been transferred in great haste and with no provisions, from Stalag IIID (Steglitz) to Stalag IVG (Oschatz). On this occasion the PWD asked the Swiss to launch a protest with Berlin, at which point the matter, ostensibly, ended.[37] That the Steglitz evacuation was a mere prelude, however, was made clear when Stalag Luft VI (Heydekrug) was cleared of its 9,000 prisoners with only an hour's notice on 13 July. The evacuation came at the end of weeks of rumours and tension within the camp over the impending arrival of the Red Army, which had surged towards the eastern border of the Reich following the launching of Operation Bagration in June. In response to this advance, the prisoners at Heydekrug were hastily rounded up, some with only wooden clogs for shoes, and told to gather whatever additional clothing and Red Cross parcels they could carry. They were then marched westwards from the camp, their destination not disclosed by their captors, who also did not inform either the Protecting Power or the ICRC of the situation. As the evacuation unfolded, the prisoners divided into smaller groups. Some ended their journey two hundred miles south at the sprawling, and also soon-to-be evacuated Stalag complex at Thorn. Others endured a three-day journey via coal barge across the Baltic to Swinemünde, the point of departure for an open-top truck ride and forced march through a dense forest to the overcrowded Stalag Luft IV (Gross Tychow), which was itself finally evacuated on 6 February 1945.[38]

The first reports of these evacuations reached the ICRC and the Protecting Power sporadically over the course of the autumn and, having alerted Whitehall of this turn of events and the increasing influence of the SS in POW affairs, discussions finally took place between British officials, BRC and ICRC delegates over POW welfare. Tellingly, the ICRC was restricted in the discussions to addressing only matters that the British deemed it responsible for – namely, the flow of parcels to the camps. Talk of immunity zones, parcel supply depots, food drops by Red Cross planes or any other fanciful plans were to be off the table. Indeed, on the three separate occasions that the ICRC representative at the meetings, Walter Fülleman, raised the prospect of establishing immunity zones under ICRC auspices, the idea was rejected without further discussion by DPW officials.[39] The most striking aspect of the British–ICRC meetings was the persistence of the differance between each party's conception of the burgeoning POW crisis, despite all that had occurred in the preceding months. Throughout the meetings the British appeared to be playing catch-up, asking questions about why rolling stock was unavailable, whether the Committee had established itself properly yet at Lübek and what would happen if the rail lines from France into Switzerland were cut.[40] The ICRC's answers – tinged as always with a grim despondency – were met with a mixed response. Despite warnings from the ICRC of the need to strengthen the Baltic route with more ships, the DPW was slow to broaden its view beyond a reliance on the Lisbon–Marseilles route. This preference for the latter arose from the fact that it had been a fixture of the POW system since 1940 and also because during November four White Ships – the *Lobitio*, the *Silver Oak*, the *Ambriz* and the *Targus* – had returned to service on the route. This had led to stores of parcels that had been held up at Philadelphia and Casablanca at last being cleared and sent to the Continent. This development led one British official to predict that the 'one parcel, per man, per week' rate of delivery would be restored, hopefully, by Christmas. Scant regard was paid in this assessment, however, to the problems of maintaining the land route between Marseilles and Geneva which, despite the DPW's perception of its 'difficulties being overcome', was still hampered at this time by the lack of trucks and railcars. The further matter of how any semblance of order in parcel delivery could be maintained when camps were being evacuated and reports of POW captures from the Germans were on the decline was also relatively absent from Whitehall's considerations. Thus it was not until 25 January 1945, when the rate of evacuations increased exponentially, that British officials adopted a genuine sense of urgency and requested the Protecting Power to investigate the situation. The man who sent out the request was the War Office's Harry Phillimore, who indicated – albeit in an afterthought that he scribbled in pen over the telegram – that the ICRC should also be contacted to get to the bottom of the evacuation issue.[41]

Amid the lack of comprehension that generally defined British perceptions of the POW crisis of 1944, Phillimore's attitude proved the exception to the rule and, unlike his colleagues, he showed both vision and a willingness to embrace a more fluid relief policy. In addition to being one of the driving forces behind the various arms and food drop schemes, during the British–ICRC meetings Phillimore alone showed support for Fülleman's suggestions for immunity zones and parcel depots and – in contrast to the optimism of others – he questioned the delegate for details of the Committee's contingency plans should the Lisbon–Marseilles route again break down. Phillimore also differed from his colleagues in his view of how parcels should be distributed, favouring the ICRC's request that parcels be distributed at the discretion of the delegates to those most in need. In contrast, the chairman of the meetings, the War Office's W. H. Gardner, urged Fülleman to make sure that 'British prisoners of war were not impeded by some arbitrary formula' for delivering parcels.[42]

The ICRC for its part was clearly at the limits of its patience with the Allies over questions of relief policy. Having realized by early January that its once fanciful schemes for a more flexible relief system were now seemingly imperative for the survival of the prisoners on the march, the ICRC compiled an embittered report on solutions to the problem that held back little and criticized the Allies for their handling of POW relief matters over the course of the previous year. The report, sent to Haccius for communication to the PWD and DPW, bluntly declared that the ICRC required 'immediate, repeat, immediate, acceptance' of its proposal to pool all parcels, irrespective of their intended recipients, for distribution to any POWs or civilians who needed them, as well as noting that its delegates:

> Cannot but deplore in this connection that our request made already 18 months ago to British and American authorities for delivery of 600 goods vans or material for construction thereof in Switzerland, which we submitted foreseeing that serious transport situation was bound to arise sooner or later was not acceded to. Had this then been accepted situation today would not be as tragic.

In a final salvo the report declared that the 'ICRC must decline responsibility if proposal should for one reason or another not be put into practice'.[43] This assertion was followed on 22 February by a statement from the ICRC to all belligerents and National Red Cross Societies indicating that rather than wait for an answer from the belligerents, the Committee would begin pooling parcels immediately at Stalag VIIA (Moosburg) for distribution to 'any United Nations prisoners of war'.[44]

This decision was a timely one. By the end of February a much fuller picture of the POW evacuations had emerged, one which blew apart any lingering conceptions in Allied minds of the tenability of a business-as-usual approach to relief. This impression was conveyed in reports received from the Protecting Power and one of Marti's delegates, Robert Schirmer, who had spent weeks following the lines of march across Germany. The reports spoke of four camps, evacuated in quick succession in the early weeks of January by commandants who had favoured ill-provisioned flight over coordination and provisioning, often shepherding their charges in a general direction rather than along established routes to an intended destination. By mid-February the streams of prisoners had formed three main lines of march. These were a southern line consisting of approximately 80,000 marchers (many plagued by dysentery), a central line of 60,000 marchers heading in the direction of Dresden and a colossal northern line of perhaps as many as 100,000 heading through thickening snow towards Hamburg and Lübeck.[45] Testament to the scale of the disaster, amid the POWs there also marched concentration camp internees – hitherto segregated for the most part from Western Allied POWs. Although internees of concentration and work camps were more likely to be massacred along the march, or to die of exhaustion and disease, the privations of the evacuations were generally suffered by both categories of war victims. Furthermore, owing to the chaotic nature of the evacuations, by the time the marchers found their way to the mass camps at the end of their journey, the idea of the ICRC or any other agents of relief compartmentalizing them by nationality, race or perceived crime had become nearly untenable. The marches were a shared experience of brutality and misery for all who were involved.[46]

At the time of the receipt of Schirmer's report, Allied thinking had settled on launching an official appeal to Berlin to cease the evacuations. The parlous situation outlined in Schirmer's report and those of the Protecting Power, combined with an emerging fear in Whitehall of a return to the public scandal of POW neglect in 1940, however, forced a more proactive response.[47] On 21 February the War Office and the State Department decided to hand the problem of developing a relief strategy for POWs over to the Supreme Head of the Allied Expeditionary Force (SHAEF), a move that prompted swift and decisive action. Within days of being put in charge of POW relief, General Dwight D. Eisenhower authorized the release of trucks, fuel and spare parts to the ICRC and approved a plan for the immediate despatch of two relief convoys to be sent from Lübeck and Geneva to one of the main prisoner assembly points at Moosburg. This was to be followed by the establishment of two more ICRC transit centres, complete with parcel stockpiles, at Kreuzlingen on the Swiss side of the southern border with Germany and at Ravensburg, in Swabia.[48] The ICRC's official historian captures the importance of this moment in the context of the Committee's push, since 1943, to take on a more central and autonomous role in humanitarian agency. By February 1945 the ICRC had at last assumed:

> the dimensions of a self-contained organization for protection and assistance, with ships sailing under its flag, trains and road convoys bearing its sign, travelling huge distances, while its delegates not only carried on their habitual duties but added emergency activities, supplying moving columns and entering camps where previously they had been denied access.[49]

Given relatively free rein to carry out its mission, the Committee's delegates dispersed into the German countryside, encountering scattered groups of marchers, spread out over hundreds of kilometres and led by commandants and guards who often had little idea of their location and intended destination. In such circumstances the ICRC's oft-requested vehicles were crucial for supplying those prisoners who had been lost, injured or simply left behind by their fellow marchers. The freedom to operate unfettered, however, was not without a cost. As the first SHAEF-serviced trucks left Switzerland for Germany, the question of immunity from air attack was still unresolved. Both the Allies and the Germans declared that they could not guarantee safe conducts for the ICRC's trucks, despite their striking white colour and clear Red Cross markings on the sides and roof. The most that could be promised was for Bomber Command to inform its pilots of the approximate location of the trucks and their markings and to remind them to keep their eyes open. Conversely, concern was raised over the displaying of the Red Cross emblem, as it was feared that the safety implied by its presence might attract scavenging German troops – an ironic concern given the many attacks that had occurred on Red Cross-marked vehicles. The ICRC's delegates were not the only ones in danger from above. Mistaken for retreating Wehrmacht troops, POWs and civilian marchers alike came under fire from the air right up until 8 May and even Lübeck, the centre of the ICRC's northern supply operations, was not safe from attacking Allied planes, which sunk three ships carrying concentration camp inmates – one of which was marked with a Red Cross – during the final week of the war.[50] In such extremes, however, the ICRC's fluid humanitarian policy thrived in spite of the risks to its delegates. Having established a system of parcel depots and acquired the necessary trucks, in the war's final weeks the ICRC's delivery of parcels to some camps was re-established at something close to the ideal rate of one parcel, per man, per week. For the many prisoners who had marched for weeks without parcels, gratitude at the sight of the Red Cross trucks – dubbed the 'White Angels' – was palpable and their arrival was often heralded as nothing less than a starvation-averting 'miracle'. A representative of the British POWs scattered around Lübeck went so far as to write personally to the commander of the newly arrived British Occupation Force praising the efforts of Paul de Blonay, the ICRC's resident delegate, and requesting that he be retained as part of the occupation force's post-war relief management.[51]

As the command centre for this increased relief effort, Marti's Berlin delegation became the ICRC's busiest and most productive hive of activity. In response to the flight of many officials from Berlin, the cutting of communications and disruptions to the mail – which by the start of 1945 was taking on average five weeks to reach the embattled Reich capital from Geneva – in early February, Marti decided to diffuse his central office near Wanssee and establish semi-autonomous sub-branches outside the city at Wagenitz, Uffing and as far south as Vienna. These were staffed by a fresh intake of ICRC delegates, whose travel visas were organized, albeit only in the war's final weeks, by Burckhardt's old contact, Wolfgang Krauel. The creation of these sub-delegations epitomized the ICRC's response to Germany's *Götterdämmerung*. Each group of humanitarians had bestowed upon them by Marti the authority to respond swiftly and in a de-centralized manner to emerging situations in their area, a step made all the more necessary following the encirclement of Berlin by the Red Army in April.[52]

Elsewhere, other delegates were voluntarily placing themselves in potentially dangerous situations. This was primarily because in March Burckhardt had obtained the agreement of the Germans to have delegates install themselves in camps until they were liberated, in order to safeguard POWs and civilians – to make themselves hostages in all but name.[53] These and other delegates relied, not on recourse to humanitarian sentiment, but on their ability to negotiate solutions to local problems and to broker deals with German commandants desperate to prove themselves humane in the shadow of total defeat and the discovery of the concentration camps. Recruitment of both SS guards and some of the fitter POWs for the purposes of unloading supplies became commonplace. Burckhardt himself led by example in this more cavalier form of pragmatic humanitarianism. In early March he entered into negotiations with SS Obergruppenführer Ernst Kaltenbrunner over the release of Jewish, French and Polish prisoners.[54] Burckhardt's motives for this last-minute attempt to play saviour to Holocaust victims have rightly been questioned. The timing of his approach to the SS – within days of the highly publicized success of the former Swiss Federal Councillor Jean-Marie Musy's evacuation of 1,200 Jews across the border into Switzerland – suggests that Burckhardt was in no mood to have his humanitarian thunder stolen by non-ICRC saviours and that his efforts were, probably more than anything, an attempt to enhance both his personal reputation and that of the Committee. He was also clearly motivated in no small part to secure the release of a particular detainee at Ravensbrück, Countess Karolina Lanckorońska, an old acquaintance of his whose release he had first taken up with Himmler in 1942.[55] Irrespective of his and other ICRC members' motivations for their eleventh hour efforts on behalf of Jewish war victims in particular, the very act of opening discussions with the SS on such a sensitive issue was indicative of the unconventional measures taken by many delegates, during the war's final weeks.[56]

It is worth stepping back at this point to assess this turn to unorthodox, relatively unrestrained humanitarianism. Such an approach had been adopted by the ICRC in the Far East since 1942. Moreover, those measures had generally been approved by both the British and the Americans as a necessary response to both Japanese attitudes and the inability of the Committee to construct a POW relief system comparable to that which had been established in Europe.[57] In the latter theatre, however, the Allies were generally reluctant to entertain such anarchic humanitarianism until the maintenance of a more conservative view became untenable over the winter of 1944–5. This reluctance to adjust to the breakdown of relief norms was owed in no small part to the fact that – unlike in the Far East – since the start of the war in Europe there had been a discernible POW regime in place with Germany, one built on the solid foundations of reciprocal adherence to IHL and a functional POW relief system.[58] The robustness of the POW regime and the need to maintain its norms in its dealings with Berlin were important factors in shaping Allied, in particular British, reluctance to change its POW policies in the war's final year. It is also ironic that the ICRC's ability to maintain the functionality of the POW relief system during the war's middle years informed British views that the Committee would be able to perform similarly during the Reich's collapse without recourse to unorthodox measures. To accept the ICRC's proposals for a more radical and assertive humanitarian response in Europe would have required nothing short of a paradigm shift in humanitarian thinking on the part of the British. In this respect, old habits die hard. The DPW, for example, was very apprehensive towards the State Department's decision to approve the ICRC's pooled parcel depots, to the extent that Haccius was advised that, even under the new policy, parcels for Western Allies should be kept out of the hands of Soviet POWs where possible and that the trucks supplied to Geneva should be used only to supply British and American POWs.[59] The British Chiefs of Staff went a step further, expressing doubts that the ICRC's ambitious scheme for mobile relief could even be executed. Faced with the decision to approve the ICRC's new relief operation, there were the usual lamentations over the 'organizational problems involved' and the need for further reports to be compiled before a decision on the Committee's proposals could be made.[60] Considering this prevailing lack of imagination in British humanitarian thinking, the decision to hand the problem of dealing with the ICRC over to SHAEF stands as an even more momentous decision than it ostensibly appears. Without such a decision being made, it is difficult to conceive of those officials who had struggled for so long with the ICRC's ambitions being able to come around to Geneva's point of view, even when the POW situation had deteriorated so markedly.

In defence of those officials who found great difficulty in switching from a conservative humanitarian mindset to one that gave the ICRC greater autonomy, a few lingering strategic issues should be noted. At the time that the winter POW crisis was developing concerns were also growing in the Allied leadership of a German retreat to the much-vaunted 'Alpine Redoubt' – a fortified, mountainous zone to which Nazi fanatics and crack SS troops would fall back in order to make a final stand. There was even a suggestion that the marching POWs and VIP prisoners – the Prominente – would be herded to the Redoubt to be either used as bartering chips for trial-evading Nazis or simply executed in mass reprisal. This concern contributed to the understandable reluctance to allow the ICRC to become involved in what would be a delicate and complex problem. The idea of avoiding the Redoubt scenario by driving American forces deep into Austria in an effort to cut off any fleeing Germans, or of deploying special POW rescue units, such as SAARF, was also at odds with the proposals of the ICRC to have its trucks move unhindered through warzones. By turning the area around the suspected Redoubt into such a warzone, the conditions for the deployment of ICRC trucks laid out by the Secretary of War, James Grigg – 'that such assistance will not weaken the attack on Germany and so delay the conclusion of hostilities' – would have to be compromised. Another related consideration was that, following the shock of the Ardennes Offensive over Christmas, there was no certainty in Allied minds that victory was within months of being achieved. The concerns over a more drawn-out and bitter resistance from the Germans and the continuation of fighting into 1945 and beyond would have made the idea of giving the ICRC carte blanche to travel through active war zones unwelcomed, so too would have been the notion of diverting trucks, fuel and other supplies to Geneva when they might be needed by Allied forces.[61]

By March, however, many of these concerns over an unfettered ICRC had subsided and in SHAEF the Committee was finding the cooperation it had been denied by both Whitehall and, to a lesser extent, Washington. Much like Harry Phillimore, Eisenhower understood the importance of maintaining a close working relationship with the Committee. As early as June 1944 he had stressed that, when rejecting the ICRC's proposal for immunity zones, the response should not in any way question the competence of the Red Cross or the appreciation felt by the Allies for its efforts.[62] Furthermore, when the Committee and SHAEF began to cooperate over the winter of 1944–5, Eisenhower not only expedited the order to supply the ICRC with trucks and fuel but also approved the despatch of a terse communiqué to Bomber Command over recent attacks on as many as sixteen Red Cross trucks, as well as the *Henry Dunant* and the *Halleren*. This denouncement of attacks on Red Cross vehicles also led to a ban on the US Eighth Air Force attacking any vehicles or personnel seen on roads near Wismar and Schwerin – a quite extraordinary capitulation of military action to humanitarian needs.[63] This decision was, however, an exception to the prevailing rule which was – despite Eisenhower's relative amiability – that SHAEF's cooperation with the ICRC had limits, specifically at the point where the latter was deemed to be overstretching its mandate. The most notable instance of this came when SHAEF refused a request by the Committee for its delegates to inspect the POW transit camps that it had set up in France. Authorization to visit the dishevelled and poorly fed Germans held in these camps, and then only under strict conditions of supervision, was only given in October 1944 after months of cajoling.[64] This sore point aside, SHAEF's assistance to the ICRC was quite consistent and was maintained on the understanding that the Committee was both necessary to ensure that Allied POWs survived Europe's liberation, and was a qualified agent for the task. Once that liberation had taken place, however, the status of the ICRC in the victor's plans for Europe, and with it the role of the Committee in the post-war international order, was called into question.

8
Relief and Redundancy, 1945–6

A new humanitarian order

Europe in the spring of 1945 was a desperate place – short of food, lacking infrastructure, awash with the displaced, the wounded, the homeless and the starving. As this state of troubled peace emerged from the maelstrom of the war, Max Huber – newly returned to the post of ICRC president following Burckhardt's acceptance of the position of Swiss Foreign Minister to Paris – took to his pen, as he had in September 1939, to sketch out the tasks that awaited the ICRC in its next epoch.[1] Huber was very mindful of the fact that, fraught though it had been, the ICRC's war had engendered the greatest expansion in the organization's history and increased its capabilities and resources such that it could lay claim to being the humanitarian agent par excellence of the post-war world. Fortified by this belief in April 1945 he made an impassioned call to arms to the Red Cross faithful, in which he both pressed the need for the ICRC to sustain its relief effort following the cessation of hostilities and sought to remind his audience of the uniqueness and value of ICRC delegates at a time when a host of relief agencies representing all manner of outside interests was converging on Europe:

> as long as there are prisoners of war and occupied territories there will be circumstances in which *an institution independent of both victors and vanquished, acting only for humanitarian purposes and hampered by no political ties*, can be of service. Moreover, the Committee's wealth of experience and network of delegations render it capable of performing useful work in the difficult transition period following the end of hostilities.

Huber's conception of the Committee as not only the 'largest non-governmental body for distributing relief' but also one whose delegates had been seasoned by years of conflict and were prepared like no others to handle post-war humanitarian crises was not a chimera.[2]

It was Marti's delegates in Berlin who, having exerted themselves tremendously during the final days of the Reich, became the first ICRC workers to experience the difficulties of transition from war to peace. On 2 May Red Army soldiers kicked down what was left of the door of the delegation's headquarters at Wannsee – the building had been hit by artillery fire and been without water and electricity for several days – and then, having looted the premises, forced the delegation to move on. After a few weeks of desperate work trying to feed the flood of refugees into the city, the delegation was officially dissolved by the Soviet occupation forces, who interned six of Marti's staff in camps far away on the outskirts of Moscow. They were not released until 16 October 1945.[3] Junod was also in the thick of the other great arena of post-war crises in Japan. After years of struggle for recognition from Tokyo, the ICRC was at last given permission to bolster its delegation in the capital in May 1944.[4] It was not until November of that year, however, that Junod received the appropriate visas to begin his epic trek across the Soviet Union, Iran and into Manchuria, before at last arriving in the Japanese capital on 9 August 1945, just in time to hear of the dropping of the second atomic bomb on Nagasaki. In the weeks that followed, Junod – working out of a new ICRC headquarters that had replaced the one destroyed in an air raid – coordinated the Committee's attempts to uncover the locations of the many POW camps kept secret from them during the war, as well as negotiating with the American occupation forces for the despatch of medical supplies to Hiroshima, the ruins of which he eventually visited on 8 September.[5]

The exertions of the likes of Junod and Marti, and the relative success of the Committee when given a modicum of autonomy in Europe during the war's final months, probably influenced Huber's thinking about the place that the ICRC should occupy in the new post-war order. When he accepted the Nobel Peace Prize on behalf of the ICRC in December 1945, he made clear his view that 'no organisation intended to guarantee peace among nations can survive unless it is inspired by the idea of active solidarity among human beings, an idea which the Red Cross wishes to safeguard even in humanity's darkest hours'. The ICRC had learnt many lessons during the war, and, although in theory it 'made no claim to be a substitute for the Allied authorities or for the National Societies' in the relief effort to come, it was nonetheless willing and prepared to put its experience to use in order to build a 'constructive peace' on the foundations of faith in 'human solidarity'.[6]

This apparent robustness of the Red Cross spirit in 1945 was ostensibly matched by the strength of the ICRC as an organization. Over the war's duration Huber's tight-knit group of humanitarians had grown to comprise a staff of close to 4,000 volunteers, 179 of whom were official delegates accredited to the 76 delegations that had extended the Committee's purview across the globe. Chenevière's Central Agency had similarly spread across Switzerland, filling numerous buildings with endless rows of capture card indexes, overseen by a staff of 2,500 volunteers. Burckhardt's equally sizeable JRC was also kept running into the post-war period, on the assumption that it would play a key role in providing succour for Europe in the first years of peace.[7] Beneath this apparent preparedness, however, lay a dearth of funding. The ICRC's expenses had sky-rocketed from 1942 onwards and by 1944, bereft of funds from Italy and in the midst of preparations for Europe's liberation, it was clear that its future expenditure would be greater than revenue. A notably sizeable contribution from Britain, as well as increases in annual contributions from India, Norway and Chile, kept the ICRC solvent into 1945. During this year, however, it also lost Japanese and German funding and had the money owed it by the defeated Axis held up by the Swiss authorities at the request of the Allies.[8] The trend of downsizing, rather than expanding further in the post-war years, was set in motion.

The financial squeeze was not the only inhibitor of Huber's vision. For all its growth and good intentions, the ICRC's preparations for post-war relief had long been dwarfed by those of the Allies. In keeping with the policy of 'victory before relief', as early as 1941 the British had begun stockpiling foodstuffs and, in the years that followed, both Whitehall and Washington created agencies which would be tasked with organizing the distribution of these supplies once the fighting ended. In the United States, the War Relief Control Board was established by executive order on 25 July and a month later the British created the Council of British Societies for Relief Abroad, which was to act as the coordinator of all British humanitarian agencies in Europe, including the BRC. This was followed by the creation by President Roosevelt on 9 November 1943 of UNRRA, the body that would both oversee all post-war relief and coordinate the work of all agencies involved. UNRRA's creation was highly significant, in as much as it signified the end of the era of privatised humanitarianism – an era that had, arguably, been dominated by the Red Cross movement – and the coming of the age of greater state oversight and global governance in humanitarian action. In 1945, global governance meant the governance of the Allies, who for the most part envisioned UNRRA not only as a necessary means of alleviating the post-war suffering of civilians but also as part of a wider campaign to build a new, more cooperative international order on the ruins left by the war. The UNRRA's roving teams of volunteers – comprising American, British, French and other representatives of Allied nations – would provide the antidote to the years of dictatorship and barbarism that had defined the lives of so many in Europe. Relief would be distributed, humanity would be restored and hearts and minds would be won.[9]

Like most utopias, the UNRRA project was not all it appeared to be. Even before the war had ended a schism in Anglo-American thinking emerged over how the organization would operate and what, in the practical sense, it could achieve. Lord Halifax, the British Ambassador in Washington, embodied the conservative view of humanitarianism within the British administration by expressing his faith in the First World War system of post-war relief, which was built in no small part upon the enthusiasm of private, Christian organizations such as the YMCA, the Quakers and National Red Cross Societies. Beneath such faith in the old lay lingering suspicions of the new, specifically, the view that UNRRA was the embodiment of a typically American, muscular, idealistic, secular and bombastic form of humanitarianism. Concerns in some quarters of both Whitehall and Geneva that UNRRA's recruitment drive had led to the enrolment of the 'wrong' sort of people – those without relief experience or Zionists whose only concern was providing succour to Jews – were exacerbated by the impression that the whole organization was bereft of the kind of unity of purpose that more traditional humanitarian agencies possessed. Certain American politicians, incensed at the fact that the US Treasury was underwriting the lion's share of UNRRA's budget, complained of its wastefulness and, possible, pro-Communist leanings.[10] Conversely, the Soviet Ambassador in Britain, Ivan Maisky, expressed concerns that UNRRA could provide a cover for Western subversion and espionage in Soviet-held territories.[11]

Geneva had its own reasons for being wary of UNRRA. Not only did its creation eclipse any hopes Huber had for the ICRC being the primary humanitarian agency of the post-war relief effort but also the emergence of this American-backed organization doubtless seemed like the ghost of Davison's LRCS come back to haunt the Committee. The ICRC's criticisms of UNRRA's work certainly struck a similar note to the sentiment expressed over the League during the 1920s. The delegate Nicholas Burckhardt recalled that, at the ICRC's headquarters near Vlotho in the

British Occupation Zone, the various Red Cross workers were united both in their enthusiasm for their duties and in their belief that they, not UNRRA – mockingly known to Burckhardt's colleagues as You Never Really Relieved Anybody – were able to fulfil them. The presentation of UNRRA in the ICRC's official history is also telling. The former delegate André Durand wrote of UNRRA as if it were simply one 'of the various relief bodies' which worked alongside the ICRC in the post-war years, albeit one that 'gave considerable help' to the Committee.[12]

Aside from a degree of institutional jealousy, the ICRC's critical view of UNRRA was also born from the fact that, for all the hopes of UNRRA heralding a new, internationalist, cooperative humanitarian age, in practice its purview of operations was both restricted and partial to the interests of the victors. German civilians, be they from the Reich itself or ethnic Germans – *Volksdeutsche* – from elsewhere, were deemed to be outside UNRRA's remit, which was confined to providing relief for 'nationals of the United Nations, stateless persons, and Italian nationals' as well as non-German displaced persons (DPs).[13] Those thought to have sowed the seeds of the Nazi regime would, therefore, be left to harvest its bitterness.

This selective humanitarianism, which left UNRRA open to criticisms of being 'nothing more than a conqueror's relief wing', placed it at odds with the more universalist ICRC from the outset.[14] Shortly after its formation in 1943 UNRRA staff met with the Committee's Suzanne Ferrière in Washington, where a request was made that the ICRC assist the new organization in locating 'Allied nationals and neutrals in areas liberated by the United Nations forces'. Ferrière agreed that the ICRC could help by using the Agency's vast stores of information and the skills of delegates on the ground, albeit with the understanding that the Committee would not restrict itself to locating only Allied nationals and neutrals. As always, the ICRC, 'on principle', had to work 'for all persons, Allied and Axis alike'.[15] The UNRRA, for its part, still believed that cooperation with the ICRC was possible despite the gap in humanitarian philosophy. In August 1944 UNRRA's Director, Herbert Lehman, discussed with Alfred Zollinger several schemes that would bring the two organizations closer together. Although the discussions were amicable, Zollinger maintained that UNRRA's distinctly partial character meant that the Committee could only offer the most limited cooperation, lest too close an association compromise its principles of impartiality and neutrality. The UNRRA was also willing to play this game. When, for example, the Committee requested that UNRRA assist its delegation in Bucharest with relief for Romanian civilians, the latter refused on the grounds that such war victims were beyond its mandate. The idea of ICRC delegates attaching themselves to UNRRA teams and vice versa was also out of the question for similar reasons – mixed objectives would lead to confusion of purpose in the field. In the end, the only cooperation of note came in the agreement that UNRRA could make use of the ICRC's massive index of DP names and information.[16] This aside, UNRRA and the ICRC would, in the main, march to the beat of their own drums.

It is difficult to predict how much more effective the post-war relief effort might have been had UNRRA and the ICRC's efforts been better coordinated. To some extent, given UNRRA's relative success in spite of its early teething problems, such a hypothesis is moot.[17] What is certain is that, for better or worse, the separation of UNRRA and the ICRC was preferred by Washington and Whitehall, whose shared view of post-war relief work was that it would be overseen, first by SHAEF and then, with the creation of the various zones of occupation in Germany in the summer of 1945, by the Allied authorities in coordination with UNRRA. The entire relief operation had to be tightly managed and the Americans in particular felt that the 'liberal use of voluntary societies should be avoided at all costs'.[18] There was no room, therefore, for an independent body like the ICRC, whose principles placed it at odds with the imperatives of the Allies' relief strategy. Adding extra bitterness to the ICRC's exclusion was the fact that its two most prosperous 'children' – the BRC and the ARC – had been given high-profile positions within the victor's humanitarian plans. The latter had eagerly anticipated this. In 1942, when requested by Geneva to supply the JRC with additional food-stuffs to supplement its stockpiles, the ARC president, Norman Davies, refused, on the grounds that an 'intra-governmental relief organiza-tion' – UNRRA – would soon be founded. The ARC would thus make no commitment to helping the ICRC plan for post-war relief, until it could confirm what its relationship to this new organization and its role in the Allies' relief plan would be.[19] This confirmation came shortly after UNRRA's creation, when Davies was informed by Allied High Command that the ARC would handle all immediate civilian relief in the wake of the Allied armies' advance. Initially, this stoked a rivalry between the ARC and the BRC, who felt themselves being excluded by their richer, brasher trans-Atlantic cousin. This dispute was rectified, however, by the agreement of the Allies in May 1944 that both the ARC and the BRC – now recognized as being 'quasi-military organizations' – would carry out emergency relief operations, after which UNRRA teams would estab-lish a more permanent humanitarian mission.[20] In the interim period between the ARC and BRC deployments and the start of UNRRA's work, the latter would 'act in all matters under the orders of the Supreme Commander Allied Expeditionary Force, and through military channels', as well as act as 'coordinating authority' for all National Red Cross Societies and the YMCA, among others, in distributing relief. Very little thought, however, was given to ICRC–UNRRA cooperation.[21]

Although the aforementioned division of interests between UNRRA and the ICRC was important in confirming the latter's exclusion from the Allies' plans, another issue in its exclusion was the belief that the Committee, for all its claims to the contrary, was no different from other voluntary humanitarian groups, such as the Quakers, the YMCA, the World Council of Churches and the non-American or British National Societies, all of whom would have to work under the UNRRA umbrella. As one British official stressed in the days after the unconditional surrender, 'any ICRC work in connexion with displaced persons must be coordinated with the United Nations Relief and Rehabilitation Administration', which would also act as the conduit for correspondence between the Committee and SHAEF. Moreover, the ICRC's purchases of foodstuffs for its own relief operations would also need to be controlled by the British, who insisted that its Combined Food Board oversee the movement of all food supplies from Switzerland into the occupied territories.[22] Any notions that had emerged from the brief flurry of SHAEF/ICRC cooperation in the war's final weeks, therefore, of the Committee being raised to an elevated position in Allied considerations had dissipated.

The Allies' attitude was more a product of the post-war context and pragmatism than of disrespect towards the Committee. For all the life-saving work done by the ICRC's delegates in the war's final months, the constant common ground in relations between the Allies and the ICRC – the welfare of Allied POWs – had crumbled by the early summer of 1945. Following their liberation, Allied POWs were kept in Recovered Allied Military Personnel camps and provided for by the ICRC and the Allies themselves, until such time as they could be repatriated in an orderly manner. It was a scheme that adhered to the principles of 'stand fast'. As had been the case before, however, the dictum was problematic when applied. Discontent over the delay in getting home and the breakdown of discipline among some POWs led to orders being given in April for their immediate repatriation in order to avert further trouble.[23] The extent to which POW discontent was viewed seriously by the Allied leadership can be gauged by the fact that by the end of May most of the evacuations had been completed. From that point on Allied

POWs – long seen by Whitehall and Washington as the ICRC's *raison d'être* – were no longer a factor of consideration. This was true, at least, in Europe. In the Far East, in contrast, the ICRC's work on behalf of Allied POWs continued for much longer, and with it the importance of the Committee's delegates to the Allied administrators. The day after the Japanese surrender Junod began a relationship of 'close collaboration with the Allied headquarters' in Japan, which provided material support to his endeavours to track down, distribute relief to and, ultimately, repatriate the many American POWs held in camps hitherto unknown to the ICRC.[24] The Committee in the Far East was, therefore, an important component of the liberation–repatriation process. In Europe, however, where the Allied authorities – for reasons of geography as much as anything else – were able to exert control more thoroughly over, first, POW repatriations and then the relief effort writ large, the ICRC was placed back in the role of helpful amateur humanitarian. As one official from the Ministry of Food remarked, with UNRRA activated, 'the work of the International Red Cross will now tend to shrink'.[25]

It is possible that the ICRC could have nullified this perception. The issue that had lain at the heart of British reluctance to support the ICRC's relief work in Europe – fear of German influence – was gone by the spring of 1945 and, owing to the importance of the Committee's on-going work in the Far East, there was little scepticism expressed by the British of the competency of ICRC delegates to work in post-war conditions. The problem, as was made clear to Nicholas Burckhardt, was that if it wanted to carry out similar work in Europe 'it would be necessary for the International Committee to consult to authorities in the respective occupied zones'.[26] This standard wartime practice of acquiring state consent for its work was complicated in 1945 by the fact that the ICRC had done itself few favours by making clear years earlier that its work had to be independent of UNRRA oversight. This became an important factor once it emerged that UNRRA, despite two years of preparation, was struggling to respond to the scale of the humanitarian crisis. At the time of the Unconditional Surrender there were only eight UNRRA teams available. Moreover, they soon gained a reputation in the eyes of the occupation forces for being 'not entirely effective' and 'more concerned with their own personal interests than with doing their respective jobs'.[27] This criticism by the very people who were supposed to be backing them belied deeper tensions between UNRRA and the Allies, who failed to deliver appropriate levels of transport and supplies and despaired of the fact that, in a situation where control was a high priority, 'the duties that UNRRA was supposed to perform were not set with precision or exactitude'.[28] Ironically, therefore, similar frustrations to those expressed by the Allies during the war over the conduct of the ICRC were applied to UNRRA in the first months of peace.

What slim chance the Committee had of stepping into the breach and offering its services to bolster UNRRA's efforts was stamped out, however, by the fact that, in addition to its refusal to countenance cooperation with the latter, the ICRC was sidestepped in considerations by the Allies, who looked to the BRC and the ARC to strengthen the teams of UNRRA volunteers. The Committee's only real contribution to solving one of the UNRRA's myriad early problems was to provide some maintenance and repair facilities for its trucks.[29] Anything more, it was thought, might have run the ICRC dangerously close to compromising its neutrality and impartiality by working within the parameters of UNRRA's partial, Anglo-American relief campaign. As UNRRA was a humanitarian proxy of the Allies, this divergence was in some respects simply the latest manifestation of the conflicting view of humanitarianism that had been prevalent between the Allies and the ICRC during the war – 'relief for some' or 'relief for all'. As had been the case during the war, the result for the Committee of this divergence was estrangement from the Allies, who, in contrast to Huber's universalist humanitarian sentiments, tended to view the provision of succour for civilian refugees 'more as a logistical than a humanitarian problem'.[30] An example of how the ICRC's opposing viewpoint could be problematic emerged in another duty that the Committee assumed during the transition from war to peace – the tracing of the many lost and displaced refugees and the issuing of travel permits for DPs.

During the war, the ICRC had built up a successful tracing operation, in collaboration with the National Societies, which enabled it to keep track of the movement of refugees and the transfer of camp inmates across Europe.[31] No amount of preparation, however, was enough for the task of tracing the millions of DPs who took to Europe's roads in the final year of the war. As a means of clearing the backlog, as early as 1944 the ICRC's Rome delegation began to loosen its regulations for the issuing of travel permits for refugees. Standards dropped further in 1945, prompting clashes between the ICRC and the Allied authorities, who wanted tighter regulations on the movement of DPs and a clamp down on the ICRC's laissez-faire practice. As in relief, the Allies installed their own agency for the task of processing DPs, the International Refugee Organisation (IRO), which took a similar stance to UNRRA: *Volksdeutsche* were not victims of war, and thus were not entitled to flee its aftermath. Only after intense investigation confirmed that a DP was in fact a genuine war victim were IRO travel permits issued. Although it seemed harsh, this policy had some justification. As early as 1947 it became apparent that the lack of investigation into individual cases of DPs by the ICRC had led to travel permits being issued to members of the SS, Nazi Party and collaborators. The Committee was thus complicit, through its amateurism, in the flight of war criminals from justice.[32] Moreover, the debacle over travel permits served to estrange the ICRC from the Allied/UNRRA humanitarian effort further. This sense of the ICRC being 'the other' in post-war humanitarianism was exacerbated further when, following the dissolution of the German state and its government as a requirement of the Unconditional Surrender, Switzerland ceased to be the Protecting Power for German interests. In a less than ideal fulfilment of one of its wartime wishes, the ICRC thus became the new neutral protector of the Germans. This apparent elevation was approved by the British, albeit with the qualification that the ICRC should not be 'promoted to the status of diplomatic intermediary', but instead simply be recognized as the primary representative for German interests.[33] This role, combined with UNRRA's exclusion of German and *Volksdeutche* DPs from its remit, meant that the ICRC became the key humanitarian agent for millions of German POWs and DPs spread across Europe – a task that, owing to anti-German sentiment, did little for its reputation and further estranged it from the war's victors.[34]

The protector of the Germans

As the winter of 1944/5 loomed, those of the Wehrmacht who were able scrambled west to reach the Anglo-American lines, lest they be made captives of the inexorably advancing and brutally vengeful Red Army. This led to millions of German POWs – more than was ever anticipated by SHAEF – being marched into Western Allied captivity during the war's final months. Despite the hopes of the Germans, deprivation of food and medical care, as well as varying degrees of maltreatment, were prevalent aspects of their internment in the months that followed. This was primarily as a consequence of the continuation of the same poor POW planning by the Allies that had occurred in the years before. This planning had lacked, above all else, the foresight to prepare for mass capitulation. In the autumn of 1944 waves of German POWs were shipped across the Channel from barely functional camps in France. There was little provision in Britain, however, for this overflow of prisoners, which led to the suggestion that they be housed in tents within barbed-wire-ringed fields – in the middle of winter.[35] The housing difficulties were exacerbated in 1945 by the lack of available food in Europe, which, combined with the dramatic growth of the German prisoner population – 7.5 million by June 1945 – led to the aforementioned decline in standards of treatment for German POWs.[36] These logistical problems were also undeniably edged with a degree of contempt for the vanquished on the part of some of the victors, which led to abuses of the prisoners and a general lack of care and consideration for their welfare. The notion, however, that anger at the Germans manifested in a secret policy of murderous revenge devised and overseen by Eisenhower is pure myth.[37] Nonetheless, the experience of German POWs in the West, though preferable to the experience of those held by the Soviets, was without question one of hardship and deprivation, in which parlous accommodation and lack of food and medical care were recurring motifs of captivity.

The policies that had been developed by Whitehall and Washington for handling the 1945 POW crisis were by no means acceptable to the ICRC, and caused a point of post-war friction far greater than any raised by UNRRA's monopolizing of the relief effort. Mindful of the possibility of post-war food shortages, the value of German prisoners as labourers and the fact that the Soviets had not ratified the POW Convention and thus would not hold to its articles in their treatment of the Germans, the Western Allies began discussing, as early as the summer of 1944, the possibility that those who laid down their arms as part of the Unconditional Surrender would not be recognized as POWs. Instead, a new classification for the prisoners which would exclude them from the standards of treatment laid down in the Convention – including the right to visitations and relief from the ICRC – was created: Surrendered Enemy Personnel (SEPs).[38] This classification was applied to both the 3.4 million Germans captured after April 1945 and, in the Far East, to the 3.5 million Japanese soldiers who laid down arms in August. In the wake of the former influx of prisoners into the European theatre, many of the newly designated SEPs were held until July 1945 in a series of massive, poorly provisioned, open-air enclosures along the west bank of the Rhine – the *Rheinwiesenlager* – within which anywhere between 4,000 and 40,000 of them died.[39]

The ICRC's appeal that these prisoners, irrespective of their SEP designation, should be treated in accordance with the articles of the Convention was rejected by the Allies, who did little to conceal that the SEP designation had been implemented specifically to address the fact that they could not and, owing to food shortages and overall occupation policy, were not willing to provide the standards of treatment laid down in the Convention to such a massive cohort of prisoners.[40] As the Foreign Office noted in response to the ICRC's querying of SEP status in 1947, 'it would have been physically impossible to have applied the Prisoner of War Convention in very many respects to these men' during the first, chaotic months of peace in Europe. In such circumstances, in which the norms of POW treatment could not be applied, 'it was quite impossible for Commanders-in-Chief to do more than ensure that captives were treated as humanely as possible.' As Churchill himself opined in 1944 to the House, the determining factor in Allied policy towards their enemies would not be to 'any pact or obligation' but to 'our consciences to civilisation'.[41] That this conscience was burdened by years of bitter war against an enemy whose capacity for barbarism was matched by his reluctance to concede defeat; and that such factors led to a standard of treatment for German POWs that was not in accordance to the wishes of the ICRC, is not surprising.

For the ICRC, however, there was no excuse for such ill-treatment. Agitation for more food and medicines, better camp facilities and swift repatriation – both on humanitarian grounds as well as to remove the financial burden that the Committee bore for providing relief for German prisoners – were prevalent themes in Allied–ICRC relations throughout 1945.[42] Although the *Rheinweisenlager* were closed by the autumn, the status of the SEPs continued to be applied and conditions in other camps, particularly in France, remained parlous. It was not until October 1945 that the ICRC achieved a breakthrough in its campaign for better treatment for the Germans. It was the transfer in the summer of as many as 400,000 emaciated prisoners from the American-administrated *Rheinweisenlager* into the hands of the French for the purposes of labour that prompted the ICRC Paris delegation's chief, Jean-Pierre Pradervand, to launch his own protests – without seeking approval from Geneva – to both the French and the Americans. The appeal resonated in the French press and evoked support from the French POW Department. Accordingly, in October the transfer of prisoners was suspended, the Americans agreed to release more food to the camps and the process of repatriation for those too old or sick to be of use in the French labour force was speeded up.[43] At the same time the ICRC was finally given permission to place a permanent delegation in the British Occupation Zone. Headed by Nicholas Burckhardt, formerly of the London Delegation, the new ICRC office at Vlotho was established on 30 October in order to deliver relief to German DPs and carry out inspections of POW camps. As the Committee happily noted, with this event the 'doors have now been opened towards extensive spheres of action'.[44]

Similar agreements for permanent ICRC delegations in other Western Allied Occupation Zones were forthcoming, first with the French in December 1945 and, in February 1946, with the Americans, although visits to civilian detainment camps in the latter zone were still prohibited. In April 1946 even the Soviets began to permit some ICRC relief to be issued in their zone.[45] Ostensibly, therefore, by the spring of 1946 the ICRC was at last making its mark in terms of post-war relief, not just for German DPs but also for POWs. As a watershed for relief these developments were significant but tensions between the ICRC and the Allies remained. The British may have allowed the ICRC into their zone and, according to at least one delegate in conversation with the British authorities, were the most cooperative of the occupation forces. The fact remained, however, that the ICRC was still, for the most part, unwanted. The policy of restraint, moreover, was still firmly applied. Following the decision to let Nicholas Burckhardt establish his delegation, the British remarked that 'the IRC is not necessary and indeed has no case to exercise its traditional role in succouring PWs as no Wehrmacht personnel in Germany now possess PW status'.[46] It was not until March 1946 that this view, at least officially, began to recede and the British admitted that 'conditions under which a distinction was originally made between prisoners of war and disarmed enemy forces no longer exist'.[47]

This acknowledgement did not, however, herald an immediate turn around in the fortunes of German POWs, or an increase in the purview of the ICRC to provide them relief. As late as September 1946, Huber was still asking the British for the codes of the POW Convention to be applied in full to German prisoners who, despite being allowed visits from ICRC inspectors, were still not permitted to speak to the delegates in order to air grievances without a British guard being present.[48] This, moreover, was only the case for those Germans who had been redesignated as POWs at the start of 1946. As late as the summer of that year the Committee remained cut off from any knowledge of the conditions of at least 20,000 prisoners – still classified as SEPs – being held in Austria. In Norway, by contrast, the SEPs had been handed over to the care of the Norwegian authorities who, in general, applied the standards of the Convention consistently. As the War Office conceded, despite the decision to transform the prisoners back into POWs, variations in standards of treatment and adherence to the Convention were commonplace depending on the place of detainment and the resources at the disposal of the local authorities.[49] The ICRC's attempts to have some form of uniformity of treatment enforced consistently met with failure. Huber's protest to the Foreign Secretary, Ernest Bevin, in September 1946, was not even acknowledged until 21 January 1947 and, when the official reply came a month later, it was simply a reiteration of policy: the SEP designation had been necessary in 1945 but now standards of humane treatment in accordance with the Convention were being applied, where possible.[50]

With regards to both the campaign for better treatment for German POWs/SEPs and its post-war civilian relief effort, the Committee was hampered by three main factors. First, the Allies clearly had little, if any, inclination to incorporate the ICRC into their post-war relief plans. In the case of civilians, UNRRA was expected to handle everything and, when this did not transpire in the manner envisioned, the Committee's refusal to submit itself to Allied governance meant that it was never going to be looked to as a suitable accompaniment to UNRRA's humanitarian campaign. It was not until 1946 that the ICRC's work on behalf of non-German civilians increased, and only then with UNRRA still firmly entrenched as the primary humanitarian agent.[51] The power exerted by the Allies over German and Japanese prisoners also ensured that any work performed by the ICRC on their behalf would have to be carried out in accordance with the policy for prisoner treatment that had been conceived by the occupation authorities. The fact that this policy amounted to a rejection of the Convention not only built a mountain of difficulties for the ICRC in terms of prisoner welfare but also removed its delegate's *locus standi*.

The second, related, problem was that the only weapons that the ICRC had to ensure adherence to the Convention – reciprocity and appeals to principles of humanity – were near to valueless in the context of 1945. Reciprocity ceased to function as a mechanism for ensuring compliance the moment that Allied POWs were moved out of harm's way. Appeals to humanity had some effect, particularly when they were edged with the threat of public criticism and support from dissenting Allied departments, as had occurred in France. This apparent breakthrough in the ICRC's post-war campaign, however, was the exception rather than the rule. The Allies in the main were successful in keeping public criticism of their occupation policy contained, in part by refusing to allow the ICRC, the YMCA and other humanitarian agencies access to the camps over the summer of 1945 when conditions were at their most scandalous. This policy of keeping neutral oversight to a minimum was adhered to as much by the Americans as the British.[52] On account of this, the ICRC also lost one of the key tools that had served it in clashes with Whitehall over humanitarian policy during the war: American intervention and fears of bad publicity. The ICRC, therefore, had very little with which to persuade the Allies to moderate their occupation policies and was greatly disempowered in the aftermath of the Second World War. Its mandates to provide relief to both civilians and POWs had been severely weakened, if not fully subsumed, by the policies of the Allies who had little use for the Committee now that the fighting had ended. Consequently, the ICRC was left adrift, as Huber put it to his colleagues, in a 'situation without precedent and particularly ungrateful', no longer enjoying the level of support it had received from belligerents during the conflict. In such context, the ICRC delegates' only recourse was to 'prudence, courage and perseverance'.[53]

All three qualities would be needed in tackling the third factor in the ICRC's post-war estrangement from the Western Allies: the attitude of Moscow. Ever since the ICRC had 'interfered' by sending relief to the Soviet Union during its Civil War of the early 1920s, the Kremlin had held a certain repugnance and distrust for 'anything that savours of Switzerland'.[54] The constant, seemingly meddlesome attempts by the ICRC throughout the Second World War to establish a delegation on Soviet soil, and Stalin's assumption that Huber and company were in cahoots with Goebbels in the Katyn Affair, had only served to strengthen that distrust with regards to the Committee, whose neutrality was as doubted by the Soviets as its delegates' capacity to spy on behalf of Moscow's enemies was accepted. The detention of staff from Marti's delegation by the Red Army and the flurry of criticisms thrown at Geneva by the Soviets – via mail, owing to the latter's unwillingness to attend – during the Seventeenth International Red Cross conference in 1948 was indicative of the extent to which this hostility lingered into the post-war era.[55]

The Western Allies were mindful of the level of Soviet distrust and factored it into their treatment of the ICRC in the years after 1945. When considering post-war relief plans, the Foreign Office expressed concern that the relative freedom granted 'a multifarious collection of Red Cross and other Societies running about Germany' would upset Moscow at a time when placation of Stalin was paramount. Accordingly, UNRRA's appointment as chief co-ordinating body was seen, among other things, as a means of assuring Moscow that voluntary societies such as the ICRC and the YMCA would only operate under the restrictions of Allied control.[56] This idea of controlling the ICRC as a means of placating the Soviets was also carried to the San Francisco Conference in June 1945, at which the United Nations charter was signed. Prior to the conference, the Foreign Office had refused a proposal from the BRC

for the ICRC to be recognized by name in the Charter for the purposes
of having its position 'safeguarded' by the United Nations. Considering
that ignorance of the ICRC's right to initiative had been displayed,
to varying degrees, by almost every belligerent of the Second World
War, the request for a clause in the Charter pledging signatories 'to
respect the independent and voluntary character of the Red Cross
organization of all nations' was reasonable.[57] The Foreign Office, however, citing the harsh reality of Soviet disapproval of the Committee,
declared that mention of the ICRC at the conference would be a distrac-
tion to the participants' efforts to keep such a politically weighty meeting 'on the rails'. Although ostensibly this attitude towards the ICRC
was for Moscow's benefit, it is unlikely that the British were entirely
reluctant to oblige Soviet prejudices. The only notable deviation from
this policy was provided by P. S. Falla, a PWD staffer who believed that
the real issue at stake in the question of ICRC acknowledgment in the
Charter was to make sure that the Committee's neutrality was not compromised by having the organization attached to the United Nations.[58]
His consideration of the ICRC's neutrality needing to be protected was
the exception, however, not the rule to Allied considerations. The sum
of this was that the war's victors, in the main, excluded the ICRC from
both the post-war relief effort and their attempts to build a new, more
stable and peaceful world order.

Conclusion

The ICRC's three main objectives in the Second World War were to provide humanitarian assistance to as many people as it was able; to respond to the conflict's spread and escalation by extending its operational purview and improving its capabilities; and, finally, to maintain its reputation and right to act, by upholding the sanctity of the Geneva and POW Conventions and adhering to the principles of neutrality and impartiality. The ICRC's aim in short, was to expand, respond and adapt within the limits of its principles, as it always had, to the changing conditions of war. By contrast, the British Government's humanitarian policy – the basis upon which its wartime relations with the ICRC were conducted – both lay at the periphery of its concerns and was restricted by the parameters of self-interest and political and strategic considerations. There were inevitable clashes between Whitehall and the ICRC on account of this divergence. The British Government came to depend greatly on the Committee, however, to maintain the health and well-being of the many British subjects who fell into captivity and, in no small part through its contretemps with Whitehall, the ICRC expanded in both ambition and operational purview during the Second World War.

Although it was not as prohibitive as the flat-out rejection of the ICRC's very presence in certain theatres, the blockade of Europe was among the most disruptive obstacles the Committee faced during the Second World War. It was certainly the greatest restriction imposed by the Western Allies upon its work. We have to be wary, however, of simplistic assessments of the blockade as an unjust millstone around the neck of wartime humanitarianism. Blockade was a legal and accepted method of waging war, and as such it was beyond the right of the ICRC, or anyone else for that matter, to question it as a legitimate strategy. Moreover, although the ethos of Whitehall's humanitarian policy – 'victory before relief' – was not significantly altered during the war, British humanitarian policy was not completely inflexible. Owing perhaps to its slogan-like simplicity, the policy was riddled from the outset with grey areas that required, and received, consideration and clarification from Whitehall as the war progressed. This was particularly true once the more moderate Earl of Selborne took over leadership of the MEW from Hugh Dalton in 1942, at which time also the war's scope broadened, relief advocates became more numerous and vocal and the task of maintaining the blockade in such a context more challenging. It would perhaps be a step too far to suggest that British humanitarian policy genuinely evolved over the course of the war. The refusal to approve of the ICRC's depots and trucks schemes, the adherence to the POW 'stand fast' order, the holding off on the delivery of food into the Netherlands until mere days before the arrival of Allied forces and the deployment of UNRRA in conjunction with the liberation were all consistent with 'victory before relief'. It is clear that, through the concessions made to Greece and Vichy, the loosening of POW and civilian internee relief protocols in the Far East and the permission, despite deeply entrenched reservations, to allow the ICRC to expand its capacity for relief operations via the White Ships, however, Whitehall was capable of responding to changed circumstances and was willing, when the context seemed appropriate, to bend the humanitarian rules it had set in August 1940. If Whitehall is to be criticized, it should be for the fact that the appropriateness of the context was determined, almost solely, by the extent to which Britain could benefit – if necessary to the detriment of her present and former allies.

In the case of Vichy it was in the name of maintaining good relations with Roosevelt and Pétain that thoughts in Whitehall turned to adjusting the blockade. In Greece, the concessions were forced by a combination of external pressures, the propaganda benefit of highlighting the damage done to Greece by the German occupation and the need to preserve good relations with a country that fell within Britain's sphere of influence. Concerns of national interest and public scrutiny also influenced Whitehall's policies for POW relief. In 1940, the impetus behind British approval of bulk parcel deliveries for British prisoners, involvement in the establishment of the Lisbon–Marseilles route and intervention into the BRC's parcel-producing operations were made with the aim of diffusing public criticism of the government and of protecting the health and well-being of British soldiers in captivity. Similar motivations were present in the Far East where, on account of the even greater danger posed to British POWs and civilian internees, Whitehall was prepared to allow the ICRC greater autonomy than it did in any other area of its wartime work. The approval for the White Ships was also given on the premise that more cargo space would mean more parcels for British POWs, a potent concern considering the loss of over 30,000 soldiers to captivity in North Africa in the summer of 1942. In each instance of flexible decision-making, therefore, the imperative of British wartime humanitarian policy remained: to balance the humanitarian needs of British victims of war with the maintenance of the blockade and its underlying principle of 'victory before relief'.

On the aforementioned occasions where this imperative was challenged or required alteration, the ICRC played the role of agitator and, more importantly, facilitator. The POW relief system in Europe, its less stable equivalent in the Far East, the White Ships and the Baltic Route provided the means through which relief could, if Whitehall deemed necessary, be delivered. The Committee alone was not responsible for constructing these schemes and systems of relief, which required negotiations with and assistance from, various National Red Cross societies and both belligerent and neutral governments in order to succeed. The ICRC's role as a driving force, not to say, visionary, in these plans was, however, important; no less than its delegates' willingness to shoulder the often perilous burdens of being agents on-board White Ships, distributors of relief in Japanese POWs camps, drivers of trucks through war-torn Germany and managers of warehousing and transport logistics in Lisbon, Marseilles and Piraeus among other ports. Enthusiasm for taking on these duties, however, was never enough to persuade the British that the ICRC could be trusted. If anything, the Committee's rush to embrace innovative and, at times, dangerous humanitarian schemes only made Whitehall more sceptical and brought to the surface the same reservations – distant in time, though not in potency – that Thomas Longmore and Florence Nightingale had once espoused: the Red Cross was amateur and had no place on the battlefield. In order to address this concern the ICRC, like Whitehall, also had to adapt its practices and modify its approach to humanitarian action.

The ICRC has always been 'slow to embrace change'.[1] This applies to everything from its leadership, to its principles, to the development of the Red Cross movement, to the wider political and strategic contexts in which it operates. For all its interwar difficulties and ill-preparedness for the Second World War, however, it is notable that the ICRC was quite forward thinking once the fighting had commenced. Having already built the foundations of its POW relief system prior to the German invasion of Western Europe – via the establishment of parcel supply routes, processes for collecting and forwarding prisoner information and the normalization of the practice of inspecting civilian internment camps – the Committee was able to construct new parcel routes, warehouses and procedures which together comprised its post-Dunkirk POW relief system. Many delegates also proved themselves adaptable to changes in the field. Junod, Marti, Egle, Zindel and Schweizer were all good at thinking on their feet, constructing inventive means of carrying out their tasks and, at times even skirting the edges of accepted ICRC practice. Innovation and flexibility in the practical aspects of its mission therefore, were common traits of the ICRC's work – indeed, they still are.[2]

With regards to the broader approaches it took to humanitarian action and the principles that guided its practice, however, the ICRC was slower to adjust. This owed as much to the deep, conservative roots that emphasized neutrality and impartiality as guiding principles as to the similarly unchanged nature of its leadership structure, which placed great emphasis on the opinions of a select few. There was little room in the meeting halls of Geneva for the kind of innovation and flexibility that could occur thousands of miles away in a world of barbed-wire and barbarism.[3] Odier's impassioned pleas for humanitarian aid for non-British war victims, Chenevière's reservations over the JRC and Huber's lamentations to belligerents over the evils of bombing and blockade reflected this conservatism and inability to adapt. In terms of British–ICRC relations, the disconnectedness of such sentiments from the reality of the conflict was detrimental. Huber and Odier's views in particular were simply too universalist and utopian to fit within the more limited paradigm of humanitarianism that had been constructed by the British. It was only once the ICRC showed a capacity to comprehend the central features of this paradigm – maintenance of British POW welfare and respect for British strategy – and work towards these ends that its schemes were met with something more than disinterest or indifference in Whitehall.

Words from Geneva were important, to some extent, in finding this common ground. Burckhardt's visit to London in 1941 – at which he outlined the White Ships scheme and apprised the British of all that had been done on behalf of their POWs since the crisis of the previous year – had some effect in countering the impression of amateurism conveyed by Odier. Haccius's incremental adjustment to British sensitivities, particularly once George Warner had been replaced by Harold Satow in early 1941, was also important in correcting misapprehensions and smoothing over the problems in day-to-day British–ICRC relations. What truly mattered to the British, however, was what the ICRC could deliver, rather than promise. The Committee had to demonstrate that it could not only carry out the duties prescribed to it in the Conventions but also, if necessary, take on new, more ambitious humanitarian projects with a degree of professionalism or, at the very least, aptitude.

The ICRC's achievements in these endeavours were mixed. This was because, although its members certainly became more mindful of

British sensitivities as the war went on, the Committee, like MEW, the PWD and the DPW, was unwilling to stray from its primary dictum: neutrality in dealing with belligerents, impartiality in relief. The need to adhere to these principles was absolutely vital to the ICRC's wartime mission. Then as now, without acknowledgement from the belligerents of its moral authority, backed by the sanctity of the Convention, the ICRC would have had no *locus standi*. It had to place itself 'above' the conflict in order to intervene. For this reason there could be no question of acquiescing fully to British wishes in order, for example, to gain greater blockade concessions. The most that could be done was to walk the thin line between accepted practice and adaptability by framing relief proposals in a manner that would appeal to the British, while not negating the ICRC's commitment to impartial relief. For the diehard humanitarians within the ICRC, this was a difficult balancing act. Odier and Zollinger lacked subtlety in their proposals and, in general, rubbed the British and the Americans the wrong way by consistently failing to appreciate Allied concerns. Max Huber was a man of two parts in this respect. Although his professional background, training and experience made him aware of the political aspects of the ICRC's work, his prevailing belief in the inherent goodness of the Red Cross ethos and the seriousness with which he took the Committee's neutrality and impartiality left him stranded, particularly as the war became more multifaceted and barbarous, in a grey area of indecision and ineffectuality. This was demonstrated most clearly in his publication of the *Good Samaritan* in 1943, in which he called on belligerents to turn back the tide of escalation and embrace the common values of humanity.[4] It was a fruitless campaign that Huber continued into 1944, with the similarly unrealistic call for immunity zones across France and the Reich coming as the fighting in Europe reached its final, bloody crescendo. The fact that these proposals came as his health worsened and the conflict intensified in its barbarism was likely no coincidence. The ICRC president was, quite simply, overwhelmed by the scale of the war and the depths of its inhumanity.

The man who benefited most from this decline in Huber – Carl J. Burckhardt – possessed a very different mindset. Burckhardt was a central figure in British–ICRC relations and his contributions to the ICRC's wartime mission were many and varied. He was, both in the final years of peace and during the war itself, a politician in a humanitarian's cloak, motivated as much, if not more so, by personal ambition than the Red Cross ethos which he, on occasion, would criticize for its naivety.[5] Burckhardt's wartime career, and with it his relations with the British, can be divided into three parts. In the war's opening years he carried the stigma of his peaceable intent of the 1930s into British–ICRC relations. This was not as damaging as might have been expected. Indeed, Anthony Eden and George Warner were less fearful of Burckhardt's political machinations than they were contemptuous of his pretensions. Nevertheless, his distinctly political character and habit of shelving ICRC neutrality when required raised eyebrows in Whitehall. This trait, however, could be a double-edged sword. It is arguable that, because Burckhardt's trip to London in 1941 did not bring the anticipated peace-feeler but, rather, a series of well-thought out relief plans that addressed British concerns, much wariness of him and the utopianism of the ICRC writ large was, temporarily, dissipated. In the wake of this small victory emerged the second phase of Burckhardt's relations with the British where, against the backdrop of fears in Geneva over its wartime failings and place in history, he launched a campaign both to better the Committee's operations and to improve the prospects for his own post-war reputation. The JRC, the White Ships and the CCPS were manifestations of a clever blend of traditional ICRC expansion – and the humanitarian impetus behind it – with Burckhardt's more political and pragmatic approach to Red Cross work. All three projects required the conduct of humanitarian diplomacy of the highest order. Greater cooperation between the LCRS and the ICRC had to be fostered, British anxieties over blockade concessions had to be tempered and German restrictions on relief for concentration camp internees had to be worked around. It is difficult to say definitively if Huber, Chenevière or Odier could have alone brokered the deals required for these innovations. What is certain, however, is that, although he was assisted to varying extents by Marti and Schwarzenberg, all three projects bore the hallmark of Burckhardt's ambition, his views on humanitarianism and concerns over the reputation of himself and the ICRC.

The Committee's handling of the Shackling Crisis and the Katyn Affair were also very much the products of Burckhardt's 'realpolitik humanitarianism', which typified the third stage of his wartime career. Although in the case of the Shackling Crisis Burckhardt undermined his own efforts by succumbing both to his overwhelming sense of self-importance and insecurity over the Protecting Power's status as compared with that of the ICRC, he was able, nevertheless, to harness both his German contacts and his political instincts to play a key role in ending the crisis. The handling of Katyn was not solely a Burckhardt effort. His concerns over appearing meddlesome to the Soviets and the British were, however, in harmony with Huber's own fears over the jeopardy into which the Committee might place itself by dancing to

Goebbels's propaganda tune. The sum of this mutual apprehension marked a high point in the ICRC's humanitarian diplomacy of the Second World War. An acknowledgement that it was both in over its head and in danger of politicizing its actions too overtly led to the prudent decision to walk away from Katyn. For Burckhardt personally, this decision was of even greater significance. It dovetailed, not only with his campaign to turn the ICRC away from utopianism and into the arms of pragmatism – which was, arguably, launched by his performance at the 'non-appeal' meeting of October 1942 – but also with his charm offensive against the British Government. The results of this attempt to rehabilitate himself were not altogether satisfactory. George Warner still believed, as late as 1944, that Burckhardt was 'pro-Fascist', a view that contributed to him losing out to another ICRC member turned politician, Paul Ruegger, for the post of Swiss Minister in London in early 1945.[6] He was, nonetheless, able to reach out after the war to and receive support from the wartime Minister of Information, Duff Cooper, and the former British Ambassador in Madrid, Sir Samuel Hoare, who both agreed to Burckhardt's request that they issue statements refuting claims in the press that he had played a role in the flight of Rudolf Hess to Scotland in 1941.[7]

In the final analysis of Burckhardt, it is fair to say that the very qualities that have made him such a controversial figure in the ICRC's history were, in practice, instrumental in pushing the Committee over its traditional institutional hurdles: tentativeness in dealing with belligerents, reluctance to break with tradition, lack of innovation at the leadership level. That this helped the ICRC to respond better to the humanitarian crises of the Second World War is clear to see. Although he did not completely win over the British personally, or raise the ICRC's status to a height comparable with that of the Protecting Power, Burckhardt's schemes nevertheless did help the ICRC to expand the scope of its operations, deliver more parcels and, in the case of the Shackling Crisis, creep ever so modestly into the role of humanitarian mediator. His contributions were also somewhat beneficial for British–ICRC relations. In the main, the schemes he championed demonstrated that the Committee was capable of shoehorning its 'relief for all' ethos into the framework of 'victory before relief' laid down by the British. Although some in the MEW were never persuaded, the fact that the White Ships led neither to the collapse of the blockade nor to a reduction in parcel delivery to British POWs in favour of suppling other Allied prisoners showed that Geneva and Whitehall's seemingly divergent relief policies could be somewhat reconciled. The problem was that the ICRC, having been given the proverbial inch by the British, almost always expected to take a foot.

The need to push belligerents just that little bit further in humanitarian concessions was an institutionalized practice of the ICRC and was thus a recurring motif in its dealings with Britain, no less than other belligerents, throughout the war. When it suited British interests – for example in the case of extending ICRC inspections from civilian to POW camps in 1940 – this practice was welcomed. However, when it was perceived by the British as the Committee reverting to type – as in the case of Odier and Burckhardt pushing to use the one-off relief shipments to Greece and Vichy as a platform for a broader relief plan – Whitehall came down hard. This need to 'rein in' the ICRC's ambitions was as potent in Whitehall's considerations as the impetus to direct its energies towards British interests. The POW exchange negotiations for example, in which the British preferred the Protecting Power to act as mediator, were particularly viewed by Whitehall as a no-go zone for the Committee. The fear was that, in its rush to play saviour to sick and wounded POWs and those kept in long-term captivity, the ICRC would not only undermine the norms of humanitarian diplomacy established for prisoner exchanges but also in so doing imperil British interests by disrupting attempts to get soldiers home. What lay at the heart of this was a divergence of opinion over the value of the Committee's input to proceedings. Why, thought the British, involve the amateurs from Geneva when the Protecting Power had both the pedigree from the First World War and the mandate under IHL to act as mediator, particularly when, as recent history suggested, the offering of such an opportunity to the ICRC would lead only to it getting ahead of itself and unleashing a barrage of new, unwelcome initiatives?

With regards to the White Ships, there was a similar disparity in expectations between Geneva and Whitehall. Although Burckhardt paid lip-service to British reservations over the White Ships being used as a medium for breaking down the blockade, it was not long after the first ships sailed that the ICRC began pushing for greater freedoms in their use. In so doing the ICRC damaged much of the goodwill that had been built up in Britain via the delegates' exertions in the Far East and Europe on behalf of British POWs. The outcome of this was a slamming shut by Whitehall of the door both to wider relief initiatives and to the ICRC in general in 1943. This ill-will, concentrated in particular within MEW, emerged in tandem with American suspicions of the ICRC's motives in North Africa and the creation of UNRRA as the primary agency for post-war relief. Against these forces, Burckhardt's attempts to paint the

ICRC as a trustworthy and professional friend of Britain became increasingly futile. Having arguably reached their highpoint in 1942, therefore, British–ICRC relations began a general trend of decline, the effects of which became apparent during Europe's liberation, occupation and rehabilitation.

The ICRC was not a factor of great consideration in Allied planning for the liberation of Europe. The relief plans put forward by Zollinger and Huber were dismissed by the Allies, not only because they came across as the latest in a parade of unrealistic proposals but also because what mattered more than anything in 1944 was the attainment of victory in as swift a manner as possible. This, and this alone, was the necessary precondition for relief, the carrying out of which had been placed by the Allies into the hands of the UNRRA and the British and American Red Cross societies. The sum of this was that the Allies expected the ICRC, during the liberation, to feed POWs and monitor their well-being as it had done since the start of the war. Anything more was instinctively viewed as ICRC meddling in pre-existing humanitarian arrangements at a crucial juncture in the war. Allied expectations of the ICRC's role in the post-war world were even more limited. With regards to the relief effort in Europe, the Committee really had only two options: it could either work within the UNRRA framework or it could let its operations 'shrink'.[8] It certainly could not either assume the role of primary humanitarian agent in Europe or, in the longer term, expect to be given a special, protected status in the United Nations Charter. Even within its own purview – that of the 'Geneva project' – the ICRC was brought down to earth. British planning – meticulous as always – for the new Geneva Convention of 1949 focused much on the need to clarify the ICRC's existing role as an agent of POW relief and curtail any initiatives that might emerge at the conference to redefine the implementation of blockade or extend the Committee's scope in the field of humanitarian diplomacy.[9]

This trend towards marginalization of the ICRC was born of several interwoven factors. First, as late as 1944 the Committee, for all its achievements, had still not corrected its reputation for being both amateur in its conduct and insensitive to Allied wishes. The ill-judged campaign to advocate further blockade concessions after the granting of permission for the White Ships, the apparent lack of discipline in its recruiting procedures and the demands made by Zollinger for a greater consideration of humanitarian planning in the war's final years confirmed the belief that the ICRC had learned little from the war and was as intrusive as it had always been into the affairs of belligerents.

The second reason was that, despite debates in Washington and Whitehall over its development, by 1944 the Allies had decided that the 'fullest possible assistance' had to be given to the UNRRA, which would become the primary humanitarian agent of the post-war period.[10] As it was the manifestation of the 'victory before relief' policy, the placing of Allied eggs into the UNRRA basket was unsurprising, the more so in that it dovetailed with the aforementioned prevalence of a negative attitude towards the ICRC's more expansive schemes for relief.

The third reason for marginalization was that, by the autumn of 1945 the task that the Allies had always regarded as the ICRC's primary focus – the maintenance of Allied POW welfare – was at an end and with it any pressing need to cooperate with the Committee. This was particularly true in the light of the decision to create the SEP class of prisoner, which denied the protections of the POW Convention to Japanese and German soldiers, thus excluding the ICRC from any efforts to mitigate their suffering. Although it was unquestionably harsh, the SEP policy and the marginalization of the ICRC that came with it did follow a certain logic in Allied post-war relief policy, which placed emphasis on the need to control everything from the distribution of precious food-stuffs, to the status of prisoners, to the movement of civilians and DPs. Allied plans for relief during Europe's liberation were also shaped by this ethos. Relief for liberated civilians would be provided by the ARC, the BRC and, later, the UNRRA teams. The ICRC and the Protecting Power would continue to monitor and deliver relief to Allied POWs who, under orders to 'stand fast' would wait patiently for their liberation. In the minds of the Allies, norms, systems and routines would govern the course of humanitarian action in the war's final months.

These were dubious assumptions to make, especially considering the wealth of experience of humanitarian crises that the PWD, the DPW and the MEW had at their disposal by this stage in the war. The fiasco in Italy a year before had made certain British officials alive to the problems of 'stand fast'. Typically, it was Harry Phillimore who was among the most sceptical, not only of 'stand fast' but also of the British rejection of the ICRC's predictions that a more flexible operation for POW relief would need to be introduced in order to cope with the collapse of relief norms. Phillimore's voice, however, fell on ears that were long deaf to innovation in humanitarianism. Part of the problem from the Allies' perspective was that, implicit in the ICRC's proposals for bulk parcel depots, the lifting of restrictions on parcel distribution by prisoner classification, and the provision of trucks and added protection for ships, was the suggestion of greater autonomy for the delegates.

This had been welcomed in the Far East, albeit once military operations had, for the most part, ceased there, and the ICRC's efforts thus offered benefits to the Allies, while seldom compromising strategic interests. In Europe in 1944, the preservation of such interests – in particular the need to finish the war as quickly as possible – formed the basis of British refusals to countenance a fluid ICRC programme of relief. Once again, the sinews of Nightingale's original objections were prevalent – humanitarians had no place in active war zones, particularly when they possessed trucks, petrol, food and medicine that might be of benefit to the enemy. The fact that the ICRC had managed to maintain a functional POW relief system in Europe since 1940 was also a likely factor in British thinking, which for the most part blocked out the possibility that the invasion of Europe might compromise a system that had kept thousands of POWs supplied since the fall of France. For all their wartime development, Whitehall's POW departments were still conservative in their outlook during the war's final years and, particularly amid concerns over German intentions towards POWs, focused on upholding the sanctity of the Conventions and maintaining the norms of the POW relief system. Underlying these objections to the ICRC's plans was also a lingering distrust of the Committee, forged from years of proffering its delegates limited freedoms only to experience in return more ambitious, unattainable demands. More so therefore than at any other time during the war the British were determined in 1944–5 to control the ICRC's actions and to deliver on the promise of 'victory before relief'.

This need to control humanitarian action, both during the invasion of Europe and its occupation, had deep roots that stretched back not only into the early years of the Second World War but, arguably, right back to the first debates between Longmore and the ICRC in 1864 over the limits of battlefield humanity. The 'Red Cross dictum' that had developed in Whitehall in the decades prior to the Second World War – in times of peace, to ensure that IHL was shaped to favour British interests and, in times of war, to wed the humanitarian actions of the BRC to the military – was institutionalized in Whitehall's thinking by 1939. These assumptions, which necessarily marginalized the ICRC and stymied its ambitions, held true throughout the war, except in circumstances where desperate humanitarian crises beset the British. In response to the POW crisis of 1940, the captures in the Far East and the increasing difficulties of maintaining a strict and unmoving blockade, Whitehall had to compromise some of its control over humanity in war in order to satisfy its own interests. In consequence, although the necessity to keep it on a leash remained paramount, the ICRC was nevertheless given freedoms it would otherwise have never been allowed by the British, who, in their growing dependence on the former, were forced to reconsider some of their own assumptions about what the Committee could and could not achieve.

There were, obviously, wider factors at play in determining the success and failure of the ICRC's wartime record than its relations with Britain. It is the contention of this book, however, that it was in no small part through its constant engagement with Whitehall – particularly in matters relating to the blockade – that the ICRC was able to build a system of relief and practice that underpinned much of its wartime work. Although it fell short of expectations in many aspects of this work – in some instances scandalously so – the ICRC seldom failed Whitehall's requirement that its delegates do their upmost to keep British POWs and civilians alive. For this, the ICRC earned the praise of the War and Foreign Offices and a personal thank you from General Eisenhower on behalf of the similar good work done by the ICRC for American POWs. In 1946, when Churchill visited Geneva, he too spoke glowingly to Max Huber of his Committee's achievements. What the ICRC did not know was that, in addition to Churchill requiring a refresher on the Committee's personnel and character, the discussions in Whitehall over its official thank you in 1945 clearly emphasized that the gesture should be collective, sent to all humanitarian agencies and that the Protecting Power should be listed above the ICRC in order of merit.[11] For the British, the ICRC was no unique humanitarian actor. Its mission was no more noble or just than any other humanitarian organization and its delegates were not 'sentinels between the human and the inhuman'.[12] At its best, when focused on Whitehall's interests, the ICRC could inspire in British officials the 'fullest assistance and confidence'. At its worst, the Committee's impetus to work from 'entirely humanitarian motives', bereft of wider considerations, made it a meddlesome interloper into Britain's conduct of the war.[13] Between these two extremes lay the truth of the British view of Huber's humanitarians during the Second World War: the ICRC, even when expanding its operations and pushing the limits of its capabilities, was, ultimately, a means to British humanitarian ends.

Notes

Introduction

1. David P. Forsythe, *The Humanitarians: The International Committee of the Red Cross* (Cambridge: Cambridge University Press, 2005), p. 42.
2. The number of British and Commonwealth prisoners is difficult to ascertain with certainty. For discussion see J. Nichol and T. Rennell, *The Last Escape: The Untold Story of Allied Prisoners of War in Germany, 1944–45* (London: Penguin, 2003), pp. 416–20; for statistics on prisoners in the Far East see IWM <http://www.iwm.org.uk/history/prisoners-of-war-in-the-far-east#> (accessed February 2013).
3. V. Vourkoutiotis, 'What the Angels Saw: Red Cross and Protecting Power Visits to Anglo-American POWs, 1939–45', *Journal of Contemporary History* 40.4 (2005), pp. 689–706 (689).
4. The National Archives of the United Kingdom, hereafter TNA:FO 371/50603 – WO to FO, 3 August 1945; H. Satow and M. J. Sée, *The Work of the Prisoners of War Department during the Second World War* (London: Foreign Office, 1950), p. 71.
5. Satow and Sée, *Work of the Prisoners of War Department*, pp. 72, 79.
6. TNA:FO 369/3796 – Roseway to Sargent, 4 December 1945.
7. Caroline Moorehead, *Dunant's Dream: War, Switzerland and the History of the Red Cross* (London: Harper Collins, 1998), pp. 389–92.
8. Churchill Archives, Cambridge, *The Papers of Sir Winston Churchill*, hereafter CHURCH 2/244 – Snow to Gilliat, 5 September 1946.
9. D. Dilks, *Churchill and Company: Allies and Rivals in War and Peace* (London: I. B. Tauris, 2012), pp. 6, 76.
10. Winston Churchill and Franklin D. Roosevelt, *Churchill & Roosevelt: The Complete Correspondence*, 3 vols, ed. Warren F. Kimball (New Jersey: Princeton University Press, 1984), vol. 3, C-914, 17 March 1945, p. 574.
11. H. Slim, 'Relief Agencies and Moral Standing in War: Principles of Humanity, Neutrality, Impartiality and Solidarity', *Development in Practice* 7.4 (1997), pp. 342–52.
12. Forsythe, *Humanitarians*, p. 24; Moorehead, *Dunant's Dream*, pp. 230–40.
13. G. Best, 'Making the Geneva Conventions of 1949: The View from Whitehall', in Christophe Swinarski (ed.), *Studies and Essays on International Humanitarian Law and Red Cross Principles in Honour of Jean Pictet* (Geneva: ICRC, 1984), pp. 5–15 (6).
14. *The ICRC: Its Mission and Its Work* (Geneva: ICRC, 2009).
15. David P. Forsythe, 'The ICRC: A Unique Humanitarian Protagonist', *International Review of the Red Cross* 89.865 (2007), pp. 63–96 (78–9); Michael Ignatieff, *The Warrior's Honor: Ethnic War and the Modern Conscience* (New York: Metropolitan, 2006), pp. 115–17.
16. Sydney Dawson Bailey, *Prohibitions and Restraints in War* (London: Oxford University Press, 1972), p. 71.

17. Charlotte Khu and Joaquín Cácres Brun, 'Neutrality and the ICRC Contribution to Contemporary Humanitarian Operations', *International Peacekeeping* 10.1 (2003), pp. 56–72; Forsythe, *Humanitarians*, ch. 3.
18. Moorehead, *Dunant's Dream*, pp. 40–2.
19. François Bugnion, 'The International Committee of the Red Cross and the Development of International Humanitarian Law', *Chicago Journal of International Law* 5.1 (2004), pp. 191–215; Forsythe, 'Humanitarian Protagonist', p. 66.
20. Geoffrey Best, *Humanity in Warfare: The Modern History of the International Law of Armed Conflicts* (London: Methuen, 1980), pp. 151–4.
21. John F. Hutchinson, *Champions of Charity: War and the Rise of the Red Cross* (Boulder: Westview Press, 1996), pp. 40–1.
22. Hutchinson, *Champions of Charity*, pp. 238–42.
23. Harold Hongju Koh, 'Why Do Nations Obey International Law?', *Yale Law School Legal Scholarship Repository: Faculty Scholarship Series*, Paper 2101 (1997) <http://digitalcommons.law.yale.edu/fss_papers/2101>; Rebecca Gill, *Calculating Compassion: Humanity and Relief in War, Britain 1870–1914* (Manchester: Manchester University Press, 2013), p. 34.
24. Neville Wylie, 'The 1929 Prisoner of War Convention and the Building of the Interwar Prisoner of War Regime', in Sibylle Scheippers (ed.), *Prisoners in War: Norms, Military Cultures and Reciprocity in Armed Conflict* (Oxford: Oxford University Press, 2010), pp. 91–106; Best, 'Making the Geneva Convention of 1949', p. 14.
25. André Durand, *From Sarajevo to Hiroshima* (Geneva: Henry Dunant Institute, 1984), ch. 9, pt 6; Moorehead, *Dunant's Dream*, ch. 15. See also the unpublished, though accessible and thorough treatment of the ICRC's work in the Far East – Christophe Laurent, 'Les Obstacles Recontrés par le CICR dans son Activité en Extême-Orient, 1941–45', PhD dissertation (Université de Lausanne, 2003).
26. See generally Jean-Claude Favez, *The Red Cross and the Holocaust*, eds and trans John Fletcher and Beryl Fletcher (Cambridge: Cambridge University Press, 1999). On the closing of the Swiss border to Jewish refugees by the Federal Council at the time of the ICRC's 'non-appeal' see Jean-François Bergier, *Switzerland and Refugees in the Nazi Era* (Berne: Independent Commission of Experts, 1999), Pt 3 and Conclusion.
27. See Favez, *Holocaust*. Caroline Moorehead also begins her overview of the ICRC's entire history by documenting the Holocaust non-appeal – Moorehead, *Dunant's Dream*, Introduction. David Forsythe addresses Second World War history in his book by focusing almost solely on the non-appeal – Forsythe, *Humanitarians*, pp. 45–8; David P. Forsythe and Barbara Ann J. Rieffer-Flanagan, *The International Committee of the Red Cross: A Neutral Humanitarian Actor* (London: Routledge, 2007), pp. 13–17.
28. Favez, *Holocaust*, pp. ix–xi.
29. See in particular Frédéric Siordet, *Inter Arma Caritas: The World of the ICRC during the Second World War* (Geneva: ICRC, 1947); Marcel Junod, *Warrior without Weapons*, trans. Edward Fitzgerald (Geneva: Henry Dunant Institute, 1951). Siodert was one of many delegates of the Second World War who responded sharply to criticisms of the ICRC's wartime record – Moorehead, *Dunant's Dream*, pp. 542–3.

30. *Report of the International Committee of the Red Cross and Its Activities during the Second World War*, 3 vols (Geneva: ICRC, 1948); Durand, *Sarajevo to Hiroshima*; Bugnion, *Protection of War Victims*. The ICRC report was, to a great extent, presented as a riposte to Soviet post-war criticisms of the Committee's various wartime failures.
31. Meredith Hindsley, 'Constructing Allied Humanitarian Policy', *Journal of Holocaust Education*, 9.2/3 (2000), pp. 77–93 (78). For further discussion on Allied humanitarian policy see Jean Beaumont, 'Starving for Democracy: Britain's Blockade of and Relief for Occupied Europe, 1939–45', *War and Society* 8.2 (1990), pp. 57–82; Ben Shepherd, 'Becoming Planning Minded: The Theory and Practice of Relief, 1940–45', *Journal of Contemporary History* 43 (2008), pp. 405–19; Ronald W. Zweig, 'Feeding the Camps: Allied Blockade Policy and the Relief of Concentration Camps in Germany, 1944–45', *Historical Journal* 41.3 (1998), pp. 825–85; Johannes-Dieter Steinhart, 'British Humanitarian Assistance: Wartime Planning and Postwar Realities', *Journal of Contemporary History* 43.3 (2008), pp. 421–35; Bob Moore, 'The Western Allies and Food Relief to the Occupied Netherlands, 1944–1945', *War and Society* 10.2 (1992), pp. 91–118.
32. Neville Wylie, *Barbed Wire Diplomacy: Britain, Germany and the Politics of Prisoners of War, 1939–1945* (Oxford: Oxford University Press, 2011). See also Arieh J. Kochavi, *Confronting Captivity: Britain and the United States and Their POWs in Nazi Germany* (Chapel Hill and London: University of North Carolina Press, 2005).
33. François Bugnion, *The International Committee of the Red Cross and the Protection of War Victims* (Richmond: MacMillan, 2003), pp. 177–8.
34. David Rolf, 'Blind Bureaucracy: The British Government and POWs in German Captivity, 1939–1945', in Bob Moore and Kent Fedorowich (eds), *Prisoners of War and Their Captors in World War II* (Oxford: Berg, 1996), pp. 47–97.

1 Britain and the Red Cross, 1864–1929

1. Stephen C. Neff, *War and the Law of Nations: A General History* (Cambridge: Cambridge University Press, 2005), p. 4; see also David Kennedy, *Of War and Law* (Princeton: Princeton University Press, 2006), ch. 2; John Fabian Witt, *Lincoln's Code: The Laws of War in American History* (New York: Free Press, 2012), pp. 16–18.
2. Henry Dunant, *A Memory of Solferino* (Geneva: Henry Dunant Institute, 1986), pp. 19, 44; on Dunant's life before Solferino see Ellen Hart, *Man Born to Live: The Life and Work of Henry Dunant, Founder of the Red Cross* (London: Victor Gollancz, 1953), ch. 2.
3. François Bugnion, *Gustav Moynier* (Geneva: Éditions Slatkine, 2010), pp. 16–23.
4. John F. Hutchinson, *Champions of Charity: War and the Rise of the Red Cross* (Boulder: Westview Press, 1996), pp. 19–23; Pierre Bossier, *The History of the International Committee of the Red Cross: From Solferino to Tsushima* (Geneva: Henry Dunant Institute, 1984), pp. 53–69; Hart, *Man Born to Live*, pp. 108–11, 137–9.

5. Richard Shelly Hartigan, *Lieber's Code and the Laws of War* (Chicago: Precedent, 1983), pp. 20–2; Michael Ignatieff, *The Warrior's Honor: Ethnic War and the Modern Conscience* (New York: Metropolitan, 2006), p. 106.
6. Diary of William Rutherford, cited in Florence Nightingale, *Collected Works of Florence Nightingale*, vol. 15, *Florence Nightingale on Wars and the War Office*, ed. Lynn MacDonald (Waterloo, ON: Wilfred Laurier University Press, 2011), pp. 584–5.
7. Lawrence Goldman, 'The Social Sciences Association, 1857–1886: A Context for Mid-Victorian Liberalism', *English Historical Review* 101.398 (1986), pp. 95–134 (98).
8. Angela Bennett, *Geneva Convention: The Hidden Origins of the Red Cross* (Stroud: Sutton, 2005), p. 49.
9. Bossier, *History of the International Committee of the Red Cross*, pp. 74–5; Hart, *Man Born to Live*, pp. 147–8; Wellcome Library, *Papers of Sir Thomas Longmore*, hereafter WL:RAM 1139/LP54 – Nightingale to Longmore, 23 July 1864; WL:RAM 1139/LP22, Longmore Minute, 3 August 1864; John Sweetman, 'The Crimean War and the Formation of the Medical Staff Corps', *Journal of the Society for Army Historical Research* 53.214 (1975), pp. 113–19.
10. Bennett, *Geneva Convention*, pp. 67–8; Léopold Bossier, 'Centenary of the First Geneva Convention in 1864', *International Review of the Red Cross* 41 (1964), pp. 393–410.
11. *Convention for the Amelioration of the Condition of the Wounded in Armies in the Field* (22 August 1864), list of state parties.
12. Nightingale letter to Longmore, 31 August 1864, cited in Nightingale, *Florence Nightingale on Wars and the War Office*, p. 587.
13. Martha Finnemore, 'Rules of War and Wars of Rules: The International Red Cross and the Restraint of State Violence', in John Boli and George M. Thomas (eds), *Constructing World Culture: International Nongovernmental Organizations since 1875* (Stanford: Stanford University Press, 1999), pp. 149–65 (164–5); Bossier, 'Centenary of the First Geneva Convention', p. 402.
14. Michael Barnett, *Empire of Humanity: A History of Humanitarianism* (Ithaca: Cornell University Press, 2011), pp. 79–80; Hutchinson, *Champions of Charity*, pp. 26–7, 52.
15. Despite his initial scepticism, Longmore became both Whitehall's chief interlocutor with the ICRC and a strong advocate for the formation of a British Red Cross society in the years after 1864 – 'Obituary of Sir Thomas Longmore', *British Medical Journal* (12 Oct. 1895).
16. *Resolutions and Recommendations of the Geneva International Conference of 1863* (26–9 October 1863), *Art.1*; Hart, *Man Born to Live*, pp. 124–5.
17. Rebecca Gill, *Calculating Compassion: Humanity and Relief in War, Britain 1870–1914* (Manchester: Manchester University Press, 2013), pp. 25–7; Paul Laity, *The British Peace Movement, 1870–1914* (Oxford: Oxford University Press, 2001), ch. 1.
18. *The Times*, 16 and 22 July 1870. By the time of the outbreak of the Franco-Prussian War national Red Cross societies had already been established in Austria, Belgium, France, Italy, Norway, Portugal, Russia, Spain, Sweden, Switzerland and Turkey – Hans Haug, *Humanity for All: The International Red Cross and Red Crescent Movement* (Berne: Henry Dunant Institute, 1993), Annex 4, pp. 633–45.

19. *The Times*, 11 August 1870.
20. Caroline Moorehead, *Dunant's Dream: War, Switzerland and the History of the Red Cross* (London: Harper Collins, 1998), pp. 69–70; Anne Summers, *Angels and Citizens: British Women as Military Nurses, 1854–1914* (London: Routledge, 2000), pp. 136–7; Hutchinson, *Champions of Charity*, pp. 235–7.
21. TNA:WO 32/7146 – Surgeon-Major W. G. MacPherson, Report on the Sixth International Conference of Red Cross Societies, 18–24 Sept. 1897.
22. *The Times*, 27 April and 4 Nov. 1899.
23. Moorehead, *Dunant's Dream*, pp. 142–7.
24. TNA:FO 83/1886 – FO to Law Offices of the Crown, 6 December 1900. For criticism of humanitarians in South Africa during the war, see generally TNA:WO 32/7880.
25. Geoffrey Best, *Humanity in Warfare: The Modern History of the International Law of Armed Conflicts* (London: Methuen, 1980), pp. 141–4; Hutchinson, *Champions of Charity*, pp. 256–68; Rachel Chrastil, 'The French Red Cross, War Readiness, and Civil Society, 1866–1914', *French Historical Studies* 31.3 (2008), pp. 445–76 (456–9).
26. Berryl Oliver, *The British Red Cross in Action* (London: Faber, 1966), pp. 186–92; 'Formation of a new Red Cross society', *The Times*, 18 July 1905.
27. *Reports by the Joint Relief Committee and the Joint War Finance Committee of the British Red Cross Society and the Order of St John of Jerusalem in England on Voluntary Aid Rendered to the Sick and Wounded and Abroad and to British Prisoners of War, 1914–1919* (London: British Red Cross, 1921), pp. 366–9; Hutchinson, *Champions of Charity*, pp. 250–1; Oliver, *British Red Cross in Action*, pp. 344–7.
28. Gill, *Calculating Compassion*, 192–7.
29. Heather Jones, 'International or Transnational? Humanitarian Action during the First World War', *European Review of History* 16.5 (2009), pp. 697–713 (697–700).
30. Moorehead, *Dunant's Dream*, pp. 40–2; Brigette Troyon and Daniel Palmieri, 'The ICRC Delegate: An Exceptional Humanitarian Player?', *International Review of the Red Cross* 89.865 (2007), pp. 97–111 (98–9).
31. David P. Forsythe, *The Humanitarians: The International Committee of the Red Cross* (Cambridge: Cambridge University Press, 2005), ch. 7.
32. Hutchinson, *Champions of Charity*, pp. 91–2. For British discussion of the articles pertaining to maritime warfare see generally TNA:FO 881/7137.
33. François Bugnion, 'The International Committee of the Red Cross and the Development of International Humanitarian Law', *Chicago Journal of International Law* 5.1 (2004), pp. 191–215.
34. Kennedy, *Of War and Law*, pp. 64–6; Barnett, *Empire of Humanity*, pp. 80–1; Neff, *War and the Law of Nations*, p. 177.
35. Hutchinson, *Champions of Charity*, pp. 109–17.
36. Forsythe, *Humanitarians*, p. 24.
37. Hart, *Man Born to Live*, pp. 259–60; Goldman, 'Social Sciences Association', pp. 127–9; Andrew Porter, *The Oxford History of the British Empire: The Nineteenth Century* (Oxford: Oxford University Press, 1999), pp. 213–15.
38. The 'Brussels Code' of 27 August 1874, which established that POWs were to be treated as 'lawful and disarmed enemies' was never signed or ratified. The only other source of codification on the question of POW treatment

was Francis Lieber's Code of 24 April 1863, which called for the humane treatment of those who were *hors de combat* – Karma Nabulsi, *Traditions of War: Occupation, Resistance and the Law* (Oxford: Oxford University Press, 2000), pp. 4–7; Bossier, *History of the International Committee of the Red Cross*, pp. 288–90.

39. Bennett, *Geneva Convention*, pp. 156–8; Roger Durand, *Henry Dunant* (Geneva: Henry Dunant Institute, 2010), pp. 64–5.

40. Geoffrey Best, 'Peace Conferences and the Century of Total War: The 1899 Hague Conference and What Came after', *International Affairs (Royal Institute of International Affairs 1944–)* 75.3 (1999), pp. 619–34 (626–7); for a view of the British delegation's thinking at the Hague Conference see generally TNA:FO 412/65.

41. For a summary of the contrasting 'peace' and 'war' movements of the late nineteenth century see Best, *Humanity in Warfare*, pp. 131–9; Michael Howard, *War and the Liberal Conscience* (London: Temple Smith, 1978), pp. 61–5.

42. James B. Scott, *The Proceedings of the Hague Peace Conferences* (New York: Oxford University Press, 1921) – *First Commission: Plenary Meetings Hague Declaration IV (III) concerning Expanding Bullets*, 29 July 1899, pp. 226–7; Stephen Barcroft, 'The Hague Peace Conference of 1899', *Irish Studies in International Affairs* 3.1 (1989), pp. 55–68 (59–64).

43. TNA:FO 881/9056 – Ardagh Memo, 4 December 1905; FO Minutes 18 and 19 November 1905.

44. Bossier, *History of the International Committee of the Red Cross*, pp. 357–64. On British support for the separation of Hague and Geneva Law see TNA:FO 881/9056 – Landsdowe to Greene, 29 November 1905; Ardagh Memo, 4 December 1905.

45. TNA:FO 83/1886 – Ardagh memorandum on Geneva Convention, 15 October 1900.

46. TNA:DO 119-189 – Chamberlain to Rosemead, 7 January 1897; Chamberlain to Robinson, 31 March 1896; TNA:FO 30/40/20/2, Ardagh Papers – W. G. MacPherson Memorandum, 18 August 1902.

47. Neville Wylie, 'The 1929 Prisoner of War Convention and the Building of the Interwar Prisoner of War Regime', in Sibylle Scheippers (ed.), *Prisoners in War: Norms, Military Cultures and Reciprocity in Armed Conflict* (Oxford: Oxford University Press, 2010), pp. 91–106.

48. TNA:FO 30/40/20/2 – Ardagh Papers – Meeting of British Delegates to the Conference for the Revision of the Geneva Convention of 1864, 16 June 1903; W. G. MacPherson notes on procedure of Geneva Conference, 1906; TNA:FO 83/1886 – Ardagh memorandum on Geneva Convention, 15 October 1900.

49. François Bugnion, *The International Committee of the Red Cross and the Protection of War Victims* (Richmond: MacMillan, 2003), pp. 82–3; Gill, *Calculating Compassion*, p. 184; on breaches of IHL and the poor treatment of POWs in the First World War see generally Alan Kramer, *Dynamic of Destruction: Culture and Mass Killing in the First World War* (New York: Oxford University Press, 2007); Heather Jones, *Violence against Prisoners of War in the First World War: Britain, France and Germany, 1914–1920* (Cambridge: Cambridge University Press, 2011).

50. The Ninth International Conference of the International Red Cross in 1912 had passed a resolution authorizing this arrangement between the ICRC and the National Societies – Robert Jackson, *The Prisoners, 1914–1918* (London: Routledge, 1989), pp. 62–3.
51. Howard S. Levie, 'Prisoners of War and the Protecting Power', *American Journal of International Law* 55.2 (1961), pp. 374–97 (375–6).
52. Alan Kramer, 'Prisoners in the First World War', in Sibylle Scheippers (ed.), *Prisoners in War: Norms, Military Cultures and Reciprocity in Armed Conflict* (Oxford: Oxford University Press, 2010), pp. 75–87 (77–81); Herbert Belfield, 'Treatment of Prisoners of War', *Transactions of the Grotius Society* 9 (1923), pp. 131–47. The post-war 'war crimes trials' in Leipzig and Istanbul were a flop, with only three camp guards given lenient sentences – Alan Kramer, 'The First Wave of War Crimes Trials: Istanbul and Leipzig', *European Review* 14.4 (2006), pp. 441–55; TNA:FO 369/106 – Berne to FO, 16 January 1915; TNA:FO 369/106 – De Grey to Duff, 7 January 1915; Geneva Red Cross (*sic*) to British Red Cross, 2 January 1915.
53. *The ICRC in World War One: The International Prisoners-of-War Agency* (Geneva: Henry Dunant Institute, 2007), p. 13; André Durand, *From Sarajevo to Hiroshima* (Geneva: Henry Dunant Institute, 1984), pp. 70–4; Forsythe, *Humanitarians*, p. 31.
54. TNA:FO 383/473 – FO Minutes, 18 April 1918.
55. Durand, *From Sarajevo to Hiroshima*, p. 89. For prohibition of the use of gas see *Hague Convention, Declaration IV, pt. II concerning asphyxiating gases* (29 July 1899).
56. TNA:WO 32/5177 – Rumbold to Balfour, 11 February 1918; 'Legal aspect of the use of poisonous gas' memo, 18 March 1918.
57. Durand, *From Sarajevo to Hiroshima*, pp. 92–5; Marion Giraud, 'Political Decisions and Britain's Chemical Warfare Challenge in World War I: Descend to Atrocities?', *Defence Studies* 8.1 (2008), pp. 105–32 (122–5); Edward M. Spiers, *A History of Chemical and Biological Weapons* (London: Reaktion, 2010), p. 42.
58. TNA:WO 32/5177 – War Cabinet Minutes on ICRC appeal for cessation of use of asphyxiating gas, 26 March 1918; *Protocol for the Prohibition of the Use of Asphyxiating, Poisonous or Other Gases, and of Bacteriological Methods of Warfare* (17 June 1925).
59. TNA:WO 162/341 – PWIB Report, 6 March 1920.
60. Durand, *From Sarajevo to Hiroshima*, p. 31: for the ICRC's limited role in the repatriation process see pp. 50–66.
61. Belfield, 'Treatment of Prisoners of War', pp. 131–47.
62. Neville Wylie, *Barbed Wire Diplomacy: Britain, Germany and the Politics of Prisoners of War, 1939–1945* (Oxford: Oxford University Press, 2011), pp. 44–5.
63. G. G. Philimore and H. L. Bellot, 'Treatment of Prisoners of War', *Transactions of the Grotius Society* 5 (1919), pp. 47–64; Belfield, 'Treatment of Prisoners of War'; TNA:CAB 16/65 – Report of Lord Justice Younger's Committee relating to Prisoners of War, 8 August 1923; TNA:WO 32/5337 – WO Minutes, 15 January 1926.
64. Durand, *From Sarajevo to Hiroshima*, pp. 251–6.
65. Martin Gilbert, *Sir Horace Rumbold: Portrait of a Diplomat, 1869–1941* (London: Heinemann, 1973), pp. 324–5; TNA:FO 372/2550 – Montgomery to Rumbold, 28 June 1929.

66. Durand, *From Sarajevo to Hiroshima*, p. 256.
67. Hampshire Records Office, Winchester, *Papers of Sir George Warner*, hereafter HRO:5M 79/B20 – Warner to Montgomery, 19 July 1929; TNA:FO 372/2550 – Warner Minute, 8 August 1929.
68. Wylie, '1929 Prisoner of War Convention', p. 96. Britain ratified both conventions in 1931 and the United States did likewise in 1932. Both Japan and the Soviet Union signed the *Convention for the Amelioration of the Condition of the Wounded and Sick in Armies in the Field* (27 July 1929) and ratified it in 1934 and 1931 respectively. Neither the Soviet Union nor Japan ratified the *Convention Relative to the Treatment of Prisoners of War* (27 July 1929), though Japan did become a state signatory, an act that declared its willingness to abide by the 'spirit' of the Convention, a pledge that it did not fulfil – Gary D. Solis and Fred L. Borch, *Geneva Conventions* (New York: Kaplan, 2010), pp. 12–13.
69. Wylie, 'The 1929 Prisoner of War Convention', pp. 92–101.
70. Barnett, *Empire of Humanity*, pp. 88–90.
71. Gill, *Calculating Compassion*, p. 196.

2 Grandeur, Tribulation, Apocalypse, 1919–40

1. Henry Dunant, *A Memory of Solferino* (Geneva: Henry Dunant Institute, 1986), p. 117.
2. Hans Haug, *Humanity for All: The International Red Cross and Red Crescent Movement* (Berne: Henry Dunant Institute, 1993), pp. 645, 421–3.
3. John F. Hutchinson, *Champions of Charity: War and the Rise of the Red Cross* (Boulder: Westview Press, 1996), pp. 239–40; G. Best, *Humanity in Warfare: The Modern History of the International Law of Armed Conflicts* (London: Methuen, 1980), p. 141.
4. H. Jones, 'International of Transnational? Humanitarian Action during the First World War', *European Review of History* 16.5 (2009), pp. 697–713 (698–9).
5. Hutchinson, *Champions of Charity*, pp. 285–93; Caroline Moorehead, *Dunant's Dream: War, Switzerland and the History of the Red Cross* (London: Harper Collins, 1998), p. 59.
6. André Durand, *From Sarajevo to Hiroshima* (Geneva: Henry Dunant Institute, 1984), pp. 151–9; Daphne A. Reid and Patrick F. Gilbo, *Beyond Conflict: The International Federation of the Red Cross and Red Crescent Societies, 1919–1994* (Geneva: IFRC, 1997), p. 80.
7. *Covenant of the League of Nations* (28 June 1919), Art. 25.
8. Caroline Moorehead, *Dunant's Dream: War, Switzerland and the History of the Red Cross* (London: Harper Collins, 1998), pp. 261–2.
9. David P. Forsythe, *The Humanitarians: The International Committee of the Red Cross* (Cambridge: Cambridge University Press, 2005), pp. 203–4; John F. Hutchinson, '"Custodians of the Sacred Fire": The ICRC and the Postwar Reorganisation of the International Red Cross', in Paul Weindling (ed.), *International Health Organisations and Movements, 1918–1936* (Cambridge: Cambridge University Press, 1995), pp. 17–35.

10. Yves Sandoz, 'Max Huber and the Red Cross', *European Journal of International Law* 18.1 (2007), pp. 171–97 (173–6); Dietrich Schindler, 'Max Huber – His Life', *European Journal of International Law* 18.1 (2007), pp. 81–95.

11. Ador had declared that 'in the family of the Red Cross, any schism is unthinkable' in 1924, despite constant clashes of personalities at ICRC/League meetings and lack of agreement on how to unite – Reid and Gilbo, *Beyond Conflict*, pp. 80–1; Archives of the International Federation of the Red Cross and Red Crescent Societies, Geneva, hereafter IFRC:A 0800/1 Minutes of ICRC/League meeting, 1 May 1924.

12. For an overview of the near-decade-long negotiations over the formation of the International Red Cross see Durand, *From Sarajevo to Hiroshima*, pp. 176–94; IFRC:A 0800/2 – Statement of Colonel Draudt, 15 March 1927.

13. '[N]ot without purposes', cited in Durand, *From Sarajevo to Hiroshima*, p. 250; '... age that is apocalyptic', cited in Moorehead, *Dunant's Dream*, p. 291; Sandoz, 'Huber and the Red Cross', p. 184.

14. Durand, *From Sarajevo to Hiroshima*, pp. 288–92; Moorehead, *Dunant's Dream*, pp. 296–8.

15. On the growing 'war psychosis' in Britain from the mid-1930s see Richard Overy, *The Morbid Age: Britain between the Wars* (London: Allen Lane, 2009), pp. 314–18; Sandoz, 'Huber and the Red Cross', p. 185.

16. Rainer Baudendistel, *Between Bombs and Good Intentions: The Red Cross and the Italo-Ethiopian War of 1935–36* (New York: Berghan, 2006), pp. 116–18; Davide Rodogno, 'Fascism and War', in Richard J. Bosworth (ed.), *The Oxford Handbook of Fascism* (Oxford: Oxford University Press, 2009), pp. 239–58 (246).

17. Baudendistel, *Between Bombs and Good Intentions*, pp. 281, 307; Moorehead, *Dunant's Dream*, pp. 311–12.

18. Richard Bessel, 'The First World War as Totality', in Richard J. Bosworth (ed.), *The Oxford Handbook of Fascism* (Oxford: Oxford University Press, 2009), pp. 52–69 (58–9).

19. Grawitz went on to supervise the experimentation programme on concentration camp inmates. He committed suicide in Berlin in April 1945 – Peter Padfield, *Himmler: Reichsführer SS* (London: MacMillan, 1990), pp. 333, 461; for the coordination of welfare and humanitarian organizations with the Nazi regime in the 1930s see Michael Burleigh, *The Third Reich: A New History* (New York: Hill and Wang, 2000), pp. 219–21.

20. Durand, *From Sarajevo to Hiroshima*, pp. 285–7; Moorehead, *Dunant's Dream*, pp. 351–2; Eugene Kogon, *The Theory and Practice of Hell: The German Concentration Camps and the System behind Them*, 1st rev. edn (New York: Farrar, Strauss and Giroux, 2006), p. 34.

21. Jean-Claude Favez, *The Red Cross and the Holocaust*, eds and trans John Fletcher and Beryl Fletcher (Cambridge: Cambridge University Press, 1999), pp. 18–21.

22. *Report of the International Committee of the Red Cross and Its Activities during the Second World War*, 3 vols (Geneva: ICRC, 1948), hereafter *ICRC Report*, vol. 2, pp. 98–9.

23. Moorehead, *Dunant's Dream*, pp. 298–9; Michael Barnett, *Empire of Humanity: A History of Humanitarianism* (Ithaca: Cornell University Press, 2011), p. 101.

24. Durand, *From Sarajevo to Hiroshima*, pp. 412–14.

25. Richard Deeming, *Heroes of the Red Cross* (Geneva: ICRC, 1969), pp. 59–79. For a more critical assessment of Junod's willingness to excuse Italian atrocities during the Italo-Ethiopian war see Baudendistel, *Between Bombs and Good Intentions*, pp. 306–7.
26. Junod, *Warrior without Weapons*, p. 94.
27. Marcel Junod, *Warrior without Weapons*, trans. Edward Fitzgerald (Geneva: Henry Dunant Institute, 1951), pp. 94, 141; François Bugnion, *The International Committee of the Red Cross and the Protection of War Victims* (Richmond: MacMillan, 2003), pp. 171–2; Archives of the International Committee of the Red Cross, Geneva, hereafter ACICR:PV – Minutes of Committee meeting, 2 September 1939.
28. Haug, *Humanity for All*, pp. 55, 60–1.
29. ACICR:G 85/1047 – Chenevière to Warner, 17 October 1939; Huber to Halifax, 20 September 1939; Huber to Halifax, 6 October 1939.
30. Assessments of British POW policy in the war's early years can be found in Arieh J. Kochavi, *Confronting Captivity: Britain and the United States and Their POWs in Nazi Germany* (Chapel Hill and London: University of North Carolina Press, 2005), pp. 10–11; David Rolf, 'Blind Bureaucracy: The British Government and POWs in German Captivity, 1939–1945', in Bob Moore and Kent Fedorowich (eds), *Prisoners of War and Their Captors in World War II* (Oxford: Berg, 1996), pp. 47–97 (48–9); Neville Wylie, *Barbed Wire Diplomacy: Britain, Germany and the Politics of Prisoners of War, 1939–1945* (Oxford: Oxford University Press, 2011), pp. 65–8.
31. TNA:FO 369/1450 – Report on the Directorate of Prisoners of War, September 1920; Tilley to FO, 11 December 1920.
32. Wylie, *Barbed Wire Diplomacy*, pp. 66–7; Harold Satow and M. J. Sée, *The Work of the Prisoners of War Department during the Second World War* (London: Foreign Office, 1950), pp. 5–6; on interrogation preparations see generally TNA:KV 4/302, particularly 'Places Suitable for the Interrogation of Prisoners' memorandum, 1 March 1939; for POW labour planning see Bob Moore, 'Turning Liabilities into Assets: British Government Policy towards German and Italian Prisoners of War during the Second World War', *Journal of Contemporary History* 32.1 (1997), pp. 117–36 (119).
33. *Geneva Convention 1929*, Article 77.
34. ACICR:G 85/1047 – Huber to Halifax, 20 September 1939; Huber to Halifax, 6 October 1939; TNA:FO 371/23939 – Warner to Huber, 12 October 1939.
35. *ICRC Report*, vol. 2, pp. 144–5; Peter Gillman and Leni Gillman, *Collar the Lot!: How Britain Interned and Expelled Its Wartime Refugees* (London: Quartet, 1980), p. 64; Bob Moore, 'Axis Prisoners in Britain during the Second World War: A Comparative Survey', in Bob Moore and Kent Fedorowich (eds), *Prisoners of War and Their Captors in World War II* (Oxford: Berg, 1996), pp. 19–46 (19).
36. TNA:WO 366/26 – Harry J. Phillimore, 'History of the Second World War: Prisoners of War 1939–1945' (unpublished, 1949), hereafter 'POWs in WWII', pp. 11, 249. Phillimore was retired when he wrote this account. Owing most likely to the unwillingness of anyone from the War Office to edit the book, it was never published and still sits in its original draft form in the National Archives in Kew.
37. TNA:FO 369/2549 – Minutes of Interdepartmental Meeting with BRC, 31 October 1939.

38. Gillman and Gillman, *Collar the Lot*, p. 64; TNA:FO 369/2547 – WO Minutes, 27 November 1939; ACICR:BG 3/003/004 – Haccius to ICRC, 11 October 1939.
39. *ICRC Report*, vol. 1, pp. 242–3.
40. Oflag XA contained only 2 British RAF officers, the vast majority of inmates being Polish – Durand, *From Sarajevo to Hiroshima*, pp. 404–5; *ICRC Report*, vol. 1, pp. 242–3.
41. Durand, *From Sarajevo to Hiroshima*, pp. 124–35, 228–9.
42. ACICR:BG 3/003/001 – Gallopin to Chenevière, 13 July 1939.
43. Pierre Bossier, *The History of the International Committee of the Red Cross: From Solferino to Tsushima* (Geneva: Henry Dunant Institute, 1984), pp. 93–100; Brigette Troyon and Daniel Palmieri, 'The ICRC Delegate: An Exceptional Humanitarian Player?', *International Review of the Red Cross* 89.865 (2007), pp. 97–111 (98); ACICR:BG 3/003/001 – Note on Haccius Instructions, 10 October 1939.
44. Junod, *Warrior without Weapons*, p. 15.
45. ACICR:G 85/1047 – Dunbar to Haccius, 2 February 1940; TNA:FO 369/2547 – FO Minutes, 18 November 1939; S. J Warner to Shepherd, 18 November 1939.
46. *ICRC Report*, vol. 1, p. 243; ACICR:G 3/003/002 – Central Commission Interview with Junod and Haccius, 27 November 1939.
47. It turned out that Warner's concern was a false alarm. Haccius had visited a camp on a day when the hot water system was not working – TNA:FO 369/2566 – Frick-Cramer to Halifax, 13 February 1940; Warner to McCleod, 6 March 1940; McCleod to Warner, 8 March 1940.
48. ACICR:G 85/1047 – Hunter to Junod, 30 November 1939; Hunter to Clouzot, 9 January 1940; TNA:FO 916/112 – Hunter to Warner, 8 January 1941.
49. Berryl Oliver, *The British Red Cross in Action* (London: Faber, 1966), p. 400.
50. TNA:FO 369/2549 – Hunter to F. M. Shepherd, 13 December 1939; HRO:5M 79/A21 – Warner to Scott, 14 March 1940.
51. TNA:FO 371/24053 – Jackson to Farquhar, 14 October 1939, FO to Haccius, 16 October 1939; for Haccius's work on relief for the Poles see generally ACICR:G 3/003/0022.
52. Haccius was briefly withdrawn to Geneva. By the end of May, however, he had returned – ACIC:RG 85/1047 – Huber to Halifax, 19 January 1940; TNA:FO 916/2587 – Satow to Chenevière, 27 May 1940.

3   Prisoners and Parcels, 1940–1

1. André Durand, *From Sarajevo to Hiroshima* (Geneva: Henry Dunant Institute, 1984), p. 484.
2. *ICRC Report*, vol. 2, pp. 32–36.
3. *ICRC Report*, vol. 2, pp. 108–14; Jean-Claude Favez, *The Red Cross and the Holocaust*, eds and trans John Fletcher and Beryl Fletcher (Cambridge: Cambridge University Press, 1999), pp. 46–50; Durand, *From Sarajevo to Hiroshima*, pp. 417–21, 485–7; Edwin Black, *IBM and the Holocaust: The Strategic Alliance between Nazi Germany and America's Most Powerful Corporation: Expanded Edition* (Washington: Dialog Press, 2012), chs 7 and 8.

4. Vasilis Vourkoutiotis, *Prisoners of War and the German High Command* (New York: Palgrave Macmillan, 2003), pp. 28–31; Rüdiger Overmans, 'German Prisoner of War Policy in World War II', in Bernard Mees and Samuel P. Koehne (eds), *Terror, War, Tradition* (Adelaide: Australian Humanities Press, 2007), pp. 171–80; Neville Wylie, 'Captured by the Nazis: Reciprocity and National Conservatism in German Policy towards British POWs, 1939–1945', in C. C. W. Szejnmann (ed.), *Rethinking History: Dictatorships and War: Essays in Honour of Richard Overy* (London: Continuum, 2009), pp. 109–24.
5. For an assessment of British and American POW treatment see Arieh J. Kochavi, *Confronting Captivity: Britain and the United States and Their POWs in Nazi Germany* (Chapel Hill and London: University of North Carolina Press, 2005), pp. 280–6, and Sean Longden, *Hitler's British Slaves: Allied POWs in Germany, 1939–45* (London: Constable, 2007); for a focus on the treatment of Australian POWs see Peter Monteath, *POW: Australian Prisoners of War in Hitler's Reich* (Sydney: MacMillan, 2011); on the French POW experience see Y. Durand, *Des Prisonniers de Guerre dans les Stalags, les Oflags et les Kommandos, 1939–1945* (Paris: Hachette, 1987).
6. TNA:FO 916/14 – Various POW accounts compiled by the Protecting Power – 12 March 1942; Sean Longden, *Dunkirk: The Men They Left Behind* (London: Constable, 2008), pp. 270–1.
7. *POW Convention 1929*, Article 11.
8. S. P. MacKenzie, *The Colditz Myth: British and Commonwealth Prisoners of War in Nazi Germany* (Oxford: Oxford University Press, 2004), pp. 68–9, citing various accounts of prisoners from the Imperial War Museum. Account of Private Alfred Charles Bryant, cited in Charles Rollings, *Prisoner of War: Voices from behind the Wire in the Second World War* (Reading: Ebury, 2008), pp. 44–5; for capture and transit see David Rolf, *Prisoners of the Reich: Germany's Captives* (London: Hodder and Stoughton, 1988), pp. 11–14; Vourkoutiotis, *POWs and German High Command*, pp. 43–4.
9. Rüdiger Overmans, 'Die kriegsgefangenenpolitik des Deutschen Reiches 1939 bis 1945', in Jörg Echternkamp et al. (eds), *Das Deutsche Reich und der Zweite Weltkrieg*, Band 9/1–2 (Munich: Deutsche Verlags-Anstalt, 2005), pp. 729–875 (843–5); Vourkoutiotis, *POWs and German High Command*, pp. 30–1; Wylie, 'Captured by the Nazis', p. 113.
10. Oliver Hoare (ed.), *Camp 020: MI5 and the Nazi Spies* (London: Public Records Office, 2000), pp. 16–19; Alexander P. Scotland, *The London Cage* (London: Evans Brothers, 1957), pp. 66–7; for revelations of prisoner maltreatment at the London Cage and the Bad Nenndorf Combined Services Detailed Intelligence Centre after the war see 'The secrets of the London Cage' and 'The interrogation camp that turned prisoners into living skeletons', *The Guardian*, 12 November and 17 December 2005.
11. Bob Moore, 'Axis Prisoners in Britain during the Second World War: A Comparative Survey', in Bob Moore and Kent Fedorowich (eds), *Prisoners of War and Their Captors in World War II* (Oxford: Berg, 1996), pp. 19–46 (20–1); Vourkoutiotis, *POWs and German High Command*, p. 193; Rolf, *Prisoners of the Reich*, pp. 31–3.
12. *POW Convention 1929*, Article 8 (italics author's emphasis).
13. MacKenzie, *Colditz Myth*, p. 65; Vourkoutiotis, *POWs and German High Command*, p. 42.

14. Account of Pilot Officer Idrwerth Patrick Bentley Denton cited in Rollings, *Prisoner of War*, p. 49; TNA:WO 32/18503 – Berne to FO, 2 August 1943; TNA:FO 916/881 – Berne to FO, 16 March 1944.
15. James Crossland, 'A Man of Peaceable Intent: Burckhardt, the British and Red Cross Neutrality during the Second World War', *Historical Research* 84.23 (2011), pp. 165–82 (173–4).
16. TNA:WO 366/26 – *POWs in WWII*, pp. 10–15; HRO:5M 79/A23 – FO to Warner, 29 April 1940.
17. ACICR:BG 003/22-1 – Odier report on visit to London, 17 July–8 August 1940.
18. David Rolf, 'Blind Bureaucracy: The British Government and POWs in German Captivity, 1939–1945', in Bob Moore and Kent Fedorowich (eds), *Prisoners of War and Their Captors in World War II* (Oxford: Berg, 1996), pp. 47–97 (49–50); Phillimore, 'POWs in WWII', pp. 16–18.
19. TNA:FO 369/2568 – Warner to Kelly, 8 April 1940; TNA:FO 372/2550 – Warner Minute, 8 August 1929; TNA:FO 369/2568 – Warner to Kelly, 8 April 1940; TNA:FO 372/2550 – Warner Minute, 8 August 1929.
20. *POW Convention 1929*, Articles 77 and 78.
21. TNA:FO 916/2546 – Warner Minute, 12 July 1940.
22. TNA:FO 916/2546 – Warner Minute, 12 July 1940; TNA:FO 916/2587 – Warner Minute, 3 June 1940.
23. Longden, *Dunkirk*, p. 181; *ICRC Report*, vol. 1, p. 245; ACICR:G 85/1047 – Frick-Cramer to British Consulate, 25 July 1940.
24. TNA:FO 916/2576 – Report of Roland Marti visit to Dulag VI D, September 1940; TNA:FO 916/2577 – British Consulate Geneva to FO, 17 October 1940.
25. ACICR:G 3 3B/44-1 – Haccius to Geneva, 23 July 1940; Haccius to Geneva, 2 October 1940; ACICR:G 3 3B/44-2 – Haccius to ICRC, 9 October 1940.
26. ACICR:G 3 3B/44-2 – Haccius to Odier, 17 December 1940; Haccius to Ducshosal, 17 January 1941.
27. ACICR:G 3 3B/44 – Warner to Haccius, 8 October 1940; ACICR:G 3 3B/44-1 – Air Ministry Bulletin, 1 August 1940; TNA:FO 916/112 – Hunter to Warner, 21 February 1941; *ICRC Report*, vol. 1, pp. 139–40; for POW exchanges see Kochavi, *Confronting Captivity*, pp. 106–7.
28. Combined donations from belligerents and their Red Cross societies for 1940 were as follows: SFR98,426.25 (Germany); SFR13,735.86 (Poland); SFR172,000.00 (France); SFR70,800.00 (Britain). Neutral contributions: SFR201,000.00 (Switzerland); SFR70,237.50 (USA); SFR10,000.00 (Japan) – *ICRC Report*, vol. 1, Annex 1, Financial Contributions 1938–1946.
29. TNA:FO 916/2587 – Central Agency Funding Report, 14 April 1940; Warner Minute, 3 June 1940; Warner Minute, 17 May 1940.
30. TNA:FO 916/2587 – Syers to Warner, 21 June 1940; for discussion of German plans for an invasion of Switzerland see Neville Wylie, *Britain, Switzerland and the Second World War* (Oxford: Oxford University Press, 2003), pp. 166–73; Stephen P. Halbrook, *Target Switzerland: Swiss Armed Neutrality in World War II* (Sarpedon: Rockville Centre, 1998), ch. 5.
31. TNA:FO 371/24530 – Warner, Political Review of Switzerland, 4 January 1940.
32. TNA:FO 371/24530 – Kelly's Report to Halifax, 21 May 1940; ACICR:G 85/1047 – Burckhardt to Livingston, 21 June 1940.

33. TNA:FO 916/2598 – Warner Minute, 2 July 1940; TNA:FO 916/2587 – Warner Memo, 11 June 1940; Warner to Syers, 28 June 1940. This reciprocal funding arrangement had been established during the First World War: see TNA:T 1/12148 – PWD to Treasury, 15 January 1918.
34. TNA:FO 916/2587 – Kelly to FO, 26 December 1940; TNA:FO 916/115 – FO Minute, 26 May 1941; *ICRC Report*, vol. 1, Annex 1, Financial Contributions 1938–1946; Harold Satow and M. J. Sée, *The Work of the Prisoners of War Department during the Second World War* (London: Foreign Office, 1950), p. 72.
35. François Bugnion, *The International Committee of the Red Cross and the Protection of War Victims* (Richmond: MacMillan, 2003), pp. 179–81.
36. Account of Pilot Officer Maurice George Butt cited in Rollings, *Prisoner of War*, p. 140; account of Captain Roger L. Shinn cited in Adrian Gilbert, *POW: Allied Prisoners of War in Europe 1939–1945* (London: John Murray, 2006), p. 99. For discussion of the impact of Red Cross parcels on prisoner health and morale see MacKenzie, *Coldtiz Myth*, pp. 156–63; Rolf, *Prisoners of the Reich*, pp. 52–6.
37. TNA:WO 366/26 – *POWs in WWII*, pp. 50–1; TNA:WO 32/14423 – BRC Report, 5 March 1942; Whitehall provided 23 per cent of the BRC's funding in the war's early years – Karen Versluys, 'When Lines Become Crossed: How the British Government Shaped the British Red Cross' Humanitarian Aid Efforts during World War II' (PhD Dissertation: Dalhousie University, Nova Scotia, 2007), pp. 17–19.
38. Neill Lochery, *Lisbon: War in the Shadows of the City of Light, 1939–45* (Melbourne: Imprint, 2011), pp. 8–10.
39. Marcel Junod, *Warrior without Weapons*, trans. Edward Fitzgerald (Geneva: Henry Dunant Institute, 1951), p. 175; ACICR:G 3/3B/44-3 – BRC Confidential Report, 24 January 1941; TNA:CAB 127/166 – Cripps' Report on BRC Parcel Distribution 1940–41; ACICR:G 3/3B/44-2 – PWD Parcel Delivery Report, 23 November 1940.
40. TNA:FO 916/2775 – PP Report on Stalag XXA, 31 July 1940; ACICR:G 3/3B/44-2 – Report of Captain Padon to American Embassy, Berlin, 20 October 1940; PWD Parcel Delivery Report, 23 November 1940; TNA:FO 916/32 – YMCA Report, 22 October 1940.
41. TNA:PREM 4/98/1 – Coombe-Tennant to Clementine Churchill, 20 November 1940; Barbara Hately-Broad, '"No one would tell you anything": The War and Foreign Offices and British Prisoner of War Families during World War II', *Journal of Family History* 27.4 (2002), pp. 459–77.
42. *ICRC Report*, vol. 3, p. 228; TNA:PREM 4/98/1 – Interdepartmental Meeting, 21 November 1940; TNA:FO 916/45 – Churchill to Herschel Johnson, 22 February 1941.
43. The MOC was usually a non-commissioned officer elected by the prisoners to coordinate parcel distribution and speak for all in meetings with the camp commandant and neutral inspectors – *POW Convention 1929*, Article 43.
44. ACICR:G 3/3B/44-2 – Haccius to ICRC, 22 July 1940; ACICR:G 85/1047 – ICRC to MEW, 5 December 1940; *ICRC Report*, vol. 1, pp. 348–50 and 144.
45. Versluys, 'When Lines Become Crossed', p. 95; TNA:FO 916/117 – BRC Parcel Delivery Report, 20 September 1940; *ICRC Report*, vol. 3, pp. 17, 202; 'Red Cross and St John War Organisation, 1939–1947: Official Record', 2 vols

P. 72

(unpublished and undated, held in British Red Cross Museum and Archives, London), hereafter BRC Report, vol. 1, pp. 360–1.

46. Neville Wylie, *Barbed Wire Diplomacy: Britain, Germany and the Politics of Prisoners of War, 1939–1945* (Oxford: Oxford University Press, 2011), pp. 107–8; ACICR:BG 003/22-1 – Odier report on visit to London, 17 July–8 August 1940.

47. TNA:WO 32/14423 – Adams to Howard-Vyse, 22 January 1942; Adams to Chetwode, 10 February 1942; BRC Report on Parcel Delivery, 5 March 1942; TNA:CAB 127/166 – Cripps Report on Stanley Adams, March 1942; *BRC Report*, vol. 1, p. 262; Versluys, 'When Lines Become Crossed', pp. 104–5.

48. David Miller, *Mercy Ships: The Untold Story of Prisoner of War Exchanges in World War II* (London: Continuum, 2008), p. 75; *BRC Report*, vol. 1, p. 262–64; ACICR:G 3 003/016 – Haccius to ICRC, 11 March 1941.

49. Satow and Sée, *Work of the Prisoners of War Department*, p. 5.

50. Rolf, *Prisoners of the Reich*, pp. 56–7; MacKenzie, *Colditz Myth*, pp. 161–5.

51. HRO:5M 79/A24 – Warner to Scott, 5 and 20 December 1940; Warner to Setchell, 6 March 1941; HRO:5M 79/D5 – Cadogan to Warner, 21 February 1941; Warner to Cadogan, 24 February 1941.

52. Warner admitted as much about Satow's aptitude when accepting his retirement – HRO:5M 79/D5 – Warner to Cadogan, 24 February 1941; TNA:FO 916/115 – Satow to Gardner, 9 June 1941.

53. TNA:FO 916/112 – Hunter to Warner, 8 January 1941; Hunter to Warner, 3 January 1941. Humiliated by his fall from grace, Hunter committed suicide in March 1942 – Wylie, *Barbed Wire Diplomacy*, p. 76.

54. TNA:FO 916/112 – Satow to Haccius, 3 May 1941; FO to Ministry of Labour, 12 June 1941.

55. Kochavi, *Confronting Captivity*, p. 26.

56. TNA:PREM 4/98/1 – Interdepartmental Memo on BRC, 1 January 1941; TNA:FO 916/112 – FO Report to Churchill on visit of Odier and Junod, 7 April 1941; TNA:FO 916/115 – Roberts Minute, 13 June 1941; Roberts to Burckhardt, 26 November 1941; for Huber's letter to Adams see BRC: 775–6 – Huber to Adams, 31 October 1941.

57. Rolf, 'Blind Bureaucracy', pp. 51–2; Kochavi, *Confronting Captivity*, pp. 18–26.

58. This claim and others like it arose on account of the prisoners' being unaware that, once the Committee made the switch from individual to collective parcel shipments, all parcels received from the BRC's packing centres were marked 'ICRC' before being despatched from Geneva. The Secretary of State for War, David Margesson, publicly corrected this misinterpretation in January 1941 – *Hansard*, 21 January 1941.

59. *BRC Report*, vol. 1, pp. 328–9; *BRC Report*, vol. 2, p. 514; TNA:FO 916/2577 – WO Minute, 3 January 1941; *ICRC Report*, vol. 1, p. 164.

60. ACICR:G 3/3/017 – ICRC to ICRC London, 21 May 1941; TNA:FO 916/112 – FO Report on Odier and Junod Visit, 7 April 1941.

61. ACICR:G 85/1098 – John Kennedy to Huber, 24 January 1941; TNA:FO 916/115 – BRC to WO, 14 May 1941.

62. TNA:FO 916/112 – Hunter to Warner, 3 January 1941; Hunter to Warner, 8 January 1941; Hunter to Warner, 19 January 1941; Hunter to Warner, 21 February 1941; ACICR:G 3/3B/44-3 – Haccius to ICRC, 18 February 1941.

63. TNA:FO 916/112 – George Warner to S. J. Warner, 26 February 1941; TNA:FO 916/113 – Roberts Minute, 15 October 1941; TNA:FO 916/15 – Roberts Minute, 13 June 1941; Berne to FO, 31 July 1941.
64. *BRC Report*, vol. 1, p. 268–9.
65. Versluys, 'When Lines Become Crossed', pp. 37, 106–11; Wylie, *Barbed Wire Diplomacy*, pp. 125–8.
66. Phillimore, 'POWs in WWII', p. 51; Miller, *Mercy Ships*, p. 75.
67. BRC: 775/166 – Burckhardt to Kennedy, 12 December 1941; TNA:FO 916/251 – Haccius to Satow, 15 March 1942.
68. For the general changes in British POW policy in 1941–2 see Wylie, *Barbed Wire Diplomacy*, pp. 122–9.
69. Wylie, *Barbed Wire Diplomacy*, pp. 191–206.
70. Bob Moore and Kent Fedorowich, *The British Empire and Its Italian Prisoners of War, 1940–1947* (Basingstoke: Palgrave MacMillan, 2002), pp. 23–5.
71. The spectrum of use for Italian POWs only grew in the war's middle years and with it their contribution to Britain's agricultural sector – Bob Moore, 'Turning Liabilities into Assets: British Government Policy towards German and Italian Prisoners of War during the Second World War', *Journal of Contemporary History* 32.1 (1997), pp. 117–36 (123–36); Sophie Jackson, *Churchill's Unexpected Guests: Prisoners of War in Britain in World War II* (Stroud: History Press, 2010), ch. 5; Johann Custodis, 'Employing the Enemy: The Contribution of German and Italian Prisoners of War to British Agriculture during and after the Second World War', *Agricultural History Review* 60.2 (2012), pp. 243–65.
72. For details of the repatriation negotiations see Satow and Sée, *Work of the Prisoners of War Department*, pp. 46–64.
73. Wylie, *Barbed Wire Diplomacy*, pp. 266–8.
74. Satow and Sée, *Work of the Prisoners of War Department*, p. 79.

4 Dependence and Divergence, 1941–2

1. TNA:WO 361/1899 – Report on ICRC inspection of Capua Transit Camp, 3 November 1941; Charles Rollings, *Prisoner of War: Voices from behind the Wire in the Second World War* (Reading: Ebury, 2008), pp. 62–3, 297, citing IWM account of Private Kenneth (Kim) Stalder, Royal Army Medical Corps and IWM account of Sapper Don Luckett, Royal Engineers; Adrian Gilbert, *POW: Allied Prisoners of War in Europe 1939–1945* (London: John Murray, 2006), pp. 47–50; Peter Monteath, *POW: Australian Prisoners of War in Hitler's Reich* (Sydney: MacMillan, 2011), pp. 56–7, 101–4.
2. Matthew Willingham, *Perilous Commitments: Britain's Involvement in Greece and Crete 1940–41* (Staplehurst: Spellmount, 2005), p. 253; *ICRC Report*, vol. 2, pp. 145–7; Harold Satow and M. J. Sée, *The Work of the Prisoners of War Department during the Second World War* (London: Foreign Office, 1950), pp. 16–17, 70–1.
3. *ICRC Report*, vol. 3, p. 48; *BRC Report*, vol. 1, pp. 399–403.
4. Brunel's war work began in September 1939 when he organized relief for Polish refugees. A month later he was in Finland visiting Russian POWs despite Moscow's refusal to acknowledge the ICRC. He was sent to Greece

in November 1940 and organized relief to POWs and civilians afflicted by famine until he was invalided back to Switzerland, where he died on 16 June 1943. Widely regarded to have literally worked himself to death on behalf of the Greeks, flags were flown at half-mast in Athens on news of his passing and the municipal council voted to name a street in the capital in his honour – André Durand, *From Sarajevo to Hiroshima* (Geneva: Henry Dunant Institute, 1984), pp. 404–6, 502.

5. Durand, *From Sarajevo to Hiroshima*, p. 492; Willingham, *Perilous Commitments*, pp. 93–6; *ICRC Report*, vol. 2, p. 147.
6. ACICR:G 85/1047 – ICRC Cable of Brunel's Report to ICRC London, 13 June 1941; TNA:FO 916/214 – ICRC to ICRC London, 11 July 1941; Geneva to FO, 9 August 1941.
7. Lambert was physically ejected from the Hadari camp, but followed a convoy leaving in his Red Cross truck. He later discovered those being transported were not British POWs but Jews – Caroline Moorehead, *Dunant's Dream: War, Switzerland and the History of the Red Cross* (London: Harper Collins, 1998), p. 396.
8. TNA:FO 916/424– Pictet to Haccius, 9 January 1942; Cairo to MEW, 14 May 1942; Ankara to FO, 30 June 1942.
9. TNA:WO 361/1873 – Berne to MI9, 4 May 1942; Treatment of Prisoners of War in Italian Hands Report, 23 April 1943.
10. TNA:FO 916/214 – Ankara to FO, 8 July 1941; DPW to FO, 8 October 1941; *ICRC Report*, vol. 3, p. 460.
11. TNA:WO 361/1873 – Treatment of Prisoners of War in Italian Hands Report, 23 April 1943; ACICR:BG 003/03/29 – Haccius to Burckhardt, 18 February 1942; Satow and Sée, *Work of the Prisoners of War Department*, pp. 16–17, 72–3.
12. Satow and Sée, *Work of the Prisoners of War Department*, pp. 12–13, 17–18.
13. *ICRC Report*, vol. 1, p. 440.
14. In addition to large sections on the ICRC in the Far East in Moorehead, *Dunant's Dream*, and Durand, *From Sarajevo to Hiroshima*, see in general Christophe Laurent, 'Les Obstacles Recontrés par le CICR dans son Activité en Extrême-Orient, 1941–45', PhD dissertation (Université de Lausanne, 2003); Gavan Daws, *Prisoners of the Japanese: POWs of World War II in the Pacific* (New York: William Morrow, 1994); Philip Towle, 'Japanese Culture and the Treatment of Prisoners of War in the Asian-Pacific War', in Sibylle Scheipers (ed.), *Prisoners in War: Norms, Military Cultures and Reciprocity in Armed Conflict* (Oxford: Oxford University Press, 2010), pp. 141–53; Hans Schweizer, *Dark Days in Singapore: Experience of a Delegate of the International Committee of the Red Cross during the Japanese Occupation of Singapore and Malaya, 1941–45* (Singapore: Swiss Club of Singapore, 1992).
15. Moorehead, *Dunant's Dream*, p. 471.
16. For ICRC action in the Sino-Japanese War see Durand, *From Sarajevo to Hiroshima*, pp. 369–83; for delegations in the Far East see pp. 522–5.
17. *ICRC Report*, vol. 1, p. 443
18. ACICR:BG 17 07/013 – British Consulate, Geneva to ICRC, 9 February 1942.
19. *BRC Report*, vol. 1, pp. 432–6.
20. François Bugnion, *The International Committee of the Red Cross and the Protection of War Victims* (Richmond: MacMillan, 2003), p. 191; *ICRC Report*, vol. 1, pp. 446–57.

21. TNA:FO 916/332 – Interdepartmental Meeting on Relief to the Far East, 2 April 1942; *BRC Report*, vol. 1, pp. 443–4, 449.
22. Kent Fedorowich, 'Doomed from the Outset? Internment and Civilian Exchanges in the Far East: The British Failure over Hong Kong, 1941–45', *Journal of Imperial and Commonwealth History* 25.1 (1997), pp. 113–40 (114).
23. David Miller, *Mercy Ships: The Untold Story of Prisoner of War Exchanges in World War II* (London: Continuum, 2008), pp. 125–6; *BRC Report*, vol. 1, pp. 444–5.
24. *ICRC Report*, vol. 1, pp. 446–52; Moorehead, *Dunant's Dream*, p. 475; F. Yap, 'Prisoners of War and Civilian Internees of the Japanese in British Asia: The Similarities and Contrasts of Experience', *Journal of Contemporary History* 47.2 (2012), pp. 317–46 (321–2).
25. For the ICRC's work on the Eastern Front see Durand, *From Sarajevo to Hiroshima*, pp. 503–21.
26. Laurent, 'Obstacles Recontrés par le CICR', p. 93.
27. The Japanese constantly objected to Schweizer using the Swiss Consulate to forward messages to Geneva – TNA:FO 916/616 – ICRC to ICRC London, 13 August 1943.
28. On his detainment by the Kempeitai see Schweizer, *Dark Days*, Part 1, pp. 30–2; Fujibayashi was not rewarded for his assistance. Imprisoned and, according to Schweizer, beaten by Allied authorities, he died in captivity in Singapore in 1945 – Schweizer, *Dark Days*, pp. 24–5; for details of Schweizer's relief programme see pp. 27–9; ACICR:BG 17 07/130 – Chenéviere to Schweizer, 12 March 1942; Schweizer to Huber, 10 August 1942.
29. *ICRC Report*, vol. 1, pp. 488–9; Durand, *From Sarajevo to Hiroshima*, pp. 524–5, 530–2; Moorehead, *Dunant's Dream*, pp. 483–4; the Protecting Power representative, Monsieur Siegenthaler, was able to purchase goods locally for POWs, provided that he did so as a 'private citizen', rather than as a representative of the Swiss Government – TNA:CO 980/149 – Note on Relief and Supply Situation of British Territory in Japanese Hands, 21 September 1944.
30. Tilak Raj Sareen, *Japanese Prisoners of War in India, 1942–1946: Bushido and Barbed Wire* (Kent: Global Oriental, 2006), pp. 109–16.
31. ACICR:BG 17 07/12 – Egle and Zindel Report on visit to Stanley Camp, 29 June 1942; ACICR:BG 17/07/14 – Egle to ICRC, 27 August 1942; ACICR:BG 17/07/131 – Schweizer to ICRC, 11 October 1945; TNA: CO 980/155 – Supplementary Report on the Work of the ICRC Delegation in Hong Kong under Japanese Occupation, 15 July 1945.
32. TNA:FO 916/616 – Johnson to Dominions Office, 18 February 1943; Wallinger to Elwes, 5 February 1943; Moorehead, *Dunant's Dream*, pp. 477–9.
33. TNA:FO 916/332 – Lisbon to FO, 3 August 1942.
34. TNA:FO 916/774 – Berne to FO, 13 November 1943; FO Minute, 16 November 1943; TNA:FO 916/774 – Berne to FO, 13 November 1943; FO Minute, 16 November 1943.
35. TNA:CO 980/148 – British Legation to the Vatican to Vatican City, 22 November 1943; *BRC Report*, pp. 444–9.
36. TNA:FO 916/616 – Paravicini Report on ICRC Delegations in the Far East, 19 August 1943; TNA:FO 916/309 – C in C India to WO, 9 January 1942; PWD to India Office, 24 February 1942.

37. TNA:FO 916/616 – Mynors to Wallinger, 6 May 1943; FO to Berne, 3 July 1943; TNA:CO 980/149 – Note on Relief and Supply Situation of British Territory in Japanese Hands, 21 September 1944.
38. ACICR:BG 17/07/16 – Egle to Paravicini, 4 November 1942; TNA:FO 916/616 – Satow to Gilchrist, 9 January 1943.
39. Any thoughts of a second voyage were curtailed when the return exchange ship, the *Awa Maru*, was torpedoed and sunk by a US submarine on 1 April 1945. In response Tokyo refused to permit any more relief vessels into its territory – *ICRC Report*, vol. 1, p. 461.
40. Miller, *Mercy Ships*, pp. 12–13.
41. Satow and Sée, *Work of the Prisoners of War Department*, p. 139.
42. TNA:CO 980/149 – Note on Relief and Supply Situation of British Territory in Japanese Hands, 21 September 1944.
43. For praise of the ICRC's work see generally ACICR:G 85/1048. Following the British retaking of Singapore in 1945, Schweizer was presented with a collection of thank-you telegrams from the BRC and the Colonial Office by Lord Louis Mountbatten – Henry Frei, 'Surrendering Syonan', in Akashi Yoji and Yoshimura Mako (eds), *New Perspectives on the Japanese Occupation in Malaya and Singapore, 1941–45* (Singapore: NUS, 2008), pp. 217–34 (225).
44. Frédéric Siordet, *Inter Arma Caritas: The World of the ICRC during the Second World War* (Geneva: ICRC, 1973), p. 89.
45. *ICRC Report*, vol. 3, pp. 30–1, 205.
46. Y. Durand, *Des Prisonniers de Guerre dans les Stalags, les Oflags et les Kommandos, 1939–1945* (Paris: Hachette, 1987), pp. 25–46; R. Scheck, 'The Prisoner of War Question and the Beginnings of Collaboration: The Franco-German Agreement of 16 November 1940', *Journal of Contemporary History* 45.2 (2010), pp. 364–88.
47. This argument was raised again when MEW tried to restrict imports for French POWs in November 1942 – *ICRC Report*, vol. 3, pp. 30–3; TNA:FO 837/1214 – Notes on MEW blockade policy, 14 February 1943; TNA:FO 916/613 – Notes on Zollinger meeting with Drogheda, 16 June 1943. On British labour in the Reich see Sean Longden, *Hitler's British Slaves: Allied POWs in Germany, 1939–45* (London: Constable, 2007), ch. 3.
48. ACICR:G 85/1047 – Illisible to Odier, 29 August 1940; *Final Report of the Joint Relief Commission of the International Red Cross: 1941–46* (Geneva: ICRC, 1948), hereafter *JRC Report*, pp. 14–16; Durand, *Des Prisonniers de Guerre*, pp. 129–30.
49. Neville Wylie, *Barbed Wire Diplomacy: Britain, Germany and the Politics of Prisoners of War, 1939–1945* (Oxford: Oxford University Press, 2011), pp. 123–4.
50. For discussion of the shared interests of the ICRC and the Swiss Government see Isabelle Vonèche Cardia, *Neutralité et engagement: les relations entre le Comité International de la Croix-Rouge et le Gouvernement Suisse, 1938–1945* (Lausanne: SHSR, 2012), ch. 1 generally; on de Haller's appointment and concerns over ICRC neutrality see, pp. 131–4; for discussion on the Protecting Power's influence on ICRC operations see ch. 6; for de Haller's closeness to the ICRC see David P. Forsythe, *The Humanitarians: The International Committee of the Red Cross* (Cambridge: Cambridge University Press, 2005), pp. 185–6.
51. ACICR:G 85/1048 – Gepp to Huber, 5 February 1942; Harry J. Phillimore, 'History of the Second World War: Prisoners of War 1939–1945' (unpublished, 1949), p. 46.

52. TNA:FO 916/33 – Satow to Gepp, 17 November 1941; TNA:FO 916/32 – Satow Minute, 13 July 1941.
53. TNA:FO 916/251 – FO to Berne, 30 September 1942; Berne to FO, 29 December 1942.
54. Neville Wylie, *Britain, Switzerland and the Second World War* (Oxford: Oxford University Press, 2003), pp. 323–4.
55. TNA:FO 916/571 – Phillimore to Roberts, 19 November 1943.
56. TNA:FO 916/251 – FO to Berne, 30 September 1942; TNA:FO 916/613 – DPW Minute, 14 December 1943; TNA:FO 916/250 – Roberts to Haccius, 3 February 1942.
57. For details of ICRC/Protecting Power roles in POW exchanges see *ICRC Report*, vol. 1, pp. 373–5.
58. TNA:FO 916/613 – WO to FO, 26 March 1943, 16 July 1943; TNA:FO 916/251 – Satow to Howard-Vyse, 15 May 1942; Satow and Sée, *Work of the Prisoners of War Department*, p. 48.
59. Bugnion, *International Committee of the Red Cross and the Protection of War Victims*, pp. 184–5; ACICR:G 003 3/017 – Haccius to Odier, 30 May 1941; Arieh, J. Kochavi, 'Why None of Britain's Long-Term POWs in Nazi German Were Repatriated during World War Two', *Canadian Journal of History* 39.1 (2004), pp. 63–85 (65–7); TNA:ADM 116/5353 – Burckhardt to FO, 13 October 1942; FO to Burckhardt, undated, May 1943.
60. TNA:WO 32/10719 – Berne to FO, 16 March 1943; TNA:WO 32/10719 – Berne to FO, 16 March 1943.
61. Neville Wylie, 'Captured by the Nazis: Reciprocity and National Conservatism in German Policy towards British POWs, 1939–1945', in C. C. W. Szejnmann (ed.), *Rethinking History: Dictatorships and War: Essays in Honour of Richard Overy* (London: Continuum, 2009), pp. 109–24 (112).
62. Cardia, *Neutralité et Engagement*, pp. 126–37.
63. *ICRC Report*, vol. 3, p. 30.

5 Civilians and Ships, 1940–3

1. Winston Churchill, *Great War Speeches* (London: Corgi, 1957), pp. 23–4.
2. Richard Overy, 'Allied Bombing and the Destruction of German Cities', in Roger Chickering, Stig Förster and Bernd Grenier (eds), *A World at Total War: Global Conflict and the Politics of Destruction, 1937–1945* (Cambridge: Cambridge University Press, 2005), pp. 277–95 (287); Gerhard Weinberg, *A World at Arms: A Global History of World War II* (New York: Cambridge University Press, 1994), pp. 150–2; David Reynolds, 'Churchill and the British Decision to Fight on: Right Policy, Wrong Reasons', in Richard Langhorne (ed.), *Diplomacy and Intelligence during the Second World War: Essays in Honour of F. H. Hinsley* (Cambridge: Cambridge University Press, 1985), pp. 147–67 (155–9).
3. Geoffrey Till, 'Naval Blockades and Economic Warfare, Europe 1939–45', in Bruce Allen Elleman and Sarah C. M Paine (eds), *Naval Blockades and Seapower: Strategies and Counterstrategies, 1805–2005* (London and New York: Routledge, 2006), pp. 117–29 (117–19); Brian Bond, *War and Society in Europe, 1870–1970* (Montreal: McGill Press, 1984), pp. 191–4.

4. Quoted from Jock Colville, *Fringes of Power: Downing Street Diaries 1939–1955* (London: Phoenix, 2005), p. 3. For details of the blockade system and its problems pre-summer 1940 see W. N. Medlicott, *The Economic Blockade*, 2 vols (London: HMSO, 1959), vol. 1, pp. 43–62 (124–32). For a contrary viewpoint see Adam Tooze, *The Wages of Destruction: The Making and Breaking of the Nazi Economy* (London: Allen Lane, 2006), pp. 332–3.
5. Hugh Dalton, *The Fateful Years: Memoirs 1931–1945* (London: Frederick Muller, 1957), pp. 334, 353; Medlicott, *Economic Blockade*, vol. 1, pp. 415–63.
6. Meredith Hindsley, 'Constructing Allied Humanitarian Policy', *Journal of Holocaust Education* 9.2/3 (2000), pp. 77–93 (84–5).
7. The Declaration of London was rejected by the British and, consequently, was never ratified by any of its signatories. *Convention (IV) Respecting the Laws and Customs of War on Land and Its Annex: Regulations concerning the Laws and Customs of War on Land* (18 October 1907), *Sect. 3, Article 43; Declaration Respecting Maritime Law* (16 April 1856), point 4; *Declaration concerning the Laws of Naval War* (26 February 1909); Wolf Heintschel von Heinegg, 'Naval blockade and Internal Law', in Bruce Allen Elleman and Sarah C. M Paine (eds), *Naval Blockades and Seapower: Strategies and Counterstrategies, 1805–2005* (London and New York: Routledge, 2006), pp. 10–22.
8. Hindsley, 'Constructing Allied Humanitarian Policy', pp. 81–2. Permission for relief for civilian internees in Vichy France was not given until 4 January 1942 – *JRC Report*, pp. 14–16.
9. German permission for relief for civilian internees was given on 28 September 1939. British and French agreement came on 23 November. There were some differences in the treatment of POWs and civilian internees despite the agreement, particularly in rations and clothing, for which POWs were generally better supplied – André Durand, *From Sarajevo to Hiroshima* (Geneva: Henry Dunant Institute, 1984), pp. 444–7; Berryl Oliver, *The British Red Cross in Action* (London: Faber, 1966), pp. 431–2; ACICR:BG 3 003/004 – Haccius to ICRC, 10 October 1939; TNA:FO 371/25158 – MEW to FO, 14 February 1940; TNA:FO 369/2568 – Warner to ICRC, 30 April 1940.
10. Mark Mazower, *Hitler's Empire: Nazi Rule in Occupied Europe* (London: Allen Lane, 2008), pp. 274–90; Lizzie Collingham, *The Taste of War: World War Two and the Battle for Food* (London: Penguin, 2012), ch. 8; Polymeris Voglis, 'Surviving Hunger: Life in the Cities and the Countryside during the Occupation', in Robert Gildea, Anette Warring and Olivier Wieviorka (eds), *Surviving Hitler and Mussolini: Daily Life in Occupied Europe* (Oxford: Berg, 2006), pp. 16–41; for specific discussion of German requisitions in France see Ian Ousby, *Occupation: The Ordeal of France, 1940–1944* (London: Pimlico, 1999), pp. 118–26.
11. Bob Moore, 'The Western Allies and Food Relief to the Occupied Netherlands, 1944–1945', *War and Society* 10.2 (1992), pp. 91–118; Collingham, *Taste of War*, pp. 176–7.
12. Hindsley, 'Constructing Allied Humanitarian Policy', pp. 95–6; Jean Beaumont, 'Starving for Democracy: Britain's Blockade of and Relief for Occupied Europe, 1939–45', *War and Society* 8.2 (1990), pp. 57–82 (77–8).
13. The sum of $2,075,837.86 was spent on relief for British subjects by the ARC between October 1939 and August 1940. The French, by contrast, had $938,311.99 spend on their interests – IFRC:A 1023 Box 2 – American Red Cross Foreign War Relief: Statement of Receipts, 6 September 1940.

14. This figure of foodstuffs received into Marseilles covers the period July–September 1940 – Medlicott, *Economic Blockade*, vol. 1, pp. 562–4; Dalton, *Fateful Years*, pp. 354–6.
15. TNA:FO 837/1218 – Odier to MEW, 2 August 1940; MEW Minutes, 10 August 1940; MEW to Odier, 14 September 1940; ACICR:G 85/1047 – Odier to MEW, 9 August 1940.
16. In reality, French agricultural output was damaged by the transfer of labour into Germany and a lack of fertilizer – Collingham, *Taste of War*, p. 170.
17. TNA:FO 837/1226 – MEW Memo, 3 August 1940; TNA:FO 837/1218 – MEW to Odier, 14 September 1940.
18. Beaumont, 'Starving for Democracy', p. 62.
19. TNA:FO 837/1226 – underline in original – Stirling to Steele, 6 August 1940; MEW Minutes, 31 July 1940.
20. TNA:FO 837/1220 – Stevenson to Stirling, 24 January 1941.
21. Marcel Junod, *Warrior without Weapons*, trans. Edward Fitzgerald (Geneva: Henry Dunant Institute, 1951), p. 177; ACICR:G 3/3B/44–2 – Haccius to Odier, 17 December 1940; TNA:FO 837/1220 – MEW to FO, 28 January 1941; TNA:FO 837/1221 – Odier to Roberts, 3 April 1941; Nichols to Odier, 5 April 1941.
22. Caroline Moorehead, *Dunant's Dream: War, Switzerland and the History of the Red Cross* (London: Harper Collins, 1998), pp. 294, 373; TNA:FO 837/1219 – Odier to Dalton, 3 December 1940; TNA:FO 837/1220 – Stevenson to Stirling, 24 January 1941. TNA:FO 837/1221 – Burckhardt and de Rouge to Dalton, 7 March 1941; Beaumont, 'Starving for Democracy', p. 63.
23. Violetta Hiondou, 'Famine in Occupied Greece: Causes and Consequences', in Richard Clogg (ed.), *Bearing Gifts to Greeks: Humanitarian Aid to Greece in the 1940s* (Basingstoke: Palgrave MacMillan, 2008), pp. 14–33; Mark Mazower, *Inside Hitler's Greece: The Experience of Occupation 1941–44* (New Haven: Yale University Press, 1993), pp. 23–37.
24. Galeazzo Ciano, *Ciano's Diary: 1939–1943*, trans. R. L Miller (London: Phoenix Press, 2002), 9 and 11 October 1941, pp. 452–3; *ICRC Report*, vol. 3, p. 451; TNA:FO 837/1230 – Geneva to MEW, 19 June 1941.
25. TNA:FO 837/1230 – MEW To Berne, 3 July 1941; Simopoulos to Dalton, 16 July 1941.
26. *ICRC Report*, vol. 3, p. 451; TNA:FO 837/1230 – Washington to FO, 27 July 1941; FO to Canea, 1 May 1941.
27. TNA:FO 837/1221 – Burckhardt to Drogheda, 15 July 1941; Drogheda Minute, 19 August 1941; W. A. Camps Minute, 18 August 1941.
28. TNA:PREM 3/74/5 – Cairo to FO, 9 January 1942.
29. TNA:FO 837/1221 – Notes of conversation between Nichols and Eden, 22 July 1941; TNA:FO 837/1230 – FO Memo, 28 July 1941; Hugh Dalton, *The Second World War Diary of Hugh Dalton: 1940–1945*, ed. Ben Pimlott (London: Jonathan Cape, 1986), 28 and 29 July 1941, pp. 262–3.
30. Dalton thought his successor 'inert' in blockade matters and disapproved of Selborne's sympathy for Eden's views – *Dalton Diaries*, 24 February 1942, pp. 382–43; 13 February 1943, p. 553.
31. Medlicott, *Economic Blockade*, vol. 2, pp. 263–4; TNA:FO 837/1231 – War Cabinet Memo, 14 February 1942.
32. Beaumont, 'Starving for Democracy', pp. 69–72; TNA:FO 837/1232 – FO to Camps, 19 September 1941.

33. Durand, *From Sarajevo to Hiroshima*, p. 493.
34. Durand, *From Sarajevo to Hiroshima*, pp. 191–3; Daphne A. Reid and Patrick F. Gilbo, *Beyond Conflict: The International Federation of the Red Cross and Red Crescent Societies, 1919–1994* (Geneva: IFRC, 1997), pp. 118–25.
35. Caroline Moorehead, *Dunant's Dream: War, Switzerland and the History of the Red Cross* (London: Harper Collins, 1998), p. 387; Paul Stauffer, *Sechs Furchtbare Jahre, auf den Spruen Carl J. Burckhardt durch den Zweiten Weltkrieg* (Zurich: Nzz Verlag, 1998), p. 17.
36. TNA:FO 916/113 – FO Minutes, 21 October 1941.
37. TNA:FO 916/114 – Berne to FO, 19 October 1941; Berne to FO, 17 October 1941; FO Minutes, 21 October 1941; Berne to FO, 19 October 1941; PWD Minutes, 22 November 1941.
38. See Chapter 6 for analysis of the Burckhardt 'peace feeler' scare.
39. TNA:FO 837/1235 – MEW to Washington, 10 July 1942; TNA:FO 837/1235 – Draft MEW Minutes, 4 February 1942.
40. Marie Mauzy, 'Inter Arma Caritas: The Swedish Red Cross in Greece in the 1940s', in Richard Clogg (ed.), *Bearing Gifts to Greeks: Humanitarian Aid to Greece in the 1940s* (Basingstoke: Palgrave MacMillan, 2008), pp. 97–112 (100–1); TNA:FO 837/1235 – MEW Minutes, 15 February 1942; TNA:FO 837/1235 – FO to Stockholm, 27 February 1942.
41. Mauzy, 'Inter Arma Caritas', pp. 102–4.
42. ACICR:G 3/27/147 – Report of Greek Delegation, 5 May 1942; *ICRC Report*, vol. 3, p. 462.
43. Beaumont, 'Starving for Democracy', p. 68. A similar view is presented by Moorehead, *Dunant's Dream*, p. 394; Mazower, *Inside Hitler's Greece*, p. 47; and Procopis Papastratis, *British Policy towards Greece during the Second World War, 1941–44* (Cambridge: Cambridge University Press, 1984), pp. 116–17.
44. *ICRC Report*, vol. 3, p. 128.
45. Junod, *Warrior without Weapons*, pp. 179–81.
46. TNA:FO 837/1221 – Minutes of Burckhardt and Odier meeting, 9 December 1942; TNA:FO 916/333 – Burckhardt to PWD, 15 July 1942; Geneva to FO, 28 July 1942.
47. Durand, *From Sarajevo to Hiroshima*, pp. 476–7; TNA:FO 916/333 – ICRC Report on setting up of Foundation, 26 May 1942; Berne to FO, 7 July 1942; TNA:FO 837/1235 – FO to Cairo, 24 June 1942; David Miller, *Mercy Ships: The Untold Story of Prisoner of War Exchanges in World War II* (London: Continuum, 2008), pp. 81–2.
48. Durand, *From Sarajevo to Hiroshima*, p. 576.
49. *ICRC Report*, vol. 3, p. 142; ACICR:G 85/1048 – MEW to Burckhardt, 30 June 1942.
50. TNA:FO 837/1224 – MEW to PWD, 6 August 1942; TNA:FO 916/333 – Burckhardt to Roberts, 15 July 1942; Geneva to FO, 28 July 1942; Burckhardt to Drogheda, 19 August 1942; Minutes of Interdepartmental Meeting, 13 August 1942. TNA:FO 837/1224 – MEW to PWD, 6 August 1942; TNA:FO 916/333 – Burckhardt to Roberts, 15 July 1942; Geneva to FO, 28 July 1942; Burckhardt to Drogheda, 19 August 1942; Minutes of Interdepartmental Meeting, 13 August 1942.
51. TNA:FO 916/333 – Minutes of Interdepartmental Meetings, 13 and 21 August 1942.

52. Medlicott, *Economic Blockade*, vol. 2, pp. 26–50; Beaumont, 'Starving for Democracy', pp. 76–7.
53. Michael Barnett, *Empire of Humanity: A History of Humanitarianism* (Ithaca: Cornell University Press, 2011), pp. 108–9.
54. Ben Shepherd, 'Becoming Planning Minded: The Theory and Practice of Relief, 1940–45', *Journal of Contemporary History* 43 (2008), pp. 405–19 (409–10).
55. Beaumont, 'Starving for Democracy', pp. 70–4; TNA:FO 837/1214 – MEW Minute, 11 April 1943.
56. TNA:FO 837/1214 – MEW Note on Blockade Policy, 14 February 1943.
57. TNA:FO 916/618 – DPW To ARC, 14 September 1943; TNA:FO 916/334 – FO to Washington, 14 November 1942.
58. TNA:FO 837/1225 – Drogheda to Burckhardt, 16 November 1943; MEW to US Embassy, 6 October 1943.; TNA:FO 916/333 – Minutes of Interdepartmental Meetings, 13 and 21 August 1942.
59. V. Vourkoutiotis, 'What the Angels Saw: Red Cross and Protecting Power Visits to Anglo-American POWs, 1939–45', *Journal of Contemporary History* 40.4 (2005), pp. 689–706 (705); *ICRC Report*, vol. 1, pp. 254–5.
60. Neville Wylie, *Barbed Wire Diplomacy: Britain, Germany and the Politics of Prisoners of War, 1939–1945* (Oxford: Oxford University Press, 2011), p. 128.
61. TNA:FO 916/334 – FO to Berne, 31 October 1942.
62. *ICRC Report*, vol. 3, p. 11; *BRC Report*, vol. 1, pp. 269–70; TNA:WO 224/63 – MOC Report to Protecting Power, 13 August 1942; TNA:WO 32/18490 – ICRC Report on Dulag Luft and *Lazaret* (work camp), 16 September 1942, 4 March 1943; TNA:WO 224/69 – ICRC Report on Oflag IVC, 3 July 1942; ICRC to ICRC London, 14 June 1943.
63. TNA:FO 916/333 – Minutes of Interdepartmental Meetings, 13 and 21 August 1942.
64. Durand, *From Sarajevo to Hiroshima*, p. 481; *ICRC Report*, vol. 3, pp. 30, 239, and vol. 1, pp. 168–9.
65. Jean-Claude Favez, *The Red Cross and the Holocaust*, eds and trans John Fletcher and Beryl Fletcher (Cambridge: Cambridge University Press, 1999), pp. 159–61; Max Domarus (ed.), *Hitler: Reden und Proklamationen, 1932–1945*, Band II (Wiesbaden: Löwit, 1973), p. 1790.
66. Favez, *Holocaust*, pp. 69–72; *ICRC Report*, vol. 3, pp. 335–6; Meier Wagner, *The Righteous of Switzerland: Heroes of the Holocaust*, ed. Andreas C. Fischer and Graham Buik (Hoboken: Ktav, 2001), pp. 218–20.
67. *ICRC Report*, vol. 3, p. 336; ACICR:G 85/1048 – MEW to Zollinger, 18 August 1943.
68. TNA:FO 916/613 – Minutes of Zollinger meeting with Drogheda, 16 June 1943. Béla Vago, 'The Horthy Offer: A Missed Opportunity for the Jews in 1944', in R. L. Braham (ed.), *Contemporary Views on the Holocaust* (Boston: Springer, 1983), pp. 23–45 (40).
69. TNA:FO 837/1214 – MEW to Burckhardt, 1 July 1943; TNA:FO 916/333 – Camps to Roberts, 6 August 1942; Medlicott, *Economic Blockade*, vol. 2, pp. 514–15; *JRC Report*, pp. 20–6.
70. See generally Louise London, *Whitehall and the Jews, 1933–1948: British Immigration Policy and the Holocaust* (New York: Cambridge University Press, 2000).

71. TNA:FO 916/618 – ADM to PWD, 8 July 1943; FO to Geneva, 9 July 1943; TNA:FO 916/334 – MEW to FO, 23 November 1942.
72. TNA:FO 916/618 – DPW to ARC, 14 September 1943.
73. *ICRC Report*, vol. 3, p. 28.
74. Junod, *Warrior without Weapons*, p. 176.
75. Ronald W. Zweig, 'Feeding the Camps: Allied Blockade Policy and the Relief of Concentration Camps in Germany, 1944–45', *Historical Journal* 41.3 (1998), pp. 825–85 (830–2).

6   Prestige and Credibility, 1942–3

1. With the exception of specific citations, the following section is derived principally from commentary on the ICRC's principles and policies from David P. Forsythe, *The Humanitarians: The International Committee of the Red Cross* (Cambridge: Cambridge University Press, 2005), pp. 157–88; Jean Pictet, *The Fundamental Principles of the Red Cross: Commentary* (Geneva: Henry Dunant Institute, 1979); H. Slim, 'Relief Agencies and Moral Standing in War: Principles of Humanity, Neutrality, Impartiality and Solidarity', *Development in Practice* 7.4 (1997), pp. 342–52.
2. Max Huber, 'Croix-Rogue et Neutralité', *International Review of the Red Cross* 18.209 (1936), pp. 353–63.
3. See Charles O. Berry, *War and the Red Cross: The Unspoken Mission* (New York: St. Martins, 1997). For a more nuanced assessment of the ICRC's relationship to the cause of peace see Yves Sandoz, 'The Red Cross and Peace: Realities and Limits', *Journal of Peace Research* 24.3 (1987), pp. 287–96.
4. Neville Wylie, 'Switzerland: A Neutral of Distinction?', in Neville Wylie (ed.), *European Neutrals and Non-Belligerents during the Second World War* (Cambridge: Cambridge University Press, 2002), pp. 331–54 (332); François Bugnion, 'Le Comité international de la Croix-Rouge et la Suisse', *Revue d'Allemagne et des pays de langue allemande* 28.3 (1996), pp. 353–65; *Manuel de la Croix-Rouge Internationale* (Geneva: ICRC, 1930), p. 146.
5. Forsythe, *Humanitarians*, pp. 43–4; on Japan see Christophe Laurent, 'Les Obstacles Recontrés par le CICR dans son Activité en Extrême-Orient, 1941–45', PhD dissertation (Université de Lausanne, 2003).
6. TNA:FO 837/1226 – Kelly to FO, 16 July 1940; TNA:FO 837/1218 – MEW Minutes, 10 August 1940; Julia S. Torrie, 'The Many Aims of Assistance: The Nationalsozialistische Volkswohlfahrt and Aid to French Civilians in 1940', *War and Society* 26.1 (2007), pp. 27–37 (29–31).
7. TNA:FO 837/1235 – MEW Minutes, 21 May 1942.
8. TNA:FO 837/1223 – MEW to IRB HQ, 30 March 1942.
9. TNA:FO 837/1236 – FO to MEW, 29 May 1942; FO to Greek Embassy in London, 15 July 1942; TNA:FO 837/1224 – MEW to Washington, 13 August 1942; ACICR:G 85/1048 – MEW to British Consulate, Geneva, 26 June 1942.
10. Marcel Junod, *Warrior without Weapons*, trans. Edward Fitzgerald (Geneva: Henry Dunant Institute, 1951), pp. 207–16; André Durand, *From Sarajevo to Hiroshima* (Geneva: Henry Dunant Institute, 1984), p. 525; Caroline Moorehead, *Dunant's Dream: War, Switzerland and the History of the Red Cross* (London: Harper Collins, 1998), pp. 495–96; Henry Frei, 'Surrendering

Syonan', in Akashi Yoji and Yoshimura Mako (eds), *New Perspectives on the Japanese Occupation in Malaya and Singapore, 1941–45* (Singapore: NUS, 2008), pp. 217–34 (224).

11. For censorship policy in 1942–3 see generally TNA:FO 916/614; for screening of delegates see TNA:FO 916/309.

12. TNA:FO 916/113 – C in C Middle East to WO, 19 July 1941; ACICR:BG 003/42/1 and 003/42/2.

13. Screenings of Haccius's delegation had taken place in early 1941 – TNA:FO 916/112 – Major Walton to Warner, 21 March 1941. In total there were forty-three delegates stationed in twenty-three delegations across the world in March 1942 – TNA:FO 916/309 – Lists of ICRC Delegations, 27 March 1942.

14. TNA:FO 916/616 – Chungking to FO, 4 February 1943; TNA:FO 916/309 – WO to FO, 4 September 1942; FO to WO, 14 September 1942; WO to FO, 18 April 1942; TNA:KV 4/49 – Report on Switzerland, Sweden and Neutrality, 22 December 1944; TNA:FO 916/309 – DPW Minute, 28 November 1944.

15. Jakub Jay, *Spies and Saboteurs: Anglo-American Collaboration and Rivalry in Human Intelligence Collection and Special Operations, 1940–45* (London: MacMillan, 1999), pp. 50, 66–7.

16. TNA:WO 204/779 – AFHQ Cable, 19 December 1943; AFHQ Cable, 15 March 1944; AFHQ Cable, 4 April 1944. A report on intercepted ICRC messages was compiled on 12 June 1944 – Communication Censorship to AFHQ, 12 June 1944; TNA:FO 916/614 – FO to Cairo, 29 July 1943, 9 September 1943.

17. See generally TNA:KV 2/570.

18. See generally TNA:WO 204/11537; Peter Grose, *Gentleman Spy: The Life of Allen Dulles* (Boston: University of Massachusetts Press, 1994), pp. 40–1.

19. TNA:WO 204/11537 – 2677 HQ report on Pagan, 18 October 1943; Tom Bower, *Blood Money: The Swiss, the Nazis and the Looted Billions* (London: Macmillan, 1997), p. 40; Adam Lebor, *Hitler's Secret Bankers: How Switzerland Profited from Nazi Genocide* (London: Simon and Schuster, 1997), pp. 234–41.

20. François Bugnion, 'ICRC Action during the Second World War', *International Review of the Red Cross* 317 (1997), pp. 562–7; Graz's greatest crime appears to have been condemning the behaviour of the French and the Americans in a less than neutral fashion in a report he compiled for Chenevière – Moorehead, *Dunant's Dream*, pp. 539–40, 701–2.

21. TNA:WO 204/11537 – Report of tactical officer, 2677 HQ, 17 November 1943.

22. Bugnion, 'ICRC Action during the Second World War', p. 566.

23. TNA:FO 916/2587 – Warner Minute, 3 June 1940; TNA:FO 916/2546 – Warner Minute, 12 July 1940.

24. Herbert S. Levin, 'The Mediator: Carl J. Burckhardt's Efforts to Avert the Second World War', *Journal of Modern History* 45.3 (1973), pp. 439–55; Gerhard Weinberg, *The Foreign Policy of Hitler's Germany: Starting World War II, 1937–39* (Chicago: University of Chicago Press, 1980), pp. 197–202; for Burckhardt's friendship with Weizsäcker, which culminated in the former testifying on the latter's behalf at the Nuremberg 'Ministries Trials' and writing a personal letter, co-signed by Huber, to President Truman asking for clemency see James Crossland, 'A Man of Peaceable Intent: Burckhardt, the British and Red Cross Neutrality during the Second World War', *Historical Research* 84.23 (2011), pp. 165–82 (169, 181); for a general overview of

Burckhardt's German connections and peace-seeking efforts at the start of the war see Ulrich Schlie, *Kein Friede mit Deutschland: die geheimen Gespräche im Zweiten Weltkrieg, 1939–1941* (Munich: Langen Müller, 1994), pp. 120–8.

25. Paul Stauffer, *Sechs Furchtbare Jahre, auf den Spruen Carl J. Burckhardt durch den Zweiten Weltkrieg* (Zurich: Nzz Verlag, 1998), pp. 188–90.
26. Crossland, 'Man of Peaceable Intent', pp. 172–3.
27. *Documents on British Foreign Policy, 1919–1939*, Series 3, vol. 5 (London: HMSO, 21 May 1939), doc. 580 – Record of Conversation between Halifax and Burckhardt, 21 May 1939, pp. 628–9; TNA:FO 371/24407 – Kelly to FO, 8 July 1940.
28. TNA:FO 916/113 – Strang and Roberts Minutes, 21 October 1941, FO to Berne, 22 October 1941; TNA:FO 371/26544 – Strang Minute, 18 November 1941; FO to Washington, 18 November 1941; Stauffer, *Sechs Furchtbare Jahre*, pp. 178–9.
29. Crossland, 'Man of Peaceable Intent', pp. 172–80; Stauffer, *Sechs Furchtbare Jahre*, p. 176.
30. TNA:FO 916/113 – Roberts to Kelly, 29 December 1941.
31. Stauffer, *Sechs Furchtbare Jahre*, pp. 93–106.
32. For Burckhardt's involvement in the CCPS see Jean-Claude Favez, *The Red Cross and the Holocaust*, eds and trans John Fletcher and Beryl Fletcher (Cambridge: Cambridge University Press, 1999), p. 95.
33. Beat Schweizer, 'The "Spirit of Geneva": Humanitarian Diplomacy and Advocacy', *Refugee Survey Quarterly* 26.4 (2007), pp. 163–5.
34. Arieh J. Kochavi, 'Why None of Britain's Long-Term POWs in Nazi German Were Repatriated during World War Two', *Canadian Journal of History* 39.1 (2004), pp. 63–85 (66–7); Neville Wylie, *Barbed Wire Diplomacy: Britain, Germany and the Politics of Prisoners of War, 1939–1945* (Oxford: Oxford University Press, 2011), pp. 168–9.
35. Isabelle Vonèche Cardia, *Neutralité et engagement: les relations entre le Comité International de la Croix-Rouge et le Gouvernement Suisse, 1938–1945* (Lausanne: SHSR, 2012), p. 127.
36. ACICR:BG 17 002/001.2 – ICRC London to ICRC, 10 February 1942; Moorehead, *Dunant's Dream*, p. 423.
37. ACICR:CL 2/001/03 – Burckhardt to Odeir, 11 December 1942; Universitat Bibliothek, Basle, *Papers of Carl J. Burckhardt*, hereafter UB:BII 4.2 – Texten zum Beriff des Humanitären, 18 August 1942.
38. Durand, *Sarajevo to Hiroshima*, p. 576. Favez, *Holocaust*, pp. 61–2.
39. ACICR:PV – Minutes of Committee Meeting, 14 October 1942. The best analysis of this episode can be found in Favez, *Holocaust*, pp. 83–9; for analysis of the differing views among attendees at the meeting see Cardia, *Neutralité et Engagement*, pp. 183–94. For Burckhardt's views on Etter see UB:BII 46E – Burckhardt circular to ICRC, 23 July 1940.
40. Forsythe, *Humanitarians*, pp. 44–9; Caroline Moorehead's expansive history of the ICRC begins with a discussion of the 'non-appeal' as a means of introduction – Moorehead, *Dunant's Dream*, pp. xxvi–xxxi.
41. Favez, *Holocaust*, p. 88.
42. Jonathan F. Vance, 'Men in Manacles: The Shackling of Prisoners of War, 1942–1943', *Journal of Military History* 59.3 (1995), pp. 483–504 (485–8); Arieh J. Kochavi, *Confronting Captivity: Britain and the United States and*

Their POWs in Nazi Germany (Chapel Hill and London: University of North Carolina Press, 2005), pp. 40–3.

43. TNA:WO 32/10719 – FO to London, 9 October 1942; Cardia, *Neutralité et Engagement*, pp. 150–1.

44. For discussion of Kelly's relations with Pilet-Golaz see Neville Wylie, 'Marcel Pilet-Golaz, David Kelly and Anglo-Swiss Relations in 1940', *Diplomacy and Statecraft* 8.1 (1997), pp. 49–79; for Kelly's relations with Burckhardt see ACICR:G 85/1048 – Kelly to Burckhardt, 6 April 1942; David Kelly, *The Ruling Few: Or, the Human Background to Diplomacy* (London: Hollis and Carter, 1952), pp. 273–4; Stauffer, *Sechs Furchtbare Jahre*, pp. 50–3, 187.

45. P. Neville, 'Norton, Sir Clifford John (1891–1990)', *Oxford Dictionary of National Biography* (Oxford: Oxford University Press, 2004): online edn (accessed January 2009).

46. In addition to gaining entry to camps that the ICRC had had trouble visiting, the Protecting Power's inspectors were also producing camp reports at a far greater rate than the ICRC by late 1942 –Neville Wylie, *Britain, Switzerland and the Second World War* (Oxford: Oxford University Press, 2003), pp. 97–8; TNA:WO 165/59 – DPW Diary, 1942.

47. TNA:PREM 3/363/2 – Churchill to Attlee, 11 October 1942; Churchill's initials on the inner sleeve of the file on the Pilet-Golaz/Burckhardt peace feeler scare of the previous year indicates that his comment may have been born of this see: TNA:FO 371/2644; Alexander Cadogan, *The Diaries of Alexander Cadogan: 1938–1945*, ed. David Dilks (New York: Faber and Faber, 1972), 12 October 1942, p. 483.

48. TNA:CAB 65/28 – Minutes of Cabinet Meeting, 12 October 1942; Wylie, *Barbed Wire Diplomacy*, pp. 132–9.

49. TNA:FO 193/555 – Berne to FO, 23 October 1942; TNA:WO 32/10719 – FO Memo, 24 November 1942; ACICR:G 85 1048 – Burckhardt to FO, 9 October 1942.

50. Vance, 'Men in Manacles', pp. 488–94; ACICR:G 85/1048 – Livingston to Huber, 15 October 1942; Vance, 'Men in Manacles', pp. 488–96; ACICR:G 85/1048 – Livingston to Huber, 15 October 1942.

51. ACICR:G 25/23/658 – Burckhardt to de Haller (phone call text), 15 October 1942; Ernst von Weizsäcker, *The Memoirs of Baron Ernst von Weizsäcker*, trans. John Andrews (Chicago: Henry Regenry Company, 1951), p. 271. Prior to the war, Krauel had helped Burckhardt in his push to become League of Nations High Commissioner to Danzig – Crossland, 'Man of Peaceable Intent', p. 169.

52. ACICR:G 25/23/658 – Burckhardt to Grawitz, 28 October 1942; Livingston to ICRC, 28 October 1942. For reports on Hitler's opinion see Marti to ICRC, 24 November 1942; *ICRC Report*, vol. 1, p. 369.

53. TNA:WO 32/10719 – Berne to FO, 20 November 1942; PWD to DO, 5 November 1942; TNA:WO 224/74 – ICRC Report on Oflag VIIB, 10 November 1942; ICRC Canada to ICRC London – 23 November 1943; *ICRC Report*, vol. 1, p. 233.

54. ACICR:C 14 – Minutes of Central Committee Meeting, 20 and 23 November 1942; ACICR:G 25/28/658 – Burckhardt to Marti, 2 November 1942.

55. ACICR:C 14 – Minutes of Central Committee Meeting, 21 December 1942; ACICR:G 25/23/658 – Krauel to Burckhardt, 1 December 1942; Burckhardt notes on visit to Livingston, 1 December 1942.

56. TNA:WO 32/10719 – Minutes of Cabinet Meeting, 30 December 1942.
57. ACICR:CL 2/001/03 – Burckhardt to Odier, 11 December 1942.
58. TNA:FO 916/273 – Menzies to Cavendish-Bentinck, 9 December 1942.
59. TNA:WO 32/10719 – Berne to FO, 10 March 1943; Berne to FO, 16 March 1943.
60. Cardia, *Neutralité et Engagement*, pp. 158–9.
61. S. P. MacKenzie, *The Colditz Myth: British and Commonwealth Prisoners of War in Nazi Germany* (Oxford: Oxford University Press, 2004), pp. 247–8; TNA:WO 193/555 – Berne to FO, 14 September 1943; ACICR:G 25/28/658 – Marti Note, 12 July 1943.
62. *ICRC Report*, vol. 1, p. 370; TNA:WO 32/10719 – Berne to FO, 6 August 1943.
63. TNA:WO 32/1071 – Berne to FO, 10 November 1943; Berne to FO, 23 November 1943; TNA:FO 916/560 – Berne to FO, 10 December 1943.
64. Wylie, *Britain, Switzerland*, pp. 326–7.
65. TNA:WO 32/1071 – Berne to FO, 16 January 1943, WO Minute, undated; TNA:FO 916/557 – Roberts to Gepp, 9 January 1943.
66. TNA:WO 32/10719 – Berne to FO, 23 November 1943; 7 December 1943; FO to Berne, 28 November 1943; ACICR:G 25/28/658 – Norton to Burckhardt, 30 November 1943.
67. ACICR:G 25/28/658 – Burckhardt to Norton, 8 December 1943; TNA:FO 916/560 – Berne to FO, 7 December 1943.
68. ACICR:G 25/28/658 – Burckhardt to Norton, 8 December 1943. The British agreed with Burckhardt's views on publicity and so ordered that the press be censored on the matter – TNA:FO 916/560 – FO to Berne, 7 December 1943.
69. Anna M. Cienciala, Natalia S. Lebedeva and Wojeciech Materski (eds), *Katyn: A Crime without Punishment* (New Haven: Yale Uuniversity Press, 2007), citing 'Communique of Sovinformburo', 15 April 1943, pp. 306–7; 'Beria Memorandum to Joseph Stalin Proposing the Execution of the Polish Officers', 5 March 1940, p. 118.
70. George Sanford, 'The Katyn Massacre and Polish-Soviet Relations 1941–43', *Journal of Contemporary History* 4.1 (2006), pp. 95–111 (96). For discussion on the search for the POWs by the Poles prior to 1943 see Louis Fitzgibbon, *Katyn Massacre* (London: Corgi, 1977), ch. 5.
71. In total, as many as 22,000 bodies of Polish army officers, police and intelligentsia were found at Katyn – Josef Goebbels, *The Goebbels Diaries, 1942–1943*, ed. and trans. Louis P. Lochner (New York: Doubleday, 1948), 14 April 1943, p. 328; Fitzgibbon, *Katyn Massacre*, p. 110.
72. Moorehead, *Dunant's Dream*, pp. 427, 436–7; Cienciala et al., *Katyn*, p. 311, citing 'Report of the Secretary of the Polish Red Cross, Kazimierz Skarżyński, on the PRC Technical Commission's Visit to Smolensk and Katyn', 15 April 1943.
73. Goebbels, *Diaries*, 17 April 1943, p. 332.
74. Alastair Noble, 'British Reaction to the Katyn Massacre', in Delphine Debons, Antoine Fleury and Jean-François Pitteloud (eds), *Katyn et la Suisse: Experts et Expertises Médicales dans les Crises Humanitaires, 1920–2007* (Geneva: Geor, 2009), pp. 224–8. For discussion of the propaganda value the British found in promoting German guilt see 'The Katyn Massacre: An SOE Perspective', *FCO Historians* 10 (1996) <http://collections.europarchive.org/tna/20080205132101/http://www.fco.gov.uk> (accessed May 2009).

75. Italics are my emphasis – Winston Churchill and Franklin D. Roosevelt, *Churchill & Roosevelt: The Complete Correspondence*, 3 vols, ed. Warren F. Kimball (New Jersey: Princeton University Press, 1984), vol. 2, C-284, 25 April 1943, p. 193.
76. TNA:FO 371/34570 – FO Circular Memorandum to Foreign Embassies, 26 April 1943. For Stalin's conspiracy theory see TNA:FO 371/34571 – Izvestia Editorial (text of broadcast), 27 April 1943.
77. Moorehead, *Dunant's Dream*, p. 390; for discussion of Burckhardt's anti-Communist leanings and view that Nazi Germany could act as a buffer to Stalin's ambitions see Stauffer, *Sechs Furchtbare Jahre*, pp. 54–5, 368–9.
78. TNA:FO 898/227– Report on ICRC in Katyn Affair, 29 April 1943.
79. Stalin had gone so far as to inform Eden that he would re-establish relations with the Poles if Sikorski retracted his request to the ICRC – Cadogan, *Diaries*, 24 April 1943, p. 523. Churchill had indicated to Stalin much earlier that the Poles' request would be withdrawn – TNA:FO 371/34570 – Churchill to Stalin, 25 April 1943; Cadogan, *Diaries*, 30 April 1943, p. 525; *ICRC Report*, vol. 1, p. 429.
80. TNA:FO 371/34573 – FO to Moscow, 1 May 1943; Sanford, 'Katyn Massacre', p. 110; Cadogan, *Diaries*, 18 June 1943, p. 537.
81. TNA:FO 371/34568 – Berne to FO, 18 April 1943; TNA:FO 898/227 – Report on ICRC in Katyn Affair, 29 April 1943.
82. Goebbels, *Diaries*, 23 April 1943, p. 341.
83. ACICR:CL-06 – Minutes of Committee Meeting, 19 April 1943. For discussion of the ICRC's relations with Moscow see Durand, *From Sarajevo to Hiroshima*, pp. 509–21.
84. ACICR:C 11 – Minutes of Committee Bureau Meeting, 21 April 1943.
85. ACICR:CL-06 – ICRC Public Communique, 23 April 1943.
86. Goebbels, *Diaries*, 24 April 1943, p. 343.
87. The ICRC had been informed by Lachert that the Soviets were responsible, declaring that 'according to the papers found on the corpses the murders must have taken place about the months of March and April, 1940' before the Germans arrived – TNA:PREM 3/353 – Professor D. L. Savoy's independent report into Katyn Massacre, 17 February 1944.
88. Favez, *Holocaust*, p. 86; ACICR:C 14 – Minutes of Central Commission Meeting, 4 November 1942.
89. TNA:FO 371/34573 – Lisbon to FO, 28 April 1943; *ICRC Report*, vol. 1, pp. 430–2.
90. Allen Dulles, *From Hitler's Doorstep: The Wartime Intelligence Reports of Allen Dulles, 1942–1945*, ed. Neal, H. Petersen (New Jersey: Princeton University Press, 1996), Doc. 2–70, Telegram 1151–3, 26 November 1943, pp. 162–3.
91. ACICR:PV – Minutes of Committee Meeting, 17 December 1943.

7. Humanity and *Götterdämmerung*, 1944–5

1. TNA:WO 193/351 – DPW Memo, 19 June 1942; TNA:CAB 119/94 – JIC Report on POW Protection, 29 July 1944.
2. TNA:WO 32/18503 – Berne to FO, 2 August 1943; TNA:WO 224/63 – WO to FO, 6 October 1943; TNA:FO 916/871 – WO to FO, 11 February 1944.

3. TNA:WO 32/18503 – ICRC Report on Dulag Luft, 15 November 1943; TNA:WO 224/67 – Protecting Power Report on Dulag Luft, 24 April 1944; TNA:WO 916/889 – WO Report on POW death from Air Raids, 14 October 1944; *ICRC Report*, vol. 1, pp. 312–13.
4. *ICRC Report*, vol. 1, pp. 693–9; ACICR:G 85/1049 – Huber to Churchill, 28 March 1944; *ICRC Report*, vol. 1, p. 314. As impractical as the scheme seemed, the ICRC had established a pseudo 'neutralized zone' in Shanghai during the Sino-Japanese War and was later able to establish two limited immunity zones in Jerusalem during the 1948 Arab-Israeli war – François Bugnion, 'The International Committee of the Red Cross and the Development of International Humanitarian Law', *Chicago Journal of International Law* 5.1 (2004), pp. 191–215 (206); André Durand, *From Sarajevo to Hiroshima* (Geneva: Henry Dunant Institute, 1984), pp. 374–5.
5. TNA:FO 916/894 – Report of Joint Intelligence Committee on POWs on the collapse of Germany – 29 July 1944.
6. TNA:WO 193/351 – DPW Memo, 19 June 1942; TNA:WO 193/352 – AIR to Washington, 27 January 1944; TNA:WO 219/2423 – Report on Operation Violet, 13 May 1945; John Nichol and Tony Rennell, *The Last Escape: The Untold Story of Allied Prisoners of War in Germany, 1944–45* (London: Penguin, 2003), pp. 179–80.
7. Winston Churchill and Franklin D. Roosevelt, *Churchill & Roosevelt: The Complete Correspondence*, 3 vols, ed. Warren F. Kimball (New Jersey: Princeton University Press, 1984), vol. 3, 22 March 1945, C-920, p. 580; Neville Wylie, *Barbed Wire Diplomacy: Britain, Germany and the Politics of Prisoners of War, 1939–1945* (Oxford: Oxford University Press, 2011), p. 237.
8. Adrian Gilbert, *POW: Allied Prisoners of War in Europe 1939–1945* (London: John Murray, 2006), pp. 279–88; Richard Lamb, *War in Italy: A Brutal Story, 1943–45* (London: John Murray, 1993), ch. 9.
9. Arieh J. Kochavi, *Confronting Captivity: Britain and the United States and Their POWs in Nazi Germany* (Chapel Hill and London: University of North Carolina Press, 2005), pp. 178–82; Wylie, *Barbed Wire Diplomacy*, pp. 220–2, 225–6.
10. TNA:WO 219/33 – SHAEF to WO, 25 March 1944; TNA:CAB 122/451 – SHAEF to CCOS, 28 June 1944; CCOS to SHAEF, 4 July 1944; Johannes-Dieter Steinhart, 'British Humanitarian Assistance: Wartime Planning and Postwar Realities', *Journal of Contemporary History* 43.3 (2008), pp. 421–35 (424–6).
11. TNA:FO 837/1217 – FO to Washington, 3 June 1944; TNA:FO 837/1217 – US State Department to FO, 27 May 1944.
12. Churchill and Roosevelt, *Complete Correspondence*, vol. 3, 8 April 1944, C-641, R-519, pp. 85–6.
13. Frédéric Siordet, *Inter Arma Caritas: The World of the ICRC during the Second World War* (Geneva: ICRC, 1973), p. 84.
14. TNA:FO 836/1231 – Naval Cipher to C in C Mediterranean, 12 July 1942; *ICRC Report*, vol. 1, p. 65.
15. TNA:FO 916/618 – Geneva to FO, 29 October 1943; *ICRC Report*, vol. 3, p. 139.
16. TNA:ADM 1/16061 – ADM Minutes, 12 November 1943; ADM Memo, 1 September 1944; Frazer to Brown, 3 November 1943; Brown to Frazer, 5 November 1943.

17. *ICRC Report*, vol. 1, p. 211.
18. *ICRC Report*, vol. 2, pp. 171–2; for *Embla* and *Christina* attacks and suspension of shipping route see generally TNA:FO 916/941 and 942; TNA:FO 916/943 – Geneva to FO, 14 June 1944.
19. TNA:FO 916/942 – BRC Memo, 14 June 1944; WO to ADM, 6 June 1944; ADM to C in C Mediterranean, 2 June 1944.
20. The BRC also had ten weeks' worth of parcels in British storehouses at this time ready to replenish the ICRC's warehouses once the supply lines were reactivated – *BRC Report*, vol. 1, p. 272.
21. TNA:FO 916/941 – Washington to FO, 11 May 1944; ADM to PWD, 25 May 1944.
22. See generally TNA:WO 204/553, 554, 555; Steven Zaloga, *Operation Dragoon 1944: France's Other D-Day* (Oxford: Osprey, 2009), pp. 34–7.
23. TNA:FO 916/343 – FO to Geneva, 4 July 1944; FO to Geneva, 16 July 1944; Ministry of War Transport to PWD, 26 July 1944; TNA:WO 204/554 – AFHQ to C in C Mediterranean, 7 July 1944.
24. *ICRC Report*, vol. 3, p. 234; Hilary Footit, *War and Liberation in France: Living with the Liberators* (Basingstoke: Palgrave MacMillan, 2004), pp. 103–5.
25. ACICR:G 85/1048 – Roberts to Burckhardt, 18 March 1942; BRC: 775/166 – Notes on visit of Burckhardt to London, 22 November 1941.
26. TNA:FO 837/1217 – State Department to FO, 27 May 1944. On Allied criticism of Sweden's trade relations see Paul A. Levine, 'Swedish Neutrality during the Second World War: Tactical Success or Moral Compromise?', in Neville Wylie (ed.), *European Neutrals and Non-Belligerents during the Second World War* (Cambridge: Cambridge University Press, 2002), pp. 304–30 (322–35).
27. For a summary of these negotiations see generally TNA:FO 837/1217, especially MEW Memo, 18 September 1944.
28. TNA:FO 916/943 – ADM to Ministry of War Transport, 20 July 1944; TNA:FO 916/943 – FO to Washington, 21 July 1944; Minutes of War Office Meeting, 29 July 1944.
29. TNA:FO 837/1217 – Halifax to FO, 9 April 1944; *BRC Report*, vol. 1, p. 387.
30. TNA:FO 916/943 – US Embassy to FO, 18 July 1944; TNA:FO 916/944 – FO to Berne, 5 August 1944; FO to Geneva, 10 August 1944; FO to Washington, 22 August 1944; TNA:WO 193/344 – Minutes of British Chiefs of Staff Meeting, 3 August 1944; *ICRC Report*, vol. 3, p. 163.
31. *ICRC Report*, vol. 2, pp. 171–2; *ICRC Report*, vol. 3, pp. 186–8; *BRC Report*, vol. 1, pp. 418–20; TNA:FO 916/944 – Washington to MEW, 21 August 1944.
32. By May 1945 the Berlin delegation had fifteen full-time members – Durand, *From Sarajevo to Hiroshima*, p. 619.
33. TNA:FO 916/938 – Berne to FO, 28 June 1944 and 18 March 1944; TNA:WO 224/63 – PP Report on Stalag Luft III, 17 July 1944; TNA:WO 224/57 – PP Report on Frontstalag 133, 27 March 1944; ACICR:G 85/1048 – Drogheda to Burckhardt, 25 September 1943; Marcel Junod, *Warrior without Weapons*, trans. Edward Fitzgerald (Geneva: Henry Dunant Institute, 1951), pp. 181–2, 218–19.
34. Nichol and Rennell, *Last Escape*, pp. 324–5, 400–1; TNA:FO 916/894 – Report of Joint Intelligence Committee, 29 July 1944; TNA:WO 193/355 – DPW 'Report on Possibility of Acts of Violence towards British Prisoners of War by SS Troops and Gestapo', 29 September 1944; ACICR:BG 3 003/49 – ICRC to ICRC London 21 September 1944.

35. ACICR:G 3/26F/109 – ICRC Berlin Memo, 16 October 1944.
36. Wylie, *Barbed Wire Diplomacy*, p. 240.
37. TNA:FO 916/888 – DPW to PWD, 19 February 1944.
38. Nichol and Rennell, *Last Escape*, pp. 20–5, 406; S. P. MacKenzie, *The Colditz Myth: British and Commonwealth Prisoners of War in Nazi Germany* (Oxford: Oxford University Press, 2004), p. 360.
39. ACICR:G 23/610 – Livingston to Burckhardt, 8 November 1944; the initial meeting in Geneva was followed by three more meetings in London in December – ACICR:G 85/1049 – Minutes of Meeting between ICRC and British Government Representatives, 26 November 1944; TNA:WO 193/344 – Minutes of Interdepartmental Meeting with ICRC, 11 December 1944.
40. ACICR:G 85/1049 – Minutes of Meeting between ICRC and British Government Representatives, 26 November 1944.
41. TNA:FO 916/947 – War Office memo on 'Southern Route for Supplies for Prisoners of War in Europe', 23 November 1944; TNA:FO 916/1156 – WO to FO, 24 January 1945.
42. TNA:WO 193/344 – Minutes of Interdepartmental Meetings with ICRC, 11 December 1944.
43. TNA:WO 193/343 – ICRC to ICRC London, 16 February 1945.
44. TNA:FO 1049/26 – ICRC to ICRC London, 22 February 1945. Although it was implemented immediately, the 'parcel pooling' policy was not made official until an ICRC telegram was sent to all camp commandants on 18 April 1945 – *ICRC Report*, vol. 3, p. 87; *BRC Report*, vol. 1, pp. 425–7.
45. TNA:FO 916/1156 – Schirmer Report, dated 2 March, originally filed with US Embassy in Berne on 28 February 1945; PWD Report on the March, 8 March 1945. The four camps evacuated in January were Stalag Luft VII (Bankau) on 19 January, Stalag 344 (Lamsdorf) on 22 January, Stalag XX-B (Marienburg) on 23 January and Stalag Luft III (Sagan) on 27 January – Nichol and Rennell, *Last Escape*, pp. 405–6.
46. See ACICR:G 23/26F/109 generally, in particular Bachman to Marti, 23 April 1945; *ICRC Report*, vol. 3, p. 89; Daniel Blatman, *The Death Marches: The Final Phase of Nazi Genocide*, trans. Chaya Galai (Harvard: Belknapp, 2011), pp. 263, 417.
47. Both the Soviets and the British Foreign Office rejected the idea of an appeal to Berlin – Kochavi, *Confronting Captivity*, pp. 212–16; TNA:WO 193/348 – Minutes of War Cabinet Meeting, 19 February 1945.
48. For an outline of SHAEF's plan see TNA:WO 193/345 – SHAEF to WO, 5 March 1945; TNA:FO 916/1181 – FO to Berne, 9 March 1945; *ICRC Report*, vol. 3, pp. 90–2.
49. *ICRC Report*, vol. 3, p. 188; Durand, *From Sarajevo to Hiroshima*, p. 623.
50. An entire file in the British National Archives is devoted to these 'friendly fire' incidents. See TNA:FO 916/1184; TNA:WO 193/345 – FO to Stockholm, 3 March 1945; TNA:FO 916/1181 – Air Ministry to Bomber Command HQ, 14 March 1945.
51. *ICRC Report*, vol. 3, pp. 90–3; ACICR:G 23/26F/109 – C. H. Burgess to Mock (ICRC delegate at Moosburg), 20 April 1945; Captain Bauer to Lieutenant-Colonel Hoseason, 3 May 1945; MacKenzie, *Colditz Myth*, p. 368.
52. It is unclear whether Siordet was exaggerating or had simply misread a document, but he claimed that forty new delegates were sent to Marti by Krauel.

The Berlin Delegation never had more than fourteen members during the war, though, as Siordet claims 'four hundred would not have been too many' in 1945 – Siordet, *Inter Arma Caritas*, p. 88; Durand, *From Sarajevo to Hiroshima*, pp. 622–3; TNA:FO 916/1181 – FO to Berne, 9 March 1945; *ICRC Report*, vol. 3, p. 92.
53. TNA:FO 916/1231 – Paris to FO, 20 March 1945; Berne to FO, 27 March 1945.
54. Jean-Claude Favez, *The Red Cross and the Holocaust*, eds and trans John Fletcher and Beryl Fletcher (Cambridge: Cambridge University Press, 1999), pp. 263–4; *Documents Diplomatiques Suisses 1848–1945*, Series 1, vol. 14 (Berne: Benteli Verlag, 1997) – Burckhardt's Report on Kaltenbrunner meeting – 17 March 1945, doc. E2001 (D) 3/474, pp. 1006–9; for a perspective that highlights Kaltenbrunner's evasiveness and Burckhardt's 'satisfaction' with the talks, see Walter Schellenberg, *The Memoirs of Hitler's Spymaster*, ed. and trans. L. Hagan (London: André Deutsch, 2006), pp. 432–3.
55. Yehuda Bauer, *Jews for Sale? Nazi-Jewish Negotiations, 1933–1945* (New Haven and London: Yale University Press, 1994), pp. 225–30; Favez, *Holocaust*, p. 66.
56. An evaluation of ICRC efforts on behalf of Jews in the war's final weeks can be found in Favez, *Holocaust*, ch. 9; for ICRC efforts in Hungary see Meier Wagner, *The Righteous of Switzerland: Heroes of the Holocaust*, ed. Andreas C. Fischer and Graham Buik (Hoboken: Ktav, 2001), pp. 195–205; for the ICRC's attempt to negotiate the surrender of Mauthausen to American forces see Caroline Moorehead, *Dunant's Dream: War, Switzerland and the History of the Red Cross* (London: Harper Collins, 1998), p. 463; for the ICRC occupation of Theresienstadt in May see Aime Bonifas, 'A "Paradisiacal" Ghetto of Theresienstadt: The Impossible Mission of the International Committee of the Red Cross', *Journal of Church and State* 34 (1992), pp. 805–18.
57. TNA:CAB 122/451 – FO to Washington, 23 November 1943.
58. For the application of 'regime theory' to Anglo-German relations on POW matters see Wylie, *Barbed Wire Diplomacy*, pp. 16–37.
59. TNA:FO 916/1181 – WO to ICRC London, 3 March 1945; *ICRC Report*, vol. 3, p. 197.
60. TNA:WO 193/343 – Chiefs of Staff Committee Memo, 19 February 1945.
61. Grigg Statement on POWs, 25 February 1945, cited in Kochavi, *Confronting Captivity*, pp. 67–8; David Stafford, *Endgame 1945: Victory, Retribution, Liberation* (London: Abacus, 2007), pp. 68–79; Arthur H. Mitchell, *Hitler's Mountain: The Fürher, Obersalzburg and the American Occupation of Berchtesgaden* (Jefferson: McFarland and Company, 2007), pp. 79–82, 101–2.
62. TNA:WO 219/33 – Eisenhower to AFHQ, 19 June 1944.
63. TNA:WO 219/243 – SHAEF to Air Ministry, 14 April 1945; SHAEF to Air Ministry, 29 April 1945; SHAEF Report, 26 April 1945. For progress reports sent from the ICRC to SHAEF see generally TNA:WO 193/345.
64. TNA:FO 916/938 – SHAEF to Peake, 21 August 1944; WO to PWD, 30 October 1944.

8 Relief and Redundancy, 1945–6

1. Burckhardt had been requested for this post by Charles de Gaulle, thus fulfilling his long-held ambition for a position in the Swiss Government.

2. Italics author's emphasis – André Durand, *From Sarajevo to Hiroshima* (Geneva: Henry Dunant Institute, 1984), pp. 634–7, citing Max Huber, undated circular to International Red Cross, April 1945.
3. Caroline Moorehead, *Dunant's Dream: War, Switzerland and the History of the Red Cross* (London: Harper Collins, 1998), p. 382; Durand, *From Sarajevo to Hiroshima*, pp. 624–5.
4. Fritz Paravicini died on 29 January 1944, leaving the Tokyo Delegation without a recognized leader.
5. Durand, *Sarajevo to Hiroshima*, pp. 631–2; Marcel Junod, *Warrior without Weapons*, trans. Edward Fitzgerald (Geneva: Henry Dunant Institute, 1951), pp. 252–71; ACICR:BG 003/51-6 – Notes on Junod talk to WO, 21 June 1946.
6. Durand, *From Sarajevo to Hiroshima*, citing Max Huber, undated circular to International Red Cross, April 1945, and Huber's Nobel Prize acceptance speech, 10 December 1945, p. 636–9.
7. The JRC was not dissolved until 31 October 1946 – Durand, *From Sarajevo to Hiroshima*, p. 638.
8. Britain's largest wartime annual contribution to the ICRC (SFR1,183,162.20) came in 1944 – *ICRC Report*, vol. 1 Annex 1; François Bugnion, *The International Committee of the Red Cross and the Protection of War Victims* (Richmond: MacMillan, 2003), pp. 172–4; Catherine Rey-Schyrr, *De Yalta à Dien Bien Phu: Historie du Comité International de la Croix-Rouge 1945–1955* (Geneva: Henry Dunant Institute, 2007), pp. 37–9.
9. Gerard Daniel Cohen, 'Between Relief and Politics: Refugee Humanitarianism in Occupied Germany, 1945–46', *Journal of Contemporary History* 43.3 (2008), pp. 437–49; Michael Barnett, *Empire of Humanity: A History of Humanitarianism* (Ithaca: Cornell University Press, 2011), pp. 109–11; Ben Shepherd, *The Long Road Home: The Aftermath of the Second World War* (London: Bodley Head, 2011), pp. 50–3.
10. Sharif Gemie, Laure Humbert and Fiona Reid, *Outcast Europe: Refugees and Relief Workers in an Era of Total War, 1936–48* (London: Bloomsbury, 2012), pp. 143–4; Keith Lowe, *Savage Continent: Europe in the Aftermath of World War II* (New York: St. Mary's, 2012), p. 108; Shepherd, *Long Road Home*, pp. 54–9.
11. Hugh Dalton, *The Second World War Diary of Hugh Dalton: 1940–1945*, ed. Ben Pimlott (London: Jonathan Cape, 1986), 25 November 1942, p. 525.
12. Moorehead, *Dunant's Dream*, pp. 505–6; Durand, *From Sarajevo to Hiroshima*, p. 639.
13. George Woodbridge, *UNRRA: The History of the United Nations Relief and Rehabilitation Administration*, 3 vols (New York: Columbia University Press, 1950), vol. 2, p. 508.
14. Gemie et al., *Outcast Europe*, p. 139.
15. ACICR:BG 003/55-1 – Ferrière meeting with Sub-Committee on Migration and Resettlement, 13 November 1943.
16. ACICR:BG 003/55-2 – Note on meeting between Zollinger and Lehman, 2 August 1944; Lehman to Zollinger, 12 August 1944; TNA:FO 371/51082 – Series of Telegrams proposing ICRC/UNRRA Operations in Romania, 4 December 1944.
17. Of particular significance was UNRRA's success in averting Europe-wide epidemics – Mark Wyman, *DP: Europe's Displaced Persons, 1945–51* (Philadelphia: Balch Institute Press, 1989), pp. 46–52.

18. TNA:CAB 122/451 – Joint Staff Mission to War Cabinet, 19 May 1944.
19. ACICR:BG 003/49-2 – Huber to Davies, 2 June 1942; Davies to Huber, 14 July 1942.
20. TNA:WO 219/33 – SHAEF to WO, 25 March 1944; Combined Civil Affairs Committee Memo, 12 May 1944.
21. See generally TNA:WO 219/3612; Woodbridge, *UNRRA History*, vol. 2, pp. 482–3.
22. TNA:FO 371/51089 – FO to WO, 11 May 1945; TNA:FO 371/51468 – FO to Ministry of Food, 23 June 1945.
23. John Nichol and Tony Rennell, *The Last Escape: The Untold Story of Allied Prisoners of War in Germany, 1944–45* (London: Penguin, 2003), ch. 14; S. P. MacKenzie, *The Colditz Myth: British and Commonwealth Prisoners of War in Nazi Germany* (Oxford: Oxford University Press, 2004), pp. 384–90; Adrian Gilbert, *POW: Allied Prisoners of War in Europe 1939–1945* (London: John Murray, 2006), pp. 315–17; *ICRC Report*, vol. 3, pp. 96–7.
24. Junod, *Warrior without Weapons*, pp. 278–85; TNA:FO 916/1235 – Junod Report on Activities of the ICRC in the Far East, 3 October 1945; see also TNA:WO 32/11678 – Minutes of Meeting between British delegation and ICRC, 7–10 June 1945.
25. TNA:FO 371/52648 – Ministry of Food to MEW, 29 May 1945.
26. TNA:WO 32/11678 – Gardner to Burckhardt, 13 July 1945.
27. TNA:FO 371/51902 – Mason to Hammer, 26 April 1945; TNA:FO 371/51087 – SHAEF to AGWAR, 28 March 1945; *UNRRA History*, vol. 1, pp. 39–41.
28. TNA:FO 371/51096 – Sub-Committee Report on UNRRA Activities, 5 July 1945; Wyman, *DP*, pp. 46–52; Woodbridge, *UNRRA History*, vol. 2, pp. 3–5, 535; David Stafford, *Endgame 1945: Victory, Retribution, Liberation* (London: Abacus, 2007), pp. 373–4.
29. TNA:FO 371/51087 – FO Minutes, 12 April 1945; on the problems of UNRRA's volunteers' lack of experience and poor equipment see Gemie et al., *Outcast Europe*, pp. 162–71; Shepherd, *Long Road Home*, pp. 58–9.
30. Lowe, *Savage Continent*, pp. 104–5.
31. Wyman, *DP*, pp. 55–6.
32. Moorehead, *Dunant's Dream*, pp. 514–18; and Gerald Steinacher, *Nazis on the Run: How Hitler's Henchmen Fled Justice* (Oxford: Oxford University Press, 2012), ch. 2.
33. TNA:FO 916/1219 – FO Minutes, 23 May 1945; Minutes of IPWC Meeting, 16 June 1945.
34. A defensive riposte to the notion that the ICRC was partial to German interests in 1945 can be found in *ICRC Report*, vol. 3, p. 100.
35. Bob Moore, 'Turning Liabilities into Assets: British Government Policy towards German and Italian Prisoners of War during the Second World War', *Journal of Contemporary History* 32.1 (1997), pp. 117–36 (134); Jon Sutherland and Diane Sutherland, *British Prisoner of War Camps during the Second World War* (Newhaven: Golden Guides, 2012), pp. 24–7.
36. James F. Trent, 'Food Shortages in Germany and Europe, 1945–48', in Stephen Ambrose and Günter Bischof (eds), *Eisenhower and the German POWs: Facts against Falsehood* (Baton Rouge: Louisiana State Press, 1992), pp. 95–112; Lizzie Collingham, *The Taste of War: World War Two and the Battle for Food* (London: Penguin, 2012), pp. 467–9.

37. See James Bacque, *Other Losses: An Investigation into the Mass Deaths of German Prisoners at the Hands of the French and the Americans after World War II* (Toronto: Stoddart, 1989). For a comprehensive rebuttal of Bacque's argument that Eisenhower deliberately starved to death hundreds of thousands of German POWs see Stephen Ambrose and Günter Bischof (eds), *Eisenhower and the German POWs: Facts against Falsehood* (Baton Rouge: Louisiana State Press, 1992).
38. The Americans used the term 'Disarmed Enemy Forces' (DEFs) – *ICRC Report*, vol. 1, pp. 539–41; Giles MacDonogh, *After the Reich: From the Liberation of Vienna to the Berlin Airlift* (London: John Murray, 2007), pp. 392–3.
39. Sutherland and Sutherland, *British Prisoner of War Camps*, pp. 20–3; for discussion of mortality rates in the *Rheinwiesenlager* see Rüdiger Overmans, 'German Historiography, the War Losses, and the Prisoners of War', in Ambrose and Bischof (eds), *Eisenhower and the German POWs*, pp. 127–69; Frederick Taylor, *Exorcising Hitler: The Occupation and De-Nazification of Germany* (London: Bloomsbury, 2011), pp. 173–7; Lowe, *Savage Continent*, pp. 114–15; MacDonogh, *After the Reich*, p. 399.
40. *ICRC Report*, vol. 1, p. 539–40; Brian Loring Villa, 'The Diplomatic and Political Context of the POW Camps Tragedy', in Ambrose and Bischof (eds), *Eisenhower and the German POWs*, pp. 52–77.
41. TNA:WO 32/11700 – FO to ICRC, 20 February 1947; *Hansard*, 22 February 1944.
42. *ICRC Report*, vol. 3, pp. 99–117. See ACICR:BG 17/005-37 – Summary of Facts Noted during Camp Visits, October–November 1945 for outline of day-to-day queries raised by the ICRC with the Allied authorities over the treatment of German POWs.
43. Moorehead, *Dunant's Dream*, pp. 533–8; *ICRC Report*, vol. 1, pp. 544–5.
44. TNA:FO 371/55738 – ICRC memorandum, 9 January 1946.
45. Durand, *From Sarajevo to Hiroshima*, pp. 639–40, 651.
46. TNA:FO 1049/246 – Control Commission Circular, 2 September 1945; Strang to Troutbeck, 15 November 1945.
47. ACICR:BG 17 005-37 – Headquarters, US Forces European Theatre Memo on Treatment of POWs, DEFs and Civilian Internees, 20 March 1946.
48. TNA:FO 368/3593 – Huber to Bevin, 6 September 1946.
49. TNA:FO 369/3593 – Summary of Observations of ICRC delegates, 6 September 1946; WO to FO, 18 December 1946.
50. TNA:FO 369/3593 – Davison to ICRC London, 21 January 1947; Davison to Huber, 20 February 1947.
51. For work on behalf of non-German DPs in the British Zone in early 1946 see generally ACICR:BG 017/04-21.
52. Loring Villa, 'Diplomatic and Political Context', pp. 70, 74–5.
53. ACICR:PV – Minutes of Committee Meeting, 22 June 1945.
54. TNA:FO 1049/246 – Strang to Troutbeck, 5 November 1945; for Soviet view of the ICRC see David P. Forsythe, *The Humanitarians: The International Committee of the Red Cross* (Cambridge: Cambridge University Press, 2005), pp. 52–3.
55. The Soviets complained that the ICRC had failed to speak out about Nazi atrocities, had sold medical supplies on the black market in Hungary and Romania and, with absurd hypocrisy, that it had displayed an 'unfriendly attitude' towards Moscow throughout the war – *ICRC Report*, vol. 1, p. 436;

Moorehead, *Dunant's Dream*, pp. 549–50; Dominique D. Junod, *The Imperilled Red Cross and the Palestine-Eretz-Yisrael Conflict, 1925–1952* (London: Kegan Paul International, 1996), pp. 14–16; ACICR:BG 003/30-09 – Marguerite Frick-Cramer, Note sur mes entretiens à Londres, October 1945.

56. Despite Maisky's suspicions of UNRRA in 1942, the Soviet Union held a position on UNRRA's Central Committee along with Britain, China, Canada and the United States – *UNRRA Charter 1943*, Article 3.3; TNA:FO 371/51081 – FO Minutes, 20 January 1945; SHAEF to AGWAR, 1 January 1945.
57. TNA:FO 371/50856 – BRC to Viscount Cranbourne, 13 April 1945.
58. TNA:FO 371/50856 – FO to DO, 20 April 1945; Falla to Gore-Booth, 12 May 1945.

Conclusion

1. David P. Forsythe, 'The ICRC: A Unique Humanitarian Protagonist', *International Review of the Red Cross* 89.865 (2007), pp. 63–96 (89).
2. Brigette Troyon and Daniel Palmieri, 'The ICRC Delegate: An Exceptional Humanitarian Player?', *International Review of the Red Cross* 89.865 (2007), pp. 97–111.
3. David P. Forsythe, *The Humanitarians: The International Committee of the Red Cross* (Cambridge: Cambridge University Press, 2005), pp. 202–3.
4. Jean-Claude Favez, *The Red Cross and the Holocaust*, eds and trans John Fletcher and Beryl Fletcher (Cambridge: Cambridge University Press, 1999), p. 21.
5. James Crossland, 'A Man of Peaceable Intent: Burckhardt, the British and Red Cross Neutrality during the Second World War', *Historical Research* 84.23 (2011), pp. 165–82.
6. Ironically, Ruegger was able to do much to better British–ICRC relations in the war's final months, acting as a bridge between Geneva, Whitehall and Berne – Neville Wylie, *Britain, Switzerland and the Second World War* (Oxford: Oxford University Press, 2003), p. 329.
7. Burckhardt's attempts to get the British Government to vet German documents implicating him in the Hess episode before they were published in the *Documents on German Foreign Policy* series was, however, unsuccessful – UB:BII 46A – Cooper to Burckhardt, 9 March 1946, Hamilton to Burckhardt, 12 March 1946, Hoare to Burckhardt, 7 March 1946; *Documents on German Foreign Policy, 1918–1945*, Series D, vol. 12 (London: HMSO, 1962), doc. 500, Memorandum of Albrecht Haushofer, 12 May 1941, p. 785.
8. TNA:FO 371/52648 – Ministry of Food to the MEW, 29 May 1945.
9. See generally TNA:CAB 130/406; TNA:FO 369/3593 – P/W Convention, views of PWD, undated. It is curious to note that, unlike the British, the United States' approach to the 1949 conference was shaped by a wider fear of the Soviet Union and the need to draft a convention that would be acceptable to Moscow, thus adding stability to the post-war order. Needless to say, the Americans were unimpressed with the more pedantic efforts of the British to shape the Convention to meet their own requirements – Olivier Barsalou, 'Making Humanitarian Law in the Cold: The Cold War, the United States and the Genesis of the Geneva Conventions of 1949', *Institute for International Law and Justice: Emerging Scholars Papers*, 11 (2008) (a sub-series of IILJ working papers); TNA:CAB 130/46 – Report of Official Working Party, 21 May 1949.

10. TNA:FO 788/23 – PM Direction, 26 August 1944.
11. Catherine Rey-Schyrr, *De Yalta à Dien Bien Phu: Historie du Comité International de la Croix-Rouge 1945–1955* (Geneva: Henry Dunant Institute, 2007), p. 43; TNA:FO 371/50603 – WO to FO, 3 August 1945; FO Minutes, 23 August 1945.
12. Michael Ignatieff, *The Warrior's Honor: Ethnic War and the Modern Conscience* (New York: Metropolitan, 2006), p. 158.
13. TNA:FO 366/26 – Harry J. Phillimore, 'History of the Second World War: Prisoners of War 1939–1945' (unpublished, 1949), p. 47.

Bibliography

Archival sources

Archives of the International Committee of the Red Cross, Geneva (ICRC)
Archives of the International Federation of the Red Cross and Red Crescent Societies, Geneva (IFRC)
British Red Cross Museum and Archives, London (BRC)
Churchill Archives, Cambridge (CHURCH)
Hampshire Records Office, Winchester (HRO)
National Archives of the United Kingdom, London (TNA)
Universität Bibliothek, Basle (UB)
Wellcome Library, London (WL)

Printed primary sources

Churchill, Winston, *Great War Speeches* (London: Corgi, 1957).
Churchill, Winston, and Roosevelt, Franklin D., *Churchill & Roosevelt: The Complete Correspondence*, 3 vols, ed. Warren F. Kimball (New Jersey: Princeton University Press, 1984).
Documents Diplomatiques Suisses 1848–1945, Series 1, vol. 14 (Berne: Benteli Verlag, 1997).
Documents on British Foreign Policy, 1919–1939, Series 3, vol. 5 (London: HMSO, 1939).
Documents on German Foreign Policy, 1918–1945, Series D, vol. 12 (London: HMSO, 1962).
Domarus, Max (ed.), *Hitler: Reden und Proklamationen, 1932–1945*, Band II (Wiesbaden: Löwit, 1973).
Dulles, Allen, *From Hitler's Doorstep: The Wartime Intelligence Reports of Allen Dulles, 1942–1945*, ed. Neal, H. Petersen (New Jersey: Princeton University Press, 1996).
Nightingale, Florence, *Collected Works of Florence Nightingale*, vol. 15, *Florence Nightingale on Wars and the War Office*, ed. Lynn MacDonald (Waterloo, ON: Wilfred Laurier University Press, 2011).
Scott, James B., *The Proceedings of the Hague Peace Conferences* (New York: Oxford University Press, 1921).

Official documents, pamphlets and reports

Bergier, Jean-François, *Switzerland and Refugees in the Nazi Era* (Berne: Independent Commission of Experts, 1999).
Final Report of the Joint Relief Commission of the International Red Cross, 1941–46 (Geneva: ICRC, 1948)
The ICRC: Its Mission and Its Work (Geneva: ICRC, 2009).

The ICRC in World War One: The International Prisoners-of-War Agency (Geneva: Henry Dunant Institute, 2007).

Manuel de la Croix-Rouge Internationale (Geneva: ICRC, 1930).

Pictet, Jean, *The Fundamental Principles of the Red Cross: Commentary* (Geneva: Henry Dunant Institute, 1979).

Red Cross and St John War Organisation, 1939–1947: Official Record, 2 vols. (unpublished and undated, held in the *British Red Cross Museum and Archives*, London)

Report of the International Committee of the Red Cross and Its Activities during the Second World War, 3 vols (Geneva: ICRC, 1948).

Reports by the Joint Relief Committee and the Joint War Finance Committee of the British Red Cross Society and the Order of St John of Jerusalem in England on Voluntary Aid Rendered to the Sick and Wounded and Abroad and to British Prisoners of War, 1914–1919 (London: British Red Cross, 1921).

Memoirs and diaries

Cadogan, Alexander, *The Diaries of Alexander Cadogan: 1938–1945*, ed. David Dilks (New York: Faber and Faber, 1972).

Ciano, Galeazzo, *Ciano's Diary: 1939–1943*, trans. R. L Miller (London: Phoenix Press, 2002).

Colville, Jock, *Fringes of Power: Downing Street Diaries 1939–1955* (London: Phoenix, 2005).

Dalton, Hugh, *The Fateful Years: Memoirs 1931–1945* (London: Frederick Muller, 1957).

Dalton, Hugh, *The Second World War Diary of Hugh Dalton: 1940–1945*, ed. Ben Pimlott (London: Jonathan Cape, 1986).

Goebbels, Josef, *The Goebbels Diaries, 1942–1943*, ed. and trans. Louis P. Lochner (New York: Doubleday, 1948).

Junod, Marcel, *Warrior without Weapons*, trans. Edward Fitzgerald (Geneva: Henry Dunant Institute, 1951).

Kelly, David, *The Ruling Few: Or, the Human Background to Diplomacy* (London: Hollis and Carter, 1952).

Schellenberg, Walter, *The Memoirs of Hitler's Spymaster*, ed. and trans. L. Hagan (London: André Deutsch, 2006).

Schweizer, Hans, *Dark Days in Singapore: Experience of a Delegate of the International Committee of the Red Cross during the Japanese Occupation of Singapore and Malaya, 1941–45* (Singapore: Swiss Club of Singapore, 1992).

Scotland, Alexander P., *The London Cage* (London: Evans Brothers, 1957).

Weizsäcker, Ernst von, *The Memoirs of Baron Ernst von Weizsäcker*, trans. John Andrews (Chicago: Henry Regenry Company, 1951).

Journal articles and book chapters

Barcroft, Stephen, 'The Hague Peace Conference of 1899', *Irish Studies in International Affairs* 3.1 (1989), pp. 55–68.

Barsalou, Olivier, 'Making Humanitarian Law in the Cold: The Cold War, the United States and the Genesis of the Geneva Conventions of 1949', *Institute for International Law and Justice: Emerging Scholars Papers*, 11 (2008) (a sub-series of IILJ working papers).

Beaumont, Jean, 'Starving for Democracy: Britain's Blockade of and Relief for Occupied Europe, 1939–45', *War and Society* 8.2 (1990), pp. 57–82.

Belfield, Herbert, 'Treatment of Prisoners of War', *Transactions of the Grotius Society* 9 (1923), pp. 131–47.

Bessel, Richard, 'The First World War as Totality', in Richard J. Bosworth (ed.), *The Oxford Handbook of Fascism* (Oxford: Oxford University Press, 2009), pp. 52–69.

Best, Geoffrey, 'Making the Geneva Conventions of 1949: The View from Whitehall', in Christophe Swinarski (ed.), *Studies and Essays on International Humanitarian Law and Red Cross Principles in Honour of Jean Pictet* (Geneva: ICRC, 1984), pp. 5–15.

Best, Geoffrey, 'Peace Conferences and the Century of Total War: The 1899 Hague Conference and What Came after', *International Affairs (Royal Institute of International Affairs 1944–)* 75.3 (1999), pp. 619–34.

Bonifas, Aime, 'A "Paradisiacal" Ghetto of Theresienstadt: The Impossible Mission of the International Committee of the Red Cross', *Journal of Church and State* 34 (1992), pp. 805–18.

Bossier, Léopold, 'Centenary of the First Geneva Convention in 1864', *International Review of the Red Cross* 41 (1964), pp. 393–410.

Bugnion, François, 'Le Comité international de la Croix-Rouge et la Suisse', *Revue d'Allemagne et des pays de langue allemande* 28.3 (1996), pp. 353–65.

Bugnion, François, 'ICRC Action during the Second World War', *International Review of the Red Cross* 317 (1997), pp. 562–7.

Bugnion, François, 'The International Committee of the Red Cross and the Development of International Humanitarian Law', *Chicago Journal of International Law* 5.1 (2004), pp. 191–215.

Chrastil, Rachel, 'The French Red Cross, War Readiness, and Civil Society, 1866–1914', *French Historical Studies* 31.3 (2008), pp. 445–76.

Cohen, Gerard Daniel, 'Between Relief and Politics: Refugee Humanitarianism in Occupied Germany, 1945–46', *Journal of Contemporary History* 43.3 (2008), pp. 437–49.

Crossland, James, 'A Man of Peaceable Intent: Burckhardt, the British and Red Cross Neutrality during the Second World War', *Historical Research* 84.23 (2011), pp. 165–82.

Custodis, Johann, 'Employing the Enemy: The Contribution of German and Italian Prisoners of War to British Agriculture during and after the Second World War', *Agricultural History Review* 60.2 (2012), pp. 243–65.

Fedorowich, Kent, 'Doomed from the Outset? Internment and Civilian Exchanges in the Far East: The British Failure over Hong Kong, 1941–45', *Journal of Imperial and Commonwealth History* 25.1 (1997), pp. 113–40.

Finnemore, Martha, 'Rules of War and Wars of Rules: The International Red Cross and the Restraint of State Violence', in John Boli and George M. Thomas (eds), *Constructing World Culture: International Nongovernmental Organizations since 1875* (Stanford: Stanford University Press, 1999), pp. 149–65.

Forsythe, David P., 'The ICRC: A Unique Humanitarian Protagonist', *International Review of the Red Cross* 89.865 (2007), pp. 63–96.

Frei, Henry, 'Surrendering Syonan', in Akashi Yoji and Yoshimura Mako (eds), *New Perspectives on the Japanese Occupation in Malaya and Singapore, 1941–45* (Singapore: NUS, 2008), pp. 217–34.

Giraud, Marion, 'Political Decisions and Britain's Chemical Warfare Challenge in World War I: Descend to Atrocities?', *Defence Studies* 8.1 (2008), pp. 105–32.

Goldman, Lawrence, 'The Social Sciences Association, 1857–1886: A Context for Mid-Victorian Liberalism', *English Historical Review* 101.398 (1986), pp. 95–134.

Hately-Broad, Barbara, '"No one would tell you anything": The War and Foreign Offices and British Prisoner of War Families during World War II', *Journal of Family History* 27.4 (2002), pp. 459–77.

Heinegg, Wolf Heintschel von, 'Naval blockade and Internal Law', in Bruce Allen Elleman and Sarah C. M Paine (eds), *Naval Blockades and Seapower: Strategies and Counterstrategies, 1805–2005* (London and New York: Routledge, 2006), pp. 10–22.

Hindsley, Meredith, 'Constructing Allied Humanitarian Policy', *Journal of Holocaust Education* 9.2/3 (2000), pp. 77–93.

Hiondou, Violetta, 'Famine in Occupied Greece: Causes and Consequences', in Richard Clogg (ed.), *Bearing Gifts to Greeks: Humanitarian Aid to Greece in the 1940s* (Basingstoke: Palgrave MacMillan, 2008), pp. 14–33.

Huber, Max, 'Croix-Rogue et Neutralité', *International Review of the Red Cross* 18.209 (1936), pp. 353–63.

Hutchinson, John F., '"Custodians of the Sacred Fire": The ICRC and the Postwar Reorganisation of the International Red Cross', in Paul Weindling (ed.), *International Health Organisations and Movements, 1918–1936* (Cambridge: Cambridge University Press, 1995), pp. 17–35.

Jones, Heather, 'International or Transnational? Humanitarian Action during the First World War', *European Review of History* 16.5 (2009), pp. 697–713.

Khu, Charlotte, and Brun, Joaquín Cácres, 'Neutrality and the ICRC Contribution to Contemporary Humanitarian Operations', *International Peacekeeping* 10.1 (2003), pp. 56–72.

Kochavi, Arieh, J., 'Why None of Britain's Long-Term POWs in Nazi German Were Repatriated during World War Two', *Canadian Journal of History* 39.1 (2004), pp. 63–85.

Koh, Harold Hongju, 'Why Do Nations Obey International Law?', *Yale Law School Legal Scholarship Repository: Faculty Scholarship Series*, Paper 2101 (1997) <http://digitalcommons.law.yale.edu/fss_papers/2101> (accessed 10 March 2014).

Kramer, Alan, 'The First Wave of War Crimes Trials: Istanbul and Leipzig', *European Review* 14.4 (2006), pp. 441–55.

Kramer, Alan, 'Prisoners in the First World War', in Sibylle Scheippers (ed.), *Prisoners in War: Norms, Military Cultures and Reciprocity in Armed Conflict* (Oxford: Oxford University Press, 2010), pp. 75–87.

Levie, Howard S., 'Prisoners of War and the Protecting Power', *American Journal of International Law* 55.2 (1961), pp. 374–97.

Levin, Herbert S., 'The Mediator: Carl J. Burckhardt's Efforts to Avert the Second World War', *Journal of Modern History* 45.3 (1973), pp. 439–55.

Levine, Paul A., 'Swedish Neutrality during the Second World War: Tactical Success or Moral Compromise?', in Neville Wylie (ed.), *European Neutrals and Non-Belligerents during the Second World War* (Cambridge: Cambridge University Press, 2002), pp. 304–30.

Loring Villa, Brian, 'The Diplomatic and Political Context of the POW Camps Tragedy', in Stephen Ambrose and Günter Bischof (eds), *Eisenhower and the German POWs: Facts against Falsehood* (Baton Rouge: Louisiana State Press, 1992), pp. 52–77.

Mauzy, Marie, 'Inter Arma Caritas: The Swedish Red Cross in Greece in the 1940s', in Richard Clogg (ed.), *Bearing Gifts to Greeks: Humanitarian Aid to Greece in the 1940s* (Basingstoke: Palgrave MacMillan, 2008).

Moore, Bob, 'Axis Prisoners in Britain during the Second World War: A Comparative Survey', in Bob Moore and Kent Fedorowich (eds), *Prisoners of War and Their Captors in World War II* (Oxford: Berg, 1996), pp. 19–46.

Moore, Bob, 'Turning Liabilities into Assets: British Government Policy towards German and Italian Prisoners of War during the Second World War', *Journal of Contemporary History* 32.1 (1997), pp. 117–36.

Moore, Bob, 'The Western Allies and Food Relief to the Occupied Netherlands, 1944–1945', *War and Society* 10.2 (1992), pp. 91–118.

Neville, P., 'Norton, Sir Clifford John (1891–1990)', *Oxford Dictionary of National Biography* (Oxford: Oxford University Press, 2004): online edn (accessed January 2009).

Noble, Alastair, 'British Reaction to the Katyn Massacre', in Delphine Debons, Antoine Fleury and Jean-François Pitteloud (eds), *Katyn et la Suisse: Experts et Expertises Médicales dans les Crises Humanitaires, 1920–2007* (Geneva: Geor, 2009), pp. 224–8.

Overmans, Rüdiger, 'German Historiography, the War Losses, and the Prisoners of War', in Stephen Ambrose and Günter Bischof (eds), *Eisenhower and the German POWs: Facts against Falsehood* (Baton Rouge: Louisiana State Press, 1992), pp. 127–69.

Overmans, Rüdiger, 'German Prisoner of War Policy in World War II', in Bernard Mees and Samuel P. Koehne (eds), *Terror, War, Tradition* (Adelaide: Australian Humanities Press, 2007).

Overmans, Rüdiger, 'Die kriegsgefangenenpolitik des Deutschen Reiches 1939 bis 1945', in Jörg Echternkamp et al. (eds), *Das Deutsche Reich und der Zweite Weltkrieg*, Band 9/1–2 (Munich: Deutsche Verlags-Anstalt, 2005).

Overy, Richard, 'Allied Bombing and the Destruction of German Cities', in Roger Chickering, Stig Förster and Bernd Grenier (eds), *A World at Total War: Global Conflict and the Politics of Destruction, 1937–1945* (Cambridge: Cambridge University Press, 2005), pp. 277–95.

Philimore, G. G., and Bellot, H. L., 'Treatment of Prisoners of War', *Transactions of the Grotius Society* 5 (1919), pp. 47–64.

Reynolds, David, 'Churchill and the British Decision to Fight on: Right Policy, Wrong Reasons', in Richard Langhorne (ed.), *Diplomacy and Intelligence during the Second World War: Essays in Honour of F. H. Hinsley* (Cambridge: Cambridge University Press, 1985), pp. 147–67.

Rodogno, Davide, 'Fascism and War', in Richard J. Bosworth (ed.), *The Oxford Handbook of Fascism* (Oxford: Oxford University Press, 2009), pp. 239–58.

Rolf, David, 'Blind Bureaucracy: The British Government and POWs in German Captivity, 1939–1945', in Bob Moore and Kent Fedorowich (eds), *Prisoners of War and Their Captors in World War II* (Oxford: Berg, 1996), pp. 47–97.

Sandoz, Yves, 'Max Huber and the Red Cross', *European Journal of International Law* 18.1 (2007), pp. 171–97.

Sandoz , Yves, 'The Red Cross and Peace: Realities and Limits', *Journal of Peace Research* 24.3 (1987), pp. 287–96.

Sanford, George, 'The Katyn Massacre and Polish-Soviet Relations 1941–43', *Journal of Contemporary History* 4.1 (2006), pp. 95–111.

Scheck, R., 'The Prisoner of War Question and the Beginnings of Collaboration: The Franco-German Agreement of 16 November 1940', *Journal of Contemporary History* 45.2 (2010), pp. 364–88.

Schindler, Dietrich, 'Max Huber – His Life', *European Journal of International Law* 18.1 (2007), pp. 81–95.

Schweizer, Beat, 'The "Spirit of Geneva": Humanitarian Diplomacy and Advocacy', *Refugee Survey Quarterly* 26.4 (2007), pp. 163–5.

Shepherd, Ben, 'Becoming Planning Minded: The Theory and Practice of Relief, 1940–45', *Journal of Contemporary History* 43 (2008), pp. 405–19.

Slim, H., 'Relief Agencies and Moral Standing in War: Principles of Humanity, Neutrality, Impartiality and Solidarity', *Development in Practice* 7.4 (1997), pp. 342–52.

Steinhart, Johannes-Dieter, 'British Humanitarian Assistance: Wartime Planning and Postwar Realities', *Journal of Contemporary History* 43.3 (2008), pp. 421–35.

Sweetman, John, 'The Crimean War and the Formation of the Medical Staff Corps', *Journal of the Society for Army Historical Research* 53.214 (1975), pp. 113–19.

Till, Geoffrey, 'Naval Blockades and Economic Warfare, Europe 1939–45', in Bruce Allen Elleman and Sarah C. M Paine (eds), *Naval Blockades and Seapower: Strategies and Counterstrategies, 1805–2005* (London and New York: Routledge, 2006), pp. 117–29.

Torrie, Julia S., 'The Many Aims of Assistance: The Nationalsozialistische Volkswohlfahrt and Aid to French Civilians in 1940', *War and Society* 26.1 (2007), pp. 27–37.

Towle, Philip, 'Japanese Culture and the Treatment of Prisoners of War in the Asian-Pacific War', in Sibylle Scheipers (ed.), *Prisoners in War: Norms, Military Cultures and Reciprocity in Armed Conflict* (Oxford: Oxford University Press, 2010), pp. 141–53.

Trent, James F., 'Food Shortages in Germany and Europe, 1945–48', in Stephen Ambrose and Günter Bischof (eds), *Eisenhower and the German POWs: Facts against Falsehood* (Baton Rouge: Louisiana State Press, 1992), pp. 95–112.

Troyon, Brigette, and Palmieri, Daniel, 'The ICRC Delegate: An Exceptional Humanitarian Player?', *International Review of the Red Cross* 89.865 (2007), pp. 97–111.

Vago, Béla, 'The Horthy Offer: A Missed Opportunity for the Jews in 1944', in R. L. Braham (ed.), *Contemporary Views on the Holocaust* (Boston: Springer, 1983), pp. 23–45.

Vance, Jonathan F., 'Men in Manacles: The Shackling of Prisoners of War, 1942–1943', *Journal of Military History* 59.3 (1995), pp. 483–504.

Voglis, Polymeris, 'Surviving Hunger: Life in the Cities and the Countryside during the Occupation', in Robert Gildea, Anette Warring and Olivier Wieviorka (eds), *Surviving Hitler and Mussolini: Daily Life in Occupied Europe* (Oxford: Berg, 2006), pp. 16–41.

Vourkoutiotis, V., 'What the Angels Saw: Red Cross and Protecting Power Visits to Anglo-American POWs, 1939–45', *Journal of Contemporary History* 40.4 (2005), pp. 689–706.

Wylie, Neville, 'The 1929 Prisoner of War Convention and the Building of the Interwar Prisoner of War Regime', in Sibylle Scheippers (ed.), *Prisoners in War: Norms, Military Cultures and Reciprocity in Armed Conflict* (Oxford: Oxford University Press, 2010), pp. 91–106.

Wylie, Neville, 'Captured by the Nazis: Reciprocity and National Conservatism in German Policy towards British POWs, 1939–1945', in C. C. W. Szejnmann (ed.), *Rethinking History: Dictatorships and War: Essays in Honour of Richard Overy* (London: Continuum, 2009), pp. 109–24.

Wylie, Neville, 'Marcel Pilet-Golaz, David Kelly and Anglo-Swiss Relations in 1940', *Diplomacy and Statecraft* 8.1 (1997), pp. 49–79.

Wylie, Neville, 'Switzerland: A Neutral of Distinction?', in Neville Wylie (ed.), *European Neutrals and Non-Belligerents during the Second World War* (Cambridge: Cambridge University Press, 2002), pp. 331–54.

Yap, F., 'Prisoners of War and Civilian Internees of the Japanese in British Asia: The Similarities and Contrasts of Experience', *Journal of Contemporary History* 47.2 (2012), pp. 317–46.

Zweig, Ronald W., 'Feeding the Camps: Allied Blockade Policy and the Relief of Concentration Camps in Germany, 1944–45', *Historical Journal* 41.3 (1998), pp. 825–85.

Books

Ambrose, Stephen, and Bischof, Günter (eds), *Eisenhower and the German POWs: Facts against Falsehood* (Baton Rouge: Louisiana State Press, 1992).

Bacque, James, *Other Losses: An Investigation into the Mass Deaths of German Prisoners at the Hands of the French and the Americans after World War II* (Toronto: Stoddart, 1989).

Bailey, Sydney Dawson, *Prohibitions and Restraints in War* (London: Oxford University Press, 1972).

Barnett, Michael, *Empire of Humanity: A History of Humanitarianism* (Ithaca: Cornell University Press, 2011).

Baudendistel, Rainer, *Between Bombs and Good Intentions: The Red Cross and the Italo-Ethiopian War of 1935–36* (New York: Berghan, 2006).

Bauer, Yehuda, *Jews for Sale? Nazi-Jewish Negotiations, 1933–1945* (New Haven and London: Yale University Press, 1994).

Bennett, Angela, *Geneva Convention: The Hidden Origins of the Red Cross* (Stroud: Sutton, 2005).

Berry, Charles O., *War and the Red Cross: The Unspoken Mission* (New York: St. Martins, 1997).

Best, Geoffrey, *Humanity in Warfare: The Modern History of the International Law of Armed Conflicts* (London: Methuen, 1980).

Black, Edwin, *IBM and the Holocaust: The Strategic Alliance between Nazi Germany and America's Most Powerful Corporation: Expanded Edition* (Washington: Dialog Press, 2012).

Blatman, Daniel, *The Death Marches: The Final Phase of Nazi Genocide*, trans. Chaya Galai (Harvard: Belknapp, 2011).

Bond, Brian, *War and Society in Europe, 1870–1970* (Montreal: McGill Press, 1984).

Bossier, Pierre, *The History of the International Committee of the Red Cross: From Solferino to Tsushima* (Geneva: Henry Dunant Institute, 1984).

Bower, Tom, *Blood Money: The Swiss, the Nazis and the Looted Billions* (London: Macmillan, 1997).

Bugnion, François, *Gustav Moynier* (Geneva: Éditions Slatkine, 2010).

Bugnion, François, *The International Committee of the Red Cross and the Protection of War Victims* (Richmond: MacMillan, 2003).

Burleigh, Michael, *The Third Reich: A New History* (New York: Hill and Wang, 2000).

Cardia, Isabelle Vonèche, *Neutralité et engagement: les relations entre le Comité International de la Croix-Rouge et le Gouvernement Suisse, 1938–1945* (Lausanne: SHSR, 2012).

Cienciala, Anna M., Lebedeva, Natalia S., and Materski, Wojeciech (eds), *Katyn: A Crime without Punishment* (New Haven: Yale University Press, 2007).

Collingham, Lizzie, *The Taste of War: World War Two and the Battle for Food* (London: Penguin, 2012).

Daws, Gavan, *Prisoners of the Japanese: POWs of World War II in the Pacific* (New York: William Morrow, 1994).

Deeming, Richard, *Heroes of the Red Cross* (Geneva: ICRC, 1969).

Dilks, David, *Churchill and Company: Allies and Rivals in War and Peace* (London: I. B. Tauris, 2012).

Dunant, Henry, *A Memory of Solferino* (Geneva: Henry Dunant Institute, 1986).

Durand, André, *From Sarajevo to Hiroshima* (Geneva: Henry Dunant Institute, 1984).

Durand, Roger, *Henry Dunant* (Geneva: Henry Dunant Institute, 2010).

Durand, Y., *Des Prisonniers de Guerre dans les Stalags, les Oflags et les Kommandos, 1939–1945* (Paris: Hachette, 1987).

Favez, Jean-Claude, *The Red Cross and the Holocaust*, eds and trans John Fletcher and Beryl Fletcher (Cambridge: Cambridge University Press, 1999).

Fitzgibbon, Louis, *Katyn Massacre* (London: Corgi, 1977).

Footit, Hilary, *War and Liberation in France: Living with the Liberators* (Basingstoke: Palgrave MacMillan, 2004).

Forsythe, David P., *The Humanitarians: The International Committee of the Red Cross* (Cambridge: Cambridge University Press, 2005).

Forsythe, David P., and Rieffer-Flanagan, Barbara Ann J., *The International Committee of the Red Cross: A Neutral Humanitarian Actor* (London: Routledge, 2007).

Gemie, Sharif, Humbert, Laure, and Reid, Fiona, *Outcast Europe: Refugees and Relief Workers in an Era of Total War, 1936–48* (London: Bloomsbury, 2012).

Gilbert, Adrian, *POW: Allied Prisoners of War in Europe 1939–1945* (London: John Murray, 2006).

Gilbert, Martin, *Sir Horace Rumbold: Portrait of a Diplomat, 1869–1941* (London: Heinemann, 1973).

Gill, Rebecca, *Calculating Compassion: Humanity and Relief in War, Britain 1870–1914* (Manchester: Manchester University Press, 2013).

Gillman, Peter, and Gillman, Leni, *Collar the Lot!: How Britain Interned and Expelled Its Wartime Refugees* (London: Quartet, 1980).

Grose, Peter, *Gentleman Spy: The Life of Allen Dulles* (Boston: University of Massachusetts Press, 1994).

Halbrook, Stephen P., *Target Switzerland: Swiss Armed Neutrality in World War II* (Sarpedon: Rockville Centre, 1998).

Hart, Ellen, *Man Born to Live: The Life and Work of Henry Dunant, Founder of the Red Cross* (London: Victor Gollancz, 1953).

Hartigan, Richard Shelly, *Lieber's Code and the Laws of War* (Chicago: Precedent, 1983).

Haug, Hans, *Humanity for All: The International Red Cross and Red Crescent Movement* (Berne: Henry Dunant Institute, 1993).

Hoare, Oliver (ed.), *Camp 020: MI5 and the Nazi Spies* (London: Public Records Office, 2000).

Howard, Michael, *War and the Liberal Conscience* (London: Temple Smith, 1978).

Hutchinson, John F., *Champions of Charity: War and the Rise of the Red Cross* (Boulder: Westview Press, 1996).

Ignatieff, Michael, *The Warrior's Honor: Ethnic War and the Modern Conscience* (New York: Metropolitan, 2006).

Jackson, Robert, *The Prisoners, 1914–1918* (London: Routledge, 1989).

Jackson, Sophie, *Churchill's Unexpected Guests: Prisoners of War in Britain in World War II* (Stroud: History Press, 2010).

Jay, Jakub, *Spies and Saboteurs: Anglo-American Collaboration and Rivalry in Human Intelligence Collection and Special Operations, 1940–45* (London: MacMillan, 1999).

Jones, Heather, *Violence against Prisoners of War in the First World War: Britain, France and Germany, 1914–1920* (Cambridge: Cambridge University Press, 2011).

Junod, Dominique D., *The Imperilled Red Cross and the Palestine-Eretz-Yisrael Conflict, 1925–1952* (London: Kegan Paul International, 1996).

Kennedy, David, *Of War and Law* (Princeton: Princeton University Press, 2006).

Kochavi, Arieh J., *Confronting Captivity: Britain and the United States and Their POWs in Nazi Germany* (Chapel Hill and London: University of North Carolina Press, 2005).

Kogon, Eugene, *The Theory and Practice of Hell: The German Concentration Camps and the System behind Them*, 1st rev. edn (New York: Farrar, Strauss and Giroux, 2006).

Kramer, Alan, *Dynamic of Destruction: Culture and Mass Killing in the First World War* (New York: Oxford University Press, 2007).

Laity, Paul, *The British Peace Movement, 1870–1914* (Oxford: Oxford University Press, 2001).

Lamb, Richard, *War in Italy: A Brutal Story, 1943–45* (London: John Murray, 1993).

Lebor, Adam, *Hitler's Secret Bankers: How Switzerland Profited from Nazi Genocide* (London: Simon and Schuster, 1997).

Lochery, Neill, *Lisbon: War in the Shadows of the City of Light, 1939–45* (Melbourne: Imprint, 2011).

London, Louise, *Whitehall and the Jews, 1933–1948: British Immigration Policy and the Holocaust* (New York: Cambridge University Press, 2000).

Longden, Sean, *Dunkirk: The Men They Left Behind* (London: Constable, 2008).

Longden, Sean, *Hitler's British Slaves: Allied POWs in Germany, 1939–45* (London: Constable, 2007).

Lowe, Keith, *Savage Continent: Europe in the Aftermath of World War II* (New York: St. Mary's, 2012).

MacDonogh, Giles, *After the Reich: From the Liberation of Vienna to the Berlin Airlift* (London: John Murray, 2007).

MacKenzie, S. P., *The Colditz Myth: British and Commonwealth Prisoners of War in Nazi Germany* (Oxford: Oxford University Press, 2004).

Mazower, Mark, *Hitler's Empire: Nazi Rule in Occupied Europe* (London: Allen Lane, 2008).

Mazower, Mark, *Inside Hitler's Greece: The Experience of Occupation 1941–44* (New Haven: Yale University Press, 1993).

Medlicott, W. N., *The Economic Blockade*, 2 vols (London: HMSO, 1959).

Miller, David, *Mercy Ships: The Untold Story of Prisoner of War Exchanges in World War II* (London: Continuum, 2008).

Mitchell, Arthur H., *Hitler's Mountain: The Fürher, Obersalzburg and the American Occupation of Berchtesgaden* (Jefferson: McFarland and Company, 2007).

Monteath, Peter, *POW: Australian Prisoners of War in Hitler's Reich* (Sydney: MacMillan, 2011).

Moore, Bob, and Fedorowich, Kent, *The British Empire and Its Italian Prisoners of War, 1940–1947* (Basingstoke: Palgrave MacMillan, 2002).

Moorehead, Caroline, *Dunant's Dream: War, Switzerland and the History of the Red Cross* (London: Harper Collins, 1998).

Nabulsi, Karma, *Traditions of War: Occupation, Resistance and the Law* (Oxford: Oxford University Press, 2000).

Neff, Stephen C., *War and the Law of Nations: A General History* (Cambridge: Cambridge University Press, 2005).

Nichol, John, and Rennell, Tony, *The Last Escape: The Untold Story of Allied Prisoners of War in Germany, 1944–45* (London: Penguin, 2003).

Oliver, Berryl, *The British Red Cross in Action* (London: Faber, 1966).

Ousby, Ian, *Occupation: The Ordeal of France, 1940–1944* (London: Pimlico, 1999).

Overy, Richard, *The Morbid Age: Britain between the Wars* (London: Allen Lane, 2009).

Padfield, Peter, *Himmler: Reichsführer SS* (London: MacMillan, 1990).

Papastratis, Procopis, *British Policy towards Greece during the Second World War, 1941–44* (Cambridge: Cambridge University Press, 1984).

Phillimore, Harry J., 'History of the Second World War: Prisoners of War 1939–1945' (unpublished, 1949).

Porter, Andrew, *The Oxford History of the British Empire: The Nineteenth Century* (Oxford: Oxford University Press, 1999).

Reid, Daphne A., and Gilbo, Patrick F., *Beyond Conflict: The International Federation of the Red Cross and Red Crescent Societies, 1919–1994* (Geneva: IFRC, 1997).

Rey-Schyrr, Catherine, *De Yalta à Dien Bien Phu: Historie du Comité International de la Croix-Rouge 1945–1955* (Geneva: Henry Dunant Institute, 2007).

Rolf, David, *Prisoners of the Reich: Germany's Captives* (London: Hodder and Stoughton, 1988).

Rollings, Charles, *Prisoner of War: Voices from behind the Wire in the Second World War* (Reading: Ebury, 2008).

Sareen, Tilak Raj, *Japanese Prisoners of War in India, 1942–1946: Bushido and Barbed Wire* (Kent: Global Oriental, 2006).

Satow, Harold, and Sée, M. J., *The Work of the Prisoners of War Department during the Second World War* (London: Foreign Office, 1950).

Schlie, Ulrich, *Kein Friede mit Deutschland: die geheimen Gespräche im Zweiten Weltkrieg, 1939–1941* (Munich: Langen Müller, 1994).

Shepherd, Ben, *The Long Road Home: The Aftermath of the Second World War* (London: Bodley Head, 2011).

Siordet, Frédéric, *Inter Arma Caritas: The World of the ICRC during the Second World War* (Geneva: ICRC, 1973).

Solis, Gary D., and Borch, Fred L., *Geneva Conventions* (New York: Kaplan, 2010).

Spiers, Edward M., *A History of Chemical and Biological Weapons* (London: Reaktion, 2010).

Stafford, David, *Endgame 1945: Victory, Retribution, Liberation* (London: Abacus, 2007).

Stauffer, Paul, *Sechs Furchtbare Jahre, auf den Spruen Carl J. Burckhardt durch den Zweiten Weltkrieg* (Zurich: Nzz Verlag, 1998).

Steinacher, Gerald, *Nazis on the Run: How Hitler's Henchmen Fled Justice* (Oxford: Oxford University Press, 2012).

Summers, Anne, *Angels and Citizens: British Women as Military Nurses, 1854–1914* (London: Routledge, 2000).

Sutherland, Jon, and Sutherland, Diane, *British Prisoner of War Camps during the Second World War* (Newhaven: Golden Guides, 2012).

Taylor, Frederick, *Exorcising Hitler: The Occupation and De-Nazification of Germany* (London: Bloomsbury, 2011).

Tooze, Adam, *The Wages of Destruction: The Making and Breaking of the Nazi Economy* (London: Allen Lane, 2006).

Vourkoutiotis, Vasilis, *Prisoners of War and the German High Command* (New York: Palgrave Macmillan, 2003).

Wagner, Meier, *The Righteous of Switzerland: Heroes of the Holocaust*, ed. Andreas C. Fischer and Graham Buik (Hoboken: Ktav, 2001).

Weinberg, Gerhard, *The Foreign Policy of Hitler's Germany: Starting World War II, 1937–39* (Chicago: University of Chicago Press, 1980).

Weinberg, Gerhard, *A World at Arms: A Global History of World War II* (New York: Cambridge University Press, 1994).

Willingham, Matthew, *Perilous Commitments: Britain's Involvement in Greece and Crete 1940–41* (Staplehurst: Spellmount, 2005).

Witt, John Fabian, *Lincoln's Code: The Laws of War in American History* (New York: Free Press, 2012).

Woodbridge, George, *UNRRA: The History of the United Nations Relief and Rehabilitation Administration*, 3 vols (New York: Columbia University Press, 1950).

Wylie, Neville, *Barbed Wire Diplomacy: Britain, Germany and the Politics of Prisoners of War, 1939–1945* (Oxford: Oxford University Press, 2011).

Wylie, Neville, *Britain, Switzerland and the Second World War* (Oxford: Oxford University Press, 2003).

Wyman, Mark, *DP: Europe's Displaced Persons, 1945–51* (Philadelphia: Balch Institute Press, 1989).

Zaloga, Steven, *Operation Dragoon 1944: France's Other D-Day* (Oxford: Osprey, 2009).

PhD dissertations

Laurent, Christophe, 'Les Obstacles Recontrés par le CICR dans son Activité en Extrême-Orient, 1941–45', PhD dissertation (Université de Lausanne, 2003).

Versluys, Karen, 'When Lines Become Crossed: How the British Government Shaped the British Red Cross' Humanitarian Aid Efforts during World War II', PhD Dissertation (Dalhousie University, Nova Scotia, 2007).

Websites

British Medical Journal Online – <www.bmj.com/archive>
Foreign and Commonwealth Office – <www.fco.gov.uk>
Guardian Newspaper – <www.guardian.co.uk>
Imperial War Museum – <www.iwm.org.uk>
Oxford Dictionary of National Biography – <oxforddnb.com>
The Times Online Archive – <www.thetimes.co.uk/site/archive>

Index

Relevant to Red Cross Parcels for POWs and Internees

58 IBM cards for POWs; converted to Hollerith punched cards

59 Hitler's interventions; shackling of British + Canadian POWs 1942; beatings; poor diet; long marches.

60 Dilatory and dysfunctional admin. (of German) POW admin

61 Interrogation of POWs and dilatory record-keeping
& lack of ICRC oversight contributed to abuse

64 Inadequate food and poor accommodation of POWs 62, 63
~~65-66~~   and near-constant Interrogation of POWs
65-66   Red-Cross marked planes used by Germans
for surveillance over S England

73 Director of POW affairs appointed to BRC board Jan 1941 was Stanley Adam also chairman of Thomas Cook travel agents, being an expert on European transport services. However, after a year of frustration and having his authority whittled down, he resigned Jan 194?

73-74 S-Adams appointment coincided with the receipt of 20,000 parcels in Geneva delivered from the Lisbon-Marseille route then coming to life.

74 To avoid interruptions in the flow of the delivery of parcels to POWs, S-Adams insisted that BRC carry and maintain a stockpile of 1 million parcels in Britain and 1.5 million by May 1941. The ICRC also built a stockpile of 300,000 parcels in Geneva. By end - 1941 almost 3 million parcels had been despatched to mainland Europe.

p. 74 Such a huge stock meant that the principle of delivery of "one parcel per man per week" could be attained, sometimes more

p. 75 New problems arose first in Greece, then North Africa and desperately in Far East following collapse of British Forces in Hong Kong, Malaya and Singapore, where 130,000 POW were taken. This led to a crisis in the parcel supply. Whitehall's POW Dept held George Warner became exhausted, lost energy and Sir Howell Satow with more energy and capable of restoring some range in ICRC / BRC relations

P.104

76-77 The Red X parcel service could not be maintained
while BRC and ICRC had a "stand-off" from
each other. The crisis of greatly increased
numbers of Allied P.o.W. held by German
forces meant that George Warner and colleagues
could not cope. An example of reading
of P.o.W letters home in Autumn 1940
showed an inmate of **Oflag VIIC (Laufen)**
writing, in a letter home that as P.o.W's
were receiving parcels marked "ICRC" rather
than "BRC" indicated that BRC must have
been dragging its feet. The ICRC was
in direct and regular touch with its Government,
within own Country, excluding BRC.

This became the 'norm'.

8 In Feb 1942 the War Office began a steady
and increasing watch over it, added work of
BRC. This probably contributed to its peak
of parcels packed and despatched in
war-time of 5,552,151. By end-1942
with over 200,000 soldiers and civilians
in captivity neither Whitehall / BRC nor
ICRC and Swiss Govt, could realistically
avoid increasing co-operation with
each other.

30 Between Autumn 1940 and Spring 1941 British forces
in North and East Africa captured close to
300,000 Italian troops, though completely
unprepared for so large a prisoner in their

82 20 April to () early May 1941, first
in Greece and later in Crete, the German
forces took 23,000 (until Surrender)
Allied P.o.Ws

CPSIA information can be obtained
at www.ICGtesting.com
Printed in the USA
LVHW050755260723
753416LV00003B/10